# IDOLATRY AND REPRESENTATION

# IDOLATRY AND REPRESENTATION

## THE PHILOSOPHY OF FRANZ ROSENZWEIG RECONSIDERED

*Leora Batnitzky*

PRINCETON UNIVERSITY PRESS    PRINCETON, NEW JERSEY

Published by Princeton University Press, 41 William Street,
Princeton, New Jersey 08540
In the United Kingdom: Princeton University Press,
Chichester, West Sussex


*Library of Congress Cataloging-in-Publication Data*

Batnitzky, Leora Faye, 1966–
Idolatry and representation : the philosophy of Franz Rosenzweig
reconsidered / Leora Batnitzky.
p. cm.
Includes bibliographical references and index.
ISBN 0-691-04850-9 (alk. paper)
1. Rosenzweig, Franz—1886–1929. 2. Judaism—Doctrines. 3. Idolatry.
4. Philosophy, Jewish. I. Title.
BM755.R6B38 2000
296.3′092—dc21 99-044920 CIP

This book has been composed in Sabon

The paper used in this publication meets the minimum requirements of
ANSI/NISO Z39.48-1992 (R 1997) (*Permanence of Paper*)

http://pup.princeton.edu

Printed in the United States of America

10 9 8 7 6 5 4 3 2 1

To My Family

# *Contents*

# *Acknowledgments*

IN WRITING and rewriting this book, I have incurred many debts and am happy to thank some of the many people and institutions that helped this study reach this point. Robert Gibbs introduced me to Rosenzweig. I thank him for extensive comments on and conversations about this project at an early stage. I have learned much from his work. I also thank Eric Santner and Jeffrey Stout for their practical and philosophical advice early on. I have admired their rather diverse scholarship and have tried to better my own work by learning from them. Peter Ochs and Steven Kepnes read what became the final draft of this manuscript. I thank them for their sensitive criticisms and generous support of this project. Lawrie Balfour, Susan Bernofsky, Avi Bernstein-Nahar, James Goldwasser, Peter Eli Gordon, Mark Larrimore, Robert Lebeau, Jacob Meskin, and Jonathan Skolnik discussed, read, and offered valuable comments and criticism of various parts of this book. I thank them all. I thank A. Deborah Malmud, Eric D. Schramm, Elizabeth Swayze, and Princeton University Press for their fine editorial advice, support, and assistance. Thanks also to Hannah Schell, who offered editorial assistance at various stages of preparing this manuscript.

This book also has benefited from much institutional support. I thank the Department of Religion and the Program in Jewish Studies at Princeton University for the supportive contexts they have provided my work and me. A visit to the Franz Rosenzweig Research Center for German-Jewish Literature and Cultural History at the Hebrew University was also very important to the evolution of this work. I thank Stéphane Mos FE s for arranging that visit and also for a number of very helpful conversations over the years. I also thank the Princeton University Center for Human Values and the Society of Fellows of the Woodrow Wilson Foundation for supporting this work in its early stages.

Earlier versions of parts of this manuscript were published in other forums and I gratefully acknowledge permission to reprint them here. An earlier version of chapter 3 was published in the *Journal of Jewish Thought and Philosophy*. A portion of chapter 5 was published in *New German Critique*. Finally, an expanded part of chapter 6 was published in the *Journal of Religion*.

Last but not least, my husband, Bob, and our son, Jonathan, provided the time, space, and good humor that allowed me to complete this project. While essential, their contribution to this book is the least of my debt to them. Thank you, Bob and Jonathan, for your respective interest and lack of interest in this work, and for teaching me much during the writing of this book about many things, including learning, computers, trucks, dinosaurs, and other joys and wonders.

# IDOLATRY AND REPRESENTATION

# *Introduction*

## Reconsidering Rosenzweig and Modern Conceptions of Idolatry

Franz Rosenzweig has long been interpreted as an existentialist philosopher who rejected philosophy for the sake of religion, and reason for the sake of revelation. These longstanding interpretations of Rosenzweig have persisted despite the fact that Rosenzweig himself was deeply critical of the term religion, claimed to have written not a Jewish book but a philosophical system, and continually qualified his understanding of revelation. This book reconsiders Rosenzweig's thought in the context of these tensions in interpretation and attempts to reorient thinking about Rosenzweig in terms of his approach to the problem of idolatry.

"Idolatry" is perhaps the one religious category that has taken on and maintains the most secular and critical power. Friedrich Nietzsche claims idolatry is the worship of a transcendent God at the cost of finite man. Karl Marx maintains it is the deification of money. Francis Bacon argues that it is sophistry in the face of logic. For Theodor Adorno, it is the claim to have arrived at a truly just society. Indeed, as epitomized best by Nietzsche's thought, modern notions of idolatry are often used to describe precisely what is wrong with religion itself. Rosenzweig's view of idolatry is a distinctly modern one in that it also offers a criticism of "religion." Rosenzweig's effort to think about idolatry as a modern possibility takes the form of a Jewish critique of modernity and some of its views of religion, ethics, national identity, art, and language. His criticism of modernity, however, is not a rejection of modernity. It is not an attempt to reach back for a pre-modern conception of idolatry (if this is even possible). Rather, it is an attempt to think critically about the complex interaction between Judaism and modern thought and to demonstrate the critical potential of this interaction for contemporary understandings of ethics, national identity, art, and language.

There are compelling reasons to reconsider the philosophy of Franz Rosenzweig. As Rosenzweig himself noted, his work *The Star of Redemption* is a book that people seem to buy, but that no one seems to read.[1] This is not entirely its audience's fault. Rosenzweig's style is dense and his prose is cryptic. But the misunderstanding of Rosenzweig goes beyond the inherent difficulty of his prose. Rosenzweig's arguments themselves are multilayered and multidirectional, embodying in fact the very problematic that animates his work: the complex relations between Judaism and modern thought. Because of the complexity, and indeed the textuality, of his arguments, most of Rosenzweig's interpreters (both his contemporaries and our own) have failed to appreciate his fundamental concern: the question of the *possibility* of religious authority in the modern world.

This means that Rosenzweig's philosophy is not accurately described as existentialist, neo-Hegelian, or, as has been advocated most recently (and anachronistically), postmodern.[2] The inherent fallacy of these interpretations of Rosenzweig's thought is that each in its own way conflates Rosenzweig's views of philosophy and Judaism.[3] The existentialist portrait conflates Rosenzweig's commitment to truth and reason with its own commitment to the rupture of revelation.[4] Conversely, the neo-Hegelian portrait conflates Rosenzweig's view of revelation's rupture with its own arguments about truth and reason.[5] While the postmodern portrait of Rosenzweig's thought gets past the existential/neo-Hegelian dialectic, it nonetheless succumbs to the same fallacy by conflating Rosenzweig's view of Jewish particularity with a notion of philosophical particularity.[6] Each of these views fails to appreciate the ways in which philosophy and Judaism always exist for Rosenzweig in incommensurable, yet hermeneutically complex tensions.[7] The aim of this study is to avoid such conflations by reconsidering, both philosophically and historically, Rosenzweig's thought in relation to German-Jewish arguments about Judaism and idolatry in the modern world.

Reading Rosenzweig's project through the rubric of a polemic about idolatry, this study attempts to return to the culturally critical import of his work. To do so, we must return to some of Rosenzweig's fundamental questions about human finitude. Rosenzweig argues that the Judaic prohibition on idolatry is central to reassessing the meaning of human finitude. Idolatry for Rosenzweig stems not from how we think about God but from how we worship God. The way we worship God is intimately connected to our lives as finite human beings. Rosenzweig maintains that a reassessment of human finitude is especially necessary after the crisis of reason in the first part of this century, a time at which the prospects of reasoned enlightenment and historical progress seemed all but destroyed. Rosenzweig's idiom is not our own, but at the end of this violent and bloody century his concerns remain ours.

For Rosenzweig, Judaism and its ban on idolatry can and should be seen as the crucial intellectual and spiritual resource available to modern readers for revitalizing the meanings of human finitude for human interaction. We may thus use Rosenzweig's thought to ask what it means to speak about idolatry as a modern possibility.[8] Just as Rosenzweig argues that the avoidance of idolatry is intimately connected to understanding our lives as finite human beings, so too he argues that idolatry is central to reassessing the modern meanings of art, language, and national identity.

Before turning to the details of Rosenzweig's notion of idolatry, it will be useful to map out a number of modern philosophical constructions of the concept. In their excellent study *Idolatry*, Moshe Halbertal and Avishai Margalit argue that there are three distinctly modern forms of discourse on idolatry, what they call "replacement," "extension," and "inversion" (these arguments are detailed below). Rosenzweig's notion of idolatry cannot be assimilated under any of these three categories, although his view of idolatry has some affinity with a number of thinkers whose views can be categorized according to this schema. Rosenzweig's approach to idolatry is best understood under the rubric of "ethical monotheism," a claim that is developed throughout this book. Halbertal and Margalit do not include modern Jewish views of idolatry as a category of modern forms of the concept "idolatry." The implication of their otherwise excellent book is that Jewish, philosophical views of idolatry end in the thirteenth century with the Spanish rabbinic authority and kabbalist Nachmanides (1194–1270).[9] Despite this obvious oversight, their categories of modern discourses of idolatry remain a useful grid against which to begin to measure Rosenzweig's more particular and complex notion.

Halbertal and Margalit's first modern category of discourse on idolatry is "replacement." If idolatry is defined as the worship of the alien god in place of the true god, some modern, secular discourses on idolatry merely replace the true god with a new ideal. Francis Bacon replaces the right god with the ideal of the true science of nature. Just as the worship of the true god requires an eradication of all idols, so too Bacon argues the true science of nature requires an eradication of the idols of the mind.[10] Karl Marx replaces the true god with the essence of man. Money is the worship of an alien god at the expense of man's true nature. In Marx's now well known words, "Money is the Jealous God of Israel before whom no other gods may exist."[11] While for Bacon, idolatry is an epistemological problem remedied by the right epistemological framework (i.e., science), for Marx, idolatry is an error remedied by the recognition of how meaning is created. Marx argues that we worship the alien god of money and do not recognize that we have created our own gods and endowed them with meaning. Famously, Marx makes the comparison between the worship of the false god of money and the worship of the false gods of religion: "The more the worker exerts himself, the more powerful becomes the alien objective world which he fashions against himself, the poorer he and his inner world become, the less there is that belongs to him. It is the same in religion."[12]

Rosenzweig does not share with Marx the argument that a traditional conception of the right god must be replaced with a nontraditional ideal, but his argument about the root of idolatry does have a significant affinity with Marx's. Like Marx, Rosenzweig argues that the root of idolatry is a misunderstanding about the ways in which meaning is created and human identity is constituted. Marx and Rosenzweig differ on what constitutes the proper interpretative framework for understanding how human meaning and identity are created. For Marx, it is the "essence of man" that constitutes human meaning and identity. When the true essence of man and his labor are replaced by money, idolatry results. For Rosenzweig, on the other hand, it is the pastness of the present that constitutes human meaning and identity. When the power of the past for the present and the future is denied, idolatry follows.

Rosenzweig's central concern about the possibility of religious authority in the modern world is intimately linked to what he argues is modernity's denial of its past. A reconsideration of Rosenzweig's thought thus has broad relevance to contemporary debates about the status of religious traditions in the modern world. Rosenzweig's early twentieth century musings on the nature of religious tradition and the possibility of their modern authority both anticipate and go beyond current arguments by tradition-oriented thinkers, such as Alasdair MacIntyre in the Anglo-American context and Hans-Georg Gadamer in the Continental European context.[13] Like MacIntyre and Gadamer, Rosenzweig's consideration of the epistemological and ethical status of tradition in the modern world does not attempt to undermine scientific and social scientific worldviews but rather to reorient them in their relation to the traditions and histories upon which they are built. Rosenzweig argues (as MacIntyre and Gadamer do) that the modern person has lost access to her past and that it is essential that we appreciate anew the ways in which our modern identities are constituted by the past. Finally, Rosenzweig concurs with MacIntyre's and Gadamer's respective analyses of the ways in which the individual herself is constituted by the historical structures of communities. This important point only underscores the ways in which the interpretation of Rosenzweig as an advocate of personal revelation is inherently problematic.

In order to stress Rosenzweig's fundamental affinity with a tradition of hermeneutics associated with Gadamer and Heidegger before him, I will use the term "hermeneutic" throughout this book to describe Rosenzweig's concern with the way in which the past constitutes the present. I have in mind here Gadamer's famous statement in *Truth and Method* that "Consciousness of being affected by history [*wirkungsgeshichtliches Bewusstsein*] is primarily consciousness of the hermeneutical *situation*."[14] However, it is at the same time on the issue of effective history that Rosenzweig's thought goes beyond and presents an important challenge to contemporary hermeneutics. For Rosenzweig, the past not only constitutes the present but also upsets the present in such a way that creates not wholeness but discontinuity. Rosenzweig would agree with MacIntyre's statement that "I am born with a past; and to try to cut myself off from that past . . . is to deform my present relationships,"[15] but whereas MacIntyre emphasizes continuity, Rosenzweig emphasizes discontinuity. For Rosenzweig, the past makes demands on the present, demands that are neither entirely clear nor easily met. To take the past seriously is not only to look to the past but to risk the present for the sake of the past. Most fundamentally, for Rosenzweig, to take the past seriously is to risk our very lives in the present.

While a reconsideration of Rosenzweig's thought is highly relevant in regard to the generic question of the present's relation to the past—a question of great importance for those interested in the modern statuses of religious tradition, reason, science, and historical study—a reconsideration of Rosenzweig's thought also has much to offer to the internal questions of how to understand the Jewish tradition in the modern world. Rosenzweig's thought has a deep affinity with a group of contemporary thinkers whom Peter Ochs has called "post-critical," meaning an approach to a religious tradition that takes seriously the internal interpretive dynamics of a tradition while nonetheless taking into account a critical-historical and scientific approach to texts.[16] Rosenzweig's question about the *possibility* of religious authority in the modern world is a philosophical question that recognizes the *philosophical* limits imposed by the complex textuality and historicity of the Jewish tradition and people.[17] A reconsideration of Rosenzweig's thought is vital to understanding the contemporary problems of Jewish thought and its modern history. Rosenzweig saw more clearly than his contemporaries the modern pitfalls of a wholly rationalist and apologetic approach to Judaism's relation to philosophy. He argued that such an approach had grave practical implications in terms of the Jewish tradition's place in the modern world, and he mapped out a solution that attempted to restore the integrity of what we might call a Jewish language game without denying the historical reality of Jewish modernity.[18] Rosenzweig attempts to *philosophically* take seriously, in Clifford Geertz's now famous formulation, a "thick description" of Jewish life and practice. In Geertz's words, a thick description is "first, description of details as part of 'interworked systems of construable signs . . . within which they can be intelligibly . . . described.' Second, it is description from the actor's, participant's, or language-user's point of view, yet without mimicry or confusion of identity on the part of the interpreter."[19]

Rosenzweig's *philosophical* commitment to take seriously the tradition and language game of the Jewish people is highly significant in relation to Halbertal and Margalit's second modern discourse on idolatry, what they call "extension." As they note, this form of argument has been particularly popular among twentieth-century Protestant theologians. It is an argument with which Rosenzweig's understanding of idolatry does *not* have much affinity. As Halbertal and Margalit argue, the discourse of idolatry as extension is an extreme version of iconoclasm. Old idols must not be replaced with new ones. All gods and all ideals are suspect: "The category of idolatry is extended to include any competing opposite, even what was supposedly conceived of as the right God himself. . . . Any candidate for opposing the idol is by definition an erection of a new idol."[20] Halbertal and Margalit suggest that Wittgenstein's statement—"All that philosophy can do is to destroy idols. And that means not making any new ones—say out of the 'absence of idols' "—epitomizes the extension of idolatry in philosophical terms.[21] According to Wittgenstein, philosophy's task is to recognize that our only real knowledge is negative. We can tear down the idols of false knowledge, but we can never erect true knowledge.[22]

In Christian theological terms, Paul Tillich epitomizes the discourse of idolatry as extension: "Idolatry is the elevation of a preliminary concern to ultimacy. Something essentially conditional is taken as unconditional, something essentially partial is boosted to universality, and something essentially finite is given infinite significance (the best example of contemporary idolatry is religious nationalism)."[23] Tillich's notion of idolatry is not confined to the epistemological realm, as is Wittgenstein's. For Tillich, devotion to an unworthy cause is idolatry. Tillich's example of modern idolatry is nationalism. The state is taken for a supreme value while in truth the state is only a relative value. What is finite is taken as infinite.

Though Rosenzweig is a critic of nationalism, and of Jewish nationalism in particular, and though he does in fact call Hegel's conception of the state an "idol," his understanding of nationalism as a form of idolatry is quite different from Tillich's.[24] Halbertal and Margalit rightly point out that the modern discourse of idolatry as extension ultimately cannot maintain any concept of an absolute: "What will stand in opposition to idolatry will not be any sense of absolute but the freedom from absolutes and the denial of ultimates."[25] It is not a human freedom from absolutes that Rosenzweig seeks to preserve in his view of idolatry, but rather God's freedom. Rosenzweig rejects modern nationalism and Jewish nationalism in particular because God is an absolute, and not because humans should be free from devotion to absolutes. For Rosenzweig, the Jewish people can never belong to any land because they belong to God.

But the difference between Rosenzweig's view of idolatry and the form of modern discourse that Halbertal and Margalit call "extension" goes deeper. Rosenzweig's approach to idolatry is not a matter of defining principles or rules that do and do not constitute idolatry. Though Rosenzweig argues that God's, and not human, freedom is absolute, and though he argues that the Jewish people belong to God and not to any land, these propositions are not independently or acontextually true, but only obtain their veracity through the lived community of the Jewish people. From the perspective of Rosenzweig's thought, extreme iconoclasm ultimately takes the critical edge off the concept of idolatry. It is too easy simply to say that something finite should not be given infinite significance. If idolatry could be avoided with such clear and succinct formulations, idolatry would not be the problem that it is. Idolatry is an ever-pervasive problem because it cannot ever be entirely eradicated. Life within a community in dialogue with God always runs the risk of idolatry.

Rosenzweig is not the only one who would find "extension" arguments about idolatry problematic from a theological perspective.[26] Reconsidering Rosenzweig's philosophy in connection with his arguments about idolatry allows us to appreciate the ways in which Rosenzweig's early twentieth century Jewish thought anticipates important aspects of late twentieth century Protestant thought. The conclusion of this book compares Rosenzweig's thought to the contemporary American Lutheran theologian George Lindbeck. This comparison between Rosenzweig and Lindbeck should aid us in thinking about the implications of at least two issues of great urgency to Rosenzweig himself and to current debates in religious studies today. These are the issues of, first, the possibility and nature of Jewish philosophy, and second, the possibility and nature of interreligious dialogue. Looking at Rosenzweig's affinity with aspects of late twentieth century Protestant thought allows us to further reconsider Rosenzweig's relation to Christianity. As I argue in Part 3, the significance of Rosenzweig's claims about Christianity is not, as most proponents of Jewish-Christian dialogue in Rosenzweig's name have maintained, that Judaism and Christianity are mutually affirming. There is rather an insurmountable tension between Judaism and Christianity not because they are so different but because they share so much. Judaism and Christianity have overlapping language games, and Rosenzweig argues that this tension is profoundly significant for understanding modern antisemitism.

Rosenzweig's argument for what we would call today a "thick description" of the Jewish tradition is an argument also for the incommensurability (though not the relativity) of religious traditions. Rosenzweig's conception of idolatry is thus simultaneously a criticism of the modern category "religion" for two interrelated reasons. First, "religion" is problematic for Rosenzweig because it implies a generic experience or structure that denies the very particularity that gives religious traditions their meaning. The second reason for Rosenzweig's disdain for "religion"—a disdain that is not only rarely noted but even denied by most of Rosenzweig's interpreters—brings us to what may be his surprising affinity with Halbertal and Margalit's third modern discourse on idolatry, what they call "inversion." Inversion is a form of argument in which many of the traditional oppositions between pagans and nonpagans are maintained but in which the valuation of the opposition is inverted. Best known for this kind of argument is Nietzsche, who often saw himself as the great inverter of values.[27] Agreeing with the monotheist that the pagan values animal instinct, naturalism, and self-deification, Nietzsche rejects the transcendent God of self-denial and opts for what he and the monotheist agree is the pagan's affirmation of self and life.[28] In a less extreme form, David Hume agrees with the monotheistic definition of monotheism as belief in one unified God. It is, however, for this reason that he prefers polytheism, which he argues is in fact superior to monotheism because it is pluralistic and thereby inherently tolerant.[29]

Rosenzweig's ambivalent attitude toward paganism is as significant as his ambivalent attitude toward Christianity. He argues not only that paganism is true but that paganism is a necessary prerequisite for any dialogical relation, including revelation. For Rosenzweig, both the ancient Greek pagan and the modern neo-pagan, exemplified by Goethe, rightly recognize human finitude and limitation. Rosenzweig's argument about paganism is an inverted one in that he argues that even at his most isolated, idolatrous moment, the pagan is far superior to what he calls the fanatic, whose conceptual scheme is intrinsically *religious*. For Rosenzweig, the fanatic is marked by a religiosity that demands immediate gratification and seeks absolute control. Indeed, the nonreligious pagan is closer to revelation than the religious fanatic, as Rosenzweig comments in one of his last diary entries: "Revelation has only this function: to make the world unreligious again."[30] Rosenzweig suggests that the combination of a potentially lethal idolatrous Christian zeal and the reality of modern nations converge to create modern nationalism, the political form of fanatical religiosity. Because he is not religious, the pagan remains open to revelation in a way that the fanatic does not. Rosenzweig's distinctly modern understanding of idolatry and its relation to "religion" is thus a distinctly modern criticism of the confluence between modern political and theological fanaticism.

Halbertal and Margalit conclude their study on idolatry stating that "it is a mistake to articulate an account of what is the essential content of idolatry" because the concept itself is so "diverse and problematic."[31] The truth of their statement is made clear even by our very brief survey of modern discourses on idolatry and Rosenzweig's conceptual relation to them. Nonetheless, Halbertal and Margalit do offer us these broad parameters. First, "the ban on idolatry is an attempt to dictate exclusively, to map the unique territory of the one God."[32] Second, "God and idolatry are codependent conceptually and in the lives of the faithful."[33] These general statements about idolatry offer us a point of departure for reconsidering Rosenzweig's thought. Rosenzweig's arguments about idolatry are intimately connected to his views of Judaism's significance in the modern world. For Rosenzweig, the teachings of Judaism as lived by the Jewish people represent for the world the proper relation to the proper God.

As will be argued throughout this book, Rosenzweig's thought has its deepest affinity with the trend in German-Jewish thought called "ethical monotheism." Wendell Dietrich defines ethical monotheism as "a religious concentration and intensity that focuses singular attention on God in contrast to all creaturely reality." At the same time, the ethical monotheist maintains "an inclusive interest in culture and society and insist[s] that ethical monotheistic faith energizes the construction of culture."[34] A view of idolatry is both explicit and implicit in the ethical monotheistic defense of Judaism's place in the modern world. As Halbertal and Margalit remark, "The very identity of the monotheists depends on the negation of idolatry."[35] Arguments about Judaism's contribution to world culture through its adherence to pure monotheism and hence the ban on idolatry dominated much of German-Jewish thought, from Moses Mendelssohn onward. Rosenzweig appropriates and transforms the framework of German-Jewish ethical monotheism to offer his views of the proper worship of the proper God as they relate to modern conceptions of art, language, ethics, and national identity.

I have chosen to call Rosenzweig an "ethical monotheist" in an attempt to do justice simultaneously to Rosenzweig's own context and to our own. "Ethical monotheism" remains, however, a self-consciously chosen rubric whose purpose is neither to provide a comprehensive account of Rosenzweig's intellectual and historical context nor, alternatively, to advocate or advance a particular theological position. My aim, instead, is to reconsider philosophically and historically Rosenzweig's thought in terms of its own context and our own. In keeping with his own understanding of how traditions work, Rosenzweig's inheritance of the German-Jewish ethical monotheistic tradition is not merely passive but active. Although Rosenzweig criticizes the German-Jewish ethical monotheistic tradition's view of rationality, as well as its arguments about the confluence between Judaism and modern philosophy, Rosenzweig nonetheless has his deepest affinity with this tradition of thought. He transforms this tradition, and especially Hermann Cohen's ethical monotheism, and reorients it in directions that anticipate and challenge contemporary trends in religious studies, ethics, philosophy, anthropology, theology, and biblical studies.

In attempting to accomplish the twofold task of doing justice to Rosenzweig's context and our own, I will make and defend the following claims throughout this study:

- Rosenzweig argues that the problem of idolatry does not stem from how we think about God but from how we worship God. This argument leads to four interrelated arguments:
- First, Rosenzweig appropriates the ethically monotheistic conception of Israel as witness to the nations. However, in the context of an argument that emphasizes worship rather than philosophically correct ideas, Rosenzweig privileges the carnal nature of Jewish election over "Jewish ideas." In connection with his arguments about Jewish witnessing, Rosenzweig reinterprets the problem of representation to be the problem of existing as representative (*vertreten*) as opposed to presenting or representing an idea (*vorstellen*).
- Second, idolatry as improper worship is for Rosenzweig fundamentally a hermeneutical problem. Rosenzweig develops his view of Jewish witness into a general hermeneutic theory that is meant to offer the modern person an orientation in the modern world after the crisis of meaning brought on by what Rosenzweig calls the historical enlightenment.
- Third, Rosenzweig's emphasis on idolatry as improper worship means that images are not intrinsically idolatrous. The second commandment's ban on graven images is not an all-out ban on visual representation. Rosenzweig argues that images are both potentially redemptive and idolatrous.
- Fourth, since idolatry is a matter of worship and not thought, the possibility of idolatry for Rosenzweig cannot be dismissed merely by thinking about God properly. Rather, idolatry is always a possibility, especially for those who know the true God. Adherence to the ban on idolatry, then, means that one must always risk idolatry. I suggest at the end of this study that this point is critical for thinking about Rosenzweig today in the context of the State of Israel as well as the possibility of the future of monotheism in the Diaspora.

The first two of these points are developed in Part 1, "Ethics and Monotheism." Part 2, "Art and Language," develops the third point in the contexts of Rosenzweig's theories of art and translation. Part 3, "Religion and Politics," develops the fourth point in the contexts of Rosenzweig's views of Judaism, Christianity, and the theological and political significance of antisemitism. The final chapter of the book considers the theological and political significance of Rosenzweig's views of monotheism in turn-of-the-millennium America.

To begin to consider the question of idolatry as a modern possibility, we must start with a question as old as Jewish thought itself. How should we understand the Bible's depiction of God in human terms? Would this not seem to be the definition of idolatry? How can Rosenzweig claim that idolatry is a critical concept, and indeed a modern, critical concept, if the Jewish tradition itself describes God in such a seemingly irrational manner? It is to these questions that we turn in chapter 1.

# Part 1

## ETHICS AND MONOTHEISM

# *One*

## The Eradication of Alien Worship: Rosenzweig as Ethical Monotheist

THE TITLE of this book, "Idolatry and Representation," makes an argument about the relation between Rosenzweig's thought and that of his mentor, the Marburg neo-Kantian Jewish philosopher Hermann Cohen. Rosenzweig studied with Cohen from 1913 to 1914 at the *Hochschule für die Wissenschaft des Judentums*, an institution dedicated to the scientific study of Judaism.[1] Cohen came to teach Jewish philosophy in Berlin after a distinguished career as professor of philosophy at Marburg, where he had founded the Marburg neo-Kantian school of thought.[2] Upon meeting Cohen for the first time Rosenzweig wrote, "I had the surprise of my life."[3] He found something he had not expected—"a human being."[4] Rosenzweig owed his greatest debt to Cohen, even when Cohen's positions became those against which he pitted his own.

The problem of idolatry and representation is at the core of Cohen's posthumous 1919 *Religion of Reason out of the Sources of Judaism*, the manuscript that Rosenzweig read immediately prior to writing *The Star of Redemption*.[5] Cohen argues that Judaism makes a unique ethical contribution to culture and society by adhering to the ban on idolatry. In so doing, Judaism guides the peoples of the world toward pure monotheism and fuels the world's path toward a just and universal culture.[6] For Cohen, the ban on idolatry is an all-out ban on images, the philosophical meaning of which is that God can never be represented by or positively known to human beings.[7] The dialectical tension inherent in the problematic of idolatry and representation marks Cohen's critical idealism—his arguments about the independence and limits of thought—as well as his ethical socialism.[8] Cohen maintains that just as we will always long for a God that we can never know, so too we must strive for the never-ending task of redeeming the world.[9] Cohen's program for socialism posits an ideal society that remains an infinite, ethical task. Like knowledge of the unique God, the ideal society can be approached but never fully reached.[10]

Rosenzweig's thought is guided by Cohen's very problematic—to show Judaism's unique contribution to culture and society, as well as to the omnipresent task of bringing about the redemption of the world for all peoples. Cohen's approach to the problem of idolatry and representation is a necessary backdrop to understanding Rosenzweig's rather different approach to the same problem. The title *Idolatry and Representation* thus also makes problematic the relation between Cohen's and Rosenzweig's respective thoughts, for Cohen and Rosenzweig mean very different things by both "idolatry" and "representation." Nonetheless, Rosenzweig follows Cohen in using this problematic to assess the relation both between Jews and modern culture, and between Judaism and modern philosophy defined broadly. Let us turn first to Cohen on the problem of idolatry and representation and then to Rosenzweig.

## Idolatry as Improper Thinking

The rabbinic term for idolatry—*avodah zarah*—is ambiguous. It means alien worship, but what is alien, the object of worship or the type of worship? Is idolatry a problem about how we think about God, is it about the proper understanding of the object of worship, or is idolatry a problem about how we actually worship God? In Halbertal and Margalit's formulation, is *avodah zarah* the right worship of the wrong God, or is *avodah zarah* the wrong worship of the right God?[11] The answer to this question is more a matter of emphasis than exclusion of the other possibility.[12] There is an intimate link between thinking about God improperly and worshiping God improperly, but which leads to which? Does thinking about God improperly lead to improper worship, or does worshiping God improperly lead to improper thought about God? Does idolatry begin with what we think God *is*? Or does idolatry begin with how we respond to what God asks us to *do*? Moses Maimonides (1135–1204) emphasizes the former position, arguing that idolatry is a problem that begins with thinking about God.[13] It is no accident that Maimonides begins his great philosophical work *The Guide of the Perplexed* with a discussion of anthropomorphism.[14] Maimonides argues throughout the *Guide* that even the masses, who are marked by their lack of philosophical sophistication, must recognize the illusory nature of biblical anthropomorphism.[15]

Maimonides argues that only an idol worshiper believes that a statue, an image created by a human being, is a god. Because the masses continually forget that idols are representations, and not true divinities, they are continually tempted by idolatry. According to Maimonides, this is the reason image-making is forbidden. But once we acknowledge that an image is an image and not the thing itself, we begin to ask questions about how words refer, present, or represent. Here is the starting point for Maimonides' claim that we can only describe God negatively, that is, by what God is not.

However, Maimonides recognizes that the claim that we can only describe God negatively does not solve the problem of idolatry and representation. Once the problematic of idolatry and representation has been reduced to a problem of language, how can the Bible's own blatantly anthropomorphic language be explained away? Maimonides' version of the medieval doctrine of negative attributes, no matter how sophisticated, simply cannot account for the many blatant anthropomorphic descriptions in the Bible of God.[16] Maimonides, indeed, is aware of this problem. Almost the entire first half of *The Guide of the Perplexed* attempts to explain to the perplexed person the Bible's use of anthropomorphic language to describe God. Maimonides explains that what seem to be biblical anthropomorphisms are actually only metaphors, metaphors that aid the ordinary person in the attempt to grasp God's reality: "When they [the rabbis] said, 'The Torah speaks in the language of people,' they meant whatever all people are able to understand at first thought. . . . Therefore they described Him in terms that refer to material being, in order to teach that He exists, since the masses cannot grasp existence at first glance unless it is the existence of a body."[17] Maimonides argues that the masses need to believe that God has physical attributes in order to believe in God. The only difference between God's attributes and human attributes for the unphilosophical person is that God's attributes are always bigger and better than human ones. Thus the masses think that "God would not exist if He did not have a body with a face . . . except that it is larger and brighter."[18] The philosopher recognizes the needs of the masses and therefore that anthropomorphic language is *always* metaphorical.

For Maimonides, the problem of idolatry and representation points to two central human limitations. The first is the human inability to represent God's essence, the second, the inability of language to represent anything true about God.[19] The problem of idolatry and representation is always a semantic one, for Maimonides. Philosophically, at best, we can only describe God negatively, that is, by what God is not. But rather than try to describe God in language, Maimonides asserts that "silence and limiting oneself to the apprehensions of the intellect are more appropriate."[20] For Maimonides, biblical anthropomorphisms are the result of the general degradation of language when it comes to representing God. No linguistic description of God could ever be true in a literal sense.

Maimonides believed that his doctrine of negative attributes had saved Judaism from two potentially great embarrassments: the shamefulness intrinsic to images and the shamefulness intrinsic to words. Since God can be known only negatively, Judaism is spared philosophical embarrassment. In fact, for Maimonides, Judaism's adherence to the ban on idolatry is Judaism's supreme philosophical achievement. Cohen appropriates Maimonides' notion of negative attributes for his distinctly modern, ethically monotheistic view. He argues that Judaism's unique contribution to culture is its recognition of God's uniqueness, a recognition that is ramified in the adherence to the ban on images.[21] In this way, Cohen follows Maimonides in using the problematic of idolatry and representation to argue for the confluence (what Cohen calls the "correlation") of Judaism and philosophy.[22]

Contemporary literary approaches to the problem of representation have an important conceptual relationship to Cohen's and Maimonides's approach to the problem of idolatry. Azade Seyhan sums up the problem of representation that has plagued German philosophy and literary theory in particular for the last few hundred years: "The problem of representation is inherent to the never fully answered question of how philosophical or literary language can mediate and account for the world of experience and for concepts. That question pursues the ideal correspondence of object to subject, word to meaning, image to concept."[23] This general worry about representation corresponds to Cohen's and Maimonides' understanding of the problem of idolatry. Their concern is not any subject, any meaning, or any concept but rather the subject of all subjects, the meaning of all meanings, and the concept of all concepts: God. Cohen and Maimonides ask the question of how any object, word, or image can ever represent God adequately. The answer to their question is that no object, word, or image can ever represent God. For Kant, Hegel, the German Romantics, Cohen, and Maimonides, the problem of representation is a cognitive problem. Though these rather disparate figures have different solutions to the problem of representation, their question is the same: how can the mind ever represent something accurately?

Within the German tradition, beginning with Kant, the word used for representation is *Vorstellung*, which means literally setting out before oneself and in relationship to oneself. This question of the proper *Vorstellung* or representation of God is Cohen's and Maimonides's question about idolatry. What is at stake in representing God is representing the right God. For Cohen and Maimonides, idolatry is the worship of the wrong God. Since the true God cannot be represented, any representation of God is necessarily a representation of the wrong god.

Idolatry for Cohen and Maimonides begins with thinking about God in the wrong way. Just as the German Romantics worry about the ability of words to represent feeling, so too Cohen and Maimonides worry about the ability of words to represent the true God. For the German Romantics as well as for Cohen and Maimonides, the proper response to this worry about representation is the recognition that the human mind ultimately fails at representation. Though Cohen and Maimonides always find words and images shameful, while the German Romantics sometimes do not, they agree that the failure of representation is cognitive in nature. For Cohen and Maimonides, the cognitive failure of representation brings with it a strong moral valence. The refusal to recognize our cognitive failure when it comes to representing God is the greatest betrayal of God: it is the sin of idolatry.

## Rethinking Biblical "Anthropomorphism"

Rosenzweig parts with Cohen and Maimonides by insisting that idolatry is not a failure of thought but rather a failure of worship. Cohen and Maimonides find images shameful because images cannot properly represent God. But if idolatry is more a mistake in a kind of worship than a mistake in the kind of object that is worshiped, then Maimonides' and Cohen's extreme verdict against images is also called into question. For Rosenzweig, images themselves are not intrinsically problematic or shameful. In fact, some images, and some images of God, represent truth and reality properly. Let us turn back to the question of biblical anthropomorphism. If images are not intrinsically shameful, how should we understand the Bible's representation of God with human qualities?

In a short essay of 1928, "A Note on Anthropomorphism," Rosenzweig argues that the tendency to rationalize away biblical anthropomorphisms, epitomized by Cohen and Maimonides, is both dishonest and a misunderstanding of the Bible.[24] Indeed, the very term "anthropomorphism" is laden with rationalist prejudice. Properly speaking, Rosenzweig argues, there is no "anthropomorphism" in the Bible. Rather, "the 'anthropomorphisms' of the Bible are throughout assertions about meetings between God and man."[25] Once we understand that the Bible's descriptions of God are about meetings that take place in time, rather than about essences that are eternal, we can understand that the Bible does not "assert something either about God or about man, but only about an event between the two."[26] Rosenzweig argues that the philosophical problems created by "biblical anthropomorphisms" are a result of a category error. The Bible is not concerned with what God *is*, but rather with how God *acts*, in time, in God's relation to the human being.[27]

In one of his few references to Freud, Rosenzweig elaborates on his understanding of idolatry and images.[28] Specifically, Rosenzweig responds to Freud's assertion in *Totem and Taboo* that the totem is always a substitute for the father. Rosenzweig disagrees with Freud's assumptions and notes in his diary:

> The experience of fatherhood would be an authentic revelation of God, precisely because God is not 'contained' in it. (A father can be the representative [*Stellvertreter*] of God as long as man does not call him "God.") Only the "father substitute," the totem, is idol-worship. Only in retrospect from revelation does the idol appear as God-substitute. In itself, in its origin, it is a reality-substitute. It distorts reality to such an extent that God no longer can send his messengers; now, God has to reveal himself; he has to establish his own religion (which is merely anti-religion) against the *religionitis* of man. (The second commandment is as unpagan as the first.)[29]

Recall that Freud connects the practice of animal sacrifice with the prohibition against killing the totem and asserts that the former is a symbolic substitute for the killing of the father, while the latter expresses the repressed guilt over the original murder of the father. All religious ritual and meaning are an expression of this originary guilt, according to Freud. This includes first and foremost the notion of God, which in reality is always a thinly disguised substitute for the murdered father. Against Freud, Rosenzweig argues that the Bible does endow natural experiences with a divine character but that this is not totemism. What differentiates biblical monotheism is the recognition that *God is infinitely free to reveal himself* to the human being in any way, and at any time, that God chooses. Images can authentically represent God but no image can contain God, for the former represents God's freedom to reveal God's self while the latter denies precisely this. Rosenzweig concludes that the experience of fatherhood can authentically represent God's relation to the human being, but no father is God.

For Rosenzweig, God is not "contained" in fatherhood not because all images are intrinsically suspect (Cohen's and Maimonides' view) but because the notion that fatherhood can contain God fixates on what is in fact an authentic image of God and thereby limits future interaction between the human and God. The key to Rosenzweig's understanding of idolatry is that there are for him, as Stéphane Mosès puts it, "natural experiences with a spontaneously divine character."[30] To understand this point, let us unpack Rosenzweig's statement that "God has to reveal himself; he has to establish his own religion (which is merely anti-religion) against the *religionitis* of man. (The second commandment is as unpagan as the first.)." Rosenzweig suggests that pagans worship themselves, and not God. God's religion—revelation—is anti-religion because it dislodges the human fixation on the human being. Revelation reorients the pagan's preoccupation with himself toward God's freedom to reveal God's self to the human being. Rosenzweig argues that the second commandment is as unpagan as the first because both commandments concern the recognition of God's freedom to reveal God's self to the human being. Here he defines "religion"—in opposition to revelation (which is anti-religion)—as a kind of "projective" symbolism that fixes an image of God. To fixate on any one natural experience that has a spontaneously divine character is to worship not only a spatially but a *temporally* fixed image of God. This sort of worship is a denial of God's freedom to reveal himself to the human in any form and at any time that God likes. Idolatry denies God's infinite freedom—and hence God's ability to affect the human being—for the sake of a fixed image of God.

Rosenzweig's views of biblical monotheism, idolatry, and images suggest not only that Freud's understanding of totemism is reductive, but that Cohen's and Maimonides' approach is also. Rosenzweig argues that images can authentically represent God. But to fixate on and worship any one image is idolatry. *Idolatry comes from the way in which an image is worshiped and not from the image itself.* Idolatry is the fixing of an image of God, which, Rosenzweig argues, is a denial of divine freedom.

Against Maimonides and Cohen, Rosenzweig argues not only that the Bible's multiple images of God are not a threat to monotheism, but that they are monotheism's most important safeguard. The Bible's many images of God express particular encounters between the human and the divine. The variety of images of God in the Bible is constitutive of monotheism itself. These diverse and different images of God attest to God's infinite freedom to reveal himself and the human's infinite ability to respond to God: biblical anthropomorphisms "are the single protection against the backsliding into polytheism, which indeed is nothing but consolidation of a genuine present revelation of the real God to a lasting image of God precisely by this means: resisting the ever-new will of God's revelation."[31] For Rosenzweig, the images of God in the Bible are not shameful, as they are for Cohen and Maimonides. Rather, these images go to the heart of the truth of monotheism itself: "The assumption that [biblical anthropomorphisms] make is none other than the double one that the Bible commonly makes: namely that God is capable of what he wills . . . and that the creature is capable of what he should be."[32] Rosenzweig contends that the Bible does not equate idolatry with any and all images, as Maimonides and Cohen argue. Rather, the biblical ban on images is a much more limited prohibition: only fixed or graven images are forbidden. According to Rosenzweig, the Bible forbids a certain interpretation or approach to images, a certain type of worshipful stance, and not images themselves. This understanding is reflected in Buber and Rosenzweig's translation of Exodus 20:4:

> *Nicht mache dir; Schnitzwerk noch irgend Gestalt des, was im Himmel ringsoben, was auf Erden ringsunten, was im Wasser ringsunter der Erde ist.*
>
> Do not make; any wooden carvings or any figure whatsoever of that which is (all around) above in heaven, that which is (all around) below on the earth, and that which is (all around) in the waters beneath the earth.

This notion of a more limited scope of the ban on images becomes all the more clear when contrasted with Luther's translation:

> *Du sollst dir kein Bildnis noch irgend ein Gleichnis machen, weder des, das oben im Himmel, noch des, das unten auf Erden, oder des, das im Wasser unter der Erde ist.*
>
> You shall make no portrait nor any analogy whatsoever, neither of that which is above in heaven nor that which is below on the earth, nor of that which is in the waters beneath the earth.[33]

For Luther, you should make no *portrait* or *analogy* of anything in the heavens, on the earth, or beneath the waters of the earth. Buber and Rosenzweig, on the other hand, translate the Hebrew more literally and thus point to a much more limited prohibition: you should make no *graven image*, nor any *figure* that is in the heavens above, that is on the earth beneath, that is in the waters beneath the earth. Luther's translation prohibits any and all attempts at image-making while Buber and Rosenzweig's translation prohibits only certain sorts of images: those that remain fixed and permanent.

Rosenzweig argues that idolatry is not a mistake about what God is, but a mistake about what constitutes our relationship with God: God's freedom to reveal himself as well as human freedom to respond to God. Against Cohen and Maimonides, Rosenzweig argues that idolatry is a sin not because it is an attempt to represent the unrepresentable. Rather, idolatry is a sin because it is a refusal of divine freedom.

## Idolatry as Improper Worship

Like Cohen, Rosenzweig forms his view of the problem of "anthropomorphism" and idolatry in line with a medieval Jewish philosophical antecedent. While Cohen follows Maimonides in arguing that idolatry is a mistake in the way we think about God, Rosenzweig follows Judah Halevi (1074–1141) in arguing that idolatry is a mistake in the way we worship God. This difference, between Maimonides and Cohen on the one hand and Halevi and Rosenzweig on the other, is rooted in different assumptions about philosophy, Jewish tradition, and the relation between them. At the beginning of the twentieth century, Rosenzweig transformed Halevi's notion of idolatry into a critique of modern philosophy, modern Jewish rationalism, and what he considered the historically reductive ethos of modern culture. Let us turn first to Rosenzweig's relation to Halevi.

Just as Cohen saw himself as a modern day Maimonides, Rosenzweig increasingly identified with Halevi and in fact saw himself as Halevi's modern incarnation. In 1922, the year after completing *The Star of Redemption*, and a few months after being diagnosed with amyotrophic lateral sclerosis ("Lou Gehrig's disease"), Rosenzweig began to translate Halevi's poetry. Rosenzweig's translation of Halevi culminated in 1927 with the publication of translations of ninety-two of Halevi's hymns and poems, along with an afterword and notes by Rosenzweig.[34] As he stated in "The New Thinking," his supplementary essay to *The Star of Redemption*, "The Notes to my Jehuda Halevi contain instructive examples of the practical application of the new thinking."[35]

Rosenzweig's relationship to Halevi's thought and poetry was definitive for the stance he took toward the relationship between philosophy and Judaism.[36] Whereas Maimonides and Cohen suggest that the problem of idolatry and representation reflects the confluence of philosophy and Judaism, Rosenzweig follows Halevi in suggesting that the problem of idolatry, and of biblical "anthropomorphism" more particularly, undermines this very equation. While their approaches to idolatry differ significantly, Cohen and Rosenzweig each use a medieval philosopher to formulate an ethical monotheism whose goal is the critique of modern culture. Before we examine how Rosenzweig does this, let us look briefly at some of what Rosenzweig found so attractive about Halevi's thought.

Judah Halevi's magnum opus, *The Kuzari*, is a dialogue between the king of Khazar and a Christian, Muslim, and Jew, each of whom tries to convince the king that their way is the true one.[37] The king is convinced by a Jewish sage to convert to Judaism. Halevi's book is an argument about the superiority of Judaism over the "other monotheisms," Christianity and Islam, but it can perhaps more importantly be seen as an argument about Judaism's superiority to philosophy.[38] Halevi's argument about idolatry plays a pivotal role in his polemic in *The Kuzari* about the limitations of philosophy. Though he acknowledges that idolatry can take the form of the worship of the wrong god,[39] Halevi argues that idolatry, as epitomized primarily by the Israelite worship of the golden calf, is primarily a sin resulting from wrong worship:

> Their sin, therefore, was the making of an image that was forbidden to them. They further sinned by ascribing Divinity to something that they themselves had constructed without the sanction of God. . . . This sin was not a departure from worshipping the God Who took them out of Egypt; it was rather a revolt against a fraction of His commandments. For God had commanded them not to make images [representing Him], and they proceeded to make an image. They should have continued waiting instead of [relying on their own intellect and] making something to concentrate upon, be drawn toward, and offer sacrifices on an altar. They were motivated by the seers and astrologers among them who thought their actions were based on logic and therefore most accurate.[40]

Rosenzweig's understanding of what constitutes the sin of idolatry is remarkably similar to Halevi's interpretation of the sin of the golden calf. According to Halevi, it was due to the nature of their worship that the Israelites committed the sin of idolatry by worshiping the golden calf. The problem was not that the Israelites worshiped a calf made of gold instead of the true God. Rather, in not waiting for instructions from God as how to worship him properly, the Israelites denied God's absolute authority and freedom to prescribe correct worship. The problem of idolatry does not begin for Halevi with what we think God *is* but rather with what God does and does not ask us to *do*. The implication of Halevi's position is that it is conceivable that God could have commanded the Israelites to worship him via a golden calf—and that this would not have been idolatry because God would have commanded it. As Rosenzweig suggests long after him, Halevi argues that the denial of God's freedom to command is idolatrous because it is tantamount to denying the very relationship between God and the Israelites, a relationship whose very core is precisely God's freedom to give his laws and the Israelites' freedom to obey them.

For both Halevi and Rosenzweig, it is the tradition of Jewish law, and not philosophy, which has the authority to deem what constitutes idolatry. This position avoids the philosophical embarrassment felt by Maimonides and Cohen over the many images of God described in the Bible and over the many images used in Jewish worship. Halevi and Rosenzweig do not need to pretend that biblical, as well as rabbinic and of course kabbalistic sources, do not describe God in human terms. That Jewish literature is full of images of the divine is not a problem, according to the view that idolatry is a matter of worship. The criterion for idolatry is not the presence of images, but what Jewish tradition deems idolatrous or not. The cherubim of the Jerusalem Temple, for example, are not idolatrous because God has designated their use for the proper worship of

God. While the issue of idolatry shows the confluence of Judaism and philosophy for Maimonides and Cohen, for Halevi and Rosenzweig the problem of idolatry shows where philosophy and Judaism part. For Halevi and Rosenzweig, philosophy simply has no contribution to make in telling us what is and is not idolatrous. This is not to suggest, however, that Halevi and Rosenzweig abandon philosophy or critical thought. Both *The Kuzari* and *The Star of Redemption* use Judaism to critique philosophy, but the critiques in both cases are critical and indeed philosophical ones. For Maimonides and Cohen, on the other hand, the opposite is true. Philosophy, specifically in the form of the doctrine of negative attributes, aids us uniquely in telling us how to speak and think about God in a non-idolatrous manner.[41]

Notice the very different conceptualizations of what idolatry is and how it takes place. Let us turn back to the issue of the golden calf. From Maimonides' and Cohen's point of view, the sin of the golden calf is primarily a mistake about *thinking about* what God *is*. The underlying mistake of those who made the golden calf was that they thought God could be represented by a golden calf. The sin of idolatry is the making of a calf in the place and hence the space of the infinite God, who properly speaking has no image. From Halevi and Rosenzweig's perspective, on the other hand, the sin of the golden calf is not about what the Israelites thought about God, but about what the Israelites were and were not commanded to do at a particular time. Rosenzweig maintains, following Halevi, that the temporal particularities of God's commandments to the Israelites are what constitute the unique relationship between God and the people of Israel. Although idolatry is also an issue of how we think about God for Rosenzweig—after all, this is what it means literally to fix an image of God—the mistake about thinking about God is rooted in the way in which we relate to God in time. Idolatry is a misunderstanding of how God *relates* to the human being in *time*.

Halevi's and Rosenzweig's views of idolatry have another important characteristic in common. Both develop their views of idolatry in order to respond to another, contemporaneous interpretation of Judaism. Halevi's emphasis on the tradition of Jewish law as determinate in assessing what constitutes idolatry is part and parcel of his polemic against the Karaites. This Jewish sect founded in the middle of the eighth century by Annan ben David rejected talmudic-traditional authority in favor of a literal reading of the Bible. For Halevi, Jewish tradition, which includes its continuous change over time, is authoritative not only over philosophy but over any so-called literal reading of the Bible. By arguing that it is worship and not the object of worship that constitutes idolatry, Halevi is able to argue for the supremacy of rabbinic interpretation of Jewish law. If Halevi's argument is successful, he is also able to differentiate the

Karaites from Jews who follow rabbinic law. As Halbertal and Margalit point out in *Idolatry*, from the point of view of the object that is worshiped, the Karaites are the same as Jews bound to rabbinic law and tradition. But from the point of view of the manner of worship, the similarity ends.[42]

Rosenzweig does not oppose a Jewish movement as extreme as the Karaites. We have seen that what he opposes is the rationalist trend in Jewish thought which argues that idolatry is a philosophical problem with a philosophical solution. Rosenzweig certainly does not want to suggest that those who view idolatry in terms of the object worshiped (like Cohen and Maimonides) do not have a place in Judaism. However, we should not underestimate the stakes involved in understanding the problem of idolatry properly. Rosenzweig argues that Maimonides' and Cohen's assumption that all images are shameful reflects a lack of trust in God's powers to reach us and in our power to respond to God. This lack of trust, Rosenzweig suggests at the end of his essay on anthropomorphism, has historically led Jews away from Judaism. When the reality of God's meeting with human beings has been denied, Jews have sought such meetings in an extreme manner. Rosenzweig argues that Philo's Logos, Christianity's Spirit, and the late Kabbalah's theosophical speculations were all responses to rationalist denials of a living relation with God.[43] Perhaps more to the point, he suggests that the conversion of so many Jews to Christianity in the modern period—and here Rosenzweig is no doubt also referring to his own flirtation with Christianity—resulted from the Jewish rationalist denial of a living relationship with God. Rosenzweig argues that an acknowledgment and positive assessment of biblical "anthropomorphism" is essential to the health of Judaism. In fact, trust in God's ability to meet the human and the human ability to respond to God is a necessity of comparable importance "to the Law and the Prophets, for our continued existence as Jews."[44]

Rosenzweig's diagnosis of Jewish rationalism and its consequences for Jewish life converge with his diagnosis of the crisis of reason after the First World War. Just as he argues that tradition is superior to any acontextual notion of reason when it comes to understanding idolatry, so too he argues that truth for the human being is always situated truth. As he comments in his diary, "One's own eyes, to be sure, are only one's eyes. But it would be stupidly bourgeois to believe that one had to pluck out one's own eyes in order to see clearly."[45] Rosenzweig's "new thinking" is an attempt to take human situatedness seriously without giving up the search for truth. In this way, Rosenzweig's approach to the problem of biblical "anthropomorphism" extends beyond debates about whether or not God can be represented. Rosenzweig's arguments on this issue are intimately linked to what he argues is the crisis of meaning in the modern world, a crisis brought on by a denial of the ethical and epistemological resources of tradition-based reasoning. As we will see in detail in the next chapter, Rosenzweig applies this critique to both modern Jews and modern people more broadly.

## Rethinking Representation

Before turning to Rosenzweig's argument about how meaning is constituted, we must return to the title of this book, *Idolatry and Representation*. From the perspective of Rosenzweig's thought, does the problem of idolatry *and* representation then disappear? After all, we have seen that for Maimonides, Cohen, Kant, and the German Romantics, the problem of representation is a problem of thinking about, in the case of God, what God *is*.[46] Rosenzweig's argument about biblical "anthropomorphism" is that idolatry is not a problem about what God is, but a problem about how God relates to human beings in time. Idolatry is not a matter of representing the unrepresentable God.

Nonetheless, the concept of "representation" is absolutely central to Rosenzweig's thought. However, Rosenzweig understands representation differently than Cohen does. Here we come to Rosenzweig's most fundamental affinity with and difference from Cohen's ethical monotheism. Rosenzweig does not use the word *Vorstellung* in *The Star of Redemption* to talk about representation. Instead, he uses the noun *Vertreter*, and the verb *vertreten*, which mean "representative" and "to represent" *in a political and ethical sense*. The problem of representation for Rosenzweig is not a problem about presenting ideas. Rather, it is always an ethical and political question as to how we represent ourselves *in relation* to others. As I argue in the next chapter, what it means to be a representative for the past, or a witness, is the central issue in the constitution of human meaning for Rosenzweig. The problem of witnessing is the problem of representing the past in the present for the sake of the future. This is an inherently temporal and hermeneutical issue. Rosenzweig's view is that to be a witness in the present is to stand in for (*vertreten*) the past for the sake of the future. Rosenzweig maintains that this hermeneutical insight is the contribution of Judaism to modern thought and culture.

Rosenzweig's argument is different in content from Cohen's, but it is made possible only by way of Cohen's own conceptual framework. Cohen argues that to be a witness is to present (*vorstellen*) philosophically correct ideas about God to the world.[47] Rosenzweig follows Cohen in arguing that Jews are witness to God's truth for the nations of the world. Cohen and Rosenzweig each argue in their own way that Judaism contributes uniquely to modern thought and culture through its conception of representation and adherence to the ban on idolatry.[48] As Halbertal and Margalit argue, "We can find the answer to the question of what the monotheists consider the proper worship of the proper God by seeing how they define the alien realm."[49] Rosenzweig's notion of witness is predicated on a rejection, though an ambivalent one, of the "alien realm" of philosophical paganism. The issue of what it means to be a witness is absolutely central to *The Star of Redemption*, both in terms of Judaism as witness to the nations and in terms of Rosenzweig's theory of meaning defined more broadly.

Rosenzweig parts with Cohen by arguing that it is by way of proper worship that Jews witness all of humanity. Whereas Cohen argues that Jews witness God through their philosophically correct ideas about God, Rosenzweig argues that Jews witness God through their very being, which includes not only their specific liturgy and sacred calendar but also—rather provocatively—through the very blood that runs through their veins.[50] Just as Rosenzweig argues that the so-called problem of biblical anthropomorphism is a category error committed by Jewish rationalists at the expense of the vital relationship between God and the human being, so too he argues that Cohen's conflation of Judaism and philosophically correct ideas is a category error whose price is the universally redemptive potential of Jewish particularity. Cohen argues that Judaism as a system of representations can be idolatrous—as in the case of biblical anthropomorphism. On his reading, Judaism as a system of representations can block one's relation to God and cloud one's ability to properly conceptualize the ideals of ethical monotheism. Rosenzweig, in contrast, argues that Judaism, as a system of representation, provides bridges to relations with God and the larger social world. Rosenzweig is in keeping with the form of Cohen's argument when he argues that Judaism has a crucial role to play in building up a just and plural civil society and the realization of the ethical dreams of the prophets. He parts with the content of Cohen's argument by arguing that Judaism can make those contributions only if it is allowed to be itself.[51] Significantly, and perhaps ironically, it is in keeping with Cohen's ethical monotheistic framework that Rosenzweig argues that the category errors on the part of Jewish rationalism, epitomized for him by Cohen, have grave consequences not just for Judaism but for the future of all humanity.

The differences between Cohen and Rosenzweig are highly significant and reflect Rosenzweig's response to what he argues is the crisis of reason at the beginning of this century. Still, the structure of Cohen's and Rosenzweig's arguments is remarkably similar: for both, the Jewish witness of God's revelation has world redemptive powers. Moreover, the Jewish witness of God's revelation has much to offer by way of cultural critique.

For both Cohen and Rosenzweig, this means a critique not only of contemporary notions of art and language, but also a critique of modern conceptions of national and group identity. Rosenzweig's thought is an ethical monotheism in the tradition of Hermann Cohen because his aesthetic theory, his philosophy of language, his hermeneutics, as well as his understanding of Jewish and European nationalism, are all oriented and stem from an interpretation of the ethical content of monotheism. In the tradition of Cohen's ethical monotheism, Rosenzweig's philosophical, theological, and cultural task is none other than the eradication of alien worship. To appreciate Rosenzweig's transformation of Cohen's ethical monotheism, we turn in the next chapter to Rosenzweig's place in German-Jewish arguments about a Jewish mission to the nations.

# *Two*

## Miracles and Martyrs, Ethics and Hermeneutics: Idolatry from Mendelssohn to Rosenzweig

ROSENZWEIG INHERITS a long tradition of German-Jewish thought that concluded that Judaism's particularity represents something of universal significance for all of humanity. Moses Mendelssohn, Abraham Geiger, Heinrich Graetz, Hermann Cohen, and Leo Baeck, to name only the most prominent figures, all argue that Judaism contributes to the formation of a progressive, universal culture by upholding pure monotheism.[1] For this tradition of thought, pure monotheism is coequal with an adherence to the ban on idolatry. Each of these thinkers argues in his own way that the heart of Judaism and the ban on idolatry is an unmediated relationship with the unique God. The contrast is to Christianity, which by this definition can adhere neither to pure monotheism nor to the ban on idolatry. The implication of these arguments is that because of its unmediated relationship with the one, unique God, Judaism avoids idolatry and is therefore philosophically and ethically superior to Christianity. In this way, Judaism has a particular ethical and philosophical mission in relation to the culture at large.

Rosenzweig's thought parallels most closely the ethically monotheistic philosophy of Hermann Cohen, who argues that Judaism must help Christian society to continually "come nearer" to Judaism.[2] Indeed, Rosenzweig argues that it is precisely Judaism's role, in one interpreter's words, "to keep Christianity on the straight and narrow."[3] But Rosenzweig also expands Cohen's ethical monotheist argument into an argument about the present's relation to the past. For Rosenzweig, to be representative [*Vertreter*] is not only to present others with ideas about who or what the right God is, but it is also to have a particular relation to a community and to the past of that community. Rosenzweig's view of representation (*vertreten*) is simultaneously a hermeneutic theory, for it raises questions about how the individual is constituted in the present by the past. While Rosenzweig follows Cohen's ethically monotheistic vision in arguing that the Jewish people contribute uniquely to world culture, he transforms Cohen's argument by turning the argument about the Jewish mission to the nations into a general hermeneutic theory.

In order to understand Rosenzweig's ethically monotheistic approach, and how it draws on Cohen's despite significant differences, we must turn to the father of German-Jewish thought, Moses Mendelssohn. Rosenzweig's view of idolatry has a fundamental affinity with Mendelssohn's interpretation of idolatry in *Jerusalem*.[4] Rosenzweig shares with Mendelssohn two important points: first, that idolatry is a matter of worship that is alien, and second, that this alien worship is intimately linked to a mistaken understanding of the nature of religious authority and its relation to the past. Though Mendelssohn's and Rosenzweig's approaches to reason and enlightenment differ, they are linked by a common problematic. This problematic can be formulated in the question: what is Judaism's contribution to the modern world? For both Mendelssohn and Rosenzweig, the answer to this question is intimately linked to their views of Judaism's ability to avoid idolatry through its unique understanding of how human meaning is constituted. Let us turn then to Mendelssohn in order to begin to understand the ways in which Rosenzweig's conception of representation is also a hermeneutical issue about the ways in which the past creates meaning in the present.

## Idolatry, Miracles, and Religious Authority in Mendelssohn's *Jerusalem*

In 1769, Moses Mendelssohn, already famous in German literary circles for his philosophical erudition, was forced to defend publicly his loyalty to Judaism (as well as his reasoning, given his enlightened views of philosophy and religion) as to why he should remain a Jew and not convert to Christianity.[5] While it was the Swiss clergyman John Casper Lavater who delivered this challenge, many Berlin theologians of the Enlightenment were deeply troubled by the fact that Mendelssohn did not seem to be taking steps toward conversion.[6] In the first part of his *Vistas of Eternity* (1768), Lavater had stated what was of course not a new idea: that a prelude to the millennial kingdom of Christ was the conversion of the Jews.[7] Mendelssohn's conversion, which Lavater seemed fully to have expected, would lead the way to the Jews' general conversion and to the ushering in of the kingdom of Christ. Mendelssohn's reply to Lavater is, along with some of his other writings, among the most eloquent Enlightenment pleas for religious tolerance and for the separation of church and state.

In *Jerusalem*, Mendelssohn explicitly links his concerns about tolerance, Judaism's endurance, and idolatry. Mendelssohn contends that the root of Judaism's uniqueness and importance is not a particular theological belief, but a practical and philosophical insight. The Jewish religion, Mendelssohn argues, recognizes the implicit tension between abstract ideas and the necessity of representing abstractions in concrete form. On one level, Mendelssohn is concerned with the problem of representation in Maimonides's sense, in which the question is: how can God, whose infinite being and essence are unknowable to the finite, human mind, be represented, or made concrete? But at a deeper level, Mendelssohn's concern with idolatry is a performative one. In keeping with Halevi's emphasis on worship rather than thought, Mendelssohn argues that Jewish law recognizes the priority of religious performance, or worship, over ways of thinking. In this connection, Mendelssohn claims that Judaism has no dogmas: "Among all the prescriptions and ordinances of the Mosaic law, there is not a single one which says: You shall believe or not believe. They all say: You shall do or not do. Faith is not commanded."[8]

Mendelssohn emphasizes that, on his interpretation, Jewish religion is actually closer to enlightened reason than Christianity is. Judaism, Mendelssohn maintains, requires no commitment to particular dogmas and therefore offers no potential conflict with reason. Mendelssohn claims to "recognize no eternal truths other than those that are not merely comprehensible to human reason but can also be demonstrated and verified by human powers."[9] Contrary to what his critics have contended, Mendelssohn claims that this view is wholly consistent with his understanding of Judaism:

> I believe that Judaism knows of no revealed religion in the sense in which Christians understand this term. The Israelites possess a divine legislation—laws, commandments, ordinances, rules of life, instruction in the will of God as to how they should conduct themselves in order to attain temporal and eternal felicity.[10]

It is on his understanding of divine legislation that Mendelssohn's view of idolatry converges with Halevi's. Like Halevi, Mendelssohn maintains that Jewish law is an "instruction of the will of God" that dictates not philosophically correct ideas, but proper ways of worship. Like Halevi, Mendelssohn insists that idolatry consists of worship that is alien rather than in the alien aspect of the object that is worshiped. Mendelssohn's point is that objects of worship are judged idolatrous by the way in which they are used rather than by what they are. He writes: "In plundering the Temple, the conquerors of Jerusalem found the cherubim on the Ark of the Covenant, and took them for idols of the Jews. They saw everything with the eyes of the barbarians, and from their point of view."[11] Like Halevi, Mendelssohn states clearly that Jews do use images in their worship. The issue is how images are used. Mendelssohn contends that believing the cherubim to be idols, the conquerors of Jerusalem failed to grasp the ways in which the cherubim functioned within the Jerusalem

Temple and, even more important, the ways that the Temple itself functioned within the context of Jewish life.

Perhaps most significantly, Mendelssohn's point about idolatry as improper worship has a contemporary relevance for him. By emphasizing, in his definition of idolatry, the way of worship rather than the object of worship, Mendelssohn hopes also to caution his Christian audience against its own biased assumptions about Judaism: "In judging the religious ideas of a nation that is otherwise still unknown, one must . . . take care not to regard everything from one's own *parochial* point of view, lest one should call idolatry what, in reality, is perhaps only *script*."[12]

It is on the issue of *script* that Mendelssohn's views of idolatry and Judaism's relation to modernity converge. *Jerusalem* contends not only that Judaism does not conflict with reasoned enlightenment but that the two are consonant with one another. Mendelssohn argues that properly understood, Judaism's ceremonial laws are not dogmas that make claims to eternal truths. Rather, the ceremonial laws are revealed, historical truths that script a particular way of life for a particular people. The genius of Jewish ceremonial script, Mendelssohn suggests, is that in its enactment in Jewish life, it is self-consciously a script requiring interpretation. "The ceremonial law itself is a kind of living script, rousing the mind and heart, full of meaning, never ceasing to inspire contemplation and to provide the occasion and opportunity for oral instruction."[13] On Mendelssohn's reading, it is because the Jewish ceremonial law requires constant interpretation and reinterpretation that it both avoids idolatry and is also a model for the nations of the world for avoiding it.

Before turning to Mendelssohn's view of the world-historical implications of Judaism's adherence to the ban on idolatry, we must turn to Mendelssohn's definition of idolatry: "They saw signs not as mere signs, but believed them to be the things themselves. As long as one still used the things themselves or their images and outlines, instead of signs, this error is easily made."[14] At first glance, this definition would seem to indicate that idolatry is a matter of the object that is worshiped, of mistaking what is in fact a sign for the thing itself. On Mendelssohn's view of idolatry, an alien object of worship is intimately connected to an alien kind of worship.[15] However, it is the alienness of the worship that makes the object of worship alien, and not the other way around. Signs are mistakenly believed to be things themselves by way of an error in practice. Mendelssohn claims that signs gain their meaning from the ways that they are used in communal practices. The brilliance of the Jewish ceremonial law, Mendelssohn contends, is that it embodies the recognition of the need for continued interpretation and reinterpretation. Because the law must always be reinterpreted through the generations (and hence through time), the practice of Jewish law in itself avoids idolatry. Signs are not taken to be things themselves.

I am offering a reading of Mendelssohn that emphasizes the hermeneutical implications of his view of idolatry. Mendelssohn's view, like Halevi's, has both hermeneutical and ethical implications. To begin to appreciate these implications, let us turn briefly to Karl Marx's view of commodity fetishism, a view that has an important conceptual affinity with both Mendelssohn's and Rosenzweig's notions of idolatry. Recall Marx's famous statement that

> Money is the Jealous God of Israel before whom no other gods may exist. Money degrades all the gods of mankind and converts them into commodities. Money is the general, self-sufficient value of everything. Hence it has robbed the whole world, the human world as well as nature, of its proper worth. Money is the alienated essence of man's labor and life and this alien essence dominates him as he worships it.[16]

Marx indicates that money is a false God that is worshiped as an idol. Marx contrasts the false God of money to the true God of humanity. Just as Mendelssohn argues that signs are replaced by idols, by the belief that signs are things themselves, Marx argues that money replaces the essence of man's labor and life. But Mendelssohn's and Marx's conceptual affinity cuts deeper. Marx argues, as does Mendelssohn, that an idol is replaced for the truth because of an interpretative error that has performative consequences. In a section of *Capital* entitled "commodity fetishism," Marx argues:

> A commodity appears at first sight an extremely obvious, trivial thing. But its analysis brings out that it is a very strange thing, abounding in metaphysical subtleties and theological niceties. So far as it is a use-value, there is nothing mysterious about it. . . . The form of wood, for instance, is altered if a table is made out of it. Nevertheless the table continues to be wood, an ordinary, sensuous thing. But as soon as it emerges as a commodity, it changes into a thing which transcends sensuousness. It not only stands with its feet on the ground, but, in relation to all other commodities, it stands on its head, and evolves out of its wooden brain grotesque ideas, far more wonderful than if it were to begin dancing on its own free will.[17]

A few pages later, Marx defines "value" as the god "that transforms every product of labour into a social hieroglyphic."[18] What makes a commodity a commodity, and hence an idol, Marx argues, is the way in which people lose sight of its real use. When people begin to focus not on the true question of how a table is used, they begin to ask the false question about what the table is. This, Marx contends, becomes the question of the table's value. Marx argues that relating to an object by way of what we think it is, by way of how we understand its value, rather than by the way in which we use it, distorts not only our relation to the object but our very being. Money is a false object of worship for Marx and what makes it false is the way in which we worship it.

Commodity fetishism is ultimately a hermeneutical error for Marx. By hermeneutical error I mean an error in recognizing the meanings through which our identities and our worlds are shaped and created. Marx argues that by failing to appreciate the way in which we create the commodity, we give the commodity a life of its own. This is what makes the commodity a fetish: we mistake the commodity's use value for a monetary value. Mendelssohn's view of idolatry is very close to Marx's view of the commodity fetish. Idolaters mistake signs for things themselves. Instead of recognizing the way in which signs are used, idolaters focus on what they think signs "really are."

Of course, there is a major difference between Marx and Mendelssohn and that is their differing views of religion. Marx's critique of the commodity fetish is premised on a criticism of religion; famously, the "criticism of religion is the premise of all criticism."[19] For Marx, religion and commodity fetishism both falsely project meaning onto an illusionary object.[20] Marx's critique of capitalist society is precisely an attempt to do away simultaneously with the fetishism of religion and commodities. Like Marx, Mendelssohn's diagnosis of the problem of idolatry coincides with his diagnosis of the eternal problems of humanity. However, Mendelssohn does not believe that religion, and the Jewish religion in particular, should be eradicated.

Because he would reject the notion of progress inherent in Marx's theory of humanity, Mendelssohn's hopes for the prospect of eradicating idolatry would not be as optimistic as Marx's. Though this formulation of Mendelssohn's relation to Marx is obviously anachronistic, it will be useful when we come to Rosenzweig's position.[21] A major premise of *Jerusalem*'s argument for the benefits of religion, and Jewish religion in particular, is Mendelssohn's claim that "individual man advances, but mankind continually fluctuates within fixed limits, while maintaining, on the whole, about the same degree of morality in all periods—the same amount of religion and irreligion, of virtue and vice, of felicity and misery."[22] Mendelssohn argues that because humanity cannot but battle idolatry eternally, Judaism uniquely offers humanity the prospect of redemption. To extend a point made by Alexander Altmann, Mendelssohn should rightly be seen as the father of the German-Jewish ethical monotheistic school.[23] Like Cohen, and then Rosenzweig after him, Mendelssohn links Judaism's adherence to the ban on idolatry with a particular Jewish contribution to the nations of the world. Where Mendelssohn and Marx differ, then, and indeed as we will see where Rosenzweig differs from Marx also, is not in an understanding of what constitutes idolatry or fetishism—in fact, their conceptions are quite similar—but in their evaluations of the possibilities of the progress of humanity.

Mendelssohn argues that the Jewish ceremonial law is a model for fighting the eternal battle against idolatry. He contends further that there is an implicit connection between the prohibition against idolatry and the possibility of moral life in society. Idols of any sort detract from the attention that should be paid first and foremost to human behavior and action. For Mendelssohn, the Jewish ceremonial law's hermeneutical function is twofold: first, it self-consciously recognizes the need for interpretation and reinterpretation of its laws, and, second, it rightfully emphasizes behavior and action over any reified interpretation:

> We have seen how difficult it is to preserve the abstract ideas of religion among men by means of permanent signs. Images and hieroglyphics lead to superstition and idolatry, and our alphabetical script makes man too speculative. It displays the symbolic knowledge of things and their relations too openly on the surface; it spares us the effort of penetrating and searching, and creates too wide a division between doctrine and law. In order to remedy these defects the lawgiver of this nation gave the *ceremonial law*. Religious and moral teachings were to be connected with men's everyday activities. . . . *Men must be impelled to perform actions and only induced to engage in reflection.*[24]

Mendelssohn argues that actions are always preferable to images and signs because actions cannot be preserved and thereby cannot be turned into idols: "There is nothing lasting, nothing enduring about [actions] that, like hieroglyphic script, could lead to idolatry through abuse or misunderstanding."[25] Just as important, "they also have the advantage over alphabetical signs of not isolating man, of not making him a solitary creature, pouring [*sic*] over writings and books. They impel him rather to social intercourse, to imitation, and to oral, living instruction."[26] It is through social intercourse that people are able to come together to make "the effort of penetrating and searching" for the meaning of what they are together creating and doing. Jewish ceremonial law emphasizes performance rather than adherence to dogma. For example, public readings of the Torah, a mainstay of Jewish ceremonial law, aim to produce a community that will continually interpret the text rather than worship it. Because signs arise through a "natural or an arbitrary association of ideas," an activity that by definition requires some level of consensus, signs themselves reflect a social "effort of penetrating and searching."[27] The problem with signs, however, is that, when reified, their social aspect is all too easily forgotten. Signs quickly turn into idols. Mendelssohn argues that it is simply more difficult to deny the social context of actions.

Mendelssohn's hermeneutical approach to idolatry is connected not only to an argument for the intrinsically ethical nature of community but also to an argument for the authority of community. As we have seen, for both Mendelssohn and Halevi, the cherubim of the Jerusalem Temple are not idolatrous because God has designated their use for the proper worship of God.[28] Mendelssohn follows Halevi's view on idolatry in insisting that it is God's law that remains authoritative. Moreover, in keeping with Halevi's framework, Mendelssohn argues that taking seriously a script of a nation means that idolatry is not to be judged by external, rational standards. We come now to what appears to be a major tension in *Jerusalem*, a tension upon which many of Mendelssohn's interpreters have commented: How is it possible to reconcile Mendelssohn's claims for reason with his claims for religious authority?

The import of this question has not receded with time. In fact, two of Mendelssohn's most recent interpreters—David Sorkin and Allan Arkush—argue that this issue remains the central one for understanding Mendelssohn.[29] Sorkin takes a historical view and argues that Mendelssohn's views of reason and religious authority are consistent with those of the religious enlightenment in general. Arkush takes a more philosophical approach and suggests that the careful reader will notice that Mendelssohn's views of reason and religious authority are in fact irreconcilable. The debate between these two impressive interpretations of Mendelssohn is beyond the scope of this book. What is pertinent to our discussion is the fact that in *Jerusalem*, Mendelssohn, whether sincerely, as Sorkin suggests, or disingenuously, as Arkush suggests, advocates both an adherence to reason and an adherence to religious authority.

Mendelssohn's argument about the complementarity of religious tradition and reason is nowhere as pronounced as in his position on miracles. Mendelssohn writes that "miracles can only verify testimonies, support authorities, and confirm the credibility of witnesses and those who transmit tradition. But no testimony and authority can upset any established truth of reason, or place a doubtful one beyond doubt and suspicion."[30] In the context of our discussion of idolatry, we have seen that Mendelssohn's position is tenable only because he rejects a notion of the progress of humanity. The truth of religious authority is both possible and necessary for Mendelssohn because human reason is not sufficient on its own. Human reason exists alongside the transmission of historical traditions. I am offering a reading of Mendelssohn's approach to idolatry that brings out what we might call today its hermeneutical and ethical orientation. This reading emphasizes the ways in which Mendelssohn argues that we constitute our identities as finite human beings through the interpretive scripts of our communities. Mendelssohn's hermeneutical and ethical approaches to the problem of idolatry converge in his contention that the inherited truth of religious tradition is a necessary complement to human reason.[31] We will see that Rosenzweig finds an important conceptual affinity with what he calls Mendelssohn's pre-historical enlightenment view and his own post-historical enlightenment view.

The argument of *Jerusalem* suggests that idolatry results from a distortion of the hermeneutical process, as does fetishism for Marx. Mendelssohn argues that because the problem of idolatry is an eternal one, the Jewish ceremonial law, and hence the Jewish people who observe this ceremonial law, plays a special role in the modern world in maintaining this fine balancing act between reason and tradition. Mendelssohn's arguments for the eternal problem of idolatry and the relevance of the Jewish people in the modern world converge in *Jerusalem*'s argument for a complementarity between Church and State. From Mendelssohn's perspective, the state requires the church for the same reason that the modern world requires Judaism. *Jerusalem* argues that the parts of each pair must remain separate. Nonetheless, for the sake of moral life in society and, indeed, for the sake of the possibility of the redemption of the world, they must exist side by side.

## Rosenzweig on Miracles and Martyrs

The convergence between Mendelssohn's views of idolatry and Judaism's relevance in the modern world is a necessary backdrop to understanding Rosenzweig's position on these two subjects. To begin to understand Rosenzweig's thought, let us begin where we left off with Mendelssohn: the question of miracles. The possibility of miracles is central to Rosenzweig's project in *The Star of Redemption*, in which the central text on revelation, the introduction to the second part, is in fact entitled "On the Possibility of Experiencing Miracles." For Rosenzweig, the problem of miracles captures the epistemological and existential embarrassment of modern theology in the face of modern history and science.[32] Rosenzweig maintains that modern theologians would have been happy to rid themselves of the notion of miracle if only the notion was not so historically tied to their beliefs. The possibility of experiencing miracles marks simultaneously what has been lost and what must be regained by modern theology.

Before venturing any further, we must note two important points about Rosenzweig's approach to miracles. First, Rosenzweig is not interested in establishing the truth of any particular miracle but only in the possibility of experiencing miracles. Second, modern theology's attempt to regain the possibility of experiencing miracles is not for Rosenzweig an uncritical return to a pre-modern worldview. Rather, as Rosenzweig spells out in great detail, his "new thinking" is a modern approach to old problems and themes. The key to recognizing what is both old and new about Rosenzweig's approach to miracles is to recognize the hermeneutical thrust of his argument. Like Mendelssohn, Rosenzweig's understanding of miracles is connected to a hermeneutical and ethical argument about community and the ways in which our identities are constituted. So too, like Mendelssohn, Rosenzweig's view of the possibility of experiencing miracles is intimately linked to his view of idolatry and the Jewish people's special world-historical mission to eradicate alien worship.

At the most basic level, *The Star of Redemption*'s argument is a hermeneutical one. The book's central question asks how meaning is constituted, and even more particularly, how meaning is constituted in the modern world. This question is nowhere as relevant as it is in the context of an understanding of miracles. Why are modern theologians embarrassed by miracles, Rosenzweig asks? His answer to this question is that the crisis of modernity is precisely a crisis of meaning. He argues further that the modern crisis of meaning is intimately connected to a notion of human progress, a notion that we have seen Mendelssohn rejects. Significantly, Rosenzweig maintains that Mendelssohn's approach to the question of miracles does not yet reflect this modern crisis of meaning. Rosenzweig argues that Mendelssohn's position that "miracles can only verify testimonies, support authorities, and confirm the credibility of witnesses and those who transmit tradition" reflects "honest uncertainty" in regard to miracles.[33] Rosenzweig continues that the critique of miracles quickly became dishonest, however, with a new epoch of thought that developed around 1800, an epoch that he calls the "historical enlightenment."[34] The historical enlightenment grew out of Mendelssohn's historical context, but it took a step further when it claimed a new concept for itself: "Since the simple acceptance of tradition was no longer admissible, it was necessary to discover a new principle according to which those *disjecta membra* of the tradition which the critique had left in its wake could again be fused into one vital whole. This principle was found in the idea of 'progress' of humanity."[35]

Rosenzweig argues that the past had been deemed nonauthoritative by the enlightenment's "new" standards. The idea of the progress of humanity was an attempt to give the past some credibility by incorporating it into the present. Theologians in particular had much to gain from this prospect. After all, no matter how much they wanted to enter the "modern" world, theologians, unlike so-called scientists, could not leave tradition entirely behind.[36] However, the notion of the progress of humanity accomplished exactly the opposite of what it intended: the past was in effect deemed null and void because the past was assimilated into the present. "The past had to assume the traits of the present. Only thus it became completely harmless for the present."[37] The present assimilated the past into itself, and in this way also the idea of the present was assimilated into the idea of its fulfillment in the future.[38] Rosenzweig contends that the notion of the progress of humanity is an effort to erase the present's discontinuity with the past. However, Rosenzweig's point is that discontinuity with the past is a necessary component for the constitution of meaning in the present. Rosenzweig argues that to create meaning in the present, the present must necessarily be in relation to and in tension with its past.

Rosenzweig's hermeneutic orientation includes not only a general theory of meaning, as described briefly above, but also an approach to miracles. He defines a miracle as "substantially a sign."[39] Again, Rosenzweig is in accord with Mendelssohn. Rosenzweig's suggestion is that a miracle, like a sign, is not an isolated thing in itself. Rather, a miracle, like a sign, exists within a whole system of meaning, within what Mendelssohn would call a script of a nation. To illustrate Rosenzweig's point, let us take for example the signs that Moses brings, in chapter 4 of Exodus, to the elders of Israel in order to show them that God will take the Israelites out of Egypt. One of the things that Moses does, with Aaron's help, is to turn a rod into a snake. Is simply the act of turning the rod into a snake the miracle? No, according to Rosenzweig, the miracle is the fact that God does take the Israelites out of Egypt. That is why turning the rod into a snake is a sign. It signifies beyond its event to a future event, the exodus from Egypt. But the exodus from Egypt itself is a sign that signifies God's ongoing relationship with the Israelites. Even more important, the exodus from Egypt is part of an unfinished narrative that forms the script of the people of Israel. It is in the telling and ongoing creation of the story that the meaning of miracles is found.

Rosenzweig understands the difference between his and Mendelssohn's view of the possibility of experiencing miracles as a difference in emphasis, resulting from his own response to the historical enlightenment, which Mendelssohn preceded. *The Star of Redemption* insists that after the historical enlightenment, time, and specifically the tension between the past and present, must be the basis of hermeneutical understanding. Though there is a great conceptual affinity between Rosenzweig's and Mendelssohn's understandings of signs and scripts of nations, the significant difference between the two is Rosenzweig's more fundamental emphasis on the relation between the constitution of meaning and time.[40] In the context of miracles, Rosenzweig argues that not taking seriously the way in which time, and specifically our relationship to the past, constitutes our very identities has distorted the fundamental relationship between reason and tradition, and between philosophy and theology. Modern people are unable to take seriously the possibility of miracles because, believing in the progress of humanity, the past is only something to be overcome.

While the denial of the past has obvious consequences for theology's efficacy in the modern world, Rosenzweig argues that philosophy too has been deeply wounded and is in need of repair. Rosenzweig describes the precursor of what became philosophy's eventual demise: "By comprehending itself in the history of philosophy, nothing more was left for it to comprehend. It 'generated' the truth-content of belief and discovered it to be its own methodological root, thereby overcoming the contradiction with that content."[41] Reacting to this one-dimensional dogmatism, philosophy after Hegel could only turn to the multiplicity of points of view (*Weltanschauungen*). Nietzsche's philosophy epitomizes this reaction within the history of philosophy.[42] For Rosenzweig, after Nietzsche, it was no longer possible to make absolute claims to truth, but only to describe particular points of view. In different ways, therefore, because they each lost their claims to their pasts, both theology and philosophy lost the possibility of creating the kind of meaning each had historically created. Rosenzweig argues that the crisis of meaning in the modern world is a crisis of orientation. The modern person, according to *The Star of Redemption*, has nowhere to stand.

What *The Star of Redemption* seeks to offer, then, is a place for the modern person to orient herself. The possibility of orientation depends for Rosenzweig on a relationship to the past. This does not mean an all-out embrace of the past or a return to the past. Rosenzweig contends that neither of these options is desirable or even possible. Rosenzweig's call for a return to a relationship with the past is a call both to the truth that underlies our existence and the possibility of truth. Again, in its embarrassment over miracles, theology for Rosenzweig is guilty of a fundamental dishonesty, while philosophy is incapable of making real truth claims. To understand Rosenzweig's recommendation for how the modern person can orient herself in the modern world, we must return to the relationship between miracles and signs. On what, historically, could a belief in miracles rely? Rosenzweig argues that historically, the possibility of miracles was not doubted, but the occurrence of particular miracles was. The proof of miracles, then, fell to the credibility of eyewitnesses. Of course, witnesses are not always reliable: this was one of the key insights of the historical enlightenment. There is only one true witness, however, argues Rosenzweig, and this is the witness who dies for the truth of the miracle:

> The Satan of the book of Job already knew this: only he is a true witness who testifies with his life's blood. Thus the most cogent proof of the miracle is the appeal to the martyrs, in the first instance of those martyrs who had to corroborate the testimony of their eyes with their martyrdom, but beyond this also to the later martyrs. With their blood, these validated the steadfastness of their belief in the credibility of those who had transmitted the miracle to them, that is, in the last analysis, of the eyewitness.[43]

Job's righteousness was proven only when Job testified with his blood, and not beforehand. Beyond an interpretation of the book of Job, this point has serious implications for hermeneutics. Rosenzweig argues that the truths for which people are willing to die become the truths of subsequent generations. We inherit the truths for which our ancestors were willing to die, and, in inheriting them, become witnesses to them. Furthermore, "The belief in miracles, and not just the belief in decorative miracles, but that in the central miracle of revelation, is to this extent a completely historical belief."[44] The central miracle of revelation that constitutes Judaism and Christianity is historical in exactly the way that the historical enlightenment denies that belief is historical. Rosenzweig argues that to hold a *historical* belief is to find oneself compelled to believe or, better, *forced to grapple with* the truths of a tradition. To hold a historical belief is at the same time to become a witness to a tradition. It is to become a potential martyr and, as Rosenzweig describes in the transition to Part 3 of *The Star of Redemption*, to have hope for the future.

Rosenzweig's emphasis on tradition is not an emphasis on a *belief* in all the tenets of a tradition. His emphasis, rather, is on grappling with a tradition, on awareness of one's identity in terms of a tradition. He addresses this issue most concisely in his notes for a lecture on "The Jewish Person" in which he writes, "Belief and doubt mutually produce the occasion."[45] Rosenzweig goes on to argue that the Jewish person is a doubter every bit as much as a believer. The recognition of tradition is not a wholesale embrace of tradition, but a recognition of the way in which the past constitutes the present.

It is here that Rosenzweig bears his greatest affinity with, while also pushing further, Gadamer's hermeneutical approach. Gadamer defines hermeneutics and the problematic of hermeneutics for the modern person in the following way:

> It is not so much our judgments as it is our prejudices that constitute our being. . . . The historicity of our existence entails that prejudices, in the literal

> sense of the word, constitute the initial directedness of our whole ability to experience. Prejudices are biases of our openness to the world. They are simply conditions whereby we experience something—whereby what we encounter says something to us.[46]

Like Rosenzweig before him, Gadamer contends that the inability to recognize the ways in which our identities are constituted by an indebtedness to the past has produced a crisis of meaning in the modern world. Gadamer maintains that the way out of this crisis is to return to a pre-Enlightenment understanding of prejudice not as a biased distortion of truth but as a precondition of the possibility for truth. Literally, a prejudice is a prejudgment (*Vorurteil*). Prejudices make judgments possible. They are the underlying bases of our identities that allow us to be critical.

But Rosenzweig would push Gadamer even further. Gadamer's analysis might imply that prejudices, or prejudgments, are more passive than they actually are. While Rosenzweig would agree with Gadamer in criticizing a purely cognitive approach to identity—Rosenzweig and Gadamer would agree that a prejudgment (*Vorurteil*) precedes a judgment (*Urteil*)—Rosenzweig would argue that prejudices are also full of risk and are quite costly both to individuals and to communities. Rosenzweig's epistemological criticism of the notion that judgment grounds prejudice is intimately connected to his view of martyrdom and hence the possibility of experiencing miracles. As he writes in "The New Thinking":

> From those most unimportant truths, of the type two times two is four, on which people readily agree, without any other cost than a little brain grease . . . the path leads over the truths which have cost man something, on towards those which he can verify not otherwise than with the sacrifice of life, and finally to those whose truth can be verified only upon generations of risked lives. . . . Only with God himself does the verification reside, only before Him is the truth One. Earthly truth thus remains split—split into two, like the extra-divine factuality, like the primeval facts of world and man.[47]

The difference between Rosenzweig and Gadamer is more a matter of emphasis than substance. Rosenzweig's position makes clear the price of taking the past seriously in the present. The price, Rosenzweig maintains, is life itself. In contrast, Gadamer's position on the present's indebtedness to the past often sounds overly cognitive. We read in *Truth and Method*:

> *To be historically means that knowledge of oneself can never be complete.* All self-knowledge arises from what is historically pregiven, what with Hegel we call 'substance,' because it underlies all subjective intentions and actions, and hence both prescribes and limits every possibility for understanding any tradition whatsoever in its historical alterity. This almost defines the aim of

philosophical hermeneutics: its task is to retrace the path of Hegel's phenomenology of mind until we discover in all that is subjective the substantiality that determines it.[48]

Rosenzweig emphasizes that just as the past constitutes the present, the present is radically altered in its awareness of its relation to the past. In contrast to Gadamer, Rosenzweig emphasizes the radical discontinuity between the past and present. As we will see in chapter 5, this is nowhere as clear as in Rosenzweig's theory of translation. More generally, Rosenzweig argues that at an extreme, the obligations we owe to the past can literally destroy our present.

There is another important difference between Rosenzweig and Gadamer. Where Gadamer presents *Truth and Method* as a general theory of hermeneutics, Rosenzweig's *Star of Redemption* is more particular than a generic hermeneutic. Rosenzweig's hermeneutical approach is simultaneously an attempt to negotiate Judaism's relation to modern thought. However, the particularity of Rosenzweig's approach is in keeping with his general hermeneutical argument. Rather than reflecting a parochial point of view, it is significant to recognize that on *hermeneutical* grounds Rosenzweig's position may be more compelling than Gadamer's. Where Gadamer appears to be satisfied with locating the generic fact that our judgments are always constituted by particular prejudices, he does not indicate his particular prejudices or the truths for which his ancestors have died and upon which his own prejudices are based. Rosenzweig goes further and situates his particular prejudices. As a situated person, Rosenzweig claims that it is only possible to see the universality of the hermeneutical problem from a particular position.[49]

From within his own position within the Jewish tradition and the truths for which members of that tradition have risked their lives, Rosenzweig offers a very particular normative prescription: the task of "the new thinking" is to make it *possible* for the modern person to embrace her ethical duty of witnessing for others. In Part 2 of *The Star of Redemption*, Rosenzweig focuses on what it means to be a witness on an interpersonal level and from a universal perspective. But as I argue in greater detail in the next chapter, for Rosenzweig, witnessing on the interpersonal level is only possible because the Jewish community is a witness to the nations. Rosenzweig's prescription for this personal duty to witness goes hand in hand with his ethically monotheistic argument that Judaism has an ethical mission to be a witness for the nations. Like Mendelssohn, Rosenzweig maintains that Judaism and its ban on idolatry recognize uniquely the meaning of human finitude. But whereas Mendelssohn views the duty to witness as a specifically Jewish duty, Rosenzweig goes further and argues that in the modern world the task of the new thinking is to make it possible for all to become witnesses. This, for Rosenzweig, is the only way to regain an orientation after the historical enlightenment. It is here that Rosenzweig's hermeneutical argument and arguments about idolatry converge.

Modern idolatry for Rosenzweig is the denial of our hermeneutical orientation. It is thus the denial of the *possibility* of becoming a witness and the *possibility* of experiencing miracles. We can now understand why the historical enlightenment implicitly denies even the *possibility* of experiencing miracles. Rosenzweig maintains that to be compelled by a tradition is to be compelled by a past, for which the individual *qua* individual cannot fully account. It is to be more than an individual because the individual carries the tradition with her. For Rosenzweig, the historical enlightenment, and German idealism, are one-dimensional in this regard: they implicitly deny anything beyond their "present." They are, in this sense, fundamentally unhermeneutical. However, although the historical enlightenment holds both that the present consumes the past by way of historical progress and that the present refers only to itself, the historical enlightenment is not according to Rosenzweig a form of idolatry per se. Rather, the position of the historical enlightenment is better understood as incoherent because, on its own terms, it is incapable of producing meaning.

But idolatry does have a particularly modern form, for Rosenzweig. With the case of the Nietzschean point-of-view philosopher, Rosenzweig identifies this new form of idolatry. Rosenzweig argues that the modern pagan, the philosopher of the multiplicity of points-of-view (*Weltanschauungen*), refuses to recognize the hermeneutical and ethical underpinnings of her identity. Though Rosenzweig's criticism of the point-of-view philosopher is obviously a modern and in his terms a specifically post historical-enlightenment one, notice that his definition of modern idolatry has significant affinities with Halevi's and Mendelssohn's understandings. The point-of-view philosopher's idolatrous error is an error of worship. Rosenzweig's suggestion is that the point-of-view philosopher's worldview is one of self-worship. While the point-of-view philosopher worships the wrong object—himself—his error, according to Rosenzweig, is rooted in the ways he understands his relation to his past and future. His error is a hermeneutical one.

Ironically, Rosenzweig inverts Nietzsche's own definition of idolatry. Nietzsche argues that the idolater worships a transcendent god at the cost of finite man.[50] Rosenzweig argues that the Nietzschean point-of-view philosopher worships himself because he does not understand his own finitude properly. To put Rosenzweig's criticism into Marx's terms, we could say that because the point-of-view philosopher misunderstands the way in which his identity is constituted, he makes a fetish of himself.

Significantly, however, there is a way in which Rosenzweig is in deep agreement with Nietzsche. Here Rosenzweig does something surprising for a religious thinker, and for a Jewish thinker in particular. In defining modern idolatry, Rosenzweig partakes in a form of argument that Halbertal and Margalit call "inversion." Nietzsche's argument for paganism as life-affirming is an inversion of what he takes to be the traditional monotheistic argument. Nietzsche's strategy is to agree with what he believes is the monotheist's description of paganism but to invert its valuation. Rosenzweig often partakes in this form of argument, perhaps most provocatively when its comes to his understanding of antisemitism, as discussed in chapters 4 and 6. Rosenzweig also uses this form of argument in regard to modern paganism. Paganism is idolatry according to Rosenzweig, but it is preferable to what Rosenzweig, in *The Star of Redemption*, calls "fanaticism."[51] Rosenzweig maintains that the fanatic, like the pagan, misunderstands fundamentally the hermeneutical and ethical constitution of her identity. But the fanatic's mistake is different from the pagan's. Both the pagan and the fanatic make a fetish of themselves but, Rosenzweig argues, the pagan remains open to revelation, to becoming a witness, while the fanatic does not. Even though the pagan is self-absorbed, the pagan recognizes her finitude. For Rosenzweig, fanatics—and the adherents of religion—deny their fundamental finitude.

Like Nietzsche, Rosenzweig transvalues the pagan emphasis on finitude in opposition to the other-worldliness of "religion." Recall Rosenzweig's comment, discussed in the last chapter, that "God has to reveal himself; he has to establish his own religion (which is merely anti-religion) against the *religionitis* of man." In *The Star of Redemption*, Rosenzweig elaborates on the *religious* nature of the fanatic:

> The ground prematurely cultivated by the fanatic yields no fruit. It does that only when its time has come. And its time, too, will come. But then all the work of cultivation will have to be undertaken afresh. The first seeding has by then rotted, and to assert that these rotten remnants are "already" or "in reality" the same as that which ripens into fruit is but the willful foolishness of pedants.[52]

The fanatic, for Rosenzweig, does not respect the natural order of things and most specifically the place of the finite human being in the natural world. But Rosenzweig outdoes Nietzsche and pushes this scenario even further. He argues that while paganism is superior to religion in its appreciation of human finitude, paganism is a prerequisite for revelation (as opposed to "religion"). Rosenzweig contends that the person—and the modern person in particular—who has experienced the true revelation of God truly appreciates and affirms human finitude. In his supplementary essay to *The Star of Redemption*, "The New Thinking," Rosenzweig makes this point even more strongly: "God clearly did not create religion, but instead the world. And when God reveals himself, the world not only continues to exist everywhere, but it is really only afterwards for the first time created. Revelation does not in the least bit destroy paganism, the paganism of creation."[53]

To appreciate why Rosenzweig maintains that the experience of revelation is superior to religion, we must return again to the hermeneutical underpinnings of *The Star of Redemption*. Rosenzweig argues that the ethics of witnessing requires a blending of philosophy and theology. This blending is what he calls "the new thinking." Again, Rosenzweig argues that the divorce of belief from truth, in the case of theology, led to a dishonest, apologetic emphasis on the present. This emphasis came at the cost of the past and, thereby, at the cost of the future, for the present is but the future's past. The divorce of truth from belief, in the case of philosophy, led to multiple viewpoints, which could no longer claim any truth beyond their own particularity. No longer able to make any claims to truth, philosophy could no longer believe in itself. In order for philosophy to once again claim truth for itself, maintains Rosenzweig, it requires theology.[54] With the help of theology, philosophy can regain its objectivity. But, at the same time, "The theologian whom philosophy requires for the sake of its scientific status is himself a theologian who requires philosophy—for the sake of his integrity."[55]

But, argues Rosenzweig, if theology is to have any integrity, it must reclaim its past by reclaiming creation. Focusing on the "present," modern European theologians had focused on the concept of revelation and tried to distance themselves from any view of creation. Creation, like miracles, had become an embarrassment. Creation, as Rosenzweig elaborates at length, must be understood from the point of view of creatureliness. The state of creatureliness is precisely the multiplicity of views captured by the Nietzschean philosophers of *Weltanschauungen*:

> It is an essence which at every moment originates anew with the whole content of the Distinctive which it includes. . . . It is existence. Existence [*Dasein*] in contrast to Being [*Sein*] means the universal which is full of the distinctive and which is not always and everywhere but, herein infected by the distinctive, must continually become new in order to maintain itself.[56]

Rosenzweig argues that *Dasein*, "being-there" conceived existentially, as opposed to *Sein*, "being" conceived metaphysically, is the state of creatureliness and human finitude.[57] Rosenzweig's word choice, of course, indicates a deep philosophical affinity with many of his German contemporaries, including Martin Heidegger, among others.[58] In keeping with the philosophical inclinations of his times, Rosenzweig maintains in *The Star of Redemption* that to be a creature is to find oneself being-there, in a distinctive place and with a distinctive point of view. It is to find oneself already in the world, a world that is composed of distinctive elements that come into being and eventually perish. Rosenzweig argues that this notion of existence, of being-there, is the natural conclusion of the point-of-view philosopher. On this basis, Rosenzweig contends that it is philosophy, and not theology, that can return the concept of creation to its rightful place. Rosenzweig's contention is that philosophical paganism is the prerequisite for theological honesty and truth.

But the relation between philosophy and theology is twofold, for Rosenzweig. In the modern world, philosophical paganism opens the door to the *possibility* of becoming a witness and to the *possibility* of experiencing miracles. Rosenzweig argues that theology can allow philosophy to see that creation is a sign of revelation. Here Rosenzweig's view of language, and the hermeneutical underpinnings of that view, becomes especially important. For Rosenzweig, the philosophers of *Weltanschauungen* provide descriptive statements about the multifaceted world. This multitude of descriptive statements cannot provide objectivity beyond the particularities of specific descriptions. Rosenzweig contends that creation corresponds to this indicative mood of language. Revelation corresponds to the imperative mood, and shows that indicatives require imperatives for their very possibility. Creation points to revelation because descriptions are logically dependent on commands. Again, Rosenzweig's point has serious implications for hermeneutics. His argument is that we can only describe the world after we have commitments about the world. Our commitments about the world, the imperatives that guide our indicative statements, are our most basic orientations in the world. Our fundamental orientations are what provide descriptive statements with the possibility of truth. Rosenzweig argues that without the imperative mood, the indicative mood would have no meaning. Creation is the sign of revelation because indicative statements, like signs, point to a whole system of meaning. Indicatives point to the imperatives that lie beneath them. Descriptions point to the commitments by which the descriptions themselves are oriented.

Rosenzweig's theory of language and hermeneutical model has an implicit ethical consequence. He argues that imperatives reflect simultaneously language's ethical structure: call and response. Imperatives are a marker of what it means to be a human being: the need for response to God and to other people in the world. Rosenzweig writes: "For the word is mere inception until it finds reception in an ear, and response in a mouth" (*das Wort ist bloß ein Anfang, bis es auf das Ohr trifft, das es auf-fängt, und auf den Mund, der ihm ant-wortet*).[59] Rosenzweig's hermeneutical theory is not just oriented toward the past. Rather, *The Star of Redemption* argues that a relationship with the past makes the future possible. It is here that we can understand Rosenzweig's, and Mendelssohn's, objection to the notion of historical progress. For them, the notion of historical progress denies not only the reality of the past but also the possibility of a future. From Rosenzweig's perspective, the notion of historical progress undermines the truth of any future because all futures become past. More fundamentally, however, *The Star of Redemption* argues that the notion of historical progress undermines the reality and responsibility of human freedom. The notion of historical progress implies a teleology that Rosenzweig denies. He argues that language, as response, requires time and freedom in time. The language of another calls me. To hear is to be acted upon. I cannot see the call in advance. I do not know what the other will say to me.

As *auf-fängt* indicates, the call of the other forces a new beginning onto me. Rosenzweig argues that my being-there is reoriented by the call of the other. Being called by another is a disruption, occurring in time, of my *Dasein*. Speaking and responding require a temporal sequence. I am called and then I must respond to the call. But, being acted upon, according to Rosenzweig, happens spatially also. Being called by another is a disruption of my *Dasein*, of my being there, precisely because an exterior other disturbs the "there" in which I am. Revelation is an acting upon the created self. Rosenzweig argues that the creaturely self is a sign of revelation because the created self has the capacity to respond, to give back words, to "ant-worten." Time is freedom and possibility. While the created self always has the potential to respond, an exterior other must come in time and elicit, or better, demand, a response. That an exterior other comes to me is in fact the meaning of time, for Rosenzweig.

We can now appreciate what Rosenzweig sees as the major difference between the pagan and the fanatic. The pagan is open to the future in a way that the fanatic is not. Rosenzweig argues that the fanatic is a "tyrant of the kingdom of heaven."[60] The fanatic's tyranny comes from her lack of openness to the contingency of the future. The fanatic is incapable of being responsive to true revelation because, believing she can know and control God, the human being, and the world, she lacks the ability to be affected by others. The fanatic denies both contingency and freedom. Rosenzweig argues that God does not desire this sort of "religious" person:

> A rabbinic legend spins a tale of a river in a distant land, a river so pious that it supposedly halted its flow on the Sabbath. If but this river flowed through Frankfurt instead of the Main River—no doubt all Jewry there would strictly observe the Sabbath. But God does not deal in such signs [*Zeichen*]. Apparently he dreads the inevitable consequence: that in that case precisely those least free, those most fearful and miserable, would become the most 'pious.' Evidently God wants for his own only those who are free.[61]

Significantly, the pagan, for Rosenzweig, has the capacity to become God's own because the pagan, as opposed to the fanatic, is in a position to be responsive. Rosenzweig contends that the pagan recognizes her finitude even if she makes a fetish of it. In this sense, Rosenzweig's understanding of idolatry is again close to Halevi's. Recall that for Halevi, the sin of the golden calf "was not a departure from worshipping the God Who took them out of Egypt; it was rather a revolt against a fraction of His commandments."[62] Idolatry is a sin for Rosenzweig but it is not tantamount to a denial of God. Idolatry is "a departure from worshipping the God who took them out of Egypt" only if one understands idolatry from a cognitive point of view. Then, either the way you think about God is right (proper worship) or it is wrong (idolatry). From the perspective of idolatry as improper worship, on the other hand, the issue of absolute transgression is less clear cut. Rosenzweig maintains that because the pagan rightfully recognizes her finitude, she is open, whether she knows it or not, to the possibility of a relationship with God and with others.[63] In this same vein, the fanatic's error is not due to the way she thinks about God. Rather, Rosenzweig contends that the fanatic is someone who acts like he knows and controls the future.

Let us turn briefly to Rosenzweig's well-known comment to the Jewish historian and educator Ernst Simon that "I am regarded as the 'Jewish fanatic,' and yet I have written the first unfanatical Jewish book that I know of (that is to say, Jewish and yet unfanatical, unfanatical and yet Jewish)."[64] We are now in a position to interpret this comment. Rosenzweig's understanding of the hermeneutical and ethical underpinnings of witnessing is an attempt, in Emil Fackenheim's words, to "do justice to all experience."[65] Rosenzweig suggests in his argument for revelation that philosophical paganism, which is universally true, is the prerequisite of revelation. Revelation is by definition unfanatical for Rosenzweig because it leaves the future open. Rosenzweig contends that the witness, as opposed to the fanatical, "religious" person, remains experientially and epistemologically humble.

Yet, at the same time, Rosenzweig maintains that though it has universal import, his view of witnessing is also "Jewish." In Fackenheim's words again, Rosenzweig's attempt is to "make Jewish experience indispensable and indeed somehow central." Here Rosenzweig's ethically monotheistic vision becomes clear. The parallels between Rosenzweig's view of the individual witness and Jewish witness, and indeed the mimicking of the latter by the former, is nowhere as clear as in his discussion of the Jewish Day of Atonement. Describing Yom Kippur, Rosenzweig writes:

> The individual in all his naked individuality stands immediately before God. Only his human sin is named in the moving recital of the sins "which we have sinned," a recital which is far more than mere recital. It shines into the most hidden corners of being and calls forth the confession of the one sin in the unchanging human heart. . . . And so "We" in whose community the individ-

> ual recognizes his sin can be nothing less than the congregation of mankind itself. Just as the year, on these days, represents [*vertreten*] eternity, so Israel represents mankind.[66]

Note that Rosenzweig's notion of representation (*vertreten*) is a temporal issue. Yom Kippur is representative in the Jewish calendar of the entire year. So too on Yom Kippur the individual represents the community not because she physically resembles the community but because the individual is linked to the community through a common past and hence a common future. The individual is representative of the community because the individual is constituted by the community. In this same way, Israel represents mankind not in the sense of physically resembling or cognitively presenting the ideal of mankind but because of its relation to God's revelation, which is the inheritance of its past and responsibility for the future. We see already that Rosenzweig's argument for the ethics of universal, individual witnessing is intimately linked to and in fact based on his view of the Jewish mission to the nations. We will explore this relation in greater detail in the next chapter.

For now we have come full-circle. We have seen that like Mendelssohn, Rosenzweig seeks to answer the question: what is Judaism's contribution to the modern world? Mendelssohn's answer to this question is that Judaism contributes to the modern world by way of its adherence to the ban of idolatry. I have offered a reading of Mendelssohn that highlights the hermeneutical underpinnings of his view. Mendelssohn suggests that the Jewish ceremonial law recognizes implicitly the need for continual reinterpretation. Mendelssohn defines idolatry as the mistake of thinking a sign is a thing itself. For Mendelssohn, this is ultimately a hermeneutical error because it stems from a misunderstanding of the nature of communal script and the continual need for interpretation, as well as the nature of religious authority and its relation to the past. Rosenzweig follows Mendelssohn in asking what Judaism's contribution is to the modern world and in answering with a view of Judaism's adherence to the ban on idolatry and its broad-based hermeneutical implications. Rosenzweig's view of idolatry can be read as an application of Mendelssohn's definition of idolatry in light of what he understands to be the crisis of meaning created by the historical enlightenment. Rosenzweig maintains that the modern idolater takes herself to be a thing in itself rather than a sign for an entire script of meaning. Like Mendelssohn, Rosenzweig contends that this is a hermeneutical error for which the Jewish adherence to the ban on idolatry provides a corrective to a universal, human problem. Rosenzweig argues that Judaism recognizes uniquely what it means to witness God's revelation. Rosenzweig's notion of witness is inherently hermeneutical in that a witness for Rosenzweig fulfills her duty to past and future generations. Rosenzweig argues that after the crisis of meaning caused by the historical enlightenment, the Jewish notion of witnessing serves as a model for providing the modern person with the possibility of orientation.

Although they mark the beginning and end of German-Jewish thought, Mendelssohn's *Jerusalem* and Rosenzweig's *The Star of Redemption* revolve around a remarkably similar concern. Both should be thought of as ethically monotheistic texts because they seek to answer the question of Judaism's ethical contribution to culture at large. For both, Judaism has unique insight into the eternal human propensity toward idolatry, a propensity that no amount of historical progress can or will overcome. At the beginning of the German Enlightenment, Mendelssohn seeks to show how Judaism can contribute to the Enlightenment's vitality. At the end of what he understands to be the crisis of meaning created by what he calls the historical enlightenment—the historical consequence of Mendelssohn's Enlightenment—Rosenzweig argues that it is Judaism that can revitalize German culture. Both Mendelssohn and Rosenzweig argue that Judaism has an important insight into human finitude and that Judaism and its ban on idolatry can return to German and universal culture the meaning of what it means to be a finite human being.

## Cohen's Contribution

Rosenzweig's notion of witness has its deepest affinity with Cohen's ethically monotheistic vision. But before turning to their fundamental similarity, let us account for some of the more fundamental differences between Cohen and Rosenzweig, as well as some of the most basic aspects of their relationship to each other. Rosenzweig and Mendelssohn both reject the notion of historical progress, despite the approximately 150-year gap between them. It is on the issue of historical progress that Rosenzweig is in greatest tension with Cohen.

Like Mendelssohn, Cohen was compelled to defend Judaism publicly when the historian Heinrich von Treitschke published an antisemitic pamphlet in 1876 entitled "Ein Wort über unsere Juden." Cohen replied in 1880 with "Ein Bekenntnis zur Judenfrage" and soon became one of the most influential Jewish intellectuals in Germany, as well as spokespersons for liberal Judaism. The transition from Cohen's thought to Rosenzweig's, and the tensions and issues arising from it, is rooted in their particular historical context. The philosophical tension between Cohen and Rosenzweig can and should be seen as German Jewry's disillusionment with liberalism and prospects for a German-Jewish symbiosis in light of increasing antisemitism and growing German nationalism. Exemplified by Rosenzweig's break with some of Cohen's most basic commitments, this moment reflects a disintegration of belief in universal reason and historical progress. Seen in this way, reflecting on the relationship between Cohen and Rosenzweig offers us an opportunity to better understand the complex and complicated issue of tradition, an issue that we have seen is related in significant ways to Rosenzweig's concerns about idolatry.

Despite the significant differences between Cohen's and Rosenzweig's approach to historical progress, there remain significant affinities between the two, especially in regard to the ethics and hermeneutics of witnessing. The commitment to universal reason and historical progress begins with Mendelssohn, peaks with Cohen, and ends with Rosenzweig. Nonetheless, all three seek to answer the same question: what is Judaism's contribution to modern thought and to the modern world? From Rosenzweig's own perspective, his *Star of Redemption* is not a rejection of Cohen's thought but a movement through it and beyond it.

Cohen's commitments to neo-Kantian philosophy and to Judaism culminate in his notion of ethical monotheism as a program for ethical socialism. Cohen's ideal of ethical monotheism revolves around the conception of messianism that is most developed in his posthumous *Religion der Vernunft aus den Quellen des Judentums*, again, the manuscript that Rosenzweig read before writing *The Star of Redemption*. Based on his particular understanding of Hebrew prophecy, Cohen argues for a notion of messianism as the infinite task of working for economic and social democracy and the eradication of all of society's ills. But implied in Cohen's messianism is the view that however close society may get to completing its task, it will never reach its goal, for the task is infinite. Indeed, Cohen develops this idea precisely to counter any thoughts of revolution.[67] Cohen's ethical socialism—the infinite, unending process of perfecting society through economic and social reform—is deeply rooted in Cohen's faith in the ever-growing, and never-ending, progress and advancement of liberalism and universal reason. For Rosenzweig, the notion of "progress" inherent in Cohen's messianism is the symptom of the same disease that plagues all philosophy, and most specifically German idealism. From Rosenzweig's point of view, Cohen ultimately denies the contingency of meaning and the openness to the future that language marks.

There lies a constant tension in Cohen's philosophy: on the one hand his critical idealist scheme points to the ever limited and constructed nature of human understanding. On the other hand, he takes this point to such an extreme that his initial cry for transcendence becomes an inescapable immanence.[68] Thought is so constructed that it is absolutely independent. Its absolute independence then shows that there is *nothing* outside of thought. The process whereby thought itself produces, or begets, more thoughts is Cohen's most central logical claim: the notion of correlation. Correlation attempts to show how one concept is dependent on another and how concepts infinitely generate, and propel, further concepts and correlations. Just as Cohen's correlation dialectically propels itself, Cohen's view of progress moves history along infinitely. Rosenzweig found Cohen's philosophy to be much closer to Hegel's than Cohen thought.[69] In the end, from Rosenzweig's perspective, both Hegel and Cohen deny the open-ended contingency of human existence. However, when we turn to aspects of the content of Cohen's idealism and ethical monotheism, we find that much of that content, especially in regard to the issues of idolatry and witnessing, finds its way into Rosenzweig's framework.

Rosenzweig himself recognized this affinity and attributed it to an "existential turn" that took place in Cohen's *Religion*.[70] However, as a number of recent scholars have reiterated, Cohen's philosophy does not take any sort of "turn" with *Religion*, but rather continues with the same tensions that plague it throughout.[71] Aspects of the content of Cohen's philosophy often collide with its framework. Cohen's emphasis on the ongoing suffering of the unredeemed world is integrated into a model of completion and perfection: a mathematical equation. This same tension is inherent in his logic of origins—in Cohen's view the basis of thought's independence, and hence its immanence—as well as Cohen's argument for God's transcendence. We can also see it in his view of the individual. On the one hand, Cohen's logic does ultimately generate the other person: "The other is not an Other; he originates in the precise correlation, better, in continuous relationship, with the I."[72] But the ambiguity of Cohen's position comes just a few lines later: "The I cannot be defined, cannot be generated, except if it is determined through the pure generation of the other, and comes out of that other."[73]

The tension in Cohen's view of the present's relationship to the past is most relevant for our purposes in this chapter. Though Cohen is a strong proponent of historical progress, there are elements of his thought that lend themselves to a hermeneutical argument about the present's relation to the past.[74] For Cohen, reason develops through history, and history is the development of reason.[75] Still, in *Religion*, while proclaiming these very views, Cohen also explicitly claims that the present has a debt to the past, a debt that *always* overshadows the present. Cohen develops this idea from a classical concept of Jewish thought, "the merit of the fathers." He writes:

> Can an individual have merit at all? . . . Merit designates the balance of an account, its final reckoning. The account that man must give, in an unending repentance, does not tolerate any such balance, so that a return can never be

> counted and determined. The merit of man must consist exclusively in the activity of his giving an account he can never balance.[76]

Cohen takes this point even further: "The individual has no merit at all, but the appearance of his merit is sufficiently explained through the merit of the fathers, which continuously affects history."[77] Any merit we have is a result of the merit of the fathers, and not of our own doing. Cohen, however, is not arguing for a view of culminative merit, a view that has as its companion a view of retribution.[78] Rather, the notion of the merit of the fathers is meant to act as a check against the possibility of self-righteousness and self-importance:

> If, then, the merit of the fathers wards off the illusion of one's own merit, it would be of little help if this illusion were to be transferred from one individual to another, if it became a means of exchange and perhaps misused for retribution. It is the fathers, not the individuals as such, to whom merit is traced back. The fathers are not such in an absolute sense; they are rather the fathers of the development, the standard-bearers of history. In no way are they to be thought of as exceptional individuals, as individual saints. As such they, too, could have no merit. It is only the fact that something begins with them, something that surpasses them, which makes them into starting points for the problem of merit.[79]

The ambiguity of Cohen's view of history is contained in the phrase that the fathers are "the fathers of the development, the standard-bearers of history."[80] On the one hand, this phrase stands very much in the spirit of the *Wissenschaft des Judentums*. It connotes a linear, progressive view of history. The fathers are those by whom the progress of historical development is marked. On the other hand, "the merit of the fathers" at the same time connotes the hermeneutical understanding that is denied by the person Rosenzweig describes as the fanatic. The fathers in this sense do not mark a linear development, but rather a discontinuity with the past of which the present must always be conscious. That the fathers too "could have no merit" reflects a hermeneutical point contrary to a commitment to historical progress. This view emphasizes the past's hold over the present, a hold that disrupts any notion of progress as a break from the past, the view held both by the fanatic and the historical enlightenment.

The notion of the "merit of the fathers" is one's duty to the past and to a tradition. Rosenzweig's views of witness and martyrdom work to emphasize this same notion of a duty toward a tradition. To be part of a tradition is to be a witness, and thereby a potential martyr, for that tradition. The view of martyrdom found in Rosenzweig's thought is absolutely central to Cohen's. Cohen writes:

> Even martyrdom proper, the acceptance of death for the sanctification of God's name, is nothing but duty and plain obligation, which is shown by the numer-

> ous examples in the history of all religions, in all moral tasks, and, particularly, in political ones. The martyr, therefore, cannot have any historical claim even to the semblance of a hero.[81]

Cohen argues that to become a martyr is the natural consequence of basic ethical duty. A martyr is a witness for the truth and is in this sense not different from any ordinary person who responds to their basic duties:

> The martyr does his duty as he may, and he is not to be distinguished from the one who does it without risking his life in a publicly exposed position. It is possible, in a simple sampling in various fields of civic morality, to find in all strata of society men who endanger their positions in life and, with this, their own life, and suffer the loss of it.[82]

Cohen's question is the same as Mendelssohn's and Rosenzweig's: what contribution does Judaism make to modern thought and to the modern world? Rosenzweig follows Cohen in arguing that the answer to this question must be understood precisely in relation to this issue of witness and martyrdom. Very much in the spirit of Mendelssohn, Cohen's ethically monotheistic scheme maintains that Judaism must remain Judaism because, by remaining faithful to the prohibition against idolatry, Judaism curtails the idolatrous lapses on the part of the rest of the world.

However, Cohen differs from Mendelssohn and Rosenzweig on the definition of idolatry. For Cohen, idolatry is the worship of an alien object, while for Mendelssohn and Rosenzweig, idolatry is an alien kind of worship. Even in *Religion*, Cohen argues that idolatry stems first and foremost from a cognitive problem, from the way that we think about God. "The fight against the gods [of polytheism] is therefore the fight of being [*Sein*] against seeming [*Schein*], the fight of archetypal being against likenesses that have no archetype."[83] We have seen that Rosenzweig rejects this approach to idolatry and argues that idolatry begins not in thought but in performance. Indeed, it is for this reason that Rosenzweig is at the very least ambivalent about paganism, and perhaps even rather positive. For Rosenzweig, because the modern pagan is rooted in the particularity of her existence (her *Dasein*, as opposed to *Sein*), she is capable of proper performance in relation to God and other people, while the fanatic is not. Because he remains tied to a cognitivist schema, Cohen would never embrace paganism of any kind. Indeed, his view is that "idolatry has to be destroyed absolutely. This decision is the precondition of true monotheism."[84] Rosenzweig disagrees. For him, true monotheism recognizes that idolatry is always a risk. In fact, true monotheism must always risk idolatry precisely because idolatry is an error of worship. For Rosenzweig, unlike Cohen, idolatry is not a cognitive problem that is remedied simply through right thinking. Because

God demands worship, and even intimate relationship, idolatry always remains a possibility.

Despite this important difference, Rosenzweig is nonetheless in Cohen's debt precisely on the issue of idolatry and witness. Cohen's view of Jewish witnessing, like Mendelssohn's before him and Rosenzweig's after him, suggests that the most important part of Jewish witness is its performative, and not its cognitive, aspect.[85] Cohen argues that, just as for every individual and his duty, to be a witness is to become—merely as a matter of basic obligation—a potential martyr. This, according to Cohen, is the proper interpretation of the suffering servant: "As Israel suffers, according to the prophet, for the pagan worshipers, so Israel to this very day suffers vicariously for the faults and wrongs which still hinder the realization of monotheism."[86] In adherence to the prohibition against idolatry, Israel is a witness and martyr for the nations. This theme is reiterated, almost literally, by Rosenzweig: "Israel intercedes with him [God] in behalf of the sinning peoples of the world and he afflicts Israel with disease so that those other peoples may be healed. Both stand before God: Israel, his servant, and the kings of the peoples; . . . so inextricably twined that human hands cannot untangle them."[87] The core of Cohen's ethical monotheism—Judaism's uniqueness in relation to the redemption of the world—becomes a central theme of *The Star of Redemption.*

Rosenzweig's description of *The Star of Redemption* as a book that is both unfanatical and Jewish could be applied in some measure to Cohen's *Religion.* If unfanatical means universally applicable, then Cohen argues perhaps even more emphatically than Rosenzweig that Jewish witnessing must be a model for all. Jewish experience is both essential and indispensable for Cohen's vision. Above we saw the way in which Rosenzweig's view of individual witnessing mimics Rosenzweig's argument that the individual represents the community on Yom Kippur, and that the Jewish community in turn represents all of humanity. Like his interpretation of the suffering servant, Rosenzweig borrows directly from Cohen the notion that Israel is a model for all of humanity. Cohen argues that the individual's confession in community that takes place on the Day of Atonement is "the symbol for the redemption of mankind."[88] Cohen continues that as the individual Jew does for the Jewish community on Yom Kippur, Israel suffers representatively for all of mankind:

> Suffering is the characteristic feature of religion, and it is the task of monotheism that is symbolically expressed [*symbolisch ausgedrückt*] through the suffering of those who professed Jewish monotheism. Monotheism had to become self-conscious in those who profess it. Therefore, just as one acknowledges the punishment meted out by an earthly judge, so those who professed monotheism had to recognize and acknowledge suffering as God's providence, ordained

for the purpose of their self-sanctification, their education to the maturity of the I in its correlation with God. Israel's suffering symbolically expresses the reconciliation of man with God. Israel's suffering is its "long day," as the German vernacular calls the Day of Atonement. . . . The Day of Atonement is the symbol for the redemption of mankind.[89]

Despite Cohen's and Rosenzweig's remarkably similar formulations, notice an important and highly significant difference between them. Cohen argues that Israel *symbolically expresses* all human beings and that "the Day of Atonement is the symbol for the redemption of mankind." In contrast, Rosenzweig argues, in the passage quoted at the end of the last section, Israel is *representative* of all human beings: "Just as the year, on these days, represents [*vertreten*] eternity, so Israel represents mankind."[90] Cohen's use of symbol reflects his view of the problem of idolatry and representation as a cognitive one. Cohen understands Israel's representation of humankind as *Vorstellung*, that is, as a presentation of an idea.[91] Rosenzweig, in contrast, understands Israel as representative, as *Vertreter*, of humankind. While for Cohen, Israel places before the nations of the world an idea that can propel the world toward redemption, for Rosenzweig Israel stands in for the nations of the world for the sake of redemption. This is the content of the difference between Cohen and Rosenzweig, a difference that has a variety of implications especially in terms of conceptions of aesthetics and politics. Nonetheless, the form of Cohen's and Rosenzweig's arguments is remarkably similar. For both, the example of Jewish witness is an ethical and hermeneutical model for all humankind. Following Mendelssohn, both Cohen and Rosenzweig argue that Judaism makes a contribution to culture by way of its adherence to the ban on idolatry. For all three, this adherence has profound hermeneutical implications for all humankind.

Rosenzweig draws on Cohen's thought on these most crucial issues of tradition, witness, and obligation. This is not to imply that Cohen's thought possesses an originality that Rosenzweig could not resist. On the contrary: these aspects of Cohen's thought are taken directly from some of the most basic and central of traditional Jewish concepts. Cohen's genius is that he could translate these concepts into a philosophical scheme and make the philosophical scheme conform to the concepts, and not the concepts to the philosophical scheme. This act of translation, as we will see in chapter 5, is very much in the spirit of what becomes Rosenzweig's philosophy of translation. From Rosenzweig's perspective, aspects of Cohen's neo-Kantian framework continually impinge upon much of the content of his thought. But it is not simply that Rosenzweig rejects Cohen's framework and then returns to the traditional Jewish concepts. As we will see in the next chapter, from a philosophical point of view,

Rosenzweig utilizes Cohen's *philosophical* framework and goes beyond it. Rosenzweig does not simply leave Cohen behind. Rather, very much in conformity with his own view of history, Rosenzweig uses Cohen as a measure and resource against which to define his own project. From the perspective of Rosenzweig's own position, *The Star of Redemption* is witness to Cohen's Jewish thought.

# *Three*

## The Philosophical Import of Carnal Israel: Hermeneutics and the Structure of Rosenzweig's *The Star of Redemption*

Franz Rosenzweig's claims about the Jewish people in Part 3, Book 1 of *The Star of Redemption* remain a disquieting and often embarrassing issue for his interpreters. Rosenzweig contends that the Jewish people exist outside of historical time, and that the Jewish community is a community constituted by blood. Are these claims meant historically, theologically, or philosophically?

In this chapter, we move from the performative hermeneutic of *The Star of Redemption* to the embodied character and implications of that hermeneutic. In order to make this movement clear, we must turn to the important philosophical place that "the Jewish people" occupies in *The Star of Redemption.* While Stéphane Mosès, in his 1982 *Système et révélation: La philosophie de Franz Rosenzweig*, has pointed the way toward such an understanding, a fuller account of the book's structure, and the implicit argument about community in that structure, is necessary if we are to understand the full *philosophical* import of Rosenzweig's claims about the Jewish people.[1]

Against a long line of interpreters who suggest that the structure of *The Star of Redemption* constitutes a dialectic in the Hegelian sense, I argue that the book's structure suggests a kind of hermeneutical argument that gives epistemological priority to communal frameworks in general and the Jewish community in particular. Rosenzweig's claim about community is twofold: first that the framework of community is a condition of all individual experience and cognition, and second, and perhaps more provocatively, that the Jewish community as the physical embodiment of God's revelation is a prerequisite for the possibility of any human community.

Seen in the context of Rosenzweig's claim for the unique world-historical role of Judaism and the Jewish community as the sources of world-redemption, the philosophical implications of *The Star of Redemption*'s structure suggest it should be read as an ethical monotheistic text in the tradition of Hermann Cohen's *Religion of Reason out of the Sources of Judaism.* But Rosenzweig's ethical monotheism is as significant for its divergences from Cohen's as it is for its affinities with it. As a number of recent interpreters have reiterated, Cohen's ethical monotheism as articulated in his *Religion of Reason* does not break with Cohen's system of philosophy but in fact implies, as does his entire philosophical system, a confluence between Judaism and philosophy.[2] This confluence, moreover, implies for Cohen that the harmonization of Jewish sources and modern philosophy is a necessary feature of Jewish identity and of modern Jewish identity more particularly. Against this thrust of Cohen's ethical monotheism, Rosenzweig contends that such a harmonization is neither possible nor desirable. In fact, it is Judaism that brings philosophy, and modern philosophy in particular, to its ultimate limit. As we will see, however, this argument, as Rosenzweig himself acknowledged more than once, is nonetheless a philosophical argument with philosophical implications. I turn to these implications below.

## The Structure of *The Star of Redemption* as a Hermeneutical Argument

I begin with two equally important and interrelated questions:

1. What is *The Star of Redemption*'s argument and
2. How does it make this argument?

As Rosenzweig argues in a number of his essays on translation, content cannot be separated from form.[3] With this hermeneutical approach in mind, I suggest that *The Star of Redemption*'s argument cannot be understood apart from the form of the argument, which is the structure of the book itself.

*The Star of Redemption* consists of three parts, each of which consists of three books. The first part describes a logic of three separate and unrelated elements: god, world, and man. The second part describes a world of experience that consists of the interrelationships between the human being, God, and the world. And the third part describes what Rosenzweig calls the two communities of redemption, Judaism and Christianity, and their relationship to God and truth.

Many interpreters have approached the structure of *The Star of Redemption* by assuming that it is progressive, that Part 1 leads to Part 2 and Part 2 to Part 3. Another way of formulating the progressive argument is to say that logic leads to experience, which includes for Rosenzweig the world of language and love, which then leads to the structures of Jewish and Christian communities which then lead to truth and God. If *The Star of Redemption*'s structure is seen as progressive, then its philosophical affinity with neo-Hegelianism, and with a kind of Hegelian dialectic more particularly, seems almost undeniable. One of Rosenzweig's earliest interpreters, Else-Rahel Freund, epitomizes this view of Rosenzweig's confluence with Hegel: "The third part, faith thinking, occupies the stage of synthesis in the system and is illustrated in the image of the *The Star* of David, which is the 'star of redemption.'"[4]

But what if the structure of *The Star of Redemption* does not suggest a progressive argument? While there are no doubt significant affinities between Rosenzweig's thought and Hegel's, I would like to argue that *The Star of Redemption*'s argument is not dialectical or progressive in a Hegelian sense precisely because the argument does not move autonomously and grow organically from one part to the next.[5] But how then do we get from part to part? Let us focus briefly on what is perhaps the greatest leap: the relation between Part 1 and Part 2. Part 1 presents a logic, Part 2 an account of experience and speech. Just how do we get from one to two from a philosophical perspective? The answer lies in seeing how Part 2 points to Part 1. That is, the truth of Part 1 is demonstrated out of Part 2, but Part 2 is not contingent upon Part 1.

Part 1 is produced from Part 2, and not the other way around. Logic is derived from experience. The world before creation can only be understood from the perspective of the world after creation. So, too, the world of individual experience and personal revelation can only be understood from the perspective of the communities of revelation. This reading takes seriously Rosenzweig's comment in "The New Thinking": "The reader has a particularly high regard for the first pages of philosophical books. He believes they are the basis for all that follows. . . . In truth, this is nowhere less the case than in philosophical books. Here a sentence follows not from the preceding one, but probably more from the following one."[6] *The Star of Redemption* begins self-consciously within a situated context and then asks questions backwards from within that context. This methodology goes no less for the question of the relation between logic and experience than for the relation between experience and the structures of community. While in Part 1 Rosenzweig constructs a logic of god, world, and man before creation, this logic is self-consciously produced from within a world that is already created, reflected by the construction in Part 2 of the world of experience.

*The Star of Redemption* provides us with an important clue to, as well as a significant case of, this hermeneutical strategy. Let us recall Rosenzweig's discussion in Part 2, Book 2 of the relationship between creation and revelation. Rosenzweig writes that "revelation is thus the means for confirming creation structurally."[7] What does Rosenzweig mean by this? He means that creation can only be seen as creation from the perspective of revelation. In other words, creation can only be seen after the fact of revelation. Prior to revelation, the creature does not recognize that God has created the world. As Rosenzweig elaborates in Book 1 of Part 2, the creature is only aware of her status as creature and not of her relationship with her creator. The creature only becomes aware of her relationship with her creator through the experience of revelation; revelation thus confers a past onto creation while simultaneously bringing the creature to a recognition of her previously limited self-understanding. Rosenzweig writes:

> The past creation is demonstrated from out (of) the living, present revelation—demonstrated, that is, pointed out. In the glow of the experienced miracle of revelation, a past that prepares and foresees this miracle becomes visible. The creation which becomes visible in revelation is creation of the revelation. At this point the experiential and presentive character is immovably fixed, and only here can revelation receive a past. But it really must do so. God does not answer the soul's acknowledgment, its "I am thine," with an equally simple "Thou art mine." Rather he reaches back into the past and identifies himself as the one who originated and indicated this whole dialogue between himself and the soul: "I have called thee by name: thou art mine."[8]

Let me reiterate that Rosenzweig argues that revelation confers a past onto creation while simultaneously bringing the creature to a recognition of her previously limited self-understanding. *The Star of Redemption*'s structure and the relationship between the parts follows this same backward, hermeneutical movement that Rosenzweig describes between creation and revelation. Each part brings the reader to a new recognition of the previous part and to a recognition of the previous limited understanding of that previous part. Each part suggests that it can account philosophically for the previous part and provide the previous part with a broader basis of truth. But put this way, Rosenzweig still sounds rather neo-Hegelian and *The Star of Redemption*'s structure still sounds rather progressive. So, too, we might be tempted to say at this point that the notion that logic is derived from experience, and not the other way around, is a quintessentially Hegelian point.

These points are right on target, but Rosenzweig does not argue that Hegelian philosophy (and idealism in general) is wholly false, rather that it is only partially true. For Rosenzweig, falsehood arises only with the quest for and claim of totality and completeness. While Hegel derives his logic from experience, or his *Science of Logic* from his *Phenomenology of Spirit*, he also claims that there is no discontinuity between the two, that experience leads to logic and logic to experience. It is the gap between logic and experience that Rosenzweig seeks to preserve in constructing his logic in Part 1, and the relation between Part 1 and Part 2. Rosenzweig's construction of logic in Part 1 seeks to maintain both that one is already in the world *and* that there is always a gap between logic and experience. This gap, for Rosenzweig, is the key to both human and divine freedom, freedoms that, he believes, Hegel's idealism implicitly denies. For Rosenzweig, the past, and the truth of the past, is determined out of the future, a future that is not and cannot be generated from the past or the truth of the past. Below I will return to the relationship between the truth and the future. Here, however, I would like to focus on the way in which *The Star of Redemption*'s structure is a backward movement from future to past as opposed to a dialectically forward-moving argument from past to future.

The reason why the structure of *The Star of Redemption* is neither dialectical nor forward-moving is that the parts do not move organically from one to the next. While Parts 1 and 2 are dialectically opposed to each other, their relationship does not constitute a dialectic. In fact, this is precisely the position that Rosenzweig wants to avoid. Indeed, in "The New Thinking," Rosenzweig reports that he wanted *The Star of Redemption*'s three parts to be published in three separate volumes. At the very least, this suggests that Rosenzweig saw each of the topics of each part of *The Star of Redemption* as whole in and of itself and not as dialectically generated from one another.[9] In this connection, Rosenzweig encourages his readers not to get caught up in *The Star of Redemption*'s notoriously difficult first part: "Above all: rush! Do not stop! The important part is still to come! . . . What is written here is still nothing other than the *reductio ad absurdum* of the old philosophy."[10] The reader does not require Part 1 to understand the rest of *The Star of Redemption*, for Parts 2 and 3 are not predicated upon Part 1.

But how then are the parts of *The Star of Redemption* related to each other, if not dialectically or progressively? What would it mean for each part to follow, in Rosenzweig's words, "not from the preceding one, but probably more from the following one"? I suggest that the parts are structurally related to each other as creation and revelation are related. That is, without revelation, creation is not recognized as creation per se but as a kind of creature-consciousness. While creature-consciousness is true in and of itself, revelation gives creature-consciousness its truer meaning, which is the truth of creation. The point is that creature-consciousness cannot organically produce the experience of revelation. Creature-consciousness can only come to a recognition of revelation from outside itself, that is, from the experience of revelation itself which, again, in Rosenzweig's words, confirms creation structurally. Revelation confirms the truth of creature-consciousness as creation. Just as "the past creation is demonstrated from out (of) the living present revelation," so too the past of logic is demonstrated from out of living experience. In both cases, neither creation nor logic is capable of producing from out of themselves the very truth which confers upon them their own truth.

With this hermeneutical schema in mind, let me outline briefly the content of the argument suggested by the structure of *The Star of Redemp-*

*tion*. The work's analysis is ultimately an epistemological one, each of the three parts asking how we know through different mediums. The first part of *The Star of Redemption* asks: how do we know by thinking? The second part asks: how do we know by hearing? And the third part asks: how do we know by seeing? This is *The Star of Redemption*'s movement from *Erkenntnis* (knowledge) to *Erlebnis* (experience) to *Erleuchtung* (illumination). This is also the work's movement from logic to love to communal structures.

Each part suggests a whole world of truth. Seen from its own perspective each world is whole and true. But seen from the perspective of each later part, each part is limited. The limitation of each previous part can only be seen from the perspective of the later part. That is, the limitation of logic can only be seen from the perspective of experience, while the limitation of experience can only be seen from the perspective of the framework of community. Experience is thus epistemologically privileged over logic and the structures of community are epistemologically privileged over experience.

What then is the basis of this epistemological privileging? *The Star of Redemption* begins with a basic epistemological point whose truth is ramified—while nonetheless itself shown to be limited—throughout the work. This basic epistemological point is that I cannot know my own death. To put it very briefly, Rosenzweig argues in Part 1 that Greek mythology recognizes the epistemological limitation imposed on the human being by human finitude—death—and thereby, through its insistence on the fundamental separation of the human and god, undercuts idealism's unity of thought. Part 1 ends with a self-contained logic that constructs three wholly separate elements that are not in relation to each other. Having attacked, utilized, and criticized again not just Hegel's and Cohen's logic, but Schelling's also, Rosenzweig argues that based on his initial epistemological premise—that one cannot know one's own death—the logic constructed in Part 1 is philosophically true.[11]

For Rosenzweig, the epistemological limitation that defines the truth of logic in Part 1 simultaneously shows the limitation of that logic in Part 2, in which he argues that the most basic orienting experience of the human being is that another, be it God or another person, exists outside of me and affects me by commanding that I respond to him.[12] Both the other's command and my response to him are wholly contingent; they do not exist in a dialectical relation to each other but rather happen freely, in time. In Part 2 of *The Star of Redemption*, Rosenzweig is able to make this argument about the contingency of my response to another because in Part 1 he has shattered idealism's epistemological framework. From an epistemological perspective, if I cannot know my own death I certainly cannot know the death of another. If I cannot know the death of another,

I cannot know the other completely. This epistemological limitation provides the philosophical basis for the possibility of the freedom of the other to come to me in time.

But while Part 2's description of the encounter with the other is whole in and of itself, the structure of *The Star of Redemption* suggests that the whole of experience is revealed as incomplete when it comes into relation with the social and liturgical structures of community, the subject of Part 3. Like human existence, time is fleeting. Rosenzweig argues in Part 3 that the task of redeeming the world is a task that requires the bringing of eternity into time, a task which is embodied by the structures of Jewish and Christian communities. Each community can create its own eternity because each creates a sacred calendar that stands apart from and reveals the fleetingness of the temporal world. Just as time and *Erlebnis* reveal the incompleteness of logic's claim to eternity, the eternities of Judaism and Christianity reveal the incompleteness of temporal existence and individual *Erlebnis*.

*The Star of Redemption* argues that the Jewish and Christian communities have the greatest claim to truth. It is important to recognize, however, that the eternal people and the eternal way also remain epistemologically incomplete. They remain incomplete because we, the readers, remain in life and not in eternity. To remain in life is to remain human, and to remain human, *The Star of Redemption* continually reminds us, is to be able to perceive only partially and always incompletely. While the Jewish and Christian communities embody eternity in time, they only *anticipate* eternity for they still remain in time. Just as we may be thinking we have found the All in the *Erleuchtung* (illumination) of the communities of redemption, Rosenzweig reminds us that this is not possible:

> The whole [*das Ganze*] too can be perceived only where it has become part, and so the whole of the truth, the whole truth can be perceived only by being seen in God. This is the only thing which is seen in God. It is only here that man does not experience directly; rather it is God who experiences while man merely watches. He grasps his part of the truth in the direct unity of experience and observation. But the whole truth, just because it is the whole truth and thus im-parted only to God, a part only for God, this he can observe himself only in God. For he remains a man in life. . . . The whole truth is imparted only to God.[13]

Each part of *The Star of Redemption* is truer than its previous part. However, the epistemological thrust of *The Star of Redemption* suggests not a progressive movement toward complete truth but a movement of recognizing the epistemological limitations of each whole of truth, represented by each part of *The Star of Redemption*, including the limitation of the last part. The point here is that the limitation of each part is only seen from the perspective of the next part. *Each part, including the last, does not and cannot generate its own limitation.* The relation between the parts of *The Star of Redemption* is thus always a backward movement. Just as creation can only be seen as creation from the perspective of revelation, so too the whole of logic can only be seen from the perspective of experience, and the whole of experience can only be seen from the perspective of the structures of community.

But if *The Star of Redemption*'s argument is neither dialectical nor progressive, then what kind of argument is it? *The Star of Redemption*'s structure may be best characterized as a kind of hermeneutical argument that privileges the epistemological status of communal frameworks over and against individual experience and logic. The structure of *The Star of Redemption* suggests that experience is a condition for logic and that community is a condition for experience. In this sense, the argument of *The Star of Redemption*'s structure concurs with Hans-Georg Gadamer's statement: "The hermeneutical experience is prior to all methodical alienation because it is the matrix out of which arise the questions that it then directs to science."[14] Rosenzweig does not contend that logic and the world of experience are invalidated by the authority of communal structures, but rather that the historical authority of communal structures creates the frameworks for logic and the world of experience. As Rosenzweig writes in one of his essays on Bible translation, God is both transcendent and transcendental to science.[15] While God is always beyond science, it is God that makes science possible in the first place. In the rest of this chapter, I explore what philosophical meaning this hermeneutical argument could possibly have.

To make *The Star of Redemption*'s hermeneutical argument clearer, let us return to the way in which Rosenzweig's argument in Part 2, Book 1 about creature-consciousness is a kind of hermeneutical argument. The significant thing about Rosenzweig's formulation that revelation confers structure upon creation is that creation is already creation but it just doesn't know it. This is a kind of hermeneutical argument that suggests that creature-consciousness is true but does not recognize the greater truth upon which it rests. So, too, the structure of *The Star of Redemption* suggests a similar type of hermeneutical argument. Logic is true but it does not recognize the greater truth upon which it rests: the world of experience. So, too, the world of experience is true but it does not recognize the greater truth upon which it rests: communal structures. And the structures of community, while true, rest upon an even greater truth: the messiness that we might call life but even more importantly the truth of all truths, which we can never perceive fully, God.

The hermeneutical approach to the structure of *The Star of Redemption* that I am suggesting makes sense of Rosenzweig's claim that truth can only be verified in the future. Just as creation can only be known from the perspective of revelation, the truth of Judaism and Christianity can only be confirmed from a future that is not yet. This is where the form and content of *The Star of Redemption*'s argument converge: the backwards/hermeneutical movement of *The Star of Redemption* goes hand in hand with the argument for epistemological incompleteness. Just as revelation shows creature consciousness to be incomplete, so too the future shows the eternal truths of Judaism and Christianity to be incomplete.

Let us return to the argument about the truth of the Jewish and Christian communities as they relate to the truths of individual experience and logic. The argument of *The Star of Redemption* is that communal frameworks are a condition for language, experience, and logic. *The Star of Redemption* suggests that the frameworks of community ground not only communal experience, but individual experience and cognition also. In more contemporary terms, the implication of the argument is that communal frameworks are logical conditions of personal experience and cognition.

This approach, that communal frameworks make possible individual experience and cognition, helps to make sense of Rosenzweig's conception of Judaism and Jewish community. Attention to *The Star of Redemption*'s claim for the philosophical priority of community should cause us to reevaluate the view of Rosenzweig and *The Star of Redemption* as suggesting personal and individual revelation as the meaning of Jewish revelation. Personal revelation does not lead to religious community, as the progressive reading of *The Star of Redemption* might have it. Indeed, *The Star of Redemption*'s claim for the priority of communal frameworks gives philosophical weight to Rosenzweig's "more popular" arguments about the priority of Jewish law over an individualistic relation to Judaism. So, too, *The Star of Redemption*'s claim for the priority of communal frameworks provides a philosophical context for Rosenzweig's efforts at adult education, which sought not to provide the individual Jew with access to personal revelation but rather with the tools, or, in more technical terms, the conditions for returning to Jewish community, such as knowledge of Hebrew and Jewish texts. Rosenzweig's suggestion, then, is that Jewish literacy, the literal ability to participate in Jewish communal life, *and not personal revelation*, is a prerequisite for modern Jewish identity.

This is not to deny the significance of the phenomenological account of experience, and the experience of revelation in particular, in Part 2 of *The Star of Redemption*. The personal experience of revelation described in Part 2 is the way in which a *modern* person may come to experience God's revelation. Through the personal encounter of the I and the Thou, the modern person may come to experience God's revelation. Moreover, as suggested by Book 3 of Part 2, this personal encounter may well lead to the formation of communities of multiple persons. Indeed, it is no accident that especially in Part 2 of *The Star of Redemption*, Rosenzweig employs Romantic language and imagery to emphasize that his description of personal revelation is particularly modern, and for him contemporary. But rather than suggesting that Rosenzweig was too much a creature of his times, attention to the Romantic language and imagery of Part 2 only emphasizes the hermeneutical thrust of *The Star of Redemption*. Rosenzweig self-consciously employs the language of his times in order to suggest the way in which a modern person may come to know God's revelation. As we have seen, however, attention to the argument implicit in *The Star of Redemption*'s hermeneutical structure shows that personal revelation, described in Part 2, is only possible because of the historical revelations of the Jewish and Christian communities, described in Part 3.

Once again, Gadamer's comments illustrate well the implication of the argument of *The Star of Redemption*'s structure: "The nature of the hermeneutical experience is not that something is outside that desires admission. Rather, we are possessed by something and precisely by means of it we are opened up for the new, the different, the true."[16] The modern person may well believe that she is discovering revelation anew for herself. However, just as the creature has already been created by her creator even if she does not know it, so too the modern person has the possibility of personal encounter only because the historical communities of Jewish and Christian revelation already exist in the world, even if she does not know them. Modern people, without knowing it, are for Rosenzweig already—to use Gadamer's words—"possessed by something." It is precisely by means of this "already having been possessed" that we are for Rosenzweig "opened up for the new, the different, the true."

As ramified by his efforts at translating the Hebrew Bible into German, with Martin Buber, as well as his continued effort at adult education, Rosenzweig was deeply aware of the particular hermeneutical problem of the modern person alienated from the world of religious tradition.[17] As Gadamer explains:

> It seems . . . to be generally characteristic of the emergence of the "hermeneutical" problem that something distant has to be brought close, a certain strangeness overcome, a bridge built between the once and the now. Thus hermeneutics . . . came into its own in modern times, which had become aware of the temporal distance separating us from antiquity and of the relativity of the lifeworlds of different cultural traditions.[18]

From a phenomenological perspective, *The Star of Redemption* argues for personal encounter as a modern gateway into the communities of revelation. The overall philosophical argument of *The Star of Redemption*, however, grants epistemological priority not to personal revelation, but to the communities of Judaism and Christianity. Just as the creature only recognizes the true nature of her existence after revelation, so too the modern person only recognizes that she is already possessed by the historical revelations of the Jewish and Christian communities after she returns to them.[19] The hermeneutical argument of the structure of *The Star of Redemption* does not suggest that personal revelation makes community possible; rather, it suggests that the historical realities of the Jewish and Christian communities make the experience of revelation possible for the modern person.[20]

## The Philosophical Import of Carnal Israel

Of course what *The Star of Redemption* has to say about community and the particularity of the Jewish community does not end here. I have argued that *The Star of Redemption* privileges the epistemological status of community over the realms of experience and logic. In the context of the structure of *The Star of Redemption*, this privileging of community is also a privileging of the third part of *The Star of Redemption* over the first two parts. We must note, however, that within the last part there is yet a further hermeneutical argument that privileges the Jewish community over all other communities. For Rosenzweig, the Jewish community is nothing short of a condition for the possibility of community for all peoples. *The Star of Redemption*'s claim that communal structures are conditions of individual experience and cognition is coupled with a second, more provocative claim, namely, that Jewish community as the physical embodiment of God's revelation is a prerequisite for—and in fact a condition of—the possibility of any human community.

I need not reiterate Rosenzweig's comments about Islam, Buddhism, or Confucianism to make it clear that it is certainly apparent that Rosenzweig does not believe that all communities are equal to the task of creating eternity in time. However, it is even a mistake to think, as many interpreters of Rosenzweig's thought do, that in Part 3 of *The Star of Redemption* he advocates two separate but equal communities of redemption. On the contrary: Rosenzweig's position is that the Jewish community, and the Jewish community alone, has achieved true community and that the Jewish community thereby makes it possible for all others (specifically through the medium of Christianity) to attempt to achieve community for themselves.[21] Indeed, "The Jewish people has already reached the goal toward which the nations are still moving."[22]

What has allowed the Jewish people to already reach the goal toward which the nations are moving? Famously, or perhaps infamously, the answer for Rosenzweig is Jewish blood:

> There is only one community in which such a linked sequence of everlasting life goes from grandfather to grandson, only one which cannot utter the "we" of its unity without hearing deep within a voice that adds: "are eternal." It must be a blood-community, because only blood gives warrant to the hope for a future. . . . While every other community that lays claim to eternity must take measures to pass the torch of the present on to the future, the blood-community does not have to resort to such measures. It does not have to enlist the services of the spirit; the natural propagation of the body guarantees it eternity.[23]

Jewish blood is not only the embodiment of God's revelation, according to *The Star of Redemption*, but it also creates the condition for universal community. The eternity guaranteed by Jewish blood is the eternity toward which the nations must all work if they want to gain eternity. Carnal Israel, according to *The Star of Redemption*, has both a unique ontological and epistemological status. Attention to the place of "the Jewish people" in *The Star of Redemption* thus shows the way in which "the Jewish people" function as a condition for universal community and thus for universal redemption. If, as I have argued, the structure of *The Star of Redemption* suggests that community makes possible individual experience and cognition, and if, as Part 3 of *The Star of Redemption* explicitly states, Jewish blood is the condition on which the possibility of universal community is predicated, then carnal Israel is a condition for the possibility of universal redemption.

Put this way, *The Star of Redemption* begins in a peculiar way to look something like an ethical monotheistic text in the tradition of Rosenzweig's mentor, Hermann Cohen. Just as Cohen argues in his *Religion of Reason out of the Sources of Judaism* that Judaism is the originary source of God's revelation that makes world redemption possible, so Rosenzweig argues in *The Star of Redemption* that the Jewish people are the true source of revelation. In fact, Rosenzweig concurs with Cohen's ethical monotheistic framework in arguing that the Jewish people must preserve their unique and particular identity precisely in order to make available to the world knowledge of God's revelation.[24]

In making this claim, however, about the relation between Rosenzweig's and Cohen's thought, I am conflating Cohen's notion of "Judaism" with Rosenzweig's understanding of "the Jewish people." There is of course a deeply significant difference between the two, a difference that is significant on many counts but which, in the context of this chapter's argument about the place of the "Jewish people" in *The Star of Redemption*, goes to the heart of Cohen's and Rosenzweig's conceptions of the frameworks of modern Jewish identity. For Cohen, "Judaism" is an ideal, which—although it is the conceptual originator of ethics and the source of the possibility of world redemption—is an idea like other ideas. For Rosenzweig, on the other hand, the idea in *The Star of Redemption* of "the Jewish people," while no doubt still a philosophical construct, is meant to call into question the priority of ideas.[25]

As Rosenzweig himself commented a number of times, *The Star of Redemption*'s ideas of "the Jewish people" in general, and the blood community in particular, are philosophical constructs.[26] But the idea of "the blood community" is a philosophical construct that is meant to undo the priority of philosophical constructs. "The Jewish people" play a special philosophical role in *The Star of Redemption*, a role that is both bolstered by and yet deflates philosophical argumentation. What philosophical meaning could the claim that Jewish blood is the condition of revelation, human community, love, and logic possibly have? As strange as this question sounds, such a question is actually in keeping with the *philosophical* argument of the structure of Rosenzweig's *Star of Redemption*.

Perhaps ironically, Rosenzweig uses Cohen's transcendental method against him. Almut Sh. Bruckstein summarizes well the centrality of Cohen's transcendental method and its intimate connection to his conception of Judaism: "It is Cohen's construction of 'Judaism' which provides us with the grounding—*Grundlegung*—for his philosophical system insofar as the principle of origin or of transcendental grounding is claimed to be the one and only constitutive principle of Judaism itself."[27] In order to understand Rosenzweig's philosophical project in *The Star of Redemption* in the context of the centrality of Cohen's transcendental method and its relation to his conception of Judaism, it is useful to recall here the philosophical relation between Husserl and Heidegger. Just as Heidegger takes Husserl's claims for transcendental thought to its logical limit in order to move philosophy in a new direction, so too Rosenzweig takes Cohen's transcendental argument for Judaism as a logical source of world redemption to its logical limit in order to move Jewish thought in a new direction. Heidegger and Rosenzweig share with their teachers Husserl and Cohen the search for conditions. However, the parameters of the meaning of human finitude and cognition are redefined by Heidegger and Rosenzweig in this search. Heidegger and Rosenzweig each take their teacher's (Husserl and Cohen respectively) transcendental arguments and turn them into hermeneutical ones. Heidegger and Rosenzweig each refigure the transcendental question of how cognition makes our experience of the world possible into a hermeneutical question of how our experience of the world makes cognition possible.[28]

We have seen that *The Star of Redemption*'s structure suggests a hermeneutical argument about the limitations of cognition, individual experience, and communal structures for offering complete interpretations of human life. So, too, *The Star of Redemption* applies its hermeneutical argument about conditions to philosophy itself, to show the limitation of philosophy. Rosenzweig takes Cohen's transcendental method to it ultimate limit in order to suggest that philosophy can recognize its own limits and that this recognition, indeed, is a philosophical accomplishment. For Rosenzweig, it is the "transcendental" claims of Jewish blood that bring philosophy to its ultimate limit.

Let me reiterate in this context that Rosenzweig's idea of the blood community is a philosophical idea, not meant literally or racially. In a letter to Eugen Rosenstock-Huessy, Rosenzweig makes this point clearly:

> The traditional religious law seems to me . . . quite consistent in that it must keep open the possibility of proselytism, because of the messianic character of Judaism. . . . The blood relationship is maintained only on account of its symbolic meaning; but the law must rigidly insist that the proselyte only "comes on his own accord," he is not fetched, not "converted."[29]

Just as Rosenzweig argues that the notion of the blood community has symbolically maintained the integrity of Judaism against coercive proselytism, so too the notion of the blood community symbolically maintains the integrity of Judaism in the wake of modern philosophy. In other words, the notion of the blood community in *The Star of Redemption* marks the limit of modern philosophy.

The notion of the blood community points to the category error of equating Judaism with philosophy or philosophy with Judaism, akin to the category error that Rosenzweig accuses Cohen of making when Cohen conflates "Judaism" with "Germanism" in his famous essay "Deutschtum und Judentum."[30] Indeed, the third line of Rosenzweig's response to Cohen captures both category errors of equating Judaism with Germanism and Judaism with philosophy. Rosenzweig plays on the German *erzeugen* (to generate) and *bezeugen* (to witness) to make his point: "The *Volk* do not generate their God, rather it [the *Volk*] receives and witnesses him."[31] Cohen's notion that we generate (*erzeugen*) ideas that constitute our reality allows him to claim in "Deutschtum und Judentum" that *Deutschtum* and *Judentum* are regulative ideals that represent one confluent value. Rosenzweig insists in contrast to Cohen that the existence of the Jewish people is far greater than any idea. The Jewish community in general, and the blood community in particular, are not regulative ideals but instead mark the limit of philosophy itself. For Rosenzweig, Jewish blood, and not the idea of Judaism, witnesses (*bezeugen*) God's revelation. In a clever wordplay that recapitulates Rosenzweig's earlier response to Cohen's "Deutschtum und Judentum," *The Star of Redemption* both links and distinguishes Rosenzweig's and Cohen's ethical monotheisms to and from each other: "Bearing witness [*Bezeugen*] takes place in bearing [*Erzeugen*]."[32] Against Cohen, Rosenzweig contends that Judaism and philosophy cannot be harmonized ultimately. *The Star of Redemption* shows that philosophy falls short when it comes to an understanding of the Jewish people and the revelation that it embodies. The Jewish people and their revelation are neither irrational nor anti-rational, but they are beyond reason.

Rosenzweig's view of the blood community plays off contemporary German notions of blood and *Volk*. George Mosse has remarked upon the notions of blood and *Volk* within the German-Jewish context:

> At the beginning of the twentieth century, a whole generation of German thinkers was in search of a mythology which would revive the suppressed emotions of men as a counterweight to cold reason. Such a mythology required thinking in visible and experiential categories which had always determined popular culture. Such thought was supposedly based on eternal truth—the substance of man that determined his wishes and drives. This substance was expressed through myths like those about the Germanic gods or the equally ancient Edda—myths which pointed to man's substance and gave him roots. Martin Buber shared these ideas, just as he had attempted to harness the thought of the German mystics to the Jewish revival. But while this mythology was rooted in the Jewish *Volk*, it expanded to manifest itself as a substance which was shared by all of humanity.[33]

Rosenzweig shares with Buber the argument that the Jewish *Volk* expands to all of humanity. Indeed, we have seen that the blood community's place within the structure of *The Star of Redemption* suggests that the blood community makes redemption possible for all of humanity.

But Rosenzweig's appropriation of the notion of the blood community is a critical one that transforms in important ways what Steven Schwarzschild has called "the Jewish turn to ethnicism."[34] We have already seen that Rosenzweig argues that the blood community is determined by a future—by the grandchild, and not by the grandparent. The "linked sequence of everlasting life" goes from grandparent to grandchild and not from grandchild to grandparent. As is the case with the structure of *The Star of Redemption*, the future determines the value of the past. The past does not and cannot determine the future.

Let us return to Rosenzweig's comment to Rosenstock-Huessey that the blood community derives its meaning "from the messianic character of Judaism. . . . The blood relationship is maintained only on account of its symbolic meaning." Entry into the blood community (conversion) signifies a common future, for this futurity *is* the messianic character of Judaism. We will see in chapter 7 that because of his emphasis on the messianic and hence future-oriented character of Judaism, Rosenzweig's argument about Jewish blood is an argument more in keeping with the critical import of Cohen's ethical monotheism than it is with Buber's ethnicism. In the remainder of this chapter, however, I focus only on the issue of the blood community's critical relation to philosophy.

Rosenzweig argues that the excess beyond philosophy marked by carnal Israel does not mark the end of philosophy. As Rosenzweig writes to Hans Ehrenberg in response to Ehrenberg's early review of *The Star of Redemption*, "The intention [of the book] is anti-mystic, not anti-intellectual."[35] "Life," *The Star of Redemption*'s last word, is not presented in opposition to "philosophy."[36] Rather, as Rosenzweig reiterates to Ehrenberg, he has continued to philosophize after *The Star of Redemption*. Let us consider briefly the anti-mystical, philosophical implications of carnal Israel in the context of *The Star of Redemption*'s argument about philosophy and "the new thinking."

## New Thinking and New Reading

As is well known, in "The New Thinking" Rosenzweig states emphatically that *The Star of Redemption* is not a "Jewish book" but a "system of philosophy."[37] We need, moreover, but recall the quotation that Rosenzweig chose for *The Star of Redemption*'s cover page: "Ride forth victoriously for the cause of truth" (Psalm 45:4). But if *The Star of Redemption* is a philosophical text, then what are the philosophical implications of Rosenzweig's critique of philosophy? Rosenzweig contends that philosophical writing is the art of arranging a "string of thousands of lines" that may emerge from a single thought. But the single thought does not produce these thousands of lines as the uninitiated may think:

> If a philosophical book is worth reading at all, it is certainly so only when one either does not understand its beginning or at the very least misunderstands it. Otherwise, the thought that it presents is not really worth reflection [*Nachdenken*], for one evidently already has it, if from the beginning of its exposition one knows "where it is leading up to." All this is only valid for books; only books can be written and read without consideration for the passing of time. Speaking and hearing follow other laws.[38]

Though Rosenzweig contrasts the writing of books with speaking and hearing, the argument of *The Star of Redemption*'s structure suggests that "the new thinking" begins to dismantle this distinction. By way of conclusion, I elaborate briefly on this aspect of *The Star of Redemption*'s structure which, I argue, does attempt, as best as a philosophical book is able, to take time into consideration. Finally, in this context, I turn one last time to the question of the philosophical import of carnal Israel.

Again, attention to Rosenzweig's description in "The New Thinking" of *The Star of Redemption*'s project is helpful. Rosenzweig describes *The Star of Redemption* as "a system of philosophy that does not just want to bring a mere 'Copernican turn' of thinking, after which he who has carried it out sees all things turned around—yet still only the same things that he has seen before; but, rather, thinking's complete reversal."[39] What constitutes "thinking's complete reversal"? As Part 2 of *The Star of Redemption* in particular argues, time, contingency, and response are thought's reversal. While the thinker knows his thoughts in advance, the speaker and hearer do not know the future, for their future depends on what the other will say to them. Indeed, the speaker and hearer remain enclosed unto themselves until they are spoken to. The relation between the parts of *The Star of Redemption* exhibits this same sense of self-enclosure that cannot break out of itself by itself. Only the reader of *The Star of Redemption* can bring the parts into relation with each other. New thinking also requires a new kind of reading, a kind of reading that is indicated by *The Star of Redemption*'s structure.

As I have argued throughout this chapter, the relation between the parts of *The Star of Redemption* suggests that incompleteness emerges through relation. Each of the three parts of *The Star of Redemption* is whole in and of itself, but incomplete in terms of the relation to each of the other parts. In and of themselves the parts remain whole. *The Star of Redemption*'s argument is not found in propositions that seek independently to prove something. Rather, the argument is found in the structure of the text. Indeed, the argument only becomes apparent as the reader moves from part to part. The reader is thus a catalyst for the argument of the text in that the reader recognizes the incompleteness of each whole, as each whole comes into relation with the other wholes. The reader's relation to the text and to the three wholes of the text is an integral part of making the argument of *The Star of Redemption.* For Rosenzweig, not only a new thinking and a new thinker but also a new kind of reader are required to produce and read such a text.

Rosenzweig contrasts the new thinker and the new text to the old thinker and the old text, which are defined by their knowledge of where their arguments will and must lead:

> Usually it is Socrates who sets the conversation going—going in the direction of philosophical discussion. For the thinker knows his thoughts in advance, and his expounding them is merely a concession to what he regards as the defectiveness of our means of communication. This defectiveness is not due to our need of speech but to our need of time. To require time means that we cannot anticipate, that we must wait for everything, that what is ours depends on what is another's. All this is quite beyond the comprehension of the thinking thinker, while it is valid for the "speaking thinker."[40]

*The Star of Redemption*'s structure simulates the human need of time. As Rosenzweig writes, to require time means we must wait for everything. The reader must wait for the next part to make sense of the previous part, for each previous part cannot move outside itself without the reader. But

*The Star of Redemption*, unlike ordinary philosophical texts, does not make a concession to communication in order to make its argument. Rather, it relies on its reader to make its argument, whose contention is that ultimately all arguments and truth depend on a future that is not yet. *The Star of Redemption*'s structure thus attempts to take time seriously in its continual pointing toward a future that cannot be generated from its past.

But of course, as Rosenzweig himself recognizes, a book cannot really account for time. However, it can take the experience of reading seriously, and this is precisely what *The Star of Redemption* and its structure do.[41] According to Rosenzweig, to take reading seriously is to leave ourselves open to a future that has the potential to transform us.[42] "The new thinking," as reflected by the structure and simulated in the reading of *The Star of Redemption*, takes this future seriously. Summing up his views of the old thinking to his teacher Friederich Meinecke, Rosenzweig writes,

> Its questions are meaningless to me. On the other hand, the questions asked by human beings have become increasingly important to me. This is precisely what I meant by "cognition and knowledge as service"; a readiness to confront such questions, to answer them as best I can out of my limited knowledge and my even slighter ability.[43]

"The new thinking" is not a flight from philosophy, but only a rejection of philosophy's view of the autonomy of cognition in favor of what Rosenzweig calls cognition as "a service to human beings."

We can now return one last time to the philosophical import of carnal Israel. As we have seen throughout this chapter, it is carnal Israel that, by embodying God's revelation, makes a future possible for all of humanity. Philosophically, the construct of carnal Israel points simultaneously to philosophy's limitations and to a future that we can neither know nor anticipate. Based on its explicit and implicit hermeneutical argument about the contingency of the future and its relation to truth, *The Star of Redemption* argues paradoxically that carnal Israel marks both the condition for our understanding of our world as well as the limitation of that very understanding.[44] For Rosenzweig, this paradox is at the heart of Judaism's relation to the modern world. The modern Jew must return to Judaism not by seeking to harmonize Judaism with philosophy nor by rejecting philosophy. Rather, the return to Judaism is only possible through philosophy.[45] The philosophical import of carnal Israel marks this moment of return in *The Star of Redemption*.

# Part 2

## ART AND LANGUAGE

# *Four*

## Risky Images: Rosenzweig's Aesthetic Theory and Jewish Uncanniness

*The Star of Redemption*'s argument about the philosophical import of carnal Israel makes clear the degree to which Rosenzweig attempts to consider *philosophically* the bodily ground that constitutes all human meaning. In this same vein, Rosenzweig attempts, perhaps more than any other Jewish thinker, to take seriously the *philosophical* import of images and art, despite (or perhaps because of) German-Jewish arguments that the second commandment is an all-out ban on making images.[1] Rosenzweig argues that images are as risky as they are true. Images are powerful because they affect us. The seriousness with which he considers the effectiveness of images is the key to recognizing the link between Rosenzweig's aesthetic and political theories generally, and the intimate connection between his understanding of the work of art and Judaism, more particularly.

For Rosenzweig, art shares with Judaism the quality of uncanniness [*Unheimlichkeit*]. Like so many of his German-speaking contemporaries, including Sigmund Freud, Martin Heidegger, Ludwig Wittgenstein, and Martin Buber, Rosenzweig connects being wrenched away from one's "homey place" [*Heim*] to a feeling of uncanniness [*Unheimlichkeit*]. Rosenzweig argues that art and Judaism alike produce a shocked feeling of *Unheimlichkeit*. This ability to produce shocked attention allows art and Judaism to provide transformative possibilities for their spectators. Unlike his contemporaries, including Buber, Rosenzweig maintains that the feeling of *Unheimlichkeit* expresses not only a general insight into human existence, but is a particularly Jewish contribution to the understanding of human existence. While considering his aesthetic theory, we will see once again that Rosenzweig transforms and yet retains the German-Jewish argument about a Jewish mission to the nations.

### *The Star of Redemption*'s Aesthetic Theory: Ethical Monotheistic Overtones

*The Star of Redemption*'s aesthetic theory bears its closest resemblance to Hermann Cohen's, not in content but in form. In order to appreciate Rosenzweig's affinity with the formal aspects of Cohen's aesthetic theory in particular, and the aesthetic theory of the German-Jewish tradition of ethical monotheism in general, we must first recognize his criticisms of it. Before we can even consider *The Star of Redemption*'s aesthetic theory, let us recall that Rosenzweig's "Star of Redemption" is a figure as well as a title. Both literally and philosophically, *The Star of Redemption*'s three parts culminate in the figure of a Star of David. Represented by a triangle that points upward, Part 1 describes a logic of three unrelated elements: god, world, and man. In Part 2, the triangle's point is turned downward or—in the language that *The Star of Redemption* borrows from Schelling—inverted, because the elements are now in relation with one another.[2] This realm of relationship, Rosenzweig contends, constitutes the experience of revelation and the world of human language. In Part 3, the overlapping triangles of Parts 1 and 2 come together to form a Star of David. Judaism and Christianity are together represented by Rosenzweig's Star of Redemption, Judaism forming the inner part of the star, its fire, and Christianity forming the outer part, its rays. In the last pages of *The Star of Redemption*, Rosenzweig contends that the truth of the star of redemption coincides with the truth of the divine countenance: "In the star of redemption, then, in which we saw divine truth become figure, there shines forth none other than the countenance which God turned shiningly toward us. Yea, we now recognize the Star of Redemption itself, as it has at last emerged as figure for us, in the divine visage."[3]

Rosenzweig rejects one of the fundamental premises of the German-Jewish ethical monotheistic tradition: that the second commandment ban on images presents an all out ban on visual representation. From Mendelssohn to Cohen, German-Jewish thinkers argued that there was no tension between Judaism and reasoned enlightenment, and that in fact the second commandment ban on image making represented the confluence of the two. It is no coincidence that this German-Jewish philosophical tradition was also hostile to the Kabbalah, with its two-fold emphasis on God's inner life and the individual kabbalist's *visualizations* of that inner life.[4] It is well known that Rosenzweig criticizes this rationalist strand of German-Jewish thought both in terms of its denial of a living, vibrant Jewish relationship with God and in terms of what he considers its apologetic stance toward German culture and society. It is as much in response to what he perceives as a German-Jewish apologetic for Judaism as it is in response to the question of whether or not God can be represented that Rosenzweig writes toward the end of *The Star of Redemption*: "It is not human illusion if Scripture speaks of God's countenance and even of his separate bodily parts. There is no other way to express the Truth. Only when we see the Star as countenance do we transcend every possibility and simply see."[5]

At the core of *The Star of Redemption*'s aesthetic theory is a revaluation of vision, which had been devalued precisely by the rationalist, German-Jewish tradition. Like Rosenzweig's own aesthetic theory, this tradition of German-Jewish thought sought to speak to two worlds at once: the Jewish and the German one. Jewish thinkers responded simultaneously to the Jewish theological problem of whether God can be represented as well as to a particular problematic raised by the German Enlightenment: why had Jews not contributed historically to culture and art?[6] Culminating in Hermann Cohen's claim that Judaism is "ethically one-sided" in regard to culture, German-Jewish thinkers suggested time and time again that it was the Jews' historical task to uphold monotheism precisely by resisting the lure of vision.[7] Heinrich Graetz, one of the founders of the *Wissenschaft des Judentums*, epitomizes this type of argument in his contrast between the pagan and the Jew:

> To the pagan, the divine appears within nature as something observable to the eye. He becomes conscious of it as something seen. In contrast, to the Jew who knows that the divine exists beyond, outside of, and prior to nature, God reveals Himself through a demonstration of His will, through the medium of the ear. . . . Paganism sees its god, Judaism hears Him.[8]

It is important to note, however, that Graetz does not discard aesthetics entirely. He goes on to claim that due to the ban on image-making, Judaism is the originator of a more sublime aesthetic sensibility:

> Artistic expression also develops differently according to different conceptions of God. The artistic act created in Greek paganism . . . the art of sculpture, that lovely fragrant blossom of the pagan form of perception. . . . Judaism, on the other hand, which perceives its God in the alternatively loud and soft sounds of the movement of the waves, in the rhythm of word sounds . . . gave birth to music combined with religious poetry.[9]

Reiterating Graetz's musings on the aesthetic implications of monotheism, Hermann Cohen writes:

> The question may be raised whether the peculiar kind of poetry of the Bible could have arisen if the plastic arts had not been checked. This peculiarity consists in the lyric poetry of the psalms, which sing neither of God alone nor of man alone. Plastic art, however, can only present an isolated depiction of both. Thus plastic art would have impeded the lyric style, for which the relation of God and man becomes the problem of its monotheistic aim.[10]

Cohen attests to the ethical superiority of biblical aesthetics and is even more explicit than Graetz: "Prophetic monotheism is necessarily opposed to, necessarily contradicts art."[11]

*The Star of Redemption*'s embrace of vision attacks Graetz and Cohen's *wissenschaftlich* polemic at its very core: the assumption that the Bible maintains that God cannot be represented. From Rosenzweig's perspective, as he would articulate most clearly in his 1928 "A Note on Anthropomorphism," the rationalist strand of the German-Jewish philosophical tradition was tantamount to a denial of a living relationship between the Jewish people and the God of Israel.[12] Rosenzweig argues that German-Jewish thinkers had too often tried to turn the dynamic tension of the German-Jewish *Zweistromland*, or land of two streams—the title of the only collection of Rosenzweig's essays published during his lifetime—into a single stream that denied the vitality of two incomparable and incommensurable traditions. Indeed, Rosenzweig maintained that the German-Jewish relation gained its creativity precisely because the two sides of the hyphen could *not* be synthesized or, in Cohen's terms, correlated.[13]

Rosenzweig in fact concludes *The Star of Redemption* by reversing Graetz's and Cohen's dichotomy between seeing and hearing: "But what he gave me to see in this Beyond of life—none other than what I was already privileged to perceive in the midst of life; the difference is only that I see it and no longer merely hear it."[14] Vision, and not sound, is the culmination of knowledge of the divine, for Rosenzweig. *The Star of Redemption*'s embrace of vision is coupled with an aesthetic theory in each of the three parts of *The Star of Redemption*. This aesthetic theory, moreover, is not incidental. As Rosenzweig himself boldly claims, "Of everything empirical, art alone is essential."[15] *The Star of Redemption* in fact elevates art to a status higher than thought; the pagan, Rosenzweig's argues in Part 1 of *The Star of Redemption*, is wiser than the modern philosophers for he recognizes his finitude. This wisdom that is wiser than the thought of all philosophers is precisely the wisdom of the pagan's art.

But while Rosenzweig does indeed elevate vision to a status higher than hearing, and art to a status higher than thought, it is a mistake to conclude that what *The Star of Redemption* has to say about vision and *The Star of Redemption*'s aesthetic theory is also a rejection of the German-Jewish argument for the unique world-historical mission of the Jewish people. On the contrary: it is precisely in connection to what *The Star of Redemption* has to say about aesthetics, and how *The Star of Redemption* makes its argument, that the full import of Rosenzweig's argument about the Jewish people is to be found. Despite and also—in a perhaps surprising way—because of what he has to say about vision, *The Star of Redemption* is an ethically monotheistic text in the tradition of Hermann Cohen. Again, in Wendell Dietrich's words, ethical monotheism is "a religious concentration and intensity that focuses singular attention on God in contrast to all creaturely reality." At the same time, the ethical monotheist maintains "an inclusive interest in culture and society and insist[s] that ethical monotheistic faith energizes the construction of culture."[16] Rosenzweig is an ethical monotheist for two interconnected reasons. First, he argues for a particular Jewish theological mission to the nations and, second, he links this mission with a specific Jewish relation to art and culture. Like German-Jewish ethical monotheists before him, Rosenzweig seeks to elucidate the ethical implications of monotheism for culture at large.[17]

First, it is important to note that Rosenzweig shares with Graetz the equation of the pagan and vision. Unlike his German-Jewish counterparts, however, Rosenzweig assigns the pagan and vision not a wholly negative function, but a kind of ambiguity. For Rosenzweig, the pagan and vision have an important share in truth. The Greek pagan is wiser than the modern philosopher because she knows that her death cannot be comprehended. However, the pagan is isolated by her recognition of her finitude. Rosenzweig argues that only speech, or revelation, can produce real communication. However, Rosenzweig maintains that art is the silence before speech. In fact, ancient Greek drama anticipates the giving and receiving of human interaction.[18] *The Star of Redemption* contends that communication through silence is the essence of Attic drama, a suggestion with which Walter Benjamin would later concur.[19] By keeping silent, the tragic hero becomes an image for his audience, thereby allowing each member of the audience to recognize her own finitude in that image. For Rosenzweig, art's ability to produce commonality but not community accounts for what he refers to as the magic flute of art, as well as for what he argues is the inherent limitation of art:

> Only the magic flute of art could bring off the miracle of making the unison of human content resound in the discrete selves. And how limited was even this piece of magic! . . . How it remained a world of make-believe, a world of mere possibility. . . . The same sound resounded and yet was everywhere heard only in one's own interior, no one felt the human element as the human element in others, each one only immediately in his own self. The self remained without a view beyond its walls; all that was world remained without.[20]

The crucial point here is that Rosenzweig is critical of the pagan's embrace of vision *only because it does not go far enough*. While "Art is not a real world, for the threads which are drawn from man to man in it run only for moments," art "provides the ground on which the self can grow up elsewhere."[21] Rather than discounting the pagan valorization of vision, Rosenzweig argues that the Greek/pagan relationship to vision is an achievement for all humanity, one which he contrasts to the "failures" of both Indian and Chinese civilization: "[India and China] are the two poles of the worldliness which cannot muster that courage for clarity of vision [*Schau*] to which alone the configuration of things is revealed."[22] The Greek/pagan relation to vision is an achievement precisely because it, in Rosenzweig's words, "provides the ground on which the self can grow up elsewhere." Vision and art produce the commonality that is the prerequisite for universal community. Where then is this "elsewhere" where the self can grow up?

Rosenzweig contrasts the pagan's recognition of his finitude, a recognition that is painful and solitary, to the Christian's recognition of finitude, which is shared communally.[23] Rosenzweig contends that while pagan art can only produce a sense of lonely commonality, Christian art can produce a community that transcends, though does not negate, the suffering plight of the human being. Christian arts are unique because they are

> the only arts which can wholly cure him of that disease of alienation from the world which plunged the art lover into the misleading delusion of supreme health just as he exposed himself defenselessly to the disease. Thus art is its own anti-toxin. It decontaminates itself, and man, from its own purity.[24]

Art is its own anti-toxin in that art has the ability to cleanse itself of the disease that it itself creates: separation and isolation from reality. Christian art detoxifies itself through the creation not just of commonality, but of community. Rosenzweig argues that it is thus the images that are created by Christianity, and the image of the cross in particular, that allow for the creation of Christian community.

Rosenzweig's argument that Christian images have redemptive potential seems to cut against the grain of Cohen's, Graetz's, Mendelssohn's, and Baeck's arguments (to name only the best-known advocates of this thesis) about the superiority of Judaism to Christianity. Rosenzweig is certainly unique among Jewish thinkers, and German-Jewish thinkers in particular, in valorizing Christian images. Nonetheless, as most of his interpreters, both Christian and Jewish, have failed to recognize, Rosenzweig's positive assessment of Christian images and art is intimately connected to his deep awareness of the lethal potentiality of Christian antisemitism.[25] It is in fact at the intersection of the positive potential of images and the lethal possibilities of antisemitism that we can locate Rosenzweig's ethically monotheistic argument. The problem with Christianity for Rosenzweig is not, as Hermann Cohen in particular contends, that it *makes* images, but rather that it tends to understand its images as lasting ones. Rosenzweig contends that the Christian is always in danger of turning the "genuine present revelation of the real God [in]to a lasting image of God precisely by . . . resisting the ever-new will of God's revelation."[26] Though the image of the cross has the power to form an ever-broadening, universal community, Christianity becomes lethally dangerous when it believes that it has accomplished its goal. This sense of accomplishment is the idolatry of a lasting image, for Rosenzweig.[27] Images are dangerous for the same reason that they are vital: while images make new realities possible, they constantly run the risk of idolatrously denying the very source of their power: the ever-new will of God to move the world toward redemption.

In the face of an argument for the world-redemptive potential of the image of the cross, Rosenzweig contends that it is the Jewish mission to guard Christianity against idolatry:

> And withal: the Jew does it. Not with words, for what would words still avail in this realm of vision! But with his existence, his silent existence. This existence of the Jew constantly subjects Christianity to the idea that it is not attaining the goal, the truth, that it ever remains—on the way. That is the profoundest reason for the Christian hatred of the Jew, which is heir to the pagan hatred of the Jew. In the final analysis, it is only self-hate, directed by his existence; it is hatred of one's own imperfection, one's own not-yet. By his inner unity, by the fact that in the narrowest confines of his Jewishness the Star of Redemption nonetheless still burns, the Jew involuntarily shames the Christian.[28]

While *The Star of Redemption* has elevated vision above both thought and hearing, Rosenzweig concurs with the German-Jewish rationalists that the Jew must guard Christianity precisely against vision! The Jew's existence shames the Christian and the realm of beauty that he has built for himself. But *The Star of Redemption*'s argument about the Jewish mission to the nations goes even further. As we saw in chapter 2, Rosenzweig concurs in particular with Hermann Cohen in attributing Jewish suffering to Christianity's failure to achieve pure monotheism. In connection with the above comment about Christian self-hatred, Rosenzweig suggests that it is the Jewish mission to suffer for pure monotheism. Though Rosenzweig does not deny vision its due, he nonetheless defines Judaism as that which resists vision for the sake of the redemption of the world.

Rosenzweig draws on the image of the blindfolded synagogue to make his argument about Judaism's unique relation to vision. In a 1916 letter to Eugen Rosenstock, he writes, "Is not part of the price that the Synagogue must pay for the blessing in the enjoyment of which she anticipates the whole world, namely, of being already in the Father's presence, that she must wear the bandages of unconsciousness over her eyes?"[29] This argument reverses the Christian supersessionist reading of Judaism. Rosenzweig maintains that the synagogue does indeed "wear bandages of unconsciousness over her eyes," but these bandages of unconsciousness mark not an ignorance of God's revelation but rather an excess of it. In the context of *The Star of Redemption*'s argument about art, the point is that the blindfolded synagogue does not require vision—indeed it is blind—precisely because it is a *true image* of God's revelation *for the Christian world.*

Rosenzweig's understanding of art differs in content from typical ethically monotheistic arguments. Again, he believes that vision and images are necessary for the formation of human community. However, Rosenzweig's argument duplicates in form the ethically monotheistic insistence that Judaism preserves pure monotheism by resisting art. Indeed, the form of this ethically monotheistic argument dominates the very structure of *The Star of Redemption.* Every part of *The Star of Redemption* except for one has a theory of art; only Part 1 of Book 3, "The Fire, or The Eternal Way," has no aesthetic theory. It is in this part of *The Star of Redemption* that Rosenzweig describes the uniqueness of the Jewish community. In fact, Rosenzweig's famous, or infamous, claim that Judaism is community constituted by blood should be understood in the context of this ethical monotheistic argument about Judaism and art. Rosenzweig maintains that Judaism does not require art, for the Jewish community is constituted by blood: "There is only one community . . . which cannot utter the 'we' of its unity without hearing deep within a voice that adds: 'are eternal.' It must be a blood-community, because only blood gives warrant to the hope for a future."[30] Though Rosenzweig does not believe, like Cohen, that all images are shameful, *The Star of Redemption* nonetheless argues for the "ethical one-sideness" of Judaism in regard to culture. As his interpretation of the suffering servant shows, Rosenzweig, in accord with the German-Jewish argument for the Jewish mission to the nations, suggests that the Jewish people both abstain from art and suffer for the sake of the realization of pure monotheism.[31]

## Aesthetic Consequence: Jewish Uncanniness

While the implication of *The Star of Redemption*'s argument is that Jews do not require art, Rosenzweig nonetheless argues that Jews and Judaism have aesthetic characteristics, all of which share the quality of uncanniness [*Unheimlichkeit*]. In the next section, I discuss the ways in which this notion of *Unheimlichkeit* connects Rosenzweig's theory of Judaism to his aesthetic theory. Here, however, I would like to continue to focus on Rosenzweig's ethical monotheistic gestures and the way in which his argument for the Jewish mission to the nations is simultaneously an argument for diaspora Jewish existence. As Rosenzweig makes clear in the first book of *The Star of Redemption*'s third part, Judaism is a blood community precisely because it is *not* a community constituted by land. Because of its unique relation to God's revelation, the Jewish community is wrenched away from its homeland [*Heimat*] and thereby produces a feeling of uncanniness [*Unheimlichkeit*] in the "homey place" [*Heim*] of others.[32] In notes for a 1920 lecture at his *Lehrhaus* on "The Jewish Person," Rosenzweig makes the connection between the Jewish mission to the nations and Jewish uncanniness explicit: "The Jewish people is a sign and miracle, the individual Jew is uncanny."[33]

We saw in the last section what Rosenzweig means when he argues that the Jewish people are a sign and miracle. Judaism, he maintains, is the embodiment of God's revelation on earth. Simply put, Judaism makes the redemption of the world possible. Once again it is on the issue of rationalism that Rosenzweig parts ways with the German-Jewish mission theory (and not on the issue of the mission itself). Rosenzweig contends that the Jew's uncanniness can be a catalyst either for world redemption or for lethal antisemitism. Unlike Cohen and Mendelssohn in particular, Rosenzweig argues that antisemitism is not something that reasoned enlightenment will overcome. Rather, antisemitism is part and parcel of the sign and miracle of the Jewish people. While Rosenzweig argues that the Jew does not require vision, the Jew nonetheless is an image for the Christian. The Jew appears to the Christian as being without a home, and thus he appears uncanny.

*The Star of Redemption* suggests that the antisemite rightly recognizes the Jew's homeless position and the aesthetic characteristics it produces. Rosenzweig agrees with Richard Wagner that the aesthetic consequences of Jewish difference, of Jewish uncanniness, are unsettling to the non-Jew. Let us recall briefly Wagner's infamous description of the European reaction to the Jew: "The Jew—who, as everyone knows, has a God all to himself—in ordinary life strikes us primarily by his outward appearance, which, no matter to what European nationality we belong, has something disagreeably foreign to that nationality."[34] Rather than suggesting that the eternity of the Jewish people means something different than Wagner contends, Rosenzweig completely agrees with Wagner's description: "The true eternity of the eternal people must always be alien and vexing to the state, and to the history of the world."[35] Like Wagner, Rosenzweig connects Jewish speech to the Jew's innate inability to become part of the nation in whose midst he dwells. Wagner states:

> Throughout an intercourse of two millennia with European nations, Culture has not succeeded in breaking the remarkable stubbornness of the Jewish *naturel* as regards the peculiarities of Semitic pronunciation. The first thing that

> strikes our ear as quite outlandish, and unpleasant, in the Jew's production of the voice-sounds, is a hissing, shrieking, buzzing snuffle [*Ein zischender, schrillender, summsender und murksender Lautausdruck*].[36]

And Rosenzweig concurs:

> While every other people is one with its own language, while that language withers in its mouth the moment it ceases to be a people, the Jewish people never quite grows one with the languages it speaks. Even when it speaks the language of its host, a special vocabulary, or, at least, a special selection from the general vocabulary, a special word order, its own feeling for what is beautiful or ugly in the language, betray that it is not its own.[37]

Finally, both Rosenzweig and Wagner agree that the Jew's relation to the soil, or lack thereof, is responsible first and foremost for the unnaturalness, indeed, the homelessness of Jewish language.

Where Rosenzweig and Wagner disagree, and indeed where Rosenzweig and the antisemite disagree, is not in terms of a description of the Jewish people and their repulsiveness to the nations but in the valuation of this repulsiveness. An understanding of the eternal potency, and indeed even necessity, of antisemitism is part and parcel of Rosenzweig's theory of the Jewish mission to the nations:

> The unique characteristic of the people is this: that it looks at itself in about the same way as the outside world looks at it. A whole world asserts that the Jewish people is outcast and elect, both; and the Jewish people . . . only confirms it. Except that seen from the outside, the characterization assumes the form of external connectedness [*eines äußerlichen Zusammenhangs*], while from within it represents an inner inseparableness [*eine innere Untrennbarkeit*], and the vessels of curse and blessing communicate so closely that the latter can overflow only when the former too is full to the brim.[38]

Rosenzweig maintains that blessings and curses flow equally from Judaism for the same reason: due to its uncanny quality, its *Unheimlichkeit*, Judaism invites a response from its neighbors. Judaism is both of this world and not of this world. Judaism is at one and the same time a sign of mystery beyond this world and the very disturbance to the gentile *Heim* of this world.

Rosenzweig's views of the uncanny effect of a secret hiddenness revealed call to mind Freud's much remarked upon essay on the uncanny, written in 1919, the same year Rosenzweig finished *The Star of Redemption*. It does not seem that Rosenzweig knew Freud's essay; he certainly did not know it before he wrote *The Star of Redemption*. As is well known, Freud discusses the strange and complex interconnection between the words *Geheimnis*, *unheimlich*, and *heimlich*. Freud quotes

Schelling's definition of "Unheimlich"—"'Unheimlich' is the name for everything that ought to have remained . . . hidden and secret and has become visible," and "To veil the divine, to surround it with a certain Unheimlichkeit'"[39]—reformulating it as a kind of repression: "For this uncanny is in reality nothing new or foreign, but something familiar and old-established in the mind that has been estranged only by the process of repression."[40] Freud then links the feeling of the uncanny with the fear of castration.

Recently, Daniel Boyarin has maintained that we should understand Freud's essay on the uncanny in connection with Freud's ambivalence about his Jewishness:[41] "We are led to the conclusion that seeing himself in the mirror produced in Freud the same feeling of uncanniness that he himself claims is produced in the antisemite who looks at the Jew. It is himself that Freud dislikes."[42] Boyarin contends that Freud's notion of the uncanny and his understanding of Jewishness is fraught with ambivalence about Judaism's status in the modern world.[43] Rosenzweig agrees with what Boyarin claims is Freud's connection between Jewishness and *Unheimlichkeit*, but Rosenzweig disagrees with the valuation of this connection. Rosenzweig transvalues this phenomenon and argues that Jews are always being wrenched away from the world by God's revelation (are made *Unheimlich*) *for the sake of the world.* Interpreting Wittgenstein on the uncanny, G. F. Bearn suggests that the uncanny is "the presence of what ought to be absent."[44] Rosenzweig again agrees with this description and revalues it in terms of the Jewish mission to the nations: he argues that Jews represent God's presence, a presence that seems like it ought to be absent from human life. Jews are uncanny for this very reason.

In language close to his contemporary Martin Heidegger's, Rosenzweig continues to muse in his 1920 lecture notes on the way in which the uncanniness of Jewish difference interrupts the sameness of everyone else for the sake of world redemption. Recall Heidegger's definition in *Being and Time* of "das Man," translated as "the they": "Everyone is the other, and no one is himself. The *they*, which supplies the answer to the question of the *who* of everyday Dasein, is the *nobody* to whom every Dasein has always already surrendered itself in Being-among-one-another."[45] In these 1920 lecture notes, Rosenzweig makes an argument that is both similar to and different from Heidegger's. Rosenzweig writes: "They [Jews] are after all 'so different.' Indeed, admittedly different. And precisely in their difference—uncanny. They are more different than 'one' is [*Sie sind verschiedener als 'man' ist*]."[46] Rosenzweig maintains that Jewish difference is so extreme that it calls the sameness of the masses, of "the they," into question.[47] Rosenzweig argues that Jewish difference in particular, and not *Dasein* more generally, disrupts the anonymity of "the they."

In his 1922 *I and Thou*, Martin Buber describes what he calls the uncanny shattering of the I-It world in terms that are much closer to Heidegger's musings on the uncanny and "das Man" than they are to Rosenzweig's:

> There are two basic privileges of the It-world. They induce man to consider the It-world as the world in which one has to live and also can live comfortably—and even offers us all sorts of stimulations and excitements, activities and knowledge. In this firm and wholesome chronicle the You-moments appear as queer lyric-dramatic episodes. Their spell may be seductive, but they pull us dangerously to extremes, loosening the well-tied structure, leaving behind more doubt than satisfaction, shaking up our security—*altogether uncanny* [*eben unheimlich*], altogether indispensable.[48]

Where Rosenzweig differs from both Heidegger and Buber is in insisting that it is Jewish particularity—and not a generic component of human existence—that provides insight into this fundamental meaning. As I have argued throughout this chapter, it is here that Rosenzweig's ethical monotheistic gestures are most clear. For Rosenzweig, Jewish uncanniness brings to the world both the recognition of human finitude and the possibility of world redemption. Rosenzweig contends that the disruption of Jewish difference is experienced as uncanniness by "the they" and the Jewish people alike. He goes so far as to argue that uncanniness, the experience of being *un-heimlich*, defines the ultimate unity and destiny of the Jewish people:

> What is it then with this unity [of the Jewish people]?
>
> It is actually ungraspable. Psychologically ungraspable. . . . psychologically ungraspable. . . . But also intellectually ungraspable. . . . There is no "Jewish intellectuality."
>
> All other peoples have better bodily, soulful, intellectual characteristics than we do. It is graspable only as the unity of destiny [*Schicksalseinheit*].[49]

Rosenzweig argues that the unease and disruption of the canny, of the homey place, is precisely what Jewish revelation offers to the world.[50] Jews are different because they are without a home in the world; they thereby disrupt the homey sameness of others.

## A Hermeneutical Critique of Idealist Aesthetics

An appreciation of Rosenzweig's view of the dynamics of uncanniness is the key to understanding the content of *The Star of Redemption*'s complex and often seemingly obscure aesthetic theory. For Rosenzweig, an artwork's value is measured in terms of its ability to produce a response from its audience. Rosenzweig characterizes this shocked attention produced by art as uncanniness [*Unheimlichkeit*]. Rosenzweig's notion of *Unheimlichkeit* links his theories of art and Judaism. Against idealist aesthetics, Rosenzweig maintains that artworks have the capacity to draw shocked attention from their audiences. When we take Rosenzweig's aesthetic theory together with his theory of Judaism, it becomes clear that the implication of *The Star of Redemption*'s argument is that Judaism is God's artwork given to the world for the sake of the world's response.

Let us return then to *The Star of Redemption*'s aesthetic theory. Part 1 describes an aesthetic theory related to paganism, Part 2 an aesthetics of experience, and Part 3 an aesthetics of Christianity. How, if at all, are these theories related to each other? Though Rosenzweig does not use the term "hermeneutic" to describe his aesthetic theory, *The Star of Redemption*'s aesthetic theory is hermeneutical because its underlying and unifying premise is that art deeply affects our self-understanding. While Rosenzweig replaces one methodology with the next as he moves from one part of *The Star of Redemption* to the next, art is the one constant that remains. Art's function remains the same in all three parts of *The Star of Redemption*, and only the theories of art change. Rosenzweig argues that art is essential to human existence because art is self-creation and self-interpretation. Gadamer's description of the relation between aesthetics and hermeneutics is helpful here:

> Hermeneutics includes aesthetics. Hermeneutics bridges the distance between the minds and reveals the foreignness of the other mind. . . . The work of art that says something confronts us itself. That is, it expresses something in such a way that what is said is like a discovery, a disclosure of something previously concealed. The element of surprise is based on this. . . . To understand what the work of art says to us is therefore a self-encounter.[51]

Art is at bottom hermeneutically oriented for Rosenzweig because art expresses the self-creation of individual and community.

We have already discussed briefly the aesthetic theories of Parts 1 and 3: those of paganism and Christianity. The aesthetic theory of Part 1 of *The Star of Redemption* focuses on what the pagan gets right. Rosenzweig maintains that the pagan rightly recognizes her finitude and creates her art in an attempt to create the only eternity available to her.[52] Rosenzweig maintains that *all* art, and not just ancient Greek art, mirrors the non-relational, self-contained world of Greek mythology.[53] But while art epitomizes a sense of isolation and self-containedness, Rosenzweig argues that art betrays its own isolation. Art's isolation points to something beyond itself. In Stéphane Mosès's words, art for Rosenzweig is communication without exchange.[54] It is in the context of these profound truths that we can approach Christian art, argues Rosenzweig in Part 3 of *The Star of Redemption*. Prior to revelation, the human being is isolated. Revelation creates the possibility of true communication—also known as speech—not only between the human and the divine but also between people. Rosenzweig maintains that Christian art aids in the production of interhuman relations, while both preserving and transcending the truth of human finitude. He argues that the Christian community literally comes to know and be itself through its art. Once again, through his silence about the Jewish relation to art, the form of Rosenzweig's ethical monotheistic argument emerges. The Jewish community, Rosenzweig argues, does not require art for its identity formation, for the Jewish community is formed by and through Jewish blood.

What then of the aesthetic theory in Part 2 of *The Star of Redemption*? While arguing that the pagan is indeed idolatrous in his relation to art, Rosenzweig is, as we have seen, ambivalent about paganism, as well as about Christianity (which, for Rosenzweig, always remains pagan). Rosenzweig, however, is not ambivalent about idealism's relation to art, and this unambiguous criticism is the subject of Part 2's aesthetic theory. Rosenzweig's hermeneutical criticism of idealism is intimately connected to his understanding of Judaism's relation to the modern world. Rosenzweig maintains that idealism's denial of the hermeneutical aspect of art, the way in which artworks may transform our identities, is part and parcel of idealism's denial of the possibility of the difference revelation produces in general, and of Jewish difference in particular.

One of the (many) confusing aspects of the philosophical argument of *The Star of Redemption* is what Rosenzweig actually means by "idealism." *The Star of Redemption*'s criticism of "idealism" is multilayered and Rosenzweig uses the term in many places, often with different connotations. *The Star of Redemption* claims that idealism is historically unique not only in its claims for cognition (the subject of Part 1), but also in its claims for the redemptive possibilities of art (the subject of Part 2) and the modern state (the subject of Part 3). In Parts 1 and 3, "idealism" refers to either Hegel or Cohen. In Part 2 of *The Star of Redemption*, however, I suggest that "idealism" refers specifically to Schelling's idealism. Recall Schelling's statement in his *System of Transcendental Idealism* that art is "the only true and eternal organ and document of philosophy."[55] It is Schelling, and not Hegel, who, for Rosenzweig, apotheosizes art in the modern world in a manner far more idolatrous than any pagan had.[56] While in Part 1 of *The Star of Redemption*, Rosenzweig uses Schelling's claims about myth to undercut Hegel's and Cohen's claims for cognition, the theory of revelation in Part 2 seeks to show the limitation of aesthetics qua aesthetics.[57] As we will see, this idealist apotheosization of art is for Rosenzweig intimately connected to a denial in the modern world of Judaism's redemptive powers.

Rosenzweig summarizes what he takes to be the uniqueness of the idealist—read Schelling's—approach to art:

> Idealism lacked straightforward confidence in language . . . at the moment when it rejected language, [it] apotheosized art . . . instead of believing . . . speech. Idealism threw the whole weight of its gullibility onto a single limb torn loose from the whole body of humanity. For art is no more than one limb, a limb without which, it is true, man would be a cripple, but remain withal. It is one limb among many. Man is more.[58]

As Part 2 elaborates at length, the human ability to speak and to be spoken to constitutes the wholeness of humanity, for Rosenzweig. Art is part of this whole, but not all of it. Idealism's error is a pernicious one, Rosenzweig argues. It threatens to destroy the essential marker of the human being: the ability to speak, to be spoken to, and to respond. This is also the ability to be affected. Rosenzweig claims that idealism's denial of human response-ability goes hand in hand with a denial of the human ability to be affected and changed. Methodologically, Rosenzweig argues idealism's denial of speech is linked to idealism's denial of contingency:

> Art became for Idealism the great justification of its procedure. If doubts haunted it about the admissibility of its method—that of the "panlogistically" pure generator—it had only to regard the work of art, produced by mind and yet nature-like reality to clear its conscience. . . . Idealism was incapable of acknowledging the word of man as answer to the word of God, and refused to repose confidence in it. Yet it gave this same confidence to a work of man.[59]

Rosenzweig's criticisms call to mind Schelling's *Philosophy of Art*, in which Schelling claims that the universe itself is "an absolute work of art."[60] Art reproduces what Schelling calls divine "indifference." This means not only that nature and ethics are united in art, but that the real and the ideal, and necessity and freedom, are as well. Schelling maintains that God is the immediate, absolute, and formal cause of art and that art forms reproduce "forms of things as they are in God."[61] As Rosenzweig states, Schelling's method and theory of art are one and the same: art is the ultimate reality, conforming to nature and produced by the mind.

Rosenzweig seeks in Part 2 of *The Star of Redemption* to dismantle Schelling's idealist aesthetic theory. It is in here that the form and content of Rosenzweig's theories of art and Judaism converge around the issue of uncanniness. Part 2 of *The Star of Redemption* attempts to dismantle idealism by way of its very foundation: its theory of art. Rosenzweig argues that idealism's theory of art fails on its own terms, by way of its own "categories." He suggests that idealism's aesthetic theory is plausible for the categories artist and artwork, but that it is simply false for the notion of redemption, even conceived as category. Rosenzweig maintains that idealist aesthetics betrays itself in its denial of the contingency of the audience's response to an artwork. Despite what the idealist philosopher might argue, art does and must enter the world: "The shadow realm of art, which was supposed to deceive Idealism about the lifelessness of its own world—it longs for life itself."[62] Rosenzweig contends that art's longing for life is realized in the category of redemption in which the artwork becomes public property. In becoming public property, art moves out of the world of shadows and into the world of the living.[63] Idealism's dialectic is destroyed by the spectator who remains separate and different from the artist and whatever intentions the artist might bring to the artwork. The separateness of the audience constitutes the contingency of response that art brings into human life.

Rosenzweig's description of the artwork parallels his description of the Jewish people. Against idealist aesthetics, Rosenzweig maintains that the artwork is wrenched away from its homey place and thus produces a feeling of uncanniness. "Yes, it [the artwork] is truly uncanny (*unheimlich*); it has no home, no dwelling; it does not know the shelter of a genus where it might settle comfortably."[64] Like the blindfolded synagogue, the artwork produces a feeling of uncanniness through its self-contained isolation. In art's most complete, self-contained moment—when the painting is finished and displayed, when the curtain comes down on a play—the audience may respond to it. Again like the blindfolded synagogue, art becomes part of that which it sought to escape—life itself—through its self-contained isolation. Rosenzweig argues that artistic meaning—like the meaning of Jewish existence—is possible only when the artwork is wrenched away from its home. Art and Judaism are both isolated from life and capable of entering into life for one and the same reason: they are *un-heimlich*. "The work of art stands there unique, detached from its originator, uncanny in its vitality which is full of life and yet alien to life (*unheimlichen lebensvollen und doch lebensfremden Lebendigkeit*)."[65] Rosenzweig argues that because they are uncanny, because they are wrenched away from their homey places, artworks, like Judaism, affect the human being.

*The Star of Redemption* thus presents an aesthetic theory that rests upon a hermeneutical critique of idealist aesthetics: "In the spectator, the empty humanity of the author has coalesced with the uncanniness

[*Unheimlichkeit*] of the work rich in content and full of animation. Without the spectator, the work would be mute, since it does not 'speak' to the author."[66] The *un-heimlich* quality of the artwork makes it possible for the artwork to speak to the spectator. Against idealist aesthetics, Rosenzweig contends that the meaning of the artwork is found in what the artwork says to its audience, and not in the artist's intentions. Perhaps a bit ironically, Rosenzweig suggests that Wagner's success as a composer is reflected not "by Bayreuth but by the fact that names like Elsa and Eva became fashionable, and that the ideal of woman as redeemer colored the nature of masculine eroticism in Germany for decades."[67]

## Rosenzweig's "Uncanny" as a Return to Jewish Difference

By way of conclusion, I would like to elaborate briefly on some of the ways in which Rosenzweig's theological, aesthetic, and political views converge in his understanding of the uncanny. As we have seen throughout this chapter, Rosenzweig draws on a number of shared cultural assumptions about the uncanny in constructing his aesthetic theory and view of Jewish *Unheimlichkeit*. Boyarin contends that the ambivalence about Judaism and Jewishness implicit in Freud's understanding of the uncanny is paradigmatic of Freud's desire to "remain Jewish while abandoning Judaism."[68] If we accept Boyarin's analysis of Freud, we can see that Rosenzweig, like Freud, links the uncanny with what the antisemite sees when he sees the Jew. However, it is precisely the option of remaining Jewish while abandoning Judaism that Rosenzweig seeks to reject with his notion of the uncanny. In fact, Rosenzweig's thought suggests that an embrace of Jewish uncanniness marks a return to Judaism and Jewish difference.

In keeping with *The Star of Redemption*'s valorization of images, Rosenzweig rejected what he considered the apologetic stance of liberal German Jews who, he argued, from Mendelssohn forward, sought to equate Judaism with Germanism. Rosenzweig argues for a diaspora Jewish community that needs to return to a self-contained world of its own, though its individual members may participate fully in German culture. Rosenzweig's conception of the uncanny converges with his ethical monotheistic framework: he maintains that only by returning to Judaism can Jews achieve a difference that could create the vitality necessary for the production of Jewish uncanniness. Rosenzweig argues that the Jew is wrenched from his home (is made *un-heimlich*) for the sake of world redemption.

In order to serve their world-historical mission, Rosenzweig maintains that Jews must invent anew a separate and self-contained Jewish community. To restore, albeit in new form, the wholeness or the inner inseparableness of Jewish existence—this became the sole aim of Rosenzweig's program for Jewish education in Germany. In a comment from an outline for a series of lectures at the *Lehrhaus* presented from January through March 1921, we see clearly the connection between Rosenzweig's aesthetic theory and program for Jewish education:

> Do you perceive what we lost when our grandparents turned their back on the beautiful life, and turned toward a life in which beauty is but an island [*l'art pour l'art*], an isolated phenomena, an idol? Do you perceive what we have to gain, and how we have to be regained? A life that is wholly artwork [*ganz Kunstwerk*], wholly beauty, because it is wholly life, wholly *our* life.[69]

Rosenzweig's notion of the whole artwork is in marked contrast to Wagner's formulation of the total artwork. Let us explore the differences between them briefly before turning back to the way in which Judaism is wholly artwork for Rosenzweig.

We have seen that art transforms the individual and community for Rosenzweig because in its *Un-heimlichkeit*, art invites response. For Wagner, on the other hand, art does not elicit a response that is contingent upon the spectator. This is because art is anything but *un-heimlich*, for Wagner. Rather, art is the expression of the *Heim* itself:

> Art . . . is nothing other than the fulfillment of a longing to recognize oneself [*sich selbst zu erkennen*] in a represented, admired, or beloved object, to find oneself again in the phenomena of the outer world through their representation. . . . Myth is the poem of a common view of life [*das Gedicht einer gemeinsamen Lebensanschauung*].[70]

Wagner's aesthetic theory aims for recognition of an identity that is already there, while Rosenzweig's aesthetic theory aims for the transformation of an identity that is never fixed. For Wagner, art embodies predetermined and total identity. Art has the task of confirming and restoring the ontological identity of its audience. The "Artwork of the Future" restores the lost aesthetic unity of Greek art, a lost unity that reflects for Wagner the disintegration of modern society. And the total artwork (*Gesamtkunstwerk*) restores the total being (*Gesamtwesen*) of the Greek spectator to modern man.[71] Wagner's view of the total artwork corresponds to Rosenzweig's view of the fanatic. Wagner agrees with Rosenzweig's fanatic that the past determines the future.

Recall that Rosenzweig argues that the pagan is open to the future (whether she knows it or not), while the fanatic is not. Rosenzweig's view of the whole artwork corresponds to his view of paganism discussed in chapter 2. A pagan for Rosenzweig is someone who has the possibility of being affected by another. Rosenzweig suggests that the pagan is open not only to the future, but to other people also. In keeping with Rosenzweig's view of the fanatic, Wagner maintains an openness to neither. For Wagner, recognition of identity means at the same time recognizing what one is not:

> That which should be distinguished must necessarily have that from which it is to distinguish itself. He who wants to be completely himself must first recognize what he is; this he recognizes however first in the difference from that which he is not: if he wanted to separate from himself that which is different from himself, he would not be anything different, and thus no longer something recognizable.[72]

To recognize oneself, one must recognize those who are similar to and different from oneself. In one of his last essays, "Erkenne dich selbst" (Know Thyself), Wagner makes what is for him the dynamic of recognition very clear. He writes: "What is not recognized, will be beaten" [*Was nicht erkannt wird, darauf wird losgeschlagen*]. For Wagner, difference pollutes that which is the same and must thereby be destroyed.[73] Rosenzweig maintains that unlike the fanatic, the pagan can tolerate difference. The pagan does not represent others, but the pagan does not want to beat or wipe out all that he is not. This is why the pagan strives for isolation; he knows that there are other people in the world and that this is an inescapable fact. The only means of retreat, then, is a retreat into oneself. Wagner seeks no such retreat. The Artwork of the Future seeks on the contrary total and absolute homogeneity. While the pagan seeks wholeness, the fanatic seeks totality.

Let us now return to Rosenzweig's contention that Judaism is wholly artwork. Like paganism, Judaism, for Rosenzweig, is a whole and not a totality. Judaism is *ganz Kunstwerk*, wholly artwork, as opposed to a *Gesamtkunstwerk*, total artwork. Rosenzweig's suggestion is not only that Judaism is its own art form, but that Judaism is *the* work of art *qua* work of art. Judaism is the perfect work of art, created by the creator God. Judaism is a world unto itself, but a world that, in its interaction with the world, by way of its non-interaction with the world, reveals the secret that is its source: God's revelation. God gives God's creation to the world, and allows the peoples of the world to freely respond to God's creation. The world responds to Judaism's uncanniness, and, as we see in Wagner's and Rosenzweig's views of Jewish *Unheimlichkeit*, this response can be equally curse or blessing.

Rosenzweig argues that if Jews are to (re)create a Jewish world for themselves, they must understand that a return to their holy language is absolutely essential to the task. A Jewish world is centered on Hebrew, which is the language of Judaism, both figuratively and literally.[74] For Rosenzweig, an acquaintance and then intimacy with Hebrew is the only path to Jewish *Ganzheit*:

> The German, and even the Jew qua German, can and will read the Bible as Luther, Herder, or Moses Mendelssohn read it; the Jew can understand it only in Hebrew. And even though in the case of the Bible both possibilities must be admitted, because both Jew and German share in its possession, the language of Jewish prayer is different; of the language of Hebrew prayer we may state quite categorically: it cannot be translated. Therefore the transmission of literary documents will never suffice; the classroom must remain the ante-room leading to the synagogue and to participation in its service. And understanding of public worship and participation in its expression will make possible what is necessary for the continuation of Judaism: a Jewish world.[75]

The recreation of a Jewish world is not for Rosenzweig a nationalist or Zionist task, but a distinctly diaspora one. The Jew, according to Rosenzweig, "never lose[s] the untrammeled freedom of a wanderer who is more faithful a knight to his country when he roams abroad, craving adventure and yearning for the home [*Heimat*] he has left behind, than when he is at home [*zuhause*]."[76] Rosenzweig's call for a return to Hebrew is a call to revitalize the sacred language within the German host culture, and not a call to create a modern, secular language. As we will see in chapter 7, for Rosenzweig, the attempt to revitalize Hebrew within the host culture is an attempt to return to Jewish *Unheimlichkeit*. In the next chapter, we will see the ways in which the aesthetic, political, and theological dimensions of this attempt are reflected perhaps most acutely in Buber and Rosenzweig's translation of the Hebrew Bible into German. For now let us continue to focus on Rosenzweig's conception of Judaism as wholly artwork.

The relation between Rosenzweig's aesthetic theory and understanding of Judaism cuts even deeper. To understand this affinity, we must return again briefly to Schelling's aesthetic theory. While we have seen that Rosenzweig criticizes Schelling's idealist aesthetics, we see also that his construction of Judaism resembles in significant ways the "indifference" of a Schellingian idea. In *Philosophy of Art*, Schelling defines an idea as follows: "Every idea has two unities: the one through which it exists within itself and is absolute—hence the one through which the absolute is formed into the particularity of the idea—and the one through which it is taken up as a particular into the absolute as into its own center."[77] In response to the obvious question regarding the incongruence between his view of Judaism as a blood community that lives apart from the world's cultural life, without art, and the blatant historical fact that

Jews have always interacted with their host cultures, Rosenzweig uses and transforms the two unities of a Schellingian idea.

Rosenzweig argues that Judaism is made up of contradictions (*Widersprueche*). The Jewish God, world, and person each embody these contradictions. The contradiction of the Jewish God is that God is both distant and near, both sublime and humble. The contradiction of the Jewish person is that God has chosen the Jews as his chosen people and yet the chosen people are afflicted with ongoing suffering. Finally, the contradiction of the Jewish world stems from the Jewish creation of eternity in its ritual life. Everything in the Jewish world is ambiguous because it relates to both this world and the world to come:

> As it [a benediction] divides the life of Israel into holy and profane, so it divides the whole earth into Israel and the peoples. But the division is not simple in the sense that the holy shuts out the profane. The contrast penetrates to the innermost core, and just as the benediction touches everything that is profane and makes it holy, so, quite suddenly, the devout and the wise among the peoples will participate in the eternal life of the coming of the world, which but a short time ago seemed reserved for Israel alone. Those who were blessed will themselves be a blessing.[78]

Rosenzweig's view of Judaism as wholly artwork is summed up in the last sentence of this quotation: Judaism is blessed and by being blessed is a blessing to the world. With this notion, we can begin to understand Rosenzweig's sense of Judaism's relation to the rest of the world, including the world of art. Just as Judaism in its particularity is a universal blessing, Judaism, in its particularity as "the one people," embodies the rest of the world:

> By being an individual people, a nation becomes a people among others. To close oneself off is to come close to another. But this does not hold when a people refuses to be merely an individual people and wants to be 'the one people.' Under these circumstances it must not close itself off within borders, but include within itself such borders as would, through their double function, tend to make it one individual people among others.[79]

Rosenzweig fuses the "two unities" of a Schellingian idea with his ethically monotheistic vision. He argues that Judaism does not close itself off from others, but rather includes others within its borders. For Rosenzweig, Judaism is not a nation among nations, but a nation for the nations. In being a nation for the nations, Judaism remains a nation separate from the nations *for the sake of* the nations. In this way, *Jews live the contradiction of being universal by virtue of their particularity*. Rosenzweig does not deny that individual Jews participate in the world of culture. He suggests that Jews participate in cultural life because, like a Schellingian idea, *they include within themselves* the borders, and the culture, of what is outside their particularity. Rosenzweig contends that diaspora life means that Jews must live their contradictions as contradictions. To be Jewish is to live the contradiction of living outside of the general culture (for the sake of that culture) while participating in that culture. The separate wholeness of Jewish existence literally embodies for Rosenzweig the secret of God's revelation. It is for this reason that Jews have an uncanny effect on their neighbors. Rosenzweig argues that only by existing without a home can Jews give the nations of the world the opportunity to respond to this secret revealed. The pent-up pathos produced by Jewish uncanniness may produce a vicious antisemitism, but in keeping with the ethically monotheistic framework of his mentor, Hermann Cohen, Rosenzweig argues that the effects of antisemitism are part and parcel of the Jewish mission to the nations.

# *Five*

## The Problem of Translation: Risking the Present for the Sake of the Past

ROSENZWEIG'S WORK on translation began when he translated the Grace after Meals while on his honeymoon with his wife Edith (Hahn) in April 1920.[1] The following year, on March 10, 1921, he sent his translation to Gershom Scholem with the following remarks: "In a sense we are ourselves guests at our own table, we ourselves, I myself. So long as we speak German (or even if we speak Hebrew, modern Hebrew, the Hebrew of '1921'!) we cannot avoid this detour that again and again leads us the hard way from what is alien back to our own."[2] We see here already the seeds of what would become Rosenzweig's full-fledged theory of translation. The task of the translator for Rosenzweig is to produce shocked attention in the reader. Only by encountering the alien, he argued, could the Jewish people be led back to what was already its own. Both literally and metaphorically, the problem of "translation" came to illuminate Rosenzweig's central concerns and proposed solutions, for the process of translation is simultaneously a receiving of the past and a transformation of it.

In 1923 Rosenzweig translated the poems of the medieval poet Judah Halevi.[3] Martin Buber, whom Rosenzweig first met in 1914, gave him comments on his translations. When, in 1925, Buber received a letter from a young publisher, requesting that he undertake a translation of the Hebrew Bible, he thought of Rosenzweig at once. Rosenzweig was already suffering from amyotrophic lateral sclerosis, and he was both excited and disturbed when Buber asked for his help.[4] While he did not expect to die in the near future, Rosenzweig knew that the project would take a number of years and was therefore apprehensive about beginning it. In order to communicate, he could only use his fingers to point to a typewriter to indicate letters of words. Later, he would only have the ability to blink his eyes. Still, the project began. Buber would translate a section and Rosenzweig would comment on it and make changes. This process continued until Rosenzweig's death in 1929; Buber finished the project himself in 1961, long after he had escaped from Nazi Germany to take a post at the Hebrew University of Jerusalem.

In what was intended as a criticism of the Buber-Rosenzweig translation of the Bible, Gershom Scholem captures precisely the aesthetic effect that Buber and Rosenzweig hoped to achieve. He writes to Buber in a letter of 1926:

> What fills me with doubt is the excessive tonality of this prose, which leaps out *almost uncannily* [*fast unheimlich*] from the particular wording (this word is wrong; I mean the *niggun* [melody] of your translation). If the narratives of Genesis fairly burst with pent-up pathos (and sometimes actually do so), I dare not think of the melody that *prophetic speech* will have to assume in your translation.[5]

Scholem's comment reflects the intended sense of strangeness and foreignness that Buber and Rosenzweig aimed to produce in their translation. In keeping with his aesthetic theory, Rosenzweig attempted to create a sense of the biblical text's uncanny difference from modern life in general and the German language in particular. Rosenzweig's approach to translation suggests that the text itself must be made uncanny so that modern people would have the capacity to respond to it.

Like an artwork, the biblical text can shock its readers. However, the biblical text, for Rosenzweig, is more than an artwork. The biblical text, from Rosenzweig's perspective, also commands its readers. It is here that we come to an important difference between Buber and Rosenzweig. Whereas Buber argues that the relation to the past can form our identity in the present, Rosenzweig goes further and argues that the recognition of the difference of the past brings with it obligations, and specific obligations, in the present. Because he maintains that it can transform us but not command us, the biblical text remains on par with an aesthetic object for Buber, while for Rosenzweig it does not. From the perspective of Rosenzweig's thought, it is for this reason that Buber's aesthetic and hermeneutical approaches retain pagan elements. Nonetheless, in keeping with Rosenzweig's aesthetic and hermeneutic approaches, Buber's idolatrous approach to the text nonetheless leaves the possibility of revelation open for the modern person. Despite some significant differences, Buber and Rosenzweig agreed that the translation must reflect the difference of the biblical text. Both aimed at shocked attention in the aesthetics of the text, claiming that only through a shocked experience could the modern person have the opportunity to respond anew to the biblical word.

## Translation as a Process of Distanciation and Defamiliarization

Buber and Rosenzweig consciously saw themselves in relation to a German-Jewish tradition of Bible translation that they sought to transform. The question of how to translate Hebrew into German, both literally and philosophically, was something that German Jewry had confronted long before Buber and Rosenzweig were born. Moses Mendelssohn, Leopold Zunz, Samson Raphael Hirsch, Simon Bernfeld, and, coeval with Buber and Rosenzweig, Harry Torczyner (Tur-Sinai) all attempted to answer the question of how Hebrew should be translated into German.[6] In answering this question, each translator suggested how Jews should approach the Jewish tradition (their past) and their modern, host society (their present). Each translator developed his respective position by suggesting, quite literally, how German Jews should read the Bible. What should a translation of biblical Hebrew into German look like? What commitments should a translation reflect? What should German Jews encounter when they open their Bibles? In answering these questions, they each offered a practical program for German Jewry's assessment of its relation to the Jewish tradition and modernity.

As they worked on the translation, Buber and Rosenzweig wrote essays about their philosophies of translation and about the technical problems they encountered while translating. Some of their essays were originally published separately; after Rosenzweig's death, all the essays were assembled by Buber and published in 1936 under the title *Die Schrift und ihre Verdeutschung*.[7] In the first essay, "People Today and the Jewish Bible," taken from a lecture series first given in November 1926, Buber addresses the question of the possibility of "contemporary" response to the biblical text.[8] He lays out what he sees as both the possibilities and obstacles to encountering the Bible for his generation:

> This book has since its beginning encountered one generation after another. Confrontation and reconciliation with it have taken place in every generation. Sometimes it is met with obedience and offered dominion; sometimes, with offense and rebellion. But each generation engages it vitally, and faces it in the realm of reality. Even where people have said "no" to it, that "no" has only validated the book's claim upon them—they have borne witness to it even in refusing themselves to it.[9]

For Buber, the problem of "this" generation, however, is that the Bible is encountered neither positively nor negatively, because the Bible is over-intellectualized and does not impact people's lives. The current generation understands *Geist* only intellectually, denying the double meaning of "intellect" and "spirit." Precisely because of *Geist*'s ambiguity, Buber and Rosenzweig use *Geist* to render the Hebrew *ruaḥ*, God's spirit. Modern "religion," Buber writes, does not encompass the whole but only a small part of life. The Hebrew Bible, on the other hand, does embrace all of life; in this way it is different from the great books of other religions. The Hebrew Bible is about this world; "Holiness enters into history without disenfranchising it."[10] All of its laws explicitly concern the life of the human being. Still, Buber acknowledges and encourages his readers to acknowledge along with him that "'People today' have little access to sure belief, and cannot be given such access."[11] Buber suggests, however, that "people today" do have the possibility of an *openness* to belief.

But to have such openness requires the ability, or the opportunity, to see the Bible anew, in its strangeness and difference—in other words, to be able to read the Bible without reference to what has become its static familiarity. People must be able to encounter the Bible as other, as unfamiliar. For Rosenzweig, meaning is constituted by way of the tension between present and past. Meaning is created precisely through a response to that which is different. If people are to become open to belief, the very framework for the creation of meaning must exist. Such a framework for encountering the Bible must come through a sense of the Bible's difference from, and not continuity with, the modern world. It is here that Buber and Rosenzweig anticipate Gadamer's notion that

> time is no longer a gulf to be bridged, because it separates, but it is actually the supportive ground of process in which the present is rooted. Hence, temporal distance is not something that must be overcome. This was, rather, the naive assumption of historicism, namely that we must set ourselves within the spirit of the age, and think with its ideas and its thoughts, not with our own, and thus advance towards historical objectivity. In fact, the important thing is to recognize the distance in time as a positive and productive possibility of understanding.[12]

Buber and Rosenzweig aimed precisely to use distance in time as a "positive and productive possibility of understanding." For this reason, they sought to highlight rather than underplay the difference between biblical and modern views.

However, Buber and Rosenzweig's view of the importance of recognizing the distance in time goes beyond Gadamer's claim that this distance is "positive and productive" to the possibility of understanding. Here, the hermeneutics of the Buber-Rosenzweig Bible translation radicalize Gadamer's notion of "understanding" [*Verstehen*]. For Gadamer, the process of translation is secondary to understanding. In *Truth and Method*, he makes this point explicitly: "The example of translation . . . makes us aware that language as the medium of understanding must be consciously created by an explicit mediation. This kind of explicit process is undoubtedly not the norm in a conversation."[13] Buber and Rosenzweig would disagree with Gadamer's following statement:

> Where there is understanding, there is not translation, but speech. . . . Every conversation obviously presupposes that the two speakers speak the same language. Only when two people can make themselves understood through lan-

> guage by talking together can the problem of understanding and agreement even be raised.[14]

In contrast, Rosenzweig claims that translation is the primary mode of speech and grounds the possibility of understanding because translation is fundamentally dialogical. Rosenzweig would agree with Gadamer that from a theoretical point of view, it is necessary that "only when two people can make themselves understood through language by talking together can the problem of understanding and agreement even be raised." However, Rosenzweig goes on to claim that communication does not take place in theory but in practice. This means that dialogue—the process of translation—becomes not only possible, but necessary:

> Translating means serving two masters. It follows that no one can do it. But it follows also that it is, like everything that no one can do in theory, everyone's task in practice. Everyone must translate, and everyone does. When we speak, we translate from our intention into the understanding we expect in the other. . . . When we hear, we translate words that sound in our ears into our understanding—or, more concretely, into the language of our mouth. We all have our individual speech. Or rather: we all would have our own individual speech, if there were in truth such a thing as monologic speaking (as logicians, those would-be monologists, characteristically postulate) and all speaking were not already dialogic speaking and thus—translation.[15]

Because in reality—though perhaps not in theory—there is not monologue but only dialogue, Rosenzweig maintains that translation has not a secondary but a primary role in all understanding: "[Translation] will, in the succession of 'impossible' and necessary compromises we ordinarily call life, give us the courage of modesty, which asks of itself not what is recognized as impossible but what is given as necessary."[16] In contrast to Gadamer, Rosenzweig argues that translation, *Übersetzung*, literally a placing over to the other, orients *Verstehen*, understanding between people. The aesthetic of the Buber-Rosenzweig Bible follows from this hermeneutic sensibility. What is needed in a translation, from Buber and Rosenzweig's perspective, is precisely a recognition of a dialogue which is ultimately a recognition, perhaps even the shocked recognition, of the extreme difference between the reader and text. Rosenzweig sums up this impetus for translation in his 1926 essay, "Scripture and Luther." "If somewhere [the Bible] has become familiar, customary possession, it must again and anew, as a foreign and unfamiliar sound, stir up the complacent satedness of its alleged possessor from outside. . . . The Bible is written for the sake of the reader who has been denied it."[17]

For Buber and Rosenzweig, the theological possibility of dialogue with the biblical text is intimately linked to the literary qualities of the text.

They argued that in their time a general complacency had developed in relationship to the Hebrew Bible because of the way in which the text literally was read. Buber's essay "On Word Choice in Translating the Bible" turns to the specifics of the relationship between trying to create a new openness to the Bible and the task of translation. Written in the summer of 1930 in memory of Rosenzweig, this essay contains specific examples on word choice and at the same time echoes Rosenzweig's "Scripture and Luther." Buber writes:

> The special obligation to make a new version of the Bible, which came alive in our time and led to our undertaking, resulted from the discovery that the passage of time had largely turned the Bible into a palimpsest. The original traits of the Bible, the original meaning and words, had been overlaid by a familiar abstraction, in origin partly theological and partly literary.[18]

That the Bible had become a "familiar abstraction" was directly related to its language. Significantly, Buber argues that this state of inattention "applies, moreover, not only to reading in translation but also to reading in the original." Already we sense the importance Buber and Rosenzweig place on the possibilities of translation. Not only could translation make the original accessible to the reader but a translation, if done properly, had something to contribute to the original itself. By accenting the uniqueness of the original language in making the host language conform to it, a translation could heighten the literary power of the original language itself. The Buber-Rosenzweig translation aimed to produce shocked attention in its readers by doing away with "smoothed-over conceptual language."

Buber and Rosenzweig felt that what they hoped to achieve with their translation was both necessary and possible because it had never been done before. Even the Greek Septuagint, the Latin Vulgate, and the German of the Luther translation did not "aim principally at maintaining the original character of the book as manifested in word choice, in syntax and in rhythmical articulation."[19] These translations, the best that history has known, ultimately failed, as all translation inevitably does, because they sought to transfer content to their particular communities, rather than form. While these efforts were initially successful, they eventually faded into static familiarity because they no longer said anything new. For Rosenzweig, Luther's translation was the most successful because Luther asked the reader "'to give the Hebrew some room.'"[20] Because he believed that the language of the Bible was the language of God, Luther was able to recognize the first imperative of translation—that the original language must be primary.

Following nineteenth-century German philologists and anticipating American literary criticism throughout the twentieth century, as well as recent French critics, Buber and Rosenzweig insist that content simply cannot be separated from form. Even more, Rosenzweig writes in his Luther essay that translation is necessary because written language always eventually reigns over the spoken word. At a certain point in a people's history, he tells us, *Schriftsprache* (written language) develops. Thus "a moment comes when writing ceases to be a handmaiden of language and becomes its mistress."[21] This moment has occurred for Luther's translation and as a result,

> those who would undertake a new Bible translation encounter a threefold obstacle in their way, composed of these three singular aspects of the Luther Bible. Prospective translators must, that is, encounter at once the book by which the church is made visible, the book by which the German *Schriftsprache* was founded, and the book by which the world spirit has been mediated.[22]

Through a translation, which is the effort and opportunity to return to the original, a historical time has the opportunity to ask essential, religious questions all over again. An opportunity to ask questions arises only when a historical time can distinguish itself from what has come before. Questioning comes from the tension of the awareness of difference, and not from the mediation of sameness. Only because the Bible looks so different can we have an opportunity to relate it to our lives "today." Without acknowledging its difference, it cannot speak to us and it cannot make us question ourselves. To promote such questioning was precisely the task of the Buber-Rosenzweig translation.

Buber and Rosenzweig's understanding of the revelatory possibilities of the biblical text and the task of the translator in bringing to life again these possibilities bears an important conceptual and historical affinity to Heidegger's view of the task of philosophy.[23] In this famous statement in *Being and Time*, Heidegger maintains that "the business of philosophy is to preserve [*bewahren*] the power of the most elemental words in which *Dasein* expresses itself, and to keep common understanding from flattening them to the point of unintelligibility, which in its turn functions as a source for illusory problems."[24] Like Heidegger, Buber and Rosenzweig offer criticisms of the illusory problems created by the western philosophical tradition and propose a return to the revelatory moments in certain texts.[25] They differ as to the nature of the illusory problems created by western philosophy as well as which texts contain "elemental words" that must be unflattened. But the difference between them goes deeper. For Buber and Rosenzweig, it is not, as Heidegger states, "language that speaks."[26] Buber and Rosenzweig differ from Heidegger in insisting that the revelatory moment contained in a text is mediated and created not through the language of the text alone but through the text's interpreters, past, present, and future. It is on this point that Buber and Rosenzweig also differ from each other. Where Buber argues, "Man, he alone, speaks,"[27] Rosenzweig maintains that "we seek the word of man in the word of God."[28] For Heidegger, language speaks. For Buber, the human being speaks. And for Rosenzweig, God speaks to the human being, who in turn speaks back to God. These differences, between Heidegger and Buber-Rosenzweig on the one hand, and between Buber and Rosenzweig on the other, have a variety of implications for understanding the implications of the hermeneutics of the Buber-Rosenzweig Bible translation.

## Reconsidering the Relation between Buber and Rosenzweig

Let us turn first to the similarities between Buber and Rosenzweig's approach to the biblical text. Buber follows Rosenzweig in maintaining that one fundamental difference between the Bible and contemporary life lies in understandings of history. While history in modern times has either been understood as "an indiscriminate sequence of processes" or as a set of fixed laws, the biblical conception of history centers on a sequence: creation, revelation, and redemption. These are three stages of God's interaction with the world. Buber notes that the strangeness of these categories for the modern person is indeed an obstacle to finding revelation in the Bible. However, Buber goes on to emphasize that the importance of revelation for the modern person is the recognition that "what has happened to me was precisely otherness, was being taken hold of something other. Nietzsche puts it more honestly: 'we take and do not ask who it is that gives.' I, however, think that what matters above all is to take with precisely the knowledge that *someone is giving*."[29] For Rosenzweig, that someone is giving means that an exterior other calls me out of my creaturely slumbers and elicits, or better demands, a response from me. For Buber, this notion of otherness hearkens back to his *I and Thou*.[30] There Buber explains that the primary human experience is with another person, and that the other is in fact primary to any conception of the I. In order to say I, I must first say Thou. In "People Today and the Jewish Bible," Buber asserts that if the I and Thou, which is revelation, can somehow be perceived, then the categories creation and redemption can follow.

We can see from this essay how much Buber draws on Rosenzweig's philosophy in the translation effort. Buber's comments in "People Today and the Jewish Bible" are one such instance of Rosenzweig's influence on him. Rosenzweig's influence on Buber, however, has been little appreciated because it has been a widespread and misguided perception that Buber and Rosenzweig had identical philosophies of language. It is generally assumed that Rosenzweig's philosophy of language mirrors Buber's notion of the I-Thou of religious experience.[31] But for Rosenzweig, while dialogue is the fundamental human experience, it is only the beginning. The central human experience—and it is very important to note here that, unlike Buber, Rosenzweig does not use the word "religious" to describe Judaism—is community and not dialogue. The central human experience for Rosenzweig is not comprised of just two voices, but rather of a polyphony of voices. The widespread impression that Buber and Rosenzweig only differed in their assessment of the importance of the law in Judaism is only partially true. Their different assessments of law and communal obligation stem from different understandings of the nature of language. As we will see, this difference has a variety of implications.

We have already discussed briefly some of Rosenzweig's argument in *The Star of Redemption* for what he would later call the "new thinking," the effort to bridge philosophy and theology. For Rosenzweig, speech is experience and as experience itself, speech has three fundamental moods. The indicative mood is creation; the imperative mood, revelation. Finally, the cohortative mood is redemption. Rosenzweig also characterizes creation as epic, revelation as lyric, and redemption as drama. While the most basic human experience is the I and Thou, the I and Thou is rooted in and must lead back to a plural imperative, the cohortative. Rosenzweig reiterates that the time-sequence of the moods is not one-dimensional or linear. The imperative of the I-Thou is hermeneutically prior to the possibility of the indicative's descriptive statements. Descriptive statements, which constitute the language of science, do not contradict, but in fact require a prior ethical obligation if they are to be possible. It is thus in keeping with the fundamental structure of *The Star of Redemption*'s philosophy of language that Buber writes in this first essay that if the I and Thou, or revelation, can be experienced, then creation and redemption necessarily follow.

Buber scholars agree that Buber's philosophy of language was deeply influenced by Rosenzweig and the translation project.[32] In fact, Rosenzweig transformed Buber's philosophy even before the translation project began. The particularly *dialogical* nature of the I and Thou relation was one of the last additions to *I and Thou*.[33] Buber's lectures, "Religion as Presence," given from January through March 1922, formed the basis of *I and Thou*, but showed no evidence of dialogical thinking. It was from Rosenzweig's comments on the 1922 galley sheets of *I and Thou* that Buber's dialogical emphasis emerged. As an example, Rivka Horwitz has noted changes from lecture 4 of "Religion as Presence," given February 1922, and the final version of *I and Thou* of May 1922. In the lecture, Buber writes about the relation between human beings: "I confront a human being . . . whom I love. What does that mean . . . when I actually confront this person as a Thou? . . . It is something I must realize."[34] In the final version of *I and Thou* he writes: "When I confront a human being as my You and speak the basic *I-You* to him."[35] Dialogical speech, as opposed to self-realization, was Rosenzweig's contribution to the development of Buber's thought, as he wrote in a letter earlier that year: "I will teach him speech in Frankfurt."[36]

While working with Rosenzweig on the translation project, Buber was able to deepen the dialogical philosophy that he began to develop in *I and Thou*. Rosenzweig's influence is especially evident when it comes to Buber's discussion in his biblical writings of creation, revelation, and redemption, understood as a sequence that emerges from, and is implied by, dialogue.[37] Still, differences between the two remain. The substance of the difference between Buber and Rosenzweig on the relations between creation, revelation, and redemption are perhaps best documented in a series of letters from September 1922, letters written after Rosenzweig had made comments on Buber's *I and Thou*. Rosenzweig boldly makes his point in the first letter of the exchange, a point that is directly related to this book's concern with idolatry. Rosenzweig writes to Buber: "Let me take the bull by the horns right away: in the I-It, you give the I-Thou a cripple for an antagonist. The fact that this cripple governs the modern world does not make it less a cripple."[38]

Rosenzweig's remark anticipates the 1924 exchange between Buber and Rosenzweig, known as "the builders," on the status of Jewish law.[39] Rosenzweig argues that Buber's I-It is a cripple because although Buber stresses the goodness of the creaturely world from which the I-Thou relationship emerges, he does not and cannot embrace the communal framework that the I-Thou is predicated upon and, in the modern world, must strive for. For Rosenzweig, this ultimately makes Buber's I-It a cripple because Buber's formulation simultaneously gives the I-Thou too much credit and the I-It too little.

Let us begin to unpack this argument by referring to two important comments that Buber makes in *I and Thou* about divine law. He writes:

> Man receives and what he receives is not a content, but a presence, a presence as a strength. . . . This is the eternal revelation which is present in the here and now. I neither know of nor believe in any revelation that is not the same in its primal phenomenon. I do not believe in God's naming himself or in God's defining himself before man. The word of revelation is: I am there as whoever I am there. That which reveals is that which reveals. That which has being is there, nothing more. The eternal source of strength flows, the eternal touch is waiting, the eternal voice sounds, nothing more.[40]

From Rosenzweig's perspective, Buber's refrain—"the eternal voice sounds and nothing more"—devalues the public world of law and institutions, while overvaluing the private world of lyrical relation. Significantly, Rosenzweig judges Buber with reference to Cohen:

> What is happening to you is the exact opposite of what happened to your fellow discoverer [Hermann] Cohen. . . . He discovered I-Thou as the great exception to the rule and for its sake built an annex to his already finished edifice, ever concerned with not spoiling what was already complete. Naturally, he didn't succeed; he tried to cram into the annex far too many things that had already found their place in the old building. The annex was threatening to the old building on its own, where those who had frequented the old building were able to find their way about. You, on the other hand, have put up a new edifice from the start; you reduce Creation to a chaos just good enough to supply you with building materials for your new structure.[41]

While Cohen did not "discover" the I-Thou after he had completed his "finished edifice," as Rosenzweig maintains, he did rethink it.[42] Rosenzweig argues that Cohen's "discovery" of the I-Thou relation did not come at the cost of Cohen's old edifice, which consisted first and foremost of a philosophy of law (as articulated most centrally in Cohen's *Ethik des reinen Willens*).[43] Buber's problem is twofold in this regard and is summed up in Rosenzweig's statement that Buber "reduces Creation to a chaos just good enough to supply you with building materials for your new structure." Rosenzweig argues that unlike Cohen, Buber builds a new structure for the I-Thou and thereby leaves the old structure, the I-It, a cripple. With Buber's I-Thou structure, there is no place for public institutions or communal obligations.

To further emphasize this point, Rosenzweig continues his letter to Buber: "Therefore, *ha-acharim* [heretics] will follow you and will 'mutilate the shoots.'" This is a reference to the famous story of the four rabbis who entered the garden of mystical knowledge, told in the Babylonian Talmud (*Ḥagigah* 14b). The first rabbi died, the second lost his mind, the third became a heretic and "mutilated shoots," and only the fourth, Rabbi Akiva, left the garden in peace. In this letter, Rosenzweig likens Buber to the heretic because he claims that Buber's thought leads Jews away from God's commandments. Rosenzweig also compares Cohen to Rabbi Akiva.

Rosenzweig's argument that Buber makes the I-It a cripple is simultaneously an argument against Buber's elevation of the I-Thou relation. He ends his letter to Buber: "What is to become of I and Thou if they will have to swallow up the entire world and Creator as well? *Religion? I am afraid so—and shudder at the word whenever I hear it.* For my and your sake, there has to be something else in this world besides—me and you!"[44] Here we see the significance of Rosenzweig's insistence on the sequence creation-revelation-redemption, which Buber draws on in the translation project and specifically in his essay "People Today and the Jewish Bible." The sequence creation-revelation-redemption translates for Rosenzweig not into a dichotomy between I-It and I-Thou, but into an ever over-lapping sequence I-It, I-Thou, We-It.[45] Rosenzweig argues that the human being can and must complete God's creation and that the completion of God's creation comes from answering God's commanding voice through the creation of human institutions and not private individuality. God's commanding voice is mediated through sacred texts but, contra Buber, Rosenzweig maintains that the parameters of the exegesis of scripture are prescribed by the text's past interpreters. From Rosenzweig's perspective, Buber's approach to exegesis remains highly individualistic; it denies that revelation brings with it particular commands but only formless obligations.

In order not to overstate this difference, we must note of course that Buber and Rosenzweig *both* begin with the individual's relation to the text. After all, they translated the Bible into German so that individuals could read it. However, Rosenzweig's intention was certainly not that private readings of the Buber-Rosenzweig Bible would be substituted for communal synagogue readings of the real thing. But while Buber and Rosenzweig both begin with the individual, they differ as to where the individual should end up.[46] For Rosenzweig, the individual is always checked by the community, past, present, and future, while for Buber, the individual's relation to the community remains more ambivalent. This point is connected to their different understandings of language. Let us recall for a moment Rosenzweig's comment that "we seek the word of man in the word of God" and Buber's remark, "Man, he alone, speaks." Rosenzweig agrees with Buber that the human being must interpret divine command; God's law is always mediated through the language that the human being shares with God. But the human being speaks only because God has spoken to her already. Rosenzweig states the complex relation between the human and the divine in a letter to Buber of July 1924:

> For me, too, God is not a Law-giver. But he commands. It is only by the manner of his observance that man in his inertia changes the commandments into Law, a legal system with paragraphs, without the realization that "I am the Lord," without "fear and trembling," without the awareness that the man stands under God's commandment. Could this, then, be the difference between us?[47]

Rosenzweig makes much of the relation between divine and human language in *The Star of Redemption*'s commentary on the Song of Songs. Turning to his commentary allows us to explore further some of the implications of Rosenzweig and Buber's conceptions of the I-Thou relation specifically, and language more generally. In the context of his account of the Song of Songs, Rosenzweig suggests that revelation (the I-Thou) is a lyrical moment, which is in reality love. Love, for Rosenzweig, is always fleeting. Such is the deficiency of love between two people: while it is always renewed, it is also always gone. This problem is not love's, but time's itself: "The moment . . . does not stand. Rather it vanishes with the speed of an arrow. As a result it is never 'between' its past and future: it has vanished before it could be between anything."[48] Like time, language and love are fleeting. Rosenzweig makes the comparison: "Like speech itself, love is sensual—supersensual."[49] Indeed, this quality is in a sense language's (as opposed to idealism's or logic's) perfection for Rosenzweig. Language, and language only, *is* reality's fragmentation, a fragmentation that is rooted in the temporal existence of finite human beings who die: "Language is alive because it too can die. Eternity would be an unwelcome gift to it."[50]

Rosenzweig maintains that language is more than allegory (*Gleichnis)*. He states that before the nineteenth century, "one knew that the distinction between immanence and transcendence disappears in language."[51] Language is immanent because by definition it claims to encompass all of being. To claim completeness is what it means to speak, to say what the case is. Yet at the same time, every speaking excludes something, because, in contrast to thought or to mathematics, language can never be all-encompassing. After being spoken, speech negates itself because the reality of that which it spoke is no longer present. The solution to language's fleetingness for Rosenzweig is a movement away from the lyric, and toward what he calls the dramatic. A movement away from the intimacy of two people toward a third person is necessary:

> Love after all always remains between two people; it knows only of I and Thou, not of the street. Thus this longing cannot be fulfilled in love, for love is directly present in experience and manifests itself only in experience. The sobs of the beloved penetrate beyond love, to a future beyond its present revelation. They yearn for a love eternal such as can never spring from the everlasting presentness of sensation.[52]

For Rosenzweig, the dialogue of presence and *Erlebnis* is a fleeting, momentary experience that cannot be sustained.[53] Rosenzweig argues that it is necessary to move away from the singular imperative of the I-Thou to the plural imperative of the cohortative's "let us."

In the context of his understanding of the fleetingness and intrinsic limitations of lyric discourse, Rosenzweig's emphasis on presence in the word is best interpreted not as a naive claim for divine presence in the biblical text, but as a movement toward redemption. Precisely because polyphony is required, the goal of reading the Bible is better described as drama, and not as dialogue, presence, or *Erlebnis*. Rosenzweig is a critic of notions of mystical religious experience. His claim that Buber is intoxicated by his discovery of the I-Thou in fact equates Buber's view of dialogue with a kind of generic mysticism that is incapable of moving into the world, an equation that Buber denies.[54] For Rosenzweig, "mysticism" is precisely the problem of getting "stuck in" the lyrical relation and being unable to move beyond it.[55]

Rosenzweig focuses on the modern problem of developing a notion of communal responsibility, a plural imperative, that grows out of the lyrical imperative of the I and Thou. Any notion of presence that Rosenzweig is advocating in his essays on the Bible, as well as in his discussions of revelation in *The Star of Redemption*, is a negative presence because it always passes away. If it is not to surrender to the life-denying impulse of mysticism, lyrical discourse must, for Rosenzweig, become dramatic. From the sensuous and ever-fleeting imperative of the I and Thou, captured by "Love me!," Rosenzweig suggests we must move to the ever-growing cohortative of community, "Let us redeem the world." To grasp this movement we must understand that for Rosenzweig language's presence implies and necessitates its simultaneous absence. Absence propels us to strive for a concreteness that only two voices, or dialogue, cannot attain. Concreteness is only available to human beings through a multiplicity of voices, which Rosenzweig describes as drama. From the dialogue of the lyric we move to the polyphony of the dramatic. From *Erlebnis* we move to responsibility.

Rosenzweig and Buber agree that the I-Thou relationship is a relationship *between* individuals. An individual never reads alone, but always is embedded within an interpretative community. So, too, a reader does not encounter a single voice in the Bible but rather the many voices of a single text, as well as the voices that have read the text throughout history. The text itself is polyphonous. That the reader always stands in relation to a community of readers means for Rosenzweig that the encounter with the biblical text moves beyond the here and now of lyrical discourse. The present reader's relationship with the text moves simultaneously back into a relationship with the past and forward into the future. Communities—past, present, and future—are always a check against the individual's reading of the text. For Buber, on the other hand, the reader's relation to the biblical text is rooted in the presence of the here and now. While much of Buber's later work is an attempt to build community from the new identities formed from reading biblical and other Jewish texts, his understanding of identity remains individualistic.

From Rosenzweig's perspective, even Buber's commitment to the formation of a Zionist community reflects his individualistic, present-oriented hermeneutic. As we will see in chapter 7, Rosenzweig argues that though Zionists make their claims to land by way of their pasts, their claim is actually present-oriented. Their views of the past are assimilated to what they believe are the needs of the present. In this way, the Zionist call for a new future—and here Rosenzweig means both political Zionists, such as Herzl, and cultural Zionists, such as Buber—is actually an obliteration of the past. This cultural-political stance is idolatrous for Rosenzweig, for hermeneutical reasons. As we will discuss in chapter 8, Rosenzweig in fact calls Buber's cultural-political stance "atheistic." Rosenzweig claims that Buber makes an idol out of the perceived needs of the present of the Jewish people. This idol of the present denies the Jewish people's obligations to God, obligations that are made clear through a serious engagement with the Jewish past.[56]

For Buber, the ongoing reading of the Bible takes the form of narrative retelling. For Rosenzweig, on the other hand, the ongoing reading of the Bible in community is described better as a dramatic performance. The difference between narrative retelling and dramatic performance is a difference not of kind but of emphasis. The former is more concerned with the creation of identity, the latter with the enactment of an already received identity.[57] For Buber, the reading of the Bible produces narrative retelling that is an ongoing production of identity.[58] We encounter the otherness of the Bible, and through an encounter with that which is different we tell stories about who we are now. For Rosenzweig, the reading of the Bible in community is not the creation of identity but the *enactment* of an already given identity. Very much in Mendelssohn's sense, the reading of the Bible in community is an enactment of a nation's script. The nation, the Jewish people in this case, are defined by the fact of who they are: Jews. Jewish identity is already constituted by the Jewish practice of gathering together to read the Torah. For Rosenzweig, what results from this practice of communal reading is a conversation between many different voices. There is no doubt that identities are formed and transformed through conversation, but the conversation of the Bible's reading does not aim principally at the formation of identity, because the process already assumes, and indeed demands, an identity.[59] We return here to the fundamental difference between Buber's view—"Man, he alone, speaks"—and Rosenzweig's—"We seek the word of man in the word of God."[60] For Buber, encountering the biblical text is a task confined only by the human voice. For Rosenzweig, on the other hand, the biblical text—mediated and transformed through communities, past, present, and future—brings God's commanding voice into the human world.

## Art or More than Art?

To understand further how these differences play out in Buber's and Rosenzweig's hermeneutics, let us briefly recount the development of Buber's own hermeneutical approach.[61] Buber studied at the University of Berlin with Wilhelm Dilthey in the summer of 1898 and the fall of 1899. His early hermeneutical approach resembles Dilthey's, and that of Dilthey's predecessor, Schleiermacher, in significant ways. In fact, Buber's early writings on and translations of ḥasidic stories are a rather straightforward application of romantic hermeneutics. Buber's goal was literally to retell and relive the intentions of the authors of the original tales.[62] As the transmitter of ḥasidic tales, Buber believed that he not only had direct access to the original sources, but that his access was so thorough that he understood the tales better than their authors had. He boldly states this very view in his "My Way to Ḥasidism": "I have found the true faithfulness: more adequately than the direct disciples, I received and completed the task; a later messenger in a foreign realm."[63] Buber's sense of retelling was intimately connected to a sense of re-creating ḥasidic tales. He borrowed this hermeneutical approach from Dilthey's notion of *nachbilden*.[64] Buber's ḥasidic tales were a "re-creation" and he had "not translated them but retold them."[65] In sum, Buber's was an attempt to "make these creations known to the European public in a form as *artistically pure* as possible."[66]

Even when Buber moved away from this romantic approach, his connection between and in fact equation of interpretation and art remained. Buber's dialogical philosophy is infused with such an equation. Here again we find a major difference between Buber and Rosenzweig. For Rosenzweig, though art is the silence before language, art and language are distinct from one another. Art prepares the way for revelation, but art does not play a role in revelation. Recall Rosenzweig's comment that art "provides the ground on which the self can grow up elsewhere" but "art is not a real world, for the threads which are drawn from man to man in it run only for moments."[67] Buber, on the other hand, does not distinguish clearly between aesthetic and revelatory relationships, and indeed between encounters between animate and inanimate subjects.

Buber's comments in *I and Thou* about having an I-Thou relation with a tree are well known, but they are worth repeating in this context:

> I contemplate the tree. . . . The power of exclusiveness has seized me. . . . The tree is no impression, no play of my imagination, no aspect of a mood; it confronts me bodily and has to deal with me, as I must deal with it—only differently. One should not try to dilute the meaning of the relation: relation is reciprocity.[68]

While it is true that in developing the philosophy articulated in *I and Thou*, Buber moved away from Dilthey's hermeneutical model, striking aspects of romantic hermeneutics nonetheless remained with him. Looking back on the development of his I-Thou philosophy, Buber wrote: "The realization . . . grew in me, that of human life as the possibility of dialogue with being. . . . At the same time, but in a special osmosis with it, my relationship to Ḥasidism was ever more basically transformed."[69] But while Buber moved toward a model of dialogue, the "possibility of dialogue with being" meant for him dialogue with animate and inanimate objects, including trees and art.

The philosophy of *I and Thou*, although not fully developed, is absolutely essential for understanding the development of a Buberian hermeneutic.[70] In *I and Thou*, Buber develops a sketchy model for understanding the relation between the interpreter and the text. For Buber, the relation between interpreter and text can only be understood on analogy with the relation between the human and "spiritual beings," as he writes in *I and Thou*: "Here [with 'spiritual beings'; *mit den geistigen Wesenheit*] the relation is wrapped in a cloud but reveals itself; it lacks but creates language. We hear no You and yet feel addressed; we answer—creating, thinking, acting: with our being we speak the basic word, unable to say You with our mouth."[71] In his 1929 essay "Dialogue," Buber equates dialogue with art more explicitly: "All art is, from its origin, essentially of the nature of dialogue. All music calls to an ear not the musician's own, all sculpture to an eye not the sculpture's, architecture, in addition, calls to the step as it walks in the building."[72] Art as dialogue is the basis of Buber's sense of the text as Thou. In *I and Thou*, however, encounter is unmediated. In his biblical writings, Buber develops a notion of mediated encounter. As Steven Kepnes remarks,

> In *I and Thou* Buber's reliance on the prelinguistic, unmediated encounter prohibits the full development of a theory of interpretation based on the written text. . . . For a development of such a mediated language-bound hermeneutics we will have to wait for Buber's biblical writings, and his late writings on language.[73]

Nonetheless, the sense remains that encounter, and dialogue, can take place between the human, the text, and art. As Kepnes shows convincingly, Buber's discussions of encounter between the reader and the text is an extension and application of the human encounter with art.[74]

Buber's emphasis on art as both self-realization and encounter is constant from his early to his late work.[75] With the biblical text, the notion of art is extended in Buber's thought. The biblical text is a particular form of art, one that has called out to generations and generations of readers. For Rosenzweig, art remains an idol because it remains directed only at the self-formation of the individual. (The exception to this rule is Christian art, the subject of the next chapter.) Artworks do not command us, though they may shock us. For Rosenzweig, the biblical text is not an artwork because it embodies the commanding voices of past generations of interpreters who place parameters on our self-formations in the present. As articulated most clearly in his approach to Jewish law, Buber denies the restrictions of past generations for the present one. For this reason, the biblical text remains for him akin to an artwork. It may help us fashion an identity in the present. We may learn much about ourselves from it. However, from Buber's perspective, the biblical text remains artwork in that it does not issue us commands but allows us to form ourselves. In it the human voice speaks.

For Rosenzweig, the biblical text commands the human to respond to the divine. Rosenzweig maintains that the biblical text is not a work of art to be re-created. From it we learn that we can speak only because we are addressed.[76] Rosenzweig alludes to this point in his 1927 essay, "On the Unity of the Bible": "For those who know no Hebrew, ours remains a 'creative' translation."[77] Knowing Hebrew for Rosenzweig is not recognizing, in Heidegger's words, that it is "language that speaks." Hebrew, for Rosenzweig, is a particular language spoken to a particular people for the sake of all of humanity. It is in the interpretation of the Hebrew text, and the past interpretations of that text, that these particular people are commanded to live their lives in the present. Knowing Hebrew means for Rosenzweig knowing that the Jewish people are commanded to hear God's law in the obligations established by the past.

At the same time, however, Rosenzweig's emphasis on the demands of the past brings with it an orientation toward the future. Translation is a future-oriented task, for understood properly, it is a task that must be performed over and over again. Recall Rosenzweig's comment: "To require time means that we cannot anticipate, that we must wait for everything, that what is ours depends on what is another's."[78] Translation is a process that happens in, through, and indeed because of time. Translation makes meaning possible by way of the future that cannot be anticipated. We continually encounter new contingencies and must continually translate. The task of translation recognizes the polyphony of voices from the past, the present, and the future.

From Rosenzweig's perspective, Buber's approach to the biblical text borders on idolatrous because it does not give the past its due. Together, however, Buber and Rosenzweig avoid a fanatical approach to translation, which would not give the future its due. Despite their differences, I will describe a hermeneutic that emerges from their translation project. In the translation, Buber draws on Rosenzweig's thought and the hermeneutic of the translation is in accordance with Rosenzweig's philosophy. At the same time, the actual aesthetic of the translation is due in large part to Buber's talents and capabilities as a poet. But while each contributed individually in these different areas, the hermeneutic and the aesthetic of the translation belong to them both. This is because the Buber-Rosenzweig translation is collaborative in precisely Rosenzweig's sense of unity. Like the Bible itself, the translation, in its unity, reflects a polyphony of voices. Each contributes in his own way, and while in the end we are left with one product—their translation—Buber and Rosenzweig's agreement in their final product does not obliterate their disagreement. It is the differences between Buber and Rosenzweig, and the fact that these differences are not smoothed over, that allow them together to avoid idolatry and fanaticism in their effort at translation. A fanatical translation would be capable of recognizing one voice only: its own. A fanatical translation would deny all difference in the name of and for the sake of the same. The Buber-Rosenzweig translation project sought to transform the aesthetic qualities of the German text in order to make it other. By way of implicitly preserving difference, the task of the Buber-Rosenzweig Bible translation emphasized the need for the *interpretive act*, and indeed the future-oriented act, of reading the Bible.

## Post-critical Hermeneutics

The Buber and Rosenzweig Bible translation differed from previous Christianized translations, and it differed from previous Jewish ones also. To begin with, Buber and Rosenzweig differed from Mendelssohn's attempt at translation in the late eighteenth century. Under the guise of universal reason, and in the hopes of advocating German-Jewish unity, Mendelssohn's translation sought to transform Hebrew into German. Buber and Rosenzweig did not hold Enlightenment views of reason. Perhaps more pressing than these philosophical considerations of reason, however, Buber and Rosenzweig lived at a time when the Jewish community, despite apologist strands, had become disenchanted with liberalism and political emancipation as the road to redemption.[79] Whereas Mendelssohn translated the Bible into German in the hopes that Jews would learn German, Buber and Rosenzweig translated the Bible into German in the hopes that Jews would learn Hebrew.[80] Buber and Rosenzweig sought the possibility of a Jewish renaissance in which Judaism would remain wholly separate from the institutional politics of secular states. Change from within Judaism itself, they thought, would allow Jewish culture to flourish.

For Buber and Rosenzweig, lurking behind Mendelssohn's efforts was an apologist stand of which they wanted no part. In chapter 2 we saw that, for Rosenzweig, Mendelssohn's thought itself is not apologetic or dishonest. Rather, Mendelssohn's thought reflects honest uncertainty. It is what developed from Mendelssohn's ideas, or the ideas of what Rosenzweig describes as the "third enlightenment," that is the problem. In his essay "'The Eternal' Mendelssohn and the Name of God," discussed below, Rosenzweig makes a similar claim about Mendelssohn's having good intentions in his own time but being problematic for contemporary concerns. After the historical enlightenment, Rosenzweig argues, it is no longer possible that everything can be equalized by way of reason. For Mendelssohn, there is no problem, in a philosophical sense, with the effort to transfer Hebrew into German. If nothing else, Buber and Rosenzweig wanted to retain in their translation the sense of the Hebrew of the Bible as wholly different. The Hebrew Bible simply cannot be assimilated into something else. The interesting thing about their theory of translation is that despite this resiliency, they had no doubt that it was possible to produce a successful translation. In fact, the possibility of translation, for Buber and Rosenzweig, is predicated on the notion that all languages are each irreducibly unique and yet at the same time one.

Alluding to Isaiah 45:18—"Thus says the Lord that created the heavens; God himself created the earth and did not establish it without form, he created it to be inhabited; I am the Lord, and there is none other"—Rosenzweig writes in "Scripture and Luther" that the desire to live without difference, the desire for "the other to possess our ears," is a "mad egoism."[81] This mad egoism is, for Rosenzweig, the mark of the fanatic. The fanatic seeks to deny the fact that "the world was not created without form, but rich in distinctions and kinds; and there is no room in it for such an attitude."[82] In alluding to Isaiah, Rosenzweig also alludes to the Hebrew *tohu*, the same word that is used in Genesis 1:2 to describe the earth as without form. Rosenzweig's point in using the word here is precisely that fundamental difference or diversity is the basis of creation.[83] He seems to be indicating that the tower of Babel, instead of a fall, was in some sense the way the world was intended to be: diverse and different.[84] While stating that "nothing shows so clearly that the world is unredeemed as the diversity of languages," Rosenzweig reiterates in *The Star of Redemption* that there is only one speech.[85] This one speech is not a specific language; it is the fact that we speak at all, which is an act of translation. We speak in order to respond to others. Thus, to think that translation should be a smoothing over of difference is utterly wrong, for the act of translation, which reflects the multiplicity of languages, also reflects the one speech, which, as a fundamental obligation to others, is the condition for redemption. Separation and relation mark the relationship between the human and God, the relationship between human beings, and also the task of translation. Responding to that which is other, and continually remaking ourselves according to the demands of the other, marks the task of the human being. To respond to a foreign language and remake our mother tongue in accordance with the foreign, the other, marks the task of translation. An acknowledgment of fundamental difference is the prerequisite for these tasks.

For Buber and Rosenzweig, the way to retain difference in translation is to strive for a kind of literal exactness. Here is where they agreed with the efforts of Samson Raphael Hirsch, the leader and foremost exponent of Orthodoxy in Germany in the nineteenth century.[86] In *The Nineteen Letters of Ben Uziel*, published in 1836, Hirsch urged his generation to understand Judaism as a way of life that must be embraced as a whole.[87] As Buber and Rosenzweig would later state in their own way, while the life of the intellect is a part of Judaism, the intellect only gets things partially right. Hirsch's translation, thus, was a literal rendition of the Hebrew, which sought to replicate the details of the original in forms alien to the German. In this way, it would be possible to begin to grasp Judaism's self-contained fullness.

Still, Buber and Rosenzweig were not in keeping with Hirsch's entire position; for them, the Orthodox position was ultimately dogmatic because it was monolithic and one-dimensional. Once more, we can see the relationship of *The Star of Redemption* to the understanding of translation in these essays. *The Star of Redemption*'s fundamental point, again, is that reality is fragmented. This means, among other things (but also most importantly), that *all* interpretations are partial. Revelation is not a dogmatic and eternal historical event, but a relationship with that which is wholly other. For Rosenzweig, the text is wholly other in this undogmatic sense. The text embodies revelation, for it is the embodiment of the polyphony of interpreters of the past, the present, and even the future. The Orthodox position, on the other hand, sees Judaism as wholly self-contained and historically complete. Rosenzweig situates the Buber-Rosenzweig translation in relationship to orthodoxy and liberalism in a letter of 1927, entitled "The Unity of the Bible":[88]

> Our difference from orthodoxy lies in the fact that we cannot, on the basis of our belief in the sacred and thus the special status of the Torah, and in its revelatory character, draw any conclusions regarding either the process of its literary genesis or the philological value of the text as it has come down to us.[89]

Yet Rosenzweig goes on to say that their translation is indeed most closely related to Hirsch's; Buber, Rosenzweig, and Hirsch all see the Bible as unified, despite or because of its polyphony. It is in this way that Rosenzweig and Buber differentiate themselves from the *Wissenschaft* school, which only sees divisions in texts.

While Higher Criticism has posited a final redactor "R" as responsible for putting together what, from the point of view of criticism, is a variety of contradictory texts that make up the Hebrew Bible, Rosenzweig too posits an "R" as responsible for the Bible as we know it. Rosenzweig's "R," however, stands for *rabbenu*, our teacher. While Higher Criticism's "R" signifies disunity from the point of view of *Wissenschaft*, Rosenzweig's "R" signifies unity from the point of view of a diverse and dynamic tradition. Because of their commitment to seeing the text's polyphony as part of the tradition, Buber and Rosenzweig initially agreed to work as much as possible with the Masoretic text. In doing so, they are both critical and traditionalist. For them, *Wissenschaft* gets things wrong in the same way that Hirsch does: both think they have told the complete story, because neither acknowledges the discontinuity of past and present. For Buber and Rosenzweig, our stories are intimately connected to each other through the continuity and discontinuity of the passing of time. And, just as there are many languages, there are many stories.

Diversity is what makes up reality, and human beings can only understand things in fragmentary ways. It is a great and terribly destructive mistake to think that there is but one way to understand things. To be dogmatic in this way is to deny possibilities for meeting the other. To put it another way, only because we are separate do we need bridges, or speech, which is translation. Redemption is both necessary and possible precisely because we are separate from each other. What for *Wissenschaft* are contradictions are for Rosenzweig and Buber the mark of real conversation. Read in this way, each part of the Hebrew Bible complements the other parts. It is only modern philosophy (Hegel) and modern history (*Wissenschaft des Judentums*) that think that the goal is to know everything in one way only, and that because there is one truth, there is one reason.

Modern orthodoxy believes that the Bible can be understood from only one point of view. For Buber and Rosenzweig, on the other hand, "If Wellhausen and all his theories were right, if the Samaritans really had a better text than the Masoretic one, our belief would not be affected at all."[90] Here Rosenzweig is making a point of great interest for hermeneutics. First, he is suggesting that one can benefit, as he and Buber do in their translation, from the efforts and insights of modern scholarship. But more important, he is arguing that because it shares in no tradition, *Wissenschaft* is incapable of producing meaning and ultimately has nothing to tell us. The whole notion that "science" or "scientific understanding" can account for everything is not only counter to life experience, it can contribute nothing to the way we understand ourselves. Because it attempts to make sense of the present by smoothing over all difference from the past, *Wissenschaft* is incapable of producing meaning. The tension between present and past makes the constitution of meaning possible. *Wissenschaft* denies this tension and in so doing robs itself of the opportunity to produce meaning.[91]

Once again, Rosenzweig is making a pragmatic point about human situatedness. To begin with, he situates himself in a tradition that is prior to all understanding. Because Rosenzweig does not believe in essentializing of any kind, this situatedness is not dogmatic in the way that Hirsch's was. Rather, he is interested in what it means to *live* in a tradition. He defines living in tradition as a kind of ongoing discussion and therefore as a translation. In translation, which encompasses all of life, we encounter first and foremost what for *Wissenschaft* would be contradictions. These are contradictions in the ways that stories are told, in the ways languages are different from one another, and, most profoundly, in the fact that there are just other people in the world. When Rosenzweig speaks of unity, therefore, he is referring not to a unity that denies difference, as Hirsch's unity ultimately does, but to the unity that comes from the continuous effort to translate. In opposition to this view, *Wissenschaft* denies that there is even a task to perform. For Rosenzweig, *Wissenschaft* ultimately denies the other, who, again, marks the fundamental orientation of human life and thereby expresses an imperative to translate. Our obligation is to the other, be it to the other as tradition or to the other as individual human being. But it is important to note again that for Rosenzweig, the text as other is always in the service of recognizing the other in another human being. Redemption begins with human relations, which in turn act to redeem not just the human community, but the entire world (above all, the world's institutions). The gathering together to read aloud and interpret the Torah is itself an anticipation of redemption. Therefore, writes Rosenzweig, "The unity of the written Torah and the unity of the oral Torah—or, as we might say, of the read Torah—together create the translator's task."[92] The read Torah calls to the voices of the past, present, and future. The unity of the read Torah comes not from a consensus of views that is formed, but only from the activity of reading and the continuation of that activity in the future. This unity of reading over time creates the task of the translator. The translator must ensure that the activity of reading goes on. And reading and interpretation can continue only if the conditions for the creation of meaning are present. To create these conditions is the translator's task.

To create the proper conditions for the constitution of meaning in the present, the translator must understand her role as historian. As Rosenzweig writes in "Scripture and Luther":

> A historical investigation is necessarily the product of a historiographical purpose, and can when directed to something genuinely present to us too easily write into it the lines of the historian's own purpose, which then becomes lines of separation and demarcation—thus Goethe's *Faust* as he sketched it and as the literary historian teaches it in class is simply not the poem he wrote, which is rather what the student with glowing cheeks reads from the paperback text.[93]

A historian must be able to acknowledge her own purpose in writing and not purport to be telling the objective facts because a historical investigation cannot otherwise account for its own involvement in its task. The kind of objectivity that *Wissenschaft* works to maintain cannot explain the fact that we care about what we read or, to put it another way, the fact that we only read things that we care about. Literature, and the Bible in particular, affects us. That the Bible has been so important historically is, in fact, precisely the reason for its uniqueness. In "The Secret of Biblical Narrative Form," Rosenzweig states that the Bible is not the truest or the most beautiful book ever written. Its importance and uniqueness lie only—and this is a major condition—in the fact that it has been read for so long.

> The Bible is not the most beautiful book in the world, not the deepest, the truest, the wisest, the most absorbing, not any of the ordinary superlatives—or at least we cannot impose any of these superlatives upon anyone not already predisposed in their favor. But the Bible is the most important book. That can be proven; and even the most fanatical Bible-hater must acknowledge as much, at least for the past—indeed his fanatical hate acknowledges as much for the present as well. What is at issue here is not a question of personal taste or spiritual disposition or intellectual orientation, but a question of transpired history.[94]

Rosenzweig suggests that no one, including the scientific historian, can overlook the Bible's transpired history and the ways in which all of us are part of that history. Without such an acknowledgment a translation is bound to fail.

Buber and Rosenzweig find such a failure in the efforts of the nineteenth-century Protestant theologian and follower of Wellhausen, Emil Kautzsch, who in the preface to *Textbibel des Alten und Neuen Testaments* had promised to offer his readers the "content" of the Old Testament. For Rosenzweig, Kautzsch did not understand that it is not possible to transmit content without transmitting form. In a metaphor hearkening back to his understanding of drama in *The Star of Redemption*, Rosenzweig states, "The melody makes the music." Rosenzweig gives examples: the command "attention" (*Stillgestanden*!) has the same content as "Your attention please!" (*Bitte stillgestanden!*) and even as "I order you to pay attention" (*ich befehle euch, stillzustehn*), but they do not mean the same thing. The tone of a statement is part of its meaning because tone expresses context. For example, one could hear the straightforward and simple "*Stillgestanden*!" in an emergency situation, "*Bitte stillgestanden!*" at a public concert, and "*ich befehle euch, stillzustehn*" if one were in the military. The tone of each provides clues to its context. Missing the tone of a phrase, therefore, is akin to missing its meaning.

When differences in tone are overlooked in biblical translation, the entire tone of the text is falsified. Kautzsch has rendered Exodus 19:19 a flat "became louder and louder" (*wurde immer mächtiger*), denying the tone of the original *Vayehi qol hashofar holekh vaḥazeq me'od*, "The sound of the trumpet became continually more and more strengthened" (*Da ward der Schall der Posaune fortgehend mehr erstarkend*). While we may think this difference is ultimately superficial, when form is ignored, the results of a *wissenschaftlich* translation are ultimately disastrous. Rosenzweig notes, for example, that Exodus 39:32 and 40:33 reproduce Genesis 2:1–3 and Exodus 39:43 reproduces Genesis 1:31 and 2:3. Because Kautzsch does not duplicate the form of the Hebrew into the German, the text's content and internal coherence are necessarily obscured. The goal, however, is not to attack particular translators and, for Rosenzweig, "It is almost embarrassing to state such truisms."[95] Rosenzweig's goal is to point out that "*Wissenschaft* itself . . . in translating is simply not *wissenschaftlich* enough."[96] For *Wissenschaft*, a *wissenschaftlich* approach epitomizes rigor, yet *Wissenschaft* is just not rigorous enough. If *Wissenschaft* were more rigorous, *Wissenschaft* would recognize its own limitations and as a result it would be possible for the text to emerge more completely.

It is here that Buber and Rosenzweig anticipate a trend in biblical and exegetical scholarship that Peter Ochs has called "post-critical." As Ochs summarizes it:

> Postcritical scriptural interpretation refers to an emergent tendency among Jewish and Christian text scholars and theologians to give rabbinic and ecclesial traditions of interpretation both the benefit of the doubt and the benefit of doubt: the former, by assuming that there are dimensions of scriptural meaning which are disclosed only by way of the hermeneutical practices of believing communities and believing traditions of Christians and Jews; the latter, by assuming, in the spirit of post-Spinozistic criticism, that these dimensions may be clarified through the disciplined practice of philosophical, historical and textual/rhetorical criticism.[97]

Where Rosenzweig and Buber differ from Ochs's formulation is in emphasis. Reversing Ochs's formulation, we might say that Rosenzweig and Buber sought to given the biblical text the benefit of doubt and the benefit of the doubt. Whereas many of the Jewish and Christian textual scholars whom Ochs mentions approach their texts from the inside out, that is, from within the tradition toward critical scholarship, Rosenzweig and Buber approach the biblical text, to use Rosenzweig's famous comment, from the outside in.[98] The Buber-Rosenzweig Bible translation first grants the benefit of doubt and then the benefit of the doubt. Their readers are those who literally do not know the text. They are doubters who are presented with a possible way in. To appreciate how Buber and Rosenzweig offered a way into the biblical text, we must now turn to the aesthetics of the translation.

## The Aesthetics of the Translation

Rosenzweig acknowledges the translation's debt to Buber's aesthetic sensitivities in "The Secret of Biblical Narrative Form": "Martin Buber has discovered this secret of biblical style in translating it, and has taught us how to reproduce it in translation."[99] For Buber, the unity of the Bible is found in the repetition of words, which work to repeat themes. This repetition is most developed in the Pentateuch. Buber calls this repetition *Leitwort*, or lead word, style. Repetitions work both in proximity to and at a distance from each other to tie various themes together. Buber notes that an understanding of *Leitwort* has had a role in traditional halakhic (legal) and aggadic (narrative) interpretation. Indeed, attention to language and comparisons of parallel usage mark midrashic explanation. Without adherence to basic repetitions, in sounds, words, and contexts, a translation cannot but deprive the Hebrew Bible, and the Pentateuch in particular, of its coherence. Again, this is not a coherence that wants to express one and only one view, like the coherence that *Wissenschaft* aims for; it is the coherence that comes from the Bible's history of being read. Coherence comes from tradition itself, but tradition here is not understood as monolithic, rather as diverse and dynamic.

In "*Leitwort* Style in the Narratives of the Pentateuch," Buber gives particular examples of *Leitwort* style that, if missed, destroy the whole sense of the narrative. He later discusses one of the examples that he mentions in "Abraham the Seer" in *On the Bible*.[100] Like Noah, Abraham is described as "true" (Genesis 15:6), "whole" (17:1), and "walking with God" (17:1). But unlike Noah, this description is not limited to "in his generation." According to Buber, there are seven scenes of revelation that compose the Abraham story (12:1–4, 12:5–9, 13:14–18, 15:1–21, 17:1–27, 18:1–33, and 22:1–19). Two commands frame this cycle: "Leave the land of your father" (12:1) and "Take your son to the land" (22:2). The seven scenes are tied together by the verb "to see," *ra'ah*. The final "seeing" is the binding of Isaac. Yet other translations do not employ "to see" uniformly. See for example the New English Bible, which uses "show," "appear," "look," "see," and "provide" to render forms of this one verb.[101] The reader who does not know Hebrew is thus denied what for Buber and Rosenzweig (and, for that matter, the Midrash) are exegetical hints within the text itself.[102]

Another hint at an internal moral is found, for example, in the flood narrative in Genesis 6:11–13. The verb *shaḥat* describes the world's dissolute moral state. To express it, Buber and Rosenzweig's translation reads

| | |
|---|---|
| *Die Erde aber verdarb vor Gott,* | Now the earth was ruined before God, |
| *die Erde füllte sich mit Unbill.* | the earth was filled with wrongdoing. |
| *Gott sah die Erde: da, sie war verdorben,* | God saw the earth: here, it was ruined. |
| *denn verderbt hatte alles Fleisch seinen Weg auf Erden* | for all flesh had ruined its way upon the earth. |
| *Gott sprach zu Noach . . .* | God said to Noah . . . |
| *da, ich verderbe sie samt der Erde.* | here, I will bring ruin upon them together with the earth.[103] |

The New English Bible, on the other hand, reads, "Now God saw that the whole world was corrupt and full of violence. In his sight the world had become corrupted, for all men had lived corrupt lives on earth. God said to Noah . . . I intend to destroy them, and the earth with them." This translation misses the nexus of retribution implied in the text. People have ruined themselves and the earth; therefore God will now ruin the earth and the people.

Another form of repetition in Genesis in particular highlights the concept of order that is essential to the priestly narrative throughout the Pentateuch. The Buber-Rosenzweig translation of Genesis 1:25, for example, emphasizes this repetition. "God made the wildlife of the earth according to its kind and the herd-animal according to its kind and every stirring-thing of the ground according to its kind" (*Gott machte das Wildlebende des Erdlands nach seiner Art und das Herdentier nach seiner Art und alles Gerege des Ackers nach seiner Art*). The New English Bible again does away with repetition in its translation: "God made wild animals, cattle, and all reptiles, each according to its own kind." To see redundancy rather than emphasis in this verse—presumably the impetus for deleting what appear to be repetitions—is to see the text only as a written document. What may seem redundant in writing is not redundant in speaking. "Redundancy" in speech helps the listener to hear what is important to the speaker. As mentioned, one of the main principles of their translation was that it must reflect the book as spoken and not as written. Both Buber and Rosenzweig asserted that the Bible was originally a spoken document. Their emphasis at all times was on the text *as read*. Again, as Rosenzweig writes in "Scripture and Word," the reading of the Bible in community is the *qeri'ah*, the calling out.

According to Rosenzweig, "The bond of the tongue must be loosed by the eye." In order to loosen the bond of the tongue, it is necessary to "free from beneath the logical punctuation that is sometimes its ally and sometimes its foe the fundamental principle of natural, oral punctuation: the act of breathing."[104] To achieve this, Buber and Rosenzweig used the accent system of the Masoretic text, which sets off different vocalized units through various accent marks. For Buber and Rosenzweig, the notion that the text was originally oral is in accordance with Jewish tradition. Everett Fox, who today carries on Buber and Rosenzweig's efforts in his translations of the Hebrew Bible into English,[105] indicates that in handwritten notes Buber cites the thirteenth-century *Sefer ha-Ḥasidim* (Book of the Pious) and the nineteenth-century Italian scholar, philosopher, Bible commentator, and translator S. D. Luzzatto to support the idea that the Masoretic accents point to the spokenness of the text and not just to musical notation.[106]

Again, a movement away from standardized verses and toward greater attention to the breathing units helps to reinforce the rhetoric of the text. Stressing the biblical rhythm adds to the force of the passage. The New English Bible translates Genesis 1:3–5 without attention to rhythm: "God said, 'Let there be light,' and there was light; and God saw that the light was good, and he separated light from darkness. He called the light day, and the darkness night." The Buber-Rosenzweig translation, on the other hand, renders:

| | |
|---|---|
| *Gott sprach: Licht werde! Licht ward.* | God said: Be there light! There was light. |
| *Gott sah das Licht, dass es gut ist.* | God saw the light: that it was good. |
| *Gott schied zwischen dem Licht und der Finsternis.* | God divided between the light and the darkness. |
| *Gott rief dem Licht: Tag!* | God called the light: Day! |
| *und der Finsternis rief er: Nacht!* | and the darkness he called: Night! |

Note that the New English Bible converts "God" to a pronoun in "He called." In contrast, Buber and Rosenzweig retain the fact that each unit begins with a verb and with God. The message that the rhythm speaks is that of divine power and the order of creation. Without attention to the rhythm it is not possible to hear the repetition whose form itself makes the point. Again, content cannot be separated from form.

Paronomasia—the sound-alike quality of words indicating a mutual relation of ideas—is also of great importance in biblical literature. Noah's name, for example, plays on the similar sounds of different words. Noah, meaning comfort, becomes the symbol of divine sorrow over the failure of creation. To express this word play, Buber and Rosenzweig translate Genesis 5:29 as follows:

| | |
|---|---|
| *Er rief seinen Namen: Noach!* | He called his name: Noaḥ! |
| *sprechend:* | saying: |

| | |
|---|---|
| *Se jenachmenu—* | This-one will comfort-our- [*yenaḥamenu*] |
| *Dieser wird uns leidtrösten* | sorrow |
| *in unserm Tun und der Beschwernis unsrer Hände* | in our doing and in the trouble of our hands |
| *an dem Acker, den Er verflucht hat.* | in the ground, which He has cursed. |

and then 6:5–8 as

| | |
|---|---|
| *Da leidete Ihn,* | He was sorry [*vayinaḥem*] |
| *dass er den Menschen gemacht hatte auf Erden,* | that he had made man on earth |
| *und er grämte sich in sein Herz . . .* | and he was troubled in his heart . . . |
| *denn leid ists mir, dass ich sie machte.* | for I am sorry [*niḥamti*] that I made them.[107] |

Another clear example of Buber and Rosenzweig preserving instances of paronomasia is their translation of Genesis 2:5: "and there was no man/Adam to serve the ground/Adama." ("Und Mensch, Adam, war keiner, den Acker, Adama, zu bedienen.") Particularly in his essays "The Bible in German" and "On Word Choice in Translating the Bible," Buber explains various word choices at great length. For example, *torah* is not "law" but always instruction, hence the title of their translation of the Pentateuch: *Die Fünf Bücher der Weisung*. *Malakh* is not "angel" but the momentary intervention of God and hence *Bote*. *Navi* is not "prophet" but rather proclaimer (*Künder*), for the "prophet" pronounces the word of God.

Finally, the issue of word choice culminates in Rosenzweig's essay "'The Eternal': Mendelssohn and the Name of God," whose conceptual scheme sets the Buber-Rosenzweig translation apart from its predecessors. Mendelssohn rendered YHVH as "the eternal" (*Der Ewige*) in his translation of the Bible. This was the first use of the term in Judaism, according to Rosenzweig, who notes that it has its roots in Christian Apocrypha as *ho Aionios*, in the portion of the fourth and fifth chapters of the Letters of Baruch that was perhaps originally written in Greek. In the French translation of the Old Testament, Calvin followed the lead of *ho Aionios* and used *L'Eternel*. Influenced by his rationalism, Mendelssohn followed Calvin's lead.

For Rosenzweig, however, "the eternal" just misses the mark and obscures the essential nature of the biblical text. He argues that what is needed and meant is a sense of God's presence, and not God's eternity. Mendelssohn translates Exodus 3:14 as "God spoke to Moses: 'I am the being that is eternal.' He said further: 'Say to the children of Israel, "The eternal being, which calls itself, I-am-eternal, has sent me to you."'" But, writes Rosenzweig, the verse should instead read, "Now God said to

Moshe: I will be-there howsoever I will be-There. And said: Thus shall you say to the Sons of Israel: I AM THERE sends me to you."[108] In sum, "the Hebrew *haya* is not, unlike the Indogermanic 'to be,' of its nature a copula, not of its nature static, but a word of becoming, of entering, of happening."[109] God is not eternal in the sense of static being. Rather, the biblical text speaks precisely of God's *relationship* with the human, and not of God's eternity.

Significantly, Mendelssohn's commentary to his translation follows Maimonides' statement in *The Guide of the Perplexed* that God's name means "the one who exists, who has existence within Him." Thus, Rosenzweig writes "for pre-Kantian Mendelssohn, 'the Eternal'—or, as he prefers in particularly important passages like the one under discussion here, 'the Eternal Being'—implies also the God of prayerful petition."[110] Mendelssohn's intentions were good, Rosenzweig implies, but are no longer appropriate for a contemporary translation. In post-Kantian times, a turn back to the existential meaning of the text is required:

> But what meaning for the despairing and wretched Israelites would be offered by a lecture on God's existential necessity? They, like this timid leader himself, need rather an assurance of God's being-among-them; and unlike their leader, who hears it directly from God's mouth, they need this in the form of a clarification of the old, obscure name, sufficient to establish that the assurance is of divine origin.[111]

Luther and Hirsch were able to speak to this issue by emphasizing presence in God's name. Luther capitalized God's name, while Hirsch emphasized the name by a slight separation of the letters of the words emphasized. This device of emphasis was practiced both in German and Hebrew. In a letter to Martin Goldner, Rosenzweig lays out the particulars of how he and Buber render the sense of presence in God's name. He asserts that *Adonai* does not mean Lord; rather, it is the vocative, which should be rendered "present-to-me." The tetragrammaton, moreover, is in danger of becoming a mere name. Rosenzweig suggests replacing the three dimensions of "present-to-me" with the appropriate, capitalized personal pronouns *Ich*, or *Er*, or *Du*. The German translation of Exodus 3:14–15 thus reads:

| | |
|---|---|
| *Gott sprach zu Mosche:* | Now God said to Moshe: |
| *Ich werde dasein, als der ich dasein werde.* | I will be-there howsoever I will be-There. |
| *Und sprach:* | And said: |
| *So sollst du zu den Söhnen Jissraels sprechen:* | Thus shall you say to the Sons of Israel: |
| *ICH BIN DA schickt mich zu euch.* | I AM THERE sends me to you. |

| | |
|---|---|
| *Und weiter sprach Gott zu Mosche:* | And God said further to Moshe: |
| *So sollst du zu den Söhnen Jissraels sprechen:* | Thus shall you say to the Sons of Israel: |
| *Er,* | He, |
| *der Gott eurer Väter,* | the God of your fathers, |
| *der Gott Abrahams, der Gott Jizchaks, der Gott Jaakobs,* | the God of Avraham, the God of Yitzhak, and the God of Yaakov, |
| *schickt mich zu euch.* | sends me to you. |
| *Das ist mein Name in Weltzeit,* | That is my name for the ages, |
| *das mein Gedenken, Geschlecht für Geschlecht.* | that is my title [from] generation to generation.[112] |

That God enters into relationship with the human implies ever new possibilities for the human. God's relation with the human allows the human to change and in turn to change the unredeemed world. The possibility of new possibilities brings an emphasis on human responsibility in bringing about redemption.

## The Translation as Read

Of course, as Buber and Rosenzweig were well aware, translations are to be read, and this is the test of any translation. One of the most famous reviews of the Buber-Rosenzweig translation came from Siegfried Kracauer, who was to become one of the century's most influential cultural critics. Kracauer's review gives us some sense of the translation in its German surroundings and also, in the context of this chapter and the next, brings the question of aesthetics to the fore. The review, "The Bible in German," appeared in the *Frankfurter Zeitung* on January 25, 1926, after the first book of the translation, Genesis (*Im Anfang*), was published. In it, Kracauer attacked Buber and Rosenzweig for what were purported to be neo-Orthodox, neo-Kantian, and crude nationalist—that is, Zionist—tendencies. Kracauer even went so far as to accuse Buber and Rosenzweig of "Wagnerizing." The review gives examples of particular words that Kracauer believed Buber and Rosenzweig deliberately romanticized. One of these is the replacement of Luther's "all of the world" (*alle Welt*) or "all the lands" (*alle Lande*) with "folk of the earth" (*Erdvolk*). Kracauer states that this "smacks of pseudo-native soil."

From Kracauer's point of view, the Buber-Rosenzweig translation was ultimately a renunciation of "reality." The language of their translation was, despite what they said, archaic and highly romanticized: "To enter into these abandoned linguistic spheres is to renounce reality."[113] Moreover, "instead of bringing the immovable distance of Scripture into the present, these Ur-German expressions drag scripture into an Ur-German that is only a few decades old." Buber and Rosenzweig, he writes, believe in an "atemporal ontological power of the German." Finally, "By avoiding profane language it represses the profane." This "avoidance," for Kracauer, is the root of the problem with the translation.

Stating that Kracauer justifies his general thesis through his statements about the translation's language, Buber and Rosenzweig reply to the attack on "earthfolk," and to the rest of the specific words or phrases Kracauer mentions. Defending "earthfolk" they write,

> "Earthfolk" (actually only "earth") had in Genesis to be put in place of Luther's "all lands" and "all the world" because "all lands" is simply not in the text, and also because a word for world in the sense of the epitome of space is something that biblical Hebrew very revealingly lacks, whereas a word for the epitome of time, for eternity, is something it possesses. To express the idea of world, biblical Hebrew needs two words together; the "cloddish" "earth" and the airy "heaven." How the reviewer in encountering "earthfolk" could lapse into national anxieties is to us, objectively at least, incomprehensible. If the League of Nations in Geneva were looking for a concrete word to express its goal, it could hardly do better than "earthfolk."[114]

Having shown that, in their estimation, Kracauer simply does not understand Hebrew, Buber and Rosenzweig conclude that ultimately Kracauer is attacking the Bible and not their translation. What he is attacking, then, is precisely the possibility for an openness to the Bible. On this issue, they write, they will not comment. Rather, the Bible will speak for itself.[115]

Kracauer's fundamental point behind his remarks is that the profane has outgrown the sacred. If the sacred is to speak at all, it must do so from the profane and not from some sphere which, in the name of reality, denies reality. Unlike the Buber-Rosenzweig translation, Luther's translation was situated amid a political and social critique. Kracauer makes his criticism by way of an allusion to Wagner's *Parsifal*:

> Whereas the Luther Bible attacked at precisely the decisive point, Buber and Rosenzweig's German rendering veers away from the public sphere of our social existence and into the *private*. The text of the Bible, which is meant to tear open the quotidian, is removed from the realm of the quotidian by this translation and made into the foundation of an imaginary stage consecration festival play.[116]

In this sense, the Luther translation still speaks of its public protest. Yet, it is necessary to recognize, again, that such speaking is no longer possible. There are then two options for Bible translation, Kracauer writes. The first is to keep Luther's and remember a past long gone. The second is to produce a critical edition like Kautzsch's for a Jewish audience, an edition that would take modern Jewish scholarship into account. There is no room for a third possibility.

While Kracauer writes at the beginning of his review that the insight of Rosenzweig's *The Star of Redemption* "is more profound than Buber's and thus more difficult to penetrate," he goes on to analyze what he sees as the deficiency of the translation only in connection with Buber's philosophy in *I and Thou*. Statements such as "Whoever stands in relation, participates in actuality" are what Kracauer objects to most.[117] He sees such a statement as choosing an abstraction over the concrete and then calling that abstraction "actuality." But, as we have already seen, the translation project and some of Buber's and Rosenzweig's essays on translation point to some of the differences between Buber and Rosenzweig, and it is useful to recall those differences in this context. As discussed, Rosenzweig's I and Thou does not end, or in fact begin, with the private relation of two people, but in the public streets. Once again, revelation for Rosenzweig never ends with two people. Instead, a movement to a third person is always necessary, lest one fall into the trappings of quietist, world-denying, "arrogant" mysticism.[118] Kracauer may well be right that Buber's *I and Thou* is a movement away from the profane into the sacred, which leaves the profane, or the public, behind for some sort of unified, quasi-mystical experience.[119] Indeed, such a view is Rosenzweig's own, as he makes clear in his September 1922 correspondence with Buber, discussed above. What is necessary, then, in light of this discussion of Kracauer's review, is precisely a rereading (or perhaps just a reading) of *The Star of Redemption*.

Something else that a rereading of *The Star of Redemption* may elucidate is just what Rosenzweig's assessment of the profane might be.[120] Rosenzweig's separation of the sacred and the profane is not the absolute dichotomy that Kracauer claims it is. It seems instead that, if anything, Rosenzweig stresses the concreteness of the profane that can become sacred precisely because of its concreteness. This is the meaning of Rosenzweig's insistence to Buber that "there must be more in the world than—you and me!" Rosenzweig argues that Buber has made the mundane world, the I-It, a cripple by denying the importance, and indeed the necessity, of public institutions (what he calls the old edifice of the Cohenian system, a philosophy of law).

In his discussion in *The Star of Redemption* of calendars, Rosenzweig makes his point about the sacred adhering in the profane, and the profane adhering in the sacred. For Rosenzweig, ritual calendars preserve sacred time despite and within the profane:

> Only the stroke of bells establishes the hour, not the ticking of the pendulum. . . . In the hour, instituted by himself, man frees himself from the transi-

toriness of the moment. . . . In the hour, then, one moment is recreated, whenever and if ever it were to perish, into something newly issued and thus imperishable, into a *nun stans*, into eternity. . . . The cycles of the cultic prayer are repeated every day, every week, every year, and in this repetition, faith turns the moment into an "hour," it prepares time to accept eternity.[121]

The point here is not that the sacred must replace the profane—which would render an idealism of the worst sort (what Kracauer accuses Buber and Rosenzweig of)—but rather that possibilities *for transforming the profane* are contained in ritual because the sacred is different from, yet predicated on, the profane. Kracauer's good friend Walter Benjamin expresses an almost identical notion: "The initial day of a calendar serves as a historical timelapse camera. And, basically, it is the same day that keeps recurring in the guise of holidays, which are days of remembrance. Thus the calendars do not measure time as clocks do."[122] Both Rosenzweig and Benjamin criticize western notions of progress. For both, nothing new can happen within the wholly historical because historical time is but the sum of history's ruins. In Benjamin's words, history is "one single catastrophe which keeps piling wreckage upon wreckage."[123] Something must exist outside of the profane for real change to be possible. Ritual calendars leave spaces for memory, which historical time wipes out. Memory has the power to propel us toward a new and different future—toward redemption.

The "sacred" and the "profane" thus need each other just to exist, but even more so, they need each other if something new is to happen. Rosenzweig objects to historicism and politics only as ends in themselves. The *dogmatism of such institutions* represses possibilities for change. Put into Kracauer's terms, while it may be true that the profane has outgrown the sacred, just as the sacred cannot exist without the profane, so too the profane cannot exist without the sacred. As Rosenzweig reminds Buber, the sacred, the I-Thou relation, is always rooted in, and remains within, the profane. There is more in the world than "you and me" because we live in a world of public institutions. It is our task to redeem this world, in its and our profanity, and to make it and ourselves sacred. But for Rosenzweig, even given such an exalted possibility, and indeed because such a possibility is so exalted, redemption remains incomplete and the world, and we, remain within the profane. This is what it means to be a creature.

It is a mistake to push the dichotomy between sacred and profane as far as Kracauer does because what Rosenzweig tries to emphasize is precisely that there is no such thing as simply the profane. Benjamin reiterates that the profane simply cannot erase the sacred:

Even though chronology places regularity above permanence, it cannot prevent heterogeneous, conspicuous fragments from remaining within it. To have com-

> bined recognition of a quality with the measurement of the quantity was the work of the calendars in which the places of recollection are left blank, as it were, in the form of holidays.[124]

In his review, Kracauer does not take sufficient account of Rosenzweig's philosophy. To summarize, Rosenzweig, unlike the early Buber, is not advocating private religion, let alone private experience. He is, rather, arguing for concrete communal responsibility, which can best be understood as ethical obligation that works to create and return to public institutions. Kracauer writes that "access to truth is now by way of the profane." This is exactly Rosenzweig's point: access to truth is now by way of the profane because as creatures in an unredeemed world, we always remain rooted in the profane.

Still, even while acknowledging that Kracauer misreads (or does not read) Rosenzweig, we must return to the question with which we began this section. How was the translation read? Kracauer was perceptive in demanding to know what the literary character of the translation was like.[125] For Kracauer, Rosenzweig's comment in his essay "The Unity of the Bible," that "the goal is not beauty but truth; what should be judged is not a 'work of art' but a translation, its fidelities and infidelities," is insufficient. For Kracauer, such a statement is based on a false dichotomy between that which has a literary character and that which does not.[126]

In his essay, "The Secret of Biblical Narrative Form," Rosenzweig speaks directly to this point. Referring to Goethe's comments on Luther's translation, he writes:

> It seems . . . that since there can be no truce between the claims of religious content and the claims of aesthetic form, the translator must choose between the claims of poetry and the claims of prose. . . . [But] the division between the "religious" aspects of the text and the "aesthetic" aspects has to be drawn otherwise than at first it seemed. Or rather: drawing the line of division is itself a mistake in the first place. An aesthetic object striving to be art for art's sake, a poetry altogether free of prose are of course notions that can arise only in opposition to the wildly extreme notion of a "purely religious" object, an absolutely unpoetical prose. (Moreover: if on the aesthetic side there arises the sin of being only for one-self, then on the religious side the ghastly mirror-image of that sin can arise and be embodied in response.)[127]

Rosenzweig maintains that drawing the line between the "religious" and "aesthetic" aspects of a text distorts both. Returning yet again to Rosenzweig's criticism of Buber, we can begin to understand these comments. The dichotomy between aesthetic and religious dimensions of either a text or life results from the same mistake as the dichotomy between I-It relations and I-Thou relations. These dichotomies force one to choose between either "paganism," "the sin of being only for one-self," or "religion," what Rosenzweig calls in *The Star of Redemption* fanaticism, the "ghastly mirror-image of that sin." Again, this is the meaning of Rosenzweig's claim to Buber that "there must be more in the world than—you and me!"

Rosenzweig maintains that the dichotomy between the "aesthetic" and the "religious" is a distinctly modern one that results from the divorce of reason from revelation in the modern world. He argues that the aesthetics of his translation of the Bible is an attempt to offer the modern reader the opportunity to view the Bible in its "aesthetic" and "religious" or "poetical" and "prosaic" wholeness.

In a letter of September 1927 to Buber, Rosenzweig makes this point clearly:

> Anyone who expects a work of art simply cannot understand us—even though it is one. But it is visible as such only to a person who does not look for one in our work—just as the elegance of a mathematical demonstration becomes apparent only to a person who approaches it with a mathematical interest; not to one who looks for elegance. For the rest, I even believe that in the case of an ordinary work of art, too, a really crude interest in the subject is the only legitimate route of access to it and that our aesthetics and our aestheticism block our path to a work of art, not only to what is more than a work of art.[128]

As Edward L. Greenstein has recently argued, although it is important to recognize that all translation is inherently interpretive, there nonetheless remains a difference between interpretation and translation:

> Although there is an admittedly strong element of interpretation in every translation, I would want the translation to stand as closely as possible for the source, and not for some paraphrase or metaphrase of the source. . . . The more we endeavor to distinguish translation from interpretation, the more we allow ourselves to minimize the amount of interpretation we attach to our translation . . . [and] the more we afford our readers the option of reading the source of translation. . . . The more influence the translator exerts, the less empowered is the reader.[129]

Buber and Rosenzweig sought to empower the reader with an opportunity to respond to the Bible. As we have seen, they maintained that only in the wholeness of the difference between the Bible and the contemporary world could the modern reader have such an opportunity to view the Bible's aesthetic and religious, poetic and prosaic, dimensions all at once.

Where Buber and Rosenzweig differ is on their perspectives of the past's commanding status in the present. This difference has a variety of implications for understanding Buber and Rosenzweig's different views of language, Jewish Law, and the possibility of Jewish nationalism. Recall

Scholem's intended criticism of the translation: that what fills him with doubt is "the excessive tonality of this prose, which leaps out *almost uncannily* [*fast unheimlich*] from the particular wording." Rosenzweig would embrace Scholem's view of the translation as the "pent-up pathos" of the uncanny effect of diaspora, Jewish existence.

It is for this reason that Rosenzweig describes the translation project as a particularly diaspora one. He makes this point to Buber in response to Buber's announcement that he intended to immigrate to Palestine:

> Even if you read German in Jerusalem and read about the book in question, you will lack there the real motivating sense of mission for such a specific *galut* [diaspora] project. . . . Even though in the firm of Buber and Rosenzweig your investment of working capital amounts to eighty percent and mine to only twenty, the goal and effectiveness of the work are determined by the goal and work contributed by me, the *galut* Jew.[130]

Though Buber's own philosophy of language was deeply influenced by working with Rosenzweig on the translation project, and though even Scholem would come to appreciate Rosenzweig's perspective on the problem of making the Hebrew language profane, neither Buber nor Scholem could endorse Rosenzweig's decidedly non-Zionist commitment.[131] Rosenzweig's theory of translation is consonant with his argument that Jews themselves must return to their strange, foreign pathos, both for their own sake and for the sake of the redemption of the world. For Rosenzweig, this meant an embrace of a decidedly diaspora Judaism. We turn now, in the final part of this book, to the political implications of Rosenzweig's claims about both Judaism and Christianity.

# Part 3

## RELIGION AND POLITICS

# Six

## Risking Religion: Christian Idolatry

More than any other Jewish thinker, Rosenzweig devoted considerable attention to Christianity and to the possibility of Christianity's world redemptive potential. Rosenzweig argues against the dominant strand of Jewish thought which suggests that Christianity is idolatrous from the start because, at the very minimum, its image of Christ on the cross violates the second commandment against image-making. Rosenzweig contends not only that Christianity, and in particular the Christian image of Christ on the cross, is not inherently idolatrous but that the image of the cross uniquely creates the possibility of a universal community. From the start, then, Rosenzweig's position on Christianity would seem to be in marked contrast to the German-Jewish rationalist tradition in general and to the ethically monotheistic tradition in particular.

However, against what seems to be this obvious inference, Rosenzweig differs from the rationalist tradition of German-Jewish thought not in his suggestion that Christianity may have world redemptive powers, but rather in his sense of the lethal dangers intrinsic to the relationship between Judaism and Christianity. Unlike Cohen and Mendelssohn in particular, Rosenzweig did not believe that reasoned enlightenment would or could dispel antisemitism. Rather, Rosenzweig argues that Judaism's defiant particularity, which constitutes both Judaism's relation with the one, unique God as well as Judaism's relation to the external world, cannot but cause the Christian, and Christian society, to hate the Jew. In fact, this Christian hatred of Judaism, Rosenzweig argues, is not something that Christianity can ever overcome, for it is part and parcel of the very definition, essence, and meaning of Christianity.

However, despite important differences, Rosenzweig's framework is once again in accord with the ethically monotheistic framework of Hermann Cohen. Both suggest that Judaism's world redemptive role is to keep Christianity on the monotheistic path. Where Cohen and Rosenzweig differ is not in regard to the Christian relation to Judaism, but in regard to the definition of idolatry. Rosenzweig argues that idolatry is something that must always be risked precisely for the sake of monotheism, while Cohen argues that monotheism is the eradication of the risk of idolatry. Moreover, idolatry is not a generic error for Rosenzweig as it is for Cohen. Rather, idolatry is as particular as (in Mendelssohn's terms) the "scripts of nations" themselves. For Rosenzweig,

Christianity's redemptive and idolatrous potential are intimately connected. Rosenzweig's schema suggests that Christianity risks religion for the sake of the redemption of the world.

## Christianity: An Interest Both Autobiographical and Philosophical

Rosenzweig's positive appraisal of Christianity is both autobiographical and philosophical. As is well known, Rosenzweig found his way to Judaism only through Christianity. Rosenzweig grew up in an assimilated but proud Jewish family. Having immersed himself first in medicine, then in history, and then in philosophy and theology, Rosenzweig found himself increasingly dissatisfied with the philosophical approach of his day. Idealism, and its philosophy of history, he believed, had failed. The young Rosenzweig became painfully aware that the twentieth century was not the nineteenth, and that in the twentieth century there was no clear path toward comprehensive personal and historical meaning.

In 1913, while working on what would become a book on Hegel's political philosophy, Rosenzweig attended lectures on jurisprudence at the University of Leipzig where he was also able to become reacquainted with Eugen Rosenstock, who had just been appointed a lecturer in medieval constitutional law.[1] Rosenzweig had first met and befriended Rosenstock in 1910 in the so-called Baden-Baden discussion circle.[2] Though born Jewish, Rosenstock had converted to Christianity when he was sixteen. He and Rosenzweig had many long conversations in Leipzig about the failures of academic philosophy to find meaning in the modern world, and the potential of Christianity to do precisely that. The decisive conversation came on July 7, 1913, when, according to Rosenzweig, "Rosenstock forced me step by step from my relativistic position into a nonrelativistic one. I was at a disadvantage from the start, since I myself had to admit that his attack was justified."[3]

Being forced out of his relativistic position into a nonrelativistic one meant conversion to Christianity, for Rosenzweig. He decided, however, that he had to convert to Christianity as a Jew, and not as a pagan:

> The fact that a man like Rosenstock was a conscious Christian . . . at once bowled over my entire conception of Christianity and of religion generally, including my own. I thought I had Christianized my view of Judaism, but in actual fact I had done the opposite: I had 'Judaized' my view of Christianity. I had considered the year 313 as the beginning of a falling away from true Christianity, since it opened a gate for the Christians in the opposite direction to that opened in the year 70 for the Jews. . . . In drawing my conclusions from this, I

> made a personal reservation. . . . I declared that I could turn Christian *qua* Jew—not through the intermediate stage of paganism. . . . The mission to the Hebrews actually rests on this basis, which I had thought purely personal, and urges the Jew to remain faithful to the Law even during the period of preparation and up to the moment of baptism.[4]

The decision to become Christian *via* Judaism would be decisive for Rosenzweig. For almost three months Rosenzweig, in his own words, "tortured" himself "in vain."[5] Glatzer reports that on Yom Kippur of 1913 (October 11), Rosenzweig attended services at a small Orthodox synagogue in Berlin and "left the services a changed person. What he had thought he could find in the church only—faith that gives one an orientation in the world—he found on that day in the synagogue."[6] On October 31, Rosenzweig wrote to Rudolf Ehrenberg: "After prolonged, and I believe thorough, self-examination, I have reversed my decision. It no longer seems necessary to me, and therefore, being what I am, no longer possible. I will remain a Jew."[7] The following year, Rosenzweig studied in Berlin with Hermann Cohen.

Though he devoted himself to the study of the sources of Judaism, Rosenzweig remained in dialogue with his Christian friends (most of whom were converts from Judaism) and with Christianity. While becoming acquainted in Berlin with the sources of Judaism, he listened particularly attentively to Cohen's insistence that Judaism was absolutely different from Christianity.[8] And he continued to engage his Christian friends on these differences. In May 1916, Eugen Rosenstock wrote to Rosenzweig (from Rosenzweig's parents' home in Kassel, and in fact from Rosenzweig's own desk) in an attempt to reopen their conversation about Christianity.[9] Their correspondence on this issue, which lasted through December 1916, along with Part 3, Book 2 of *The Star of Redemption*, make up the bulk of Rosenzweig's position on Christianity's relationship to Judaism.

## Christian Images

Rosenzweig's positive philosophical attitude toward Christianity is rooted in his understanding of images. Toward the end of *The Star of Redemption*, Rosenzweig states, "We speak in images [*in Bildern]*. But the images are not arbitrary. There are essential images and coincidental ones. . . . There is no other way to express the Truth."[10] For Rosenzweig, Christian images, and the image of the cross in particular, are essential and not coincidental ones. Christian images are essential and not arbitrary both because they express a truth about the human condition and because they make possible a new kind of human reality. But it is precisely because they are so wrought with the potential for truth and transformation that Christian images are also so potentially dangerous. For Rosenzweig, Christian images introduce both a world redemptive and a lethally idolatrous potential into the course of world history. It is because Christian images are essential and not arbitrary that they carry so much risk.

It will be helpful to employ the Protestant theologian Paul Tillich's distinction between symbol and sign in order to understand Rosenzweig's distinction between essential images and coincidental ones, and the ways in which this distinction relates to his view of Christianity. The comparison between Rosenzweig and Tillich is useful not only for the similarities it yields between these two thinkers (both deeply influenced by Schelling and Cohen) but also for the important difference we will find.[11] Though Tillich's distinction between symbol and sign helps us to understand Rosenzweig's interpretation of the cross, the difference between Rosenzweig and Tillich as to what constitutes Christian idolatry helps us to appreciate Rosenzweig's view of idolatry, and its indebtedness, despite important differences, to Cohen's ethical monotheism more fully.

Rosenzweig and Tillich would agree on this essential point: the cross is not an arbitrary image because it is an image that participates in that which it signifies. Tillich calls the participation in that which it signifies a symbol, as opposed to a sign.[12] The history of the distinction between a symbol and a sign is a complex one, and Rosenzweig and Tillich in fact give different valuations to these terms. Tillich follows Hegel in distinguishing symbol from sign and in insisting on an organic connection between the symbol and that to which it refers. Rosenzweig goes against Hegelian aesthetics by reversing the priority of symbol over sign. A symbol, in Rosenzweig's words, is "only symbol" for those who embrace symbols over signs naively and, often idolatrously, deny the hermeneutical task of all interpretations of symbols and signs.[13] Nonetheless, a sign for Rosenzweig participates in the reality of which it is a part. But despite this participation, a sign's possibilities of signification are infinite. Even given this obvious and significant difference between Tillich and Rosenzweig, Tillich's explanation of what constitutes a symbol goes to the heart of Rosenzweig's understanding of the kind of images created by Christianity. For Tillich, symbols have six characteristics:

1. They point beyond themselves.
2. They participate in the reality of that to which they point.
3. They open up to us new levels of reality.
4. By opening up new levels of reality, they also open up new dimensions of ourselves.

5. They cannot be produced intentionally but grow out of an individual or a collective unconscious.
6. They grow and die according to their ability to create meaning.[14]

From the perspective of Rosenzweig's thought, Christian images would uniquely meet Tillich's criteria of the symbol. While Tillich argues that these criteria can be and are met by a wide variety of religious traditions, Rosenzweig would argue that Christianity, and only Christianity, produces the kinds of images that Tillich calls symbols. Recall Rosenzweig's statement that Christian arts are

> the only arts which can wholly cure him of that disease of alienation from the world which plunged the art lover into the misleading delusion of supreme health just as he exposed himself defenselessly to the disease. Thus art is its own anti-toxin. It decontaminates itself, and man, from its own purity.[15]

For Rosenzweig, Christian art is able to move beyond the production of mere commonality—the recognition that each individual is alone but that all people share in their individual solitude—and toward community. Rather than confirming each person's sense of individual solitude, Christian art creates a common space and time for all to share in. This common space and time prepares the individual for the collective religious experience embodied in the Christian liturgical year.

Rosenzweig argues that without Christianity's images and their role in Christian liturgy, Christians would not have the possibility either of collective religious experience or of eternal salvation. Before they are able to receive the sacraments, individual Christians must feel that they are part of a community. Church architecture and Christian liturgical music literally create the space and time for the possibility of Christian community. As important, the content of Christian salvation, the eternal way, can only be gained through art. For Rosenzweig, art and Christianity are able to achieve eternity in time because they can embody the recognition of the suffering intrinsic to human finitude. Art gives structure to the experience of the individual isolation that comes from the tragic fate of the finite human being.[16] Rosenzweig contends that Christianity gives structure not only to the suffering of the individual, but to universal suffering and the suffering of all humanity. Art's muteness is thus overcome in Christianity:

> The cross which art taught men to bear was only each and everyone's cross. Even he who did not imbibe misanthropy out of the abundance of love, learned from art only to observe with amazement the thousand springs in the desert by the side of the thirsty. Art did not let him see the thirsty thousands who were with him in the same desert. It did not teach him the unity of all that is the cross. This is experienced by the lonely pagan soul, in whose blood the last unity of

> the We does not circulate, only in view of the cross on Golgotha. It recognizes itself as one with all souls only under this cross. . . . Thus the one pain without equal takes the place of his own pain and every personal pain, and thereby the bond is now forged from soul to soul.[17]

For *The Star of Redemption*, the difference between art and Christianity is a difference in degree and not in kind. Christianity depicts human passion and suffering not merely from the individual but from the communal point of view. Christianity depicts the contradiction of human passion, and of suffering in particular, without negating or succumbing to passion. Like art, Christianity *structures* passion:

> In the Christian, those forces intersect which elsewhere appear to cancel each other out. Christianity affords them no refuge beyond these contradictions. It absorbs them all within itself and inserts the Christian into their midst, into a middle which—for him who stands there—is at the same time a beginning. The cross neither negates the contradiction, nor annihilates it; rather it articulates it as structure. Structure is not created by fiat, nor is it brute force. Structure must be shaped, brought forth, constructed. The way of the Christian is at every station a crossroad.[18]

Christianity not only relies on art to create its community but also is itself the art form beyond aestheticism. Rosenzweig argues that the Christian life is a life of structured passion. To structure passion is not to control passion; it is rather to live with the tensions of passion. In Rosenzweig's words, "Structure must be shaped, brought forth, constructed." Structure is not something that can be mastered once and for all; it must be continually constructed and managed.

The continual effort and the renewal of the effort to structure and depict passion constitute the Christian way. Christian life constructs and manages all points into a midpoint between Christ's coming and return. This midpoint is also constructed and managed as a depiction of universal suffering. The Christian midpoint that defines both Christian eternity in time and an acknowledgment of the tragic fate of finite man is never achieved but must always be performed. For Rosenzweig, Christian life is the ongoing performance of the depiction of both the possibility of universal community (and thus the possibility of redemption) *and* the tragic fate of the finite human being. Christian art and Christian people articulate this contradiction through their structure. The cross depicts the very contradiction of being at a crossroads. As witness, the Christian person embodies and bears witness to this contradiction.

For Rosenzweig, art and Christianity allow the human being to bear the tragic dimension of human finitude. Art and Christianity allow the human being to structure suffering into a life that can offer moments of happiness and conciliation without denying suffering. Because it memorializes suffering, art is able to offer the human being momentary reprieves from suffering:

> All art is "tragic" in its content; it depicts suffering. Even comedy thrives on the sympathy of the ever-present poverty and deficiency of existence. Art is tragic in its content, just as it, and all art, is comic in form. It simply depicts—even the most monstrous—with a certain romantic-ironic levity.[19]

Again, what art offers on an individual level, Christianity offers on a communal level. Christianity makes it possible for all humanity to bear life's suffering and to find consolation in suffering:

> Like Janus, art has two faces: it makes life's suffering harder at the same time that it helps man to bear it, and this is what entitles it to accompany him through life. Art teaches man to overcome without forgetting. For man is not to forget; he is to remember everything in his very members. He is to bear sorrows, and to be consoled. God consoles him together with all those who are in need of consolation. The tears of the mourner will be wiped from his face as "from every face." [But] until the great renovation of all things, they will gleam in his eyes. Till then, his consolation is to be disconsolate.[20]

Art embodies the very tension that for Rosenzweig defines the Christian's eternal way. Though his tears may be wiped, the mourner's tears continue to gleam in his eyes. Though she may be saved, the Christian's salvation, she must remember, is always not-yet.

We can now return to the points on which Rosenzweig and Tillich would agree. In keeping with Tillich's first two criteria of the symbol, Rosenzweig would argue that Christian images are essential and not arbitrary because they participate in what they signify. According to Rosenzweig, Christian images, and particularly the cross, simultaneously point to and create Christian community as well as the possibility of Christian salvation. In keeping with Tillich's third and fourth criteria of a symbol, Rosenzweig would argue that the cross opens up new levels of reality, in terms of the human, the divine, and the world, that would remain inaccessible without it. And, finally, it is in keeping with Tillich's fifth and sixth criteria that Rosenzweig would argue that the cross gains what Tillich would call its symbolic power through the individual and collective unconscious. Christian images are like living beings in that they grow where the situation is ripe for them: in the hearts of individual pagans ever becoming the collective of Christian community.

What is significant is that the Jewish thinker Rosenzweig articulates an even stronger case than the Protestant theologian Tillich for the metaphysical dimensions of the meaning of Christian images in general, and the cross in particular. For the Jewish Rosenzweig, no other image embodies the powers of truth and transformation as does the Christian cross. Against Tillich, Rosenzweig would argue that the cross is unique. This means also for Rosenzweig, as against Tillich, that no other image embodies as much dangerous potential as the cross. Though Rosenzweig and Tillich would agree that, in Tillich's terms, symbols can quickly become idolatrous, they would disagree as to what the nature of idolatry actually is.

Let us turn first to what makes the cross idolatrous for Tillich. He argues that symbols have the potential to become idolatrous if we interpret them literally. Though a symbol participates in that which it signifies, it does not signify in a literal manner. The symbol always points to something beyond itself. Not recognizing this is idolatry. In Tillich's words,

> Literalism deprives God of his ultimacy and, religiously speaking, of his majesty. It draws him down to the level of that which is not ultimate, the finite and conditional. . . . Faith, if it takes its symbols literally, becomes idolatrous! It calls something ultimate which is less than ultimate.[21]

The term "recognizing" describes Tillich's understanding of idolatry appropriately, for it points to the fact that for Tillich, idolatry is a cognitive issue. Idolatry has to do with whether or not we recognize or understand something about God's nature properly. As is often the case with Tillich, his musings on what does and does not constitute idolatry begin to sound rather formulaic: "The fundamental symbol of our ultimate concern is God. . . . Where there is ultimate concern, God can be denied only in the name of God. One God can deny the other one. Ultimate concern cannot deny its own character as ultimate. Therefore, it affirms what is meant by the word 'God.' "[22]

For Tillich, not only is the problem of idolatry a cognitive issue that can be solved with such succinct formulations, but it is also primarily a problem of the finite's relation to the infinite. The finite mind must simply understand that no symbol, including "the fundamental symbol of our ultimate concern," God, can be "the true ultimate," for the finite human can never fully know the infinite ultimate. Though he believes that many, if not all, religions have the possibility of creating religiously meaningful symbols, Tillich does believe that the symbol of the cross has a superior place among religious symbols:

> That symbol is most adequate which expresses not only the ultimate but also its own lack of ultimacy. Christianity expresses itself in such a symbol in contrast to all other religions, namely, in the Cross of the Christ. Jesus could not have been the Christ without sacrificing himself as Jesus to himself as the Christ. Any acceptance of Jesus as the Christ which is not the acceptance of Jesus the crucified is a form of idolatry. . . . The event which has created this symbol has

> given the criterion by which the truth of Christianity, as well as of any religion, much be judged. The only infallible truth of faith, the one in which the ultimate itself is unconditionally manifest, is that any truth of faith stands under a yes-or-no judgment. . . . The criterion contains a Yes—it does not reject any truth of faith in whatever form it may appear in the history of faith—and it contains a No—it does not accept any truth of faith as ultimate except the one that no man possesses it. The fact that this criterion is identical with the Protestant principle and has become reality in the Cross of the Christ constitutes the superiority of Protestant Christianity.[23]

For Tillich, the cross's symbolic superiority stems from its recognition of the cognitive limitations of the human being. The difference between the symbol of Jesus and the symbol of Jesus on the cross is that the latter expresses the epistemological limitation of the finite human mind while the former denies precisely that. The epistemological truth embodied by the cross is that "no man possesses the ultimate." For Tillich, idolatry is an epistemological error that denies this ultimate truth.

The cross is such a powerful image for Rosenzweig not because it represents an acknowledgment of an epistemological limitation, but because it is itself the Christian's task: to always be at a beginning. Rosenzweig makes this clear in a comment on the meaning of the Sabbath for Christianity. In the context of our discussion of Tillich, it is perhaps ironic that this comment is the only place in which Rosenzweig refers specifically to Christian *symbol*:

> Sunday, which has never taken the prescription to rest very seriously, even in periods which were otherwise legalistic in orientation, has turned entirely into the festival of the beginning. Under the symbol [*Sinnbild*] of the beginning of the world, it celebrates primarily the beginning of the week. We recognized the strength with which Christian consciousness strove from the middle of the path on which it stands toward the beginning. The cross is ever beginning, ever the point of departure for the co-ordinates of the world. Just as the Christian era begins there, so too Christian belief repeatedly begins its course there. The Christian is the eternal beginner; completion is not for him; all's well that's well begun.[24]

Rosenzweig argues not only that Christian belief must always return to its beginnings, but that this repeated returning is the eternal way. The Christian way is eternal because it must be begun anew eternally. Christian idolatry comes from the belief that the way has been completed and from the refusal to begin anew. As Rosenzweig states repeatedly, completion is not for the Christian. Only the Jew's revelation is complete.

And it is here that we come to Rosenzweig's understanding of Christian idolatry. For Rosenzweig, idolatry is not a generic mistake whose form is the same for any person and every tradition. Instead, there are particular forms of idolatry. Against the mainstream of Jewish thought, Rosenzweig argues that the particular form of Christian idolatry is not its images of God. Rather, Christian idolatry is a straying from Christian images of God, images that express, and actually are, the ever-new beginnings of Christian faith and life. These ever-new beginnings make world redemption possible. In order to keep off the path of idolatry, Christians must use their images to create ever-new beginnings. When new beginnings are not created, Christians believe that their revelation is complete. The Christian belief in a complete revelation is for Rosenzweig Christian idolatry. It is also what Rosenzweig calls "religion." Recall that for Rosenzweig, "religion" is the idol made from revelation.[25] In *The Star of Redemption*, Rosenzweig likens the idolization of religion to fanaticism. The fanatic is one who believes she does not have to wait for God to act. The fanatic believes that she can control the future.[26] Rosenzweig argues that, believing its revelation to be complete, Christianity tends dangerously toward the idolatry of "religion" and "fanaticism."

But Rosenzweig's argument about Christian idolatry is not a generic argument against "religion." Again, idolatry is as particular as a script of a nation. Reversing the doctrine of Christian supersessionism, Rosenzweig argues that whereas Christian idolatry is the belief in the completeness of Christian revelation, Jewish revelation is complete. He argues further that Christianity cannot but desire Jewish completeness. Christians want the right to completeness and cannot help believe this right is theirs. This belief is not a cognitive failure that can be translated into countless other contexts, as Tillich might describe it. Rather, Rosenzweig argues that the idolatrous Christian belief in the completeness of their revelation has a direct practical consequence, which is as particular to Christianity as is her powerful image of the cross. The consequence of Christian idolatry is Christian antisemitism, which is ultimately the Christian resentment and hatred of Jewish completeness.

For Rosenzweig, it is not possible for Christianity, or Judaism for that matter, to ever come to Tillich's conclusion that "no man possesses the ultimate." Christianity's images are so powerful precisely because Christians can take their images to be ultimately true, and not symbolic of an epistemological limitation, as Tillich might have it. Idolatry would not be such a risk, nor would Christianity be so potentially powerful, were it so easily resisted with succinct, philosophical formulations. For Rosenzweig, the power of Christian image matches the degree of the risk of Christian idolatry, a risk that brings the possibility not only of world redemption, but also of world destruction, propelled by a lethal antisemitism.

Christianity's tendency toward its idolatrous antisemitism is at the heart of Rosenzweig's understanding of the Jewish-Christian relation.

While Rosenzweig does suggest that it is philosophically possible to articulate the philosophical complementarity of Judaism and Christianity, as he does in *The Star of Redemption* with the rubrics "the eternal people" and "the eternal way," it is never possible to have such a point of view from within each tradition. Rather, Judaism and Christianity each believe that their truth is ultimate. If they did not, argues Rosenzweig, they would not be able to create meaning for their communities nor the possibility of world redemption.

For Rosenzweig, Judaism and Christianity meet each other in their individual particularities which, despite their philosophical complementarity, do not and cannot reduce to each other. Like individual human beings, Judaism and Christianity are uniquely particular. Though they share in the whole of truth, the whole belongs to neither, but only to God:

> Before God, then, Jew and Christian both labor at the same task. He [God] cannot dispense with either. He has set enmity between the two for all time and withal has most intimately bound each to each. . . . The truth, the whole truth (*die ganze Wahrheit*) thus belongs to neither of them nor to us. . . . We both have but a part of the whole truth. But we know that it is in the nature of truth to be im-parted [*zu teil zu sein*], and that a truth in which no one had a part would be no truth.[27]

Like all human truth, Judaism and Christianity remain imparted, not whole. They face one another in a dialogue that tests the truth of each but never dares to move beyond the particularity of each. Rosenzweig's argument is that their dialogic relation is one of judgment, born of an enmity set by God for all time, and not one of affirmation as has commonly been interpreted. It is to this dynamic of enmity and judgment that we now turn.

## Dialogue as Judgment

Rosenzweig has long been interpreted as a dialogical philosopher who extolled the virtues of dialogue for the all important tasks of mutual understanding and affirmation. Frequently conflated with Martin Buber's notion of dialogue, Rosenzweig's philosophy is often interpreted as advocating mutuality and reciprocity. But such statements as Buber's "Relation is reciprocity. My You acts on me as I act on it" do not begin to capture the thrust of Rosenzweig's dialogical thinking.[28] So, too, Christian theologians who suggest that Rosenzweig's thought establishes the basis for a common purpose and understanding between Christians and Jews do not begin to grasp the impetuses for, or conclusions of, Rosenzweig's thought.[29] The failure to understand Rosenzweig properly on the Jewish-Christian relation is linked to the failure to appreciate Rosenzweig's view of idolatry, and the ways in which Christian idolatry is intimately linked to an antisemitism it can never fully overcome.

Paul van Buren, whose three-volume work *A Theology of the Jewish-Christian Reality* builds a Christian theology largely on the basis of Rosenzweig's scheme, defines dialogue as "a serious effort on both sides to listen to and understand the other in the other's terms."[30] It is, however, precisely this possibility that Rosenzweig argues is *impossible* for Judaism vis-à-vis Christianity and for Christianity vis-à-vis Judaism. Judaism and Christianity cannot "listen to and understand the other in the other's terms" because each of their self-definitions brings with it precisely a *judgment* against the other.

In a letter of October 1916, Rosenzweig comments to Eugen Rosenstock that "every Jew feels in the depths of his soul that the Christian relation to God, and so in a sense their religion, is particularly and extremely pitiful, poverty-stricken, and ceremonious."[31] This deep-rooted feeling, Rosenzweig continues, "is no discovery of modern apologetics but the simplest Jewish instinct." The Jewish judgment of Christianity is part and parcel of Judaism's self-definition. Judaism understands itself as possessing *the* truth that is contained in recognizing the proper human relationship to the one, unique God. For Jews, this is an intimate relationship that requires no mediation. And from a Jewish perspective, the Christian relationship to God is nothing but mediated. The Jew judges the Christian harshly for having to "learn from someone else, whoever he may be, to call God 'our Father.'"[32] Contained in the Jew's relationship to God the Father is a judgment against Christianity. Jews at best condescend to Christianity, and at worst despise it. Rosenzweig's point is that this is not something that Jews can get over, for if Judaism did not judge Christianity in this way, Judaism would not be Judaism.

This Jewish refusal to see anything but the Jewish relationship to God forms the basis of the Christian judgment against Judaism. Christians rightly recognize Judaism's judgment against Christianity. Judaism sees only itself and, as Rosenzweig writes to Rudolf Ehrenberg in November of 1913, "to the church [Judaism] can only say: we have already arrived at the destination, you are still enroute."[33] In making this statement, Judaism blinds herself to the rest of the world, as Rosenzweig explains to Rosenstock: "Is not part of the price that the Synagogue must pay for the blessing . . . of being already in the Father's presence, that she must wear the bandages of unconsciousness over her eyes?"[34]

For Christians, Jews are proud and stubborn. Rather than choosing the universal transformation of spirit offered by Christian conversion, Jews stubbornly remain blind to and unconscious of the world. What for Christians is Jewish stubbornness is for Jews fidelity to the proper relationship with God.[35] The Christian internalization of Jewish fidelity to

God, what Christians refer to as "the pride of the Jews," is crucial to Christian self-definition. Christians understand themselves precisely as *not* being stubborn, as *not* being blind to the world. This Christian self-understanding is at one and the same time a judgment against Judaism. Again, Rosenzweig to Rosenstock: "What does the Christian theological side of Judaism mean for the Christian? . . . This practical way, in which the theological idea of the stubbornness of the Jews works itself out, is *hatred of the Jews*."[36] Hatred of the Jews inheres in Christianity just as a condescending attitude toward Christianity inheres in Judaism. If each were to stop judging the other, each would no longer be what it is.

The Jewish-Christian relation is never, and can never become, a happy one. Rather, tension, hostility, and even the potential for catastrophic suffering characterize it. Rosenzweig does argue in *The Star of Redemption* that from a philosophical perspective, Judaism and Christianity are involved in the same task. His point, however, is that dialogue never takes place from a philosophical perspective, but only from the unique positions of absolutely different points of view. Again, he writes: "Before God, then, Jew and Christian both labor at the same task. . . . [However, God] has set enmity between the two for all time and has withal most intimately bound each to each."[37] From their respective vantage points, Jews and Christians cannot but judge the other.

Rosenzweig also claims in *The Star of Redemption* that Judaism constitutes the eternal people and Christianity the eternal way. But this is the basis precisely for the tension and incriminating judgments between Judaism and Christianity, and not the basis for the possibility of mutual understanding. For Rosenzweig, Judaism and Christianity cannot—in the words of Gerhard Spiegler, a Christian theologian who advocates interreligious dialogue in Rosenzweig's name—"accept and recognize the value and validity of the religious particularity" of the other.[38] It is in fact only through Judaism's and Christianity's non-acceptance of the other that redemption may come. Judgment propels us toward redemption, for judgment, and not affirmation, can force us to change ourselves.

Because they cannot affirm each other, Judaism and Christianity do affect one another. Already in his correspondence with Rosenstock, Rosenzweig makes this dynamic clear:

> The art of the Synagogue does not enter into living relation [*lebendigen Zusammenhang*] with other art, nor Jewish theology with Christian theology, and so on; but Jewish art and theology, taken together, build up the Jews into a united whole and maintain them in their form of life . . . and only then do they work as a ferment on Christianity and through it [*durch es hindurch*] on the world.[39]

Jewish and Christian theology do not enter into a conversation in order to find their middle ground. However, through the other's judgment,

Judaism and Christianity can each perhaps change itself, though not the other. At best, judgment by the other can produce a self-judgment.

In *The Star of Redemption*'s discussion of Christianity, Rosenzweig elaborates on what Christians may learn from Jewish judgment:

> This existence of the Jew constantly subjects Christianity to the idea that it is not attaining the goal, the truth, that it ever remains—on the way. That is the profoundest reason for the Christian hatred of the Jew. . . . In the final analysis it is only self-hate. . . . It is hatred of one's own imperfection, one's own not-yet.[40]

As against Judaism, Christianity defines itself in terms of its universal mission, in terms of its potential for universal salvation. Judaism reminds Christianity, however, that it has not yet achieved its goal. Judaism's prideful particularity saves Christianity from its own totalitarian tendency to believe that it has achieved its goal, and can teach the Christian about the ways in which she must learn to live with the discomfort of her own incompleteness. However, Christians and Christianity can be saved from themselves if and only if Jews and Judaism remain Jewish.

Jewish judgment does not compromise Christian difference, and even allows Christians to intensify their identity as different from Jews. While Christians modify their perceptions of themselves, Christians remain Christian. The Jewish judgment against them only further commits Christians to their mission of creating a universal community and culture. In Rosenzweig's words, through being what she is, which constitutes a judgment against Christianity, the Jew "involuntarily shames the Christian, who is driven outwards and onwards."[41] From the Jew's judgment, the Christian may learn something about her own salvation and commit herself further to her universal mission.

Jews also have something to learn from the Christian judgment of Judaism. Drawing on Maimonides and Judah Halevi, Rosenzweig argues in *The Star of Redemption* that since the ways of God cannot be known, the Christian conquest of the world may have something to teach the Jew about her own salvation. For Rosenzweig, the paradox of Jewish existence is that through its particularity, Judaism represents the universal. Stubborn Jewish pride allows Jews to maintain the particularity of their unique and intimate relationship with God. But Jews also understand their revelation to be universal. As part of their own self-definition of embodying salvation for all humanity, Jews are forced to recognize that there must be an option for salvation available to the peoples of the world. By way of the Christian judgment against them, which again at the same time constitutes Christian identity, Jews are forced to recognize that it is possible that they cannot be representative of the universal without Christianity. The Christian judgment against Judaism can thus make the Jew recognize that Judaism depends on a universal other, despite the Jew's complete and perfected relationship to God.

But Judaism's self-judgment does not leave Judaism affirming the truth of Christianity. Rather, like Christianity, Judaism becomes more committed to the particularity of its own existence. Judaism's self-judgment makes Jews uneasy but this uneasiness is important for Judaism if it is to maintain its unique role in bringing about the redemption of the world. Jews understand their God to be both their God and the God of all peoples. Jews must always be aware of the tension of living the universal through the particular. This tension characterizes Jewish existence and can be maintained only if Judaism closes itself off from others. Rosenzweig writes:

> What does this mean: to root in one's self? . . . It means no more and no less than that one people, though it is only one people, claims to constitute All. . . . There are two sides to every boundary. By setting separating borders for ourselves, we border on something else.[42]

Christianity's judgment against Judaism, which becomes for Judaism a self-judgment, does not annul but only intensifies Jewish particularity and therefore Jewish stubbornness. If—and from a Jewish perspective this "if" always remains—Christianity offers a universal way for all humanity, Judaism must remain all the more separate and different from it. Without Jewish difference, the nations of the world would not have the model for the goal that they strive to meet.[43]

The Jewish-Christian relation is never one of mutuality, but always one of absolute difference. Dialogue takes place in direct discourse, in saying "You" in contrast to a "We." While noting that this dynamic is indeed "dreadful" (*grauenhaft*), Rosenzweig argues that any "we" "cannot avoid this sitting in judgment, for only with this judgment does it give a definite content to the totality of its We."[44] As we have seen, judgment comes from difference, but without judgment, and thus difference, dialogue, and the potential for self-transformation, would not be possible. The impossibility of consensus is the basis of all dialogue, for Rosenzweig. Therefore, Judaism and Christianity exist in a dialogic relation not because they strive for the building of something new together, but rather because their relationship to each other strengthens the judgment of one over and against the other, for the sake of each's self-judgment. It is precisely the otherness of the other that makes it possible for Judaism and Christianity each to intensify its own identity. Rosenzweig argues that the intensification of Jewish and Christian particularity may, despite the tension, hostility, and suffering that such intensification brings, lead the way to redemption.

Like Judaism and Christianity, individuals meet each other in their particularity, in the harsh and harrowing assessment of one point of view over and against another. It is in fact the harsh and harrowing assessment of one point of view over and against the other that allows for the formation of Jewish and Christian communities in the first place. For Rosenzweig, the Jewish community is formed and maintained by acts of repentance through which individuals recognize their excessive responsibility for all members of the community. As we saw in chapter 2, Yom Kippur embodies the performance of one-sided repentance and judgment. The Christian community is formed by the Christ event that allows each individual to form a new identity in the present. This new identity, however, is nothing but a judgment against the past. Christians unite in their judgments against their pagan past, and Christian community is but the unification of this judgment.

Before turning to a fuller discussion of the formation of Christian community, we must understand Rosenzweig's view of interpersonal dialogue and how it relates to the Jewish-Christian relation a bit more fully. Rosenzweig's understanding of the I-Thou relationship is not a description of the lyricism of mutual understanding, but has as its defining mark the unresolved demand of infinite judgment. The self does not merely say "Thou" to another and thereby participate in an act of mutual affirmation. Rather, merely by being other, the presence of another (whether God or a human being) judges the self. To this otherness, to this absolute difference, the self can only respond with "I have sinned."[45] The acknowledgment of the other produces not a reciprocal relation, but rather a troubling and distressing self-judgment of the self. The other teaches the self something about itself: primarily that no self is self-contained and independent in the ways it may think it is. Rosenzweig writes:

> The soul is ashamed of its former self, and that it did not, under its own power, break the spell in which it was confined. . . . "I have sinned." Thus speaks the soul and abolishes the shame. By speaking thus, referring purely back to the past, it purifies the present from the weakness of the past. "I have sinned" means I was a sinner. With this acknowledgment of having sinned, however, the soul clears the way for the acknowledgment "I am a sinner."[46]

The mere fact of the other's absolute difference from the self constitutes a judgment against the self. And from this judgment, the self is able to recognize the shamefulness of its own existence.

For Rosenzweig, the relationships between individual human beings and the relationships between an individual and God have a possibility open to them that the relationship between Judaism and Christianity does not have. This is precisely the possibility of love. The Jewish-Christian relationship is, as we have seen, forever marked by the enmity that God has set between them. Judaism and Christianity can each say to themselves in regard to the other, "I have sinned," but they cannot each say, "I am a sinner." In their self-judgments, Judaism and Christianity can each "purify the present from the weakness of the past," but they cannot clear the way for the love of the present that comes from acknowledging that one not only was but is now a sinner. To acknowledge that one is now too a sinner means that one has become wholly open to the love of the other. But to be fully open to the love of the other is to move beyond the mere discomfort of self-judgment and to substitute the judgment of the other for oneself. In substituting the judgment of the other for oneself, the self does not become the other, but rather a new self. This is not something that Judaism or Christianity can do in regard to the other. The substitution of the self for the other's judgment is love, and it is hatred, and not love, that propels the Jewish-Christian relationship until the end of history, for the sake of the redemption of the world.

For Rosenzweig, the recognition of the shamefulness of the self's existence in the now opens the way to the possibility of love in the present. Even when lover and beloved love one another, love is an asymmetrical relation born of judgment. In fact, lover and beloved can only love one another through an intensification of one-sided self-judgment. This intensification of self-judgment, an intensification that neither Judaism nor Christianity can afford, is the movement from "I was a sinner" to "I am a sinner." Rosenzweig writes:

> This second acknowledgment is already the full admission of love. It throws the compulsion of shame far away and gives itself up entirely to love. . . . Now he acknowledges that he is still a sinner even though he had divested himself of the past shame, and now shame withdraws from him. Indeed, the very fact that his admission dares its way into the present is the sign that it has overcome shame. As long as it lingered in the past, it still lacked the courage to express itself fully and confidently; it could still harbor doubts about the answer it had coming to it. . . . It sheds its doubts only as it dares to emerge from the acknowledgment of the past into acknowledging the present. It becomes certain of the answer by acknowledging its sinfulness, not as transpired "sin," but as a sinfulness yet present, so certain that it no longer needs to hear this answer out loud.[47]

To dare one's admission of sin into the present is to open oneself up to the love of the other. But to be open to love in the present one must give oneself up to the other's judgment. Love is not affirming, but judgmental. Love is commanding.

A new self emerges from this act of admission of shame in the present. This new self does not become one with the other, but through the other's judgment remakes itself. The other cannot remake me; only I can remake myself. Rosenzweig continues:

> [The beloved] is freed of its burden at the very moment of daring to assume all of it on its shoulders. . . . The beloved no longer needs the acknowledgment of the lover which she longed for before she admitted her love. At the very

> moment when she herself dares to admit to it, she is as certain of his love as if he were whispering his acknowledgment into her ear. . . . This certainty comes to [the beloved], not from God's mouth, but from its own.[48]

In response to my acknowledgment of my sin, the other says to me, "You are mine."[49] As Rosenzweig makes clear, this is "a sentence which does not have 'I' for a subject."[50] In true dialogue, the other's judgment is not about the other, but about me. In allowing me to change myself through my own self-judgment, the other loves me. Dialogue's power lies in the fact that the otherness of the other, the other's difference, can give me the strength to change. Like dialogue, love is commanding and judgmental: love demands that I change, that I be different.

For Rosenzweig, the Jewish-Christian relation is not one of love born of judgment, but only of judgment. Judgment becomes love only when the beloved allows her or himself to be loved. But to be loved is to be wholly changed and transformed and it is this change and transformation that Judaism and Christianity each refuse in respect to the other. At best, Judaism and Christianity can cause the other to judge itself. Judaism's self-judgment drives Judaism inward, just as Christianity's self-judgment drives Christianity outward. Judaism's inwardness, the fire of the star of redemption, constitutes Judaism's part in the whole of truth. Christianity's outwardness, the rays of the star of redemption, constitutes Christianity's part in the whole of truth.

Both Judaism and Christianity share in the whole of truth, but neither possesses that whole. At the same time, in the wholeness of life that each creates for itself, Judaism and Christianity are bound to judge each other until the end of history. Each cannot but judge the other, and it is the judgment of one over and against the other that can prepare the way for redemption, for Rosenzweig. By way of its inwardness, Judaism judges Christianity. And by way of its outwardness, Christianity judges Judaism. The star of redemption requires both fire and rays.

## Redemption's Star Out of Judaism's Source

The image of the star of redemption expresses the ethically monotheistic vision that is at the core of Rosenzweig's understanding of Christianity. Given that this chapter's task has been to demonstrate that Rosenzweig diverges from the mainstream of German-Jewish thought by insisting that Christian images are not inherently idolatrous, this claim may seem surprising. And no doubt, on a number of levels this is a surprising claim. After all, though he follows Maimonides and Halevi in contemplating the possibility that God might have another revelation for the nations of the world, Rosenzweig goes quite a bit further by insisting that the Christian mission to the nations of the world is absolutely essential to the world's redemption. The Jewish thinker Rosenzweig claims not only that the Christian image of the cross has world redemptive possibilities, but that without the image of the cross, there would be no possibility of a universal humanity. Rosenzweig's position on Christianity seems to be worlds apart from Cohen's ethical monotheism which insists, following Maimonides, that images of God are shameful, false, and intrinsically idolatrous, and that the world will be redeemed only by the universal recognition of this philosophical fact.

However, though transformed, it is precisely Cohen's ethically monotheistic framework to which Rosenzweig's vision of the Jewish-Christian relation is indebted. As this chapter has demonstrated, the characterization of Rosenzweig's attitude toward Christianity as wholly positive is one-sided at best and a gross misinterpretation at worst. Central to Rosenzweig's understandings of Christianity and the image of the cross is Christianity's intrinsic propensity toward idolatrous antisemitism, a propensity it can never fully overcome. Judaism reminds Christianity of its incompleteness, and this constant, unwanted reminder is, Rosenzweig contends, the source of Christian antisemitism. When Christianity denies its incompleteness, it also denies its Jewish origins:

> Christianity is well aware . . . of the dependence of its own development on the existence—and no more than the existence—of Judaism. It was always the hidden enemies of Christianity, from the Gnostics to the present day, who wanted to deprive it of its "Old Testament." A God who was only spirit, and no longer the Creator who gave his law to the Jews, a Christ who was only Christ and no longer Jesus, a world which was only All and its center no longer the Holy Land.[51]

Rosenzweig argues that when Christianity denies its Jewish origins it falls into three different types of dangers. Each idolatrous danger is the result of reducing the complex, incomplete Christian images of God, man, and world into fixed images. Christianity's idolatrous dangers are represented by the notions that God is only spirit, that Christ is only Christ, and that the world is All. Each of these dangers is a denial of God's freedom and transcendence: "That the Spirit leads onto all ways, and not God; that the Son of man be the truth, and not God; that God would become All-in-All and not One above all—these are dangers."[52] With a denial of God's transcendence, the Christian elevates himself and his world above their finitude, above his own incompleteness, to God's level.

Rosenzweig argues that only by keeping its Jewish origins in constant sight can Christianity be both potentially redemptive and non-idolatrous.

Though he does not advocate a religion of reason out of the sources of Judaism, Rosenzweig does advocate the redemption of the world by Christianity out of the source of Jewish revelation. As Cohen did before him, Rosenzweig argues that Judaism serves as both the source of the possibility of the production of universal community, as well as that which keeps that universal community off the path of idolatry.

The major difference between Cohen and Rosenzweig on the question of Christianity is the weight that is given to antisemitism's power. In keeping with his view of idolatry, Cohen's position implies that antisemitism is something that can be corrected with proper thinking. If Christians would understand better the idea of pure monotheism, argues Cohen, then both idolatry and antisemitism would disappear. Rosenzweig, on the other hand, does not believe that either idolatry or antisemitism is so easily eradicated. As we have seen, Rosenzweig argues that the propensity toward both idolatry and antisemitism are part and parcel of Christianity. Right thinking does not overcome idolatry or antisemitism, for Rosenzweig. Only right worship can overcome these two errors. However, especially in the case of Christianity, worship will always tend toward idolatry. Still, Rosenzweig argues that precisely for the sake of the redemption of the world, Christianity must risk idolatry and hence antisemitism also.[53]

Despite their different views of idolatry and antisemitism, Cohen's term "out of the sources of Judaism" captures the core of Rosenzweig's understanding of both what is potentially redemptive and destructive about Christianity. Rosenzweig argues that Christian antisemitism is self-hatred; it is hatred of Christianity's own not-yet, of Christianity's own incompleteness. It is this hatred of incompleteness that leads Christianity to idolatry.

## Religion, Fanaticism, and Modern Nationalism

While Christianity has idolatrous potential in terms of its images of God and man, Rosenzweig argues that in the modern world, Christianity's most relevant and most deadly potential idol is the one it can make out of its world, the modern state. Contrary to Hegel's statement of 1822 that the "harmony between the State and the Church has now attained *immediate* realization,"[54] Rosenzweig writes in 1921, "The history of the Christian world . . . consists of the attempt to maintain this separation."[55] Rosenzweig agrees with Hegel that Christianity's universal mission is defined by its dual powers—the Church and the State. But against Hegel, Rosenzweig contends that these dual powers must remain separate powers. Otherwise, Christianity turns God's created world into an idolized world (*die vergötterte Welt*). As with God and man, Rosenzweig argues that Christianity makes an idol of the world by forgetting God's freedom and transcendence:

> It would forget the One above all in favor of the All-in-All; it would forfeit the pious confidence in the free inner strength of the soul which renews itself, and in the providence of God which goes its own way above all human insight, in favor of the lovingly active unification of what the world has separated into the one-and-universal building of the kingdom.[56]

In keeping with his argument for Christianity's tendency toward "religion," Rosenzweig argues that in the modern world, Christianity's denial of God's on-going revelation produces a new phenomenon: nationalism. Rosenzweig suggests that the Christian forgetfulness of God's transcendence culminates in the modern world in nationalism:

> For nationalism expresses not merely the peoples' belief that they come from God (that you rightly say, the pagans also believe), but that they go to God. But now peoples do have this belief, and hence 1789 is followed by 1914–1917, and yet more "from . . . to's"; and the Christianizing of the concept of the "people" is not yet the Christianizing of the people themselves.[57]

Modern nationalism is the product of raising the Christian people to the status of the divine. At the expense of God's transcendence, modern nationalism turns a people's image of itself into an idol. When a people begins to worship itself, it cannot but worship what it takes to be the embodiment of the external form of itself: its state.

Rosenzweig maintains that the nationalist idolization of the state has important affinities not only with the Christian tendency toward religion, but also with the Christian propensity for fanaticism. In *The Star of Redemption*, Rosenzweig contrasts ancient and modern conceptions of war. He sums up the ancient state's attitude toward war: "The ancient states had public cults, offerings, festivals and so on as the midpoint of their political existence. But war that was waged against the enemy . . . was not itself the offering, not itself the cultic action, not itself the altar."[58] In contrast to the pagan approach to war, Rosenzweig suggests that modern nationalism is something quite different. While pagans go to war as a necessity, they do not view war as a cultic action, or as an offering. Modern nationalism, on the other hand, views war as cultic action, and death in war as an offering of the individual to the nation.

Rosenzweig's reference here to an offering is no doubt a reference to Hegel, whose theory of the modern state is intimately tied to his understanding of the meaning of death. Recall Hegel's discussion of the state and death:

> War is that condition in which the vanity of temporal things [*Dinge*] and temporal goods—which tends at other times to be merely a pious phrase—takes on

> a serious significance, and it is accordingly the moment in which the ideality of the particular attains its right and becomes actuality. The higher significance of war is that, through its agency (as I have put it on another occasion), "the ethical health of nations is preserved in their indifference towards the permanence of finite determinacies, just as the movement of the winds preserves the sea from that stagnation which a last calm would produce—a stagnation which a lasting, not to say perpetual, peace would also produce among nations." . . . Since sacrifice for the individuality of the state is the substantial relation of everyone and therefore a universal duty, it itself becomes, as one aspect of the ideality (as distinct from the reality) of particular subsistence [*Bestehen*], at the same time a particular relation with an estate of its own—the estate of valour—attached to it.[59]

For Hegel, while death is a natural necessity (*Naturgewalt*), the state gives death a meaning. In fact, the state demands precisely that the death of individuals be meaningful. For Hegel, through the voluntary sacrifice of their lives, individuals defend the value of freedom, and are thereby able to gain meaning in their deaths.

Rosenzweig agrees with Hegel's description of the dynamics of the modern state, but disagrees with his valuation. Once again, Rosenzweig's disagreement is based upon his hermeneutical approach. From Rosenzweig's perspective, an individual offers himself to the state and gains meaning in his death if and only if he is first willing to obliterate others for his idealization of the state. The individual must believe that the war in which he participates will redeem the world. This spirit of redemption by way of overcoming others and incorporating others into one's vision of oneself defines modern nationalism, for Rosenzweig.

Significantly, Rosenzweig argues that the difference between pagan and modern nationalist attitudes toward war is ultimately a theological difference, and a Christian theological difference at that. Rosenzweig argues that modern nationalism is distinctly Christian:

> The nations have been in a state of inner conflict ever since Christianity with its supernational power came upon them. Ever since then, and everywhere, a Siegfried is at strife with that stranger, the man of the cross, in his very appearance so suspect a character. A Siegfried who, depending on the nation he comes from, may be blond and blue-eyed, or dark and small-boned, or brown and dark-eyed, wrestles again and again with this stranger who resists the continued attempts to assimilate him to that nation's own idealization.[60]

Christianity tends dangerously toward the desire for completion, which Rosenzweig characterizes as "religion." *The Star of Redemption* suggests that Christian religion, when combined with modern politics, will culminate in the fanatical desire to assimilate others into its own idealization of itself, at any cost. Rosenzweig's characterization of a "Siegfried" at strife with a stranger is a specific reference to the particular monuments that were erected at German cemeteries to commemorate Germany's fallen soldiers in the Great War. These war monuments depicted the dying young Siegfried, who was the symbol of youth and simplicity. As one historian notes: "Such heroes' memorials, so we are told in 1915, are symbolic of the eternal youth of the people. Siegfried was a young Apollo, and so was Germany."[61] Rosenzweig suggests that modern nationalism, and German nationalism in particular, has strong affinities with Christianity's fanatical tendencies.

For Rosenzweig, only its connection to Judaism can keep Christianity from falling into lethal idolatry:[62]

> And as that ever-present struggle of the Gnostics shows, it is the Old Testament which enables Christianity to withstand this, its own danger. . . . Had the Jews of the Old Testament disappeared from the earth like Christ, they would [now] denote the idea of the People, and Zion the idea of the Center of the World, just as Christ denotes the idea of Man. But the stalwart, the undeniable vitality of the Jewish people, attested in the very hatred of the Jews, resists such "idealizing." Whether Christ is more than an idea—no Christian can know it. But that Israel is more than an idea, that he knows, that he sees. For we live. We are eternal, not as an idea may be eternal: if we are eternal, it is in full reality.[63]

Judaism is a sign in the world of God's revelation, which, for Rosenzweig, marks God's transcendence. Only its relation to Judaism can keep Christianity from fixing its images of God, man, and world. According to Rosenzweig, Judaism reminds Christianity of the tensions intrinsic to always being en route for two main reasons. First, the Jewish notion of God's freedom and transcendence, expressed by the ban on images, keeps Christians (and Jews) open to God's continual and changing revelation. Second, the fact that Jews remain Jews, that Jews do not and will not become Christian, forces Christianity to recognize that its universal mission remains incomplete and will remain incomplete until the world is redeemed.

Rosenzweig maintains that the tensions of Christian existence mean that Christians are always forced to doubt their revelation. Christians must always wonder whether Christ is more than an idea. Rosenzweig argues that this is an issue that Christians cannot resolve. They do know, however, that Judaism and Jews are more than ideas, that they are real. Here Rosenzweig reiterates his argument that Judaism's revelation is one that is passed on not through Jewish ideas, but through Jewish people. Christians must live with the tension of knowing that their revelation is impossible without Judaism, and hence Jewish people, but that Judaism, and Jewish people, also makes the completion of their revelation, in an unredeemed world, impossible. The refusal to accept this fact leads Christianity, simultaneously, to both idolatry and antisemitism. But to keep from falling into the temptations of idolatry and antisemitism is difficult for the Christian. Christian existence is marked by tensions that have severe consequences for the entire world, and particularly for Jews. If Christians do not and cannot maintain the tensions intrinsic to finite, non-idolatrous human existence, Jews suffer first and foremost. Antisemitism of the worst sort comes from the Christian denial of its Jewish origins.

And it is in this emphasis on the avoidance of idolatry through a constant reminder of Jewish origins that we find the most significant convergence between Cohen's and Rosenzweig's ethical monotheisms. For both Cohen and Rosenzweig, Israel's role is always the one of witness to the nations. Rosenzweig follows Cohen in his recognition and embrace of the fact that the witness's burden is a heavy one to bear and one that brings the highest of risks—for a witness is always a potential martyr.

Though on the surface it may seem that Rosenzweig's view of Christianity breaks with Cohen's approach to both Christianity and idolatry, their different interpretations of Judaism's place in safeguarding the nations of the world from the idolatrous lapses into which they cannot but fall links their thought under the rubric of ethical monotheism. For both Rosenzweig and Cohen, Judaism's strict adherence to the ban on idolatry fuels the possibility of world redemption. It is in this sense that for both of them, Judaism is excessively "ethical." Judaism carries the burden of monotheism not only for itself but also for all peoples of the world. In Rosenzweig's words, Judaism is representative (*Vertreter*) of all humanity. But Judaism, like Christianity, has its particular idolatrous risks that must always be guarded against.

As we will see in the next chapter, Rosenzweig parts with Cohen, as he does with Tillich on Christianity, by insisting that Judaism's idolatrous risks are not easily resolved by philosophical formulations. Just as Rosenzweig insists that the truth and reality of Christian images are the sites of both Christian revelation and Christian idolatry, so too he argues that the truth and reality of the Jewish people is the site of both Jewish revelation and Jewish idolatry. It is to the risks of Jewish idolatry that we now turn.

# Seven

## Risking Politics: Jewish Idolatry

ROSENZWEIG ARGUES that the Jewish community's role as witness to the nations is predicated on a simultaneous relation to and separation from the world. As we saw in chapter 4, for Rosenzweig, the ability to affect and to be affected by the nations of the world constitutes the contradiction of Jewish existence. In keeping with his hermeneutical and aesthetic approaches, Rosenzweig recognizes that a Jewish whole risks becoming an idol. Rosenzweig argues that when Jewish existence loses its contradiction—its simultaneous relation to and separation from the world—it becomes idolatrous. Toward the end of *The Star of Redemption*, he argues that a total Jewish separation from the world is the greatest danger for Judaism:

> By glowing toward the inside, Judaism threatened to gather its warmth to its own bosom, far away from the pagan reality of the world. If there [with Christianity] the dangers were spiritualization of God, humanization of God, secularization of God—here [with Judaism] they are denial of the world, disdain of the world, mortification of the world.[1]

A closed off Jewish world that does not feel the tension between itself and its host society is idolatry. It is in this sense that Jewish nationalism can also be idolatry because it denies the unique hermeneutical constitution of the Jewish community.

We saw in the last chapter that Rosenzweig argues that Christianity always risks religion. In this chapter we will see that Rosenzweig contends that Judaism always risks politics. But just as they have different world-historical roles, Christianity and Judaism have different risks, both in form and content. Christianity's risk is an active one while Judaism's is passive. Whereas Christianity risks becoming religion for the sake of world redemption, the contradiction of Jewish existence requires that Jews and Judaism risk themselves to the politics of the nations of the world. While Christianity avoids idolatry when it manages not to risk religion, Judaism becomes idolatrous when it no longer risks politics.

## Separation and Relation: Less and More than a Nation

In a 1928 open letter to the editor of the German Zionist newspaper *Jüdische Rundshau*, Rosenzweig summarizes what is for him the strange religious and political identity of the Jew:

> That we are a *Volk* is not to us what it is for Herzl—"We are a *Volk*, a *Volk*!"—the end of the theoretical problematic and the liberating breakthrough into the realm of the practical; No, on the contrary, it is here that the theoretical problem first begins for us. We are a *Volk*: this does not mean to us what it means to the Zionists: because or insofar as we are not a religious denomination [*Konfession*], but precisely insofar as we are a religious denomination. We are not a *Volk*: this does not mean to us what it does to our aged party elders, because we are a religious denomination; but precisely because we are not really one (but more, and therefore less). This is why we are—in reality—also not a *Volk* (but less, and therefore more).[2]

Rosenzweig suggests that the Jews are both more and less than a religious denomination, making them both less and more than a nation. Or, alternatively, that Jews constitute both more and less than a nation, making them more and less than a religious denomination. What could he mean by this?

In the same paragraph, Rosenzweig attempts to explain the problem of describing the Jews as a *Volk* by way of an anecdote:

> In regard to the concept of the Jewish *Volk*, we therefore find ourselves in the confounded but very Jewish situation of the chazan [cantor] who, having been asked before the court what a shofar is, finally, after much beating around the bush [*Drumherumgerede*], explains that it is a trumpet, and, being reprimanded by the indignant judge for not having said so to begin with, replies: *So is it a trumpet?*[3]

This description of the Jewish *Volk* reiterates two interconnected themes in Rosenzweig's thought already detailed in the second part of this book. The first theme is Rosenzweig's argument that Judaism is so self-contained and complete that it is untranslatable. The particulars of the performance of Judaism—which Rosenzweig refers to here by the example of the shofar, the ram's horn that is blown on the High Holidays—are not readily apparent to the external world. They can only be accessed through an act of translation. And, in keeping with Rosenzweig's theory of translation, what is accessed through translation only reinforces the sense that the translation is not the original. The chazan's attempt to translate the shofar then serves to emphasize Rosenzweig's understanding of Judaism's irreducible uniqueness and strangeness to the outside world.

The second theme is Rosenzweig's contention that the meaning of Judaism is as much defined through external responses to Judaism as by way of Judaism's self-contained completeness. Rosenzweig's account of the chazan ends with his asking the court, "So is it a trumpet?" *after* the chazan himself has provided the court with this very definition. Meaning is constituted not by the chazan's answer to the court but by the court's confirmation or negation of the chazan's self-questioning. Just as we do not receive the answer from the court in this anecdote, Judaism continuously awaits a response from the world.

Rosenzweig's anecdote makes clearer the dynamic of Judaism's *Unheimlichkeit* described in chapter 4. Like a work of art, Judaism's existence in the world is "unique, detached from its originator, uncanny in its vitality which is full of life and yet alien to life."[4] By way of its self-contained completeness, Judaism invites a response from the same world from which it separates itself. The chazan provides the court the opportunity to answer the question "So is it a trumpet?" for itself, thus providing the chance for the court to rethink, by way of the foreign, its own conceptualizations. It is on this point that Rosenzweig's view of translation and his contention that dialogue is judgment converge. Translation and dialogue force the mother-tongue or the self to rethink its own conceptualizations by way of the foreign tongue. Judaism's irreducible foreignness allows for the possibility of response. Judaism's irreducible foreignness makes translation not impossible, but possible.

We can now begin to make sense of Rosenzweig's effort to define the Jewish *Volk*, quoted above. The notion of the Jewish *Volk* is not for Rosenzweig what it is for Herzl, "the end of the theoretical problematic and the liberating breakthrough into the realm of the practical." Rather, the notion of the Jewish *Volk* is where, for Rosenzweig, the theoretical problem first begins. For Herzl, the Jewish *Volk* is an isolating concept. The Jewish *Volk can* be separated from the rest of the nations and *can* form an independent identity. This view, indeed, defines Herzl's political Zionism that claims that Jews *must* separate and isolate themselves from the rest of the nations so that an authentic Jewish national identity can be formed.[5] For Herzl, a piece of land is necessary for such a separation. If Jews are to separate themselves from the rest of the nations, they must have somewhere to go, somewhere to reside. Jews must possess a *Heim* in which to be.

For Rosenzweig, on the other hand, the Jewish *Volk* does not exist as a separation but rather as a separation *and* a relation. The Jewish *Volk* is wholly separate from the nations of the world, but at the same time the Jewish *Volk* exists in relation to the nations of the world. The nations of the world are asked to respond to the completeness of Jewish revelation. The court is asked to respond to the chazan's own translation of the untranslatable Jewish ritual object. While Jews exist in untranslatable, complete isolation, Jews at the same time exist in relation to their external worlds. As we saw in chapter 4, it is by way of existing as a mystery (*Geheimnis*) that Jews appear uncanny (*unheimlich*) to their neighbors. The English term "uncanny" is instructive in this context. To be uncanny is to be beyond knowledge.[6] The shofar, and the aesthetics of Judaism, is, according to Rosenzweig, beyond knowledge. Nonetheless, they affect the external world. They await a response from the external world. Only by being without a home, by existing in an un-homelike (*un-heimlich*) manner, can Judaism obtain the response from her neighbors that God's revelation requires. Rosenzweig argues that Judaism requires a response in necessary conjunction with her self-contained isolation in order to reveal God's secret revelation to the world. In the following quotation, we can substitute "Judaism" for "art" in order to understand Rosenzweig's notion of the Jewish *Volk*'s separation and relation more fully: "Once it has become public property, [Judaism] can no longer be excluded from the world."[7] Because it is without a home (*un-heimlich*), Judaism becomes public property. For Rosenzweig, Judaism cannot be excluded from the world. Judaism relates to the world by waiting for the world's response.

Since Judaism's separation from *and* relation to the nations of the world is not easily resolved, Rosenzweig contends that the notion of the Jewish *Volk* creates rather than resolves theoretical problems. Judaism is more than a *Volk* because Judaism is also a religious denomination. Judaism's essence is not confined to the isolation that comes from mere nationality. As a *Konfession*, Judaism makes a contribution to all other nations. The secret of revelation that Judaism bears within itself affects the rest of the world. But for this reason, Judaism is not merely a religious denomination, but something more. Rosenzweig argues that the paradox is that Judaism makes its contribution to the nations of the world through its self-contained, isolated completeness. This is why Judaism is more than a religious denomination: it makes its contribution through existing as a self-contained nationality that is defined, as we saw in chapter 3, through blood. Still, since Judaism makes a contribution to the nations at large, Judaism is less than a self-contained nation. Rosenzweig argues that the status of the Jewish *Volk* is therefore not easily resolved in theoretical terms but is better understood as a contradiction that is lived by Jews.

## Land vs. Blood

Let us begin to explore Rosenzweig's view of the contradiction of Jewish existence by understanding what Rosenzweig called his "non-Zionism," which is intimately connected to his vision of Judaism as a blood community. When it comes to constituting a nation, Rosenzweig argues that blood and land are two very different things. The nations of the world constitute themselves by way of land, and not by way of blood alone. Following this model for nation building, Zionism seeks first and foremost a land in which the Jewish people may dwell. But as Rosenzweig reiterates in *The Star of Redemption*, the Jewish people are not constituted by the land in which they dwell, but by the blood that flows through Jewish veins.

Rosenzweig's critique of Zionism as a form of nationalism that is attached to land is connected in significant ways to his view of how meaning is produced. By suggesting that Judaism is a blood and not a land community, Rosenzweig is not attempting to describe the ways in which Jews are merely different from non-Jews. Rather, he uses the hermeneutics of Judaism as a blood community to criticize what he believes is the faulty hermeneutical approach of land-oriented group identity. Blood, for Rosenzweig, is hope for the future. Jews hope for the future by living their home in the blood of their veins. Blood itself is procreation. Blood produces the only kind of eternity possible for the human being: memory that will be maintained by generations of the future. Again, "bearing witness takes place in bearing" (*Das Bezeugen geschieht im Erzeugen*). While the truth of the present is verified only in the future, the future gains its hold on truth through the blood that is risked in witnessing the present. The future makes its claim to truth by way of its past and most basically by way of the blood of its past. Blood, for Rosenzweig, is human hope for the future.

Rosenzweig's view of Jewish blood is not only a criticism of the hermeneutics of Zionism, but of the misguided hermeneutics of antisemitism and racism also.[8] Once again, Rosenzweig provides a similar description of Jewish blood as an antisemite or racist would, but transvalues this description. And once again, it is Rosenzweig's hermeneutical theory that is the key to this difference. The antisemite or racist argues for blood on the basis of the past. Rosenzweig's argument in contrast is an argument for blood as hope for the future. Rather than representing an overdetermined identity, as racist and antisemitic views of Jewish blood do, Rosenzweig's view of Jewish blood represents an openness to the future and a faith in that openness.

It is significant to note in this context that Rosenzweig's emphasis on blood as a future-oriented marker of identity is in marked contrast not only to racist views of blood, but to Buber's early arguments about Jewish blood also. In a lecture called "Judaism and the Jews," given in 1909 and published in 1911, Buber argues, as Rosenzweig would in *The Star of Redemption*, that the uniqueness of the Jewish community is constituted not by land but by blood.[9] But there are important differences between Buber's conception and Rosenzweig's. Buber writes: "[The Jew] senses in this immortality of the generations a community of blood, which he feels to be the antecedents of his I, its perseverance in the infinite past."[10] Rosenzweig, on the other hand, argues that

> There is only one community in which such a linked sequence of everlasting life goes from grandfather to grandson, only one which cannot utter the "we" of its unity without hearing deep within a voice that adds: "are eternal." It must be a blood-community, because only blood gives warrant to the hope for a future.[11]

Buber and Rosenzweig differ on the issue of Jewish blood in at least three ways. First, Buber defines the Jewish relationship to blood as a relationship constituted by the past, while for Rosenzweig the relationship is future-oriented. Second, Rosenzweig's argument about Jewish blood is contrasted only to land as a defining characteristic of a people. Buber's is contrasted against not only land, but also against language and a way of life: "All the elements that might constitute a reality for him [the Jew], are missing; all of them: land, language, way of life."[12] For Rosenzweig, the Jewish community is constituted not only by blood but also by language and a way of life. As we saw in chapter 4, and as we will see further below, Rosenzweig argues that the particular Jewish relationship to their sacred tongue, Hebrew, as well as to their host language defines Jewish existence. So, too, Rosenzweig differs significantly from Buber in arguing for a particular Jewish way of life, defined by Jewish law.[13] Finally, the most obvious difference between Buber and Rosenzweig's arguments is that Buber's argument about Jewish blood is linked to an argument for a Jewish nationalism, while Rosenzweig's argument about Jewish blood serves precisely the opposite purpose. Rosenzweig's argument about Jewish blood is intimately connected to his non-Zionist stance. Again, he argues that Zionism's hermeneutical schema is fundamentally distorted.

Rosenzweig maintains that if blood is future, land is precisely that which ultimately holds no future:

> The peoples of the world are not content with the bonds of blood. They sink their roots into the night of earth, lifeless in itself but the splendor of life, and from the lastingness of earth they conclude that they themselves will last. Their will to eternity clings to the soil and to the reign over the soil, to the land. The earth of their homeland is watered by the blood of their sons, for they do not trust in the life of a community of blood, in a community that can dispense with anchorage in solid earth. We were the only ones who trusted in blood and abandoned the land; and so we preserved the priceless sap of life which pledged us that it would be eternal. Among the peoples of the world, we [the Jews] were the only ones who separated what lived within us from all community with what is dead. For while the earth nourished, it also binds. Whenever a people

> loves the soil of its native land more than its own life, it is in danger. . . . Nine times out of ten this love will save the native soil from the foe and, along with it, the life of the people; in the end the soil will persist as that which was loved more strongly, and the people will leave their lifeblood upon it. . . . Thus the earth betrays a people that entrusted its permanence to earth. The soil endures, the peoples who live on it pass.[14]

People think that land is permanence. And this is true in the sense that land always endures. The problem is that land always endures longer than human beings because people are willing to shed blood over land. In the end, "the earth betrays a people that entrusted its permanence to earth." If land is taken for a greater value than human blood, a particular land will always outlast a particular people. For Rosenzweig, war leads only to more war. A particular people's victory today means also their defeat at some future time. When the bonds of blood are not the highest of human values, our view of the future, according to Rosenzweig, is always shortsighted. Rosenzweig argues that blood is the only permanence that the human being has in time. Eternity can only come from blood and not from land.

For Rosenzweig, Judaism's key insight is this insight into blood: only through blood can human beings ensure eternity because only through a faith in our own blood can we ensure future generations and the memory of the past. We can now understand the ways in which Rosenzweig's view of blood is hermeneutically oriented. The Zionists—both political and cultural Zionists—are wrong because they attempt to replace the hermeneutics of witnessing with a hermeneutical approach that suggests that the present is but the present and nothing more. A land-oriented group identity is a present-oriented group identity. To kill and to die for land is to approach the present in a one-dimensional manner. Rosenzweig argues that though Zionists and other nationalists make their claims to land by way of their pasts, their claim is actually a present-oriented claim. Their views of the past are assimilated to what they believe are the needs of the present.[15] In this way, the modern nationalist call for a new future is actually an obliteration of the past.[16] The land becomes the focus of the here and now, but Rosenzweig's point is that the here and now of land always passes. Without looking to the future, as the eternal people's blood community does, land-defined groups are condemned to die a death in time. Time passes, and so do those who dwell only in the land and not in the blood of their own veins.

Rosenzweig argues that the Zionists have forgotten that the Jewish people are

> a people in exile. . . . To the eternal people, home never is home in the sense of land, as it is to the peoples of the world who plough the land and live and thrive

> on it, until they have all but forgotten that being a people [*Volk*] means something besides being rooted in a land. The eternal people has not been permitted to while away time in any home. It never loses the untrammeled freedom of a wanderer who is more faithful a knight to his country when he roams abroad, craving adventure and yearning for the home [*Heimat*] he has left behind, than when he is at home [*zuhause*].[17]

The Jew, the eternal wanderer, feels this yearning (*Sehnsucht*) for his *Heimat* precisely when he is *zuhause*. No matter where she is, the Jew is homeless. The Jew's homelessness in fact is felt most when the Jew is in some home. The tension between separation and relation makes for the Jew's homelessness. The Jew does not live only as a separation. Jewish existence for Rosenzweig is not constituted by a dichotomy between separateness and belonging. Indeed, it is the Zionists and the nationalists who embrace such a dichotomy. If the Jew cannot be part of the body politic, as antisemitism makes clear, argues the Zionist, the Jew must live separately. For Rosenzweig, Jewish existence is not an either/or matter. Instead, Jewish existence is always both: separation and relation. Rosenzweig argues that the Zionist does not understand this essential quality of Jewish life. And this is seen by way of what is for Rosenzweig a basic Jewish theological fact: even the holy land, the land of Israel, can only be understood in the context of Jewish homelessness:

> In the most profound sense possible, this people has a land of its own only in that it has a land it yearns for—a holy land. And so even when it has a home, this people, in recurrent contrast to all other peoples on earth, is not allowed full possession of that home. It is only a "stranger and a sojourner." God tells it, "The land is mine."[18]

By way of his account of Jewish homelessness, Rosenzweig attempts in Part 3, Book 1 of *The Star of Redemption* to describe the essence of the Jewish people.[19] Rosenzweig uses the hermeneutics of a blood community, as opposed to a community defined by land, to critique a totalizing view of the political, which he contends is idolatrous. Indeed, for Rosenzweig, Hegel's state is "an idol that demands for itself the sacrifice of the individual and the nation."[20] For Rosenzweig, the formation of nations defined by the boundaries of land is a necessary evil, an evil that defines the political sphere. As we saw in the last chapter, Christianity combats this evil by developing a universal community of faith that exists in tension with, while affecting, politics. In this way, as Rosenzweig states in "New Thinking," Christianity exists as a redemptive aesthetics.[21] In describing Judaism as a blood community that defines itself through blood rather than through land, Rosenzweig offers what he takes to be the Jewish critique of politics. Rosenzweig argues that Judaism exists not merely in tension with the political, as Christianity does, but entirely outside of the political. In this way, Judaism exists as a messianic politics.[22] Rosenzweig suggests that by existing in an *un-heimlich* state, the Jewish people remember "that being a *Volk* means something besides being rooted in a land" and serves as a reminder of this all-important lesson to the nations of the world. It is the combination of a redemptive aesthetics *and* a messianic politics that makes for the possibility of the redemption of the world.

Rosenzweig argues that Judaism, Christianity, art, and the political sphere all seek to create eternity in time. It is their particular responses to time that make art and the state the eternal gods of paganism.[23] Art celebrates the passing of time, while the state refuses time in its quest for eternity. According to Rosenzweig, it is only possible to overcome the eternal gods of paganism through a reappropriation of the pagan's respective approaches to time. As we saw in the last chapter, Christianity creates eternity in time by redeeming art. Christianity risks images but remains tied to the political sphere. Judaism in contrast does not need aesthetics to create community. It therefore does not need to risk images for the sake of the world but rather risks the consequences of the politics of the nations. We have seen that for Rosenzweig Judaism refuses the political by refusing land as its defining mark. Rosenzweig maintains that by existing in the diaspora, Judaism risks the wrath of the nations of the world. This risk is intimately connected to Rosenzweig's notion of witness and representation. In the following section, by comparing Judaism's representational scheme with that of the pagan and the fanatic, we will attempt to understand Rosenzweig's view of politics further.

## The Representational Schemes of the Pagan, Martyr, and Fanatic

Above, I called Rosenzweig's view of the formation of the political sphere a "necessary evil." It is probably more accurate, however, to describe Rosenzweig's view of politics as a necessary illusion. Rosenzweig argues that in the modern world, the illusion that defines politics can become evil. It is both the illusion of the political and the potentially devastating consequences that come from this illusion in the modern world that Rosenzweig seeks to criticize with his idealized view of Judaism in Part 1, Book 3 of *The Star of Redemption*. Let us turn first to an explanation of the difference between politics as illusion and politics as evil.

The political sphere is an illusion for Rosenzweig because it is premised on a faulty idea of representation [*Vertretungsgedanke*]. The basis of political community is the entry of individuals into a collective. The collective allows the individual to achieve a limited sense of commonality with other individuals. That is, the political is the sphere in which individuals represent themselves as individuals and nothing more. It is in this sense that the political is inherently pagan for Rosenzweig. He argues that the Greek polis achieves precisely this conceptual scheme:

> People, state, or whatever else the ancient communities may have been, are lions' dens which the individual may see tracks leading into, but not out of. In a very real sense the community confronts man as a whole: he knows that he is but a part. He is but a part vis-à-vis these wholes, only a representative [*Vertreter*] vis-à-vis these categories. . . . For the individual, caste is the state itself wherever it exists. For the ancient state knows only the immediate relationship of citizen and state; the ancient state is simply the whole whose configuration absorbs its parts."[24]

Rosenzweig maintains that the "people state" is an illusion from an ethical point of view because a conceptual scheme that claims that an individual is an individual and nothing more lacks ethical response-ability. If individuals are never more than individuals, they cannot respond to others. We have already seen in chapter 4 how this self-contained, isolated inability to respond to others marks Greek aesthetics and Attic drama in particular. Rosenzweig argues that unlike art, however, the political sphere does not redeem itself. Unlike art, the political sphere is not its own antitoxin. Politics' silencing of the individual does not break open into the responsiveness of speech as art's silence does.

Rosenzweig argues that the political sphere can exist at best as a necessary illusion if it exists in conjunction with a performative apparatus (what Mendelssohn would call "religion" or "a script of a nation") that checks the political sphere's idolatrous lapses. *The Star of Redemption* suggests that in the Greek context, this performative apparatus was the cult:

> Indeed the idea of representation [*Vertretungsgedanke*] encounters very characteristic difficulties in ancient law. Every individual is only himself, only individual. Only in the cult is the idea of representation unavoidable, especially in sacrifice—both with regard to the sacrificer and the sacrificed person.[25]

Perhaps surprisingly, Rosenzweig argues that it is the pagan Greek cult that comes closest to the proper idea of ethical witnessing. It should be clear by this point, however, that this view is completely consistent with Rosenzweig's idea of idolatry as a performative error. *The Star of Redemption* suggests that the Greek cult is both pagan and potentially ethical not because of what it worships but because of how it worships. In its performative dimension, the Greek cult anticipates the representational scheme of the witness. Nonetheless, Rosenzweig maintains that the Greek cult remains pagan because, even in its anticipation of witnessing, its representational schema remains too individualistic:

> Even here, however, this difficulty manifests itself, for we observe throughout the endeavor to provide the sacrificer with personal purity, and the sacrificed person with personal liability for death, whether for example as a criminal or at least as the object of a magically effective curse. Nothing could be further from ancient individualism than the idea that precisely someone personally pure is suitable for offering a sacrifice on behalf of all, or that one personally impure is suitable for suffering it, this idea of the absolutely communal surety for man-kind by all men—nothing, that is, except the idea of the common surety of mankind.[26]

Thus the cult, while anticipating the representational structures of revelation, remains idolatrous. Still, in the cult, a proper conception of representation is unavoidable. Despite its idolatrous tendencies, the cult, unlike the ancient state, cannot but anticipate revelation's representational scheme.

Rosenzweig's point about the idolatrous yet potentially redemptive representational scheme of the ancient state is for the purpose of contrast to the modern state, which, he argues, borders on the fanatical. Rosenzweig contends that one important difference between the ancient and modern state is that the ancient state, like the pagan, recognizes its finite mortality, while the modern state, like the fanatic, does not.[27] The pagan goes to war as a necessity, but does not seek redemption through war. In the last chapter we saw that Rosenzweig argues that modern nationalism is the political transformation of a particularly Christian religious belief in the sacrifice of the individual in war for the sake of the nation. Rosenzweig argues further that modern nations regard themselves as immortal for theological reasons. The modern nation states' wars are holy wars. He continues that since the advent of Christianity, the peoples of the world cannot distinguish between *salus*, self-preservation, and *fides*, the keeping of the pledged word: "for the Church, *salus* and *fides* are one and the same thing."[28] Every war becomes a holy war; every act of self-preservation is pledged to a higher being:

> Precisely because they are not really God's people, because they are still only in process of so becoming, therefore they cannot draw this fine distinction; they simply cannot know how much a war is holy war, and how much merely a secular war. But in any case they know that God's will somehow realizes itself in the martial fortunes of their state.[29]

For Rosenzweig, the notion that all wars are holy and the resulting continued attempt to assimilate others into a nation's own idealization of itself is a tendency toward which Christian civilization and its aftermath cannot avoid.

It is in the context of this Christian and post-Christian tendency toward fanatical nationalism that we should understand Rosenzweig's argument about Judaism's messianic politics. Rosenzweig writes: "In the whole Christian world, the Jew is practically the only human being who cannot take war seriously, and this makes him the only genuine pacifist."[30] This is because "the Jewish people has left its holy war behind in its mythical antiquity." Judaism does not live by the time of the nations, which, Rosenzweig agrees with Hegel, is the time of war. Rather, Judaism lives through the time that comes from its own blood, through a liturgical calendar that separates Judaism from the time of the world. The Christian and post-Christian worlds are eternally engaged in war *precisely because they are not really God's people, because they are still only in the process of so becoming*. In contrast to Christianity,

> The Jewish people has already reached the goal toward which the nations are still moving. It has that inner unity of faith and life which, while Augustine may ascribe it to the Church in the form of the unity between *fides* and *salus*, is still no more than a dream to the nations within the Church. But just because it has that unity, the Jewish people is bound to be outside of the world that does not yet have it.[31]

The Christian and post-Christian worlds can only imitate the unity that the Jewish people already possess.[32]

Rosenzweig's non-Zionism is his messianic politics. By achieving eternity outside of the state, by way of its own blood, Rosenzweig argues that Judaism defies the state's, and modern nationalism's, totalizing tendencies. While the modern nation-state assimilates everything into itself, Judaism simply will not be assimilated into a state. Judaism thus exists as a check against totalizing politics, as a messianic politics.[33] Judaism therefore, by definition, resists the temptation to become like the nations of the world. Rosenzweig argues that if Zionism is an attempt to become like the nations of the world, as Herzl would have it, Judaism must resist that temptation also. Judaism's messianic politics serves as a check against the false conceptual schemes of the pagan and the fanatic.

In contrast to both pagan politics and fanatical politics, Rosenzweig argues that Judaism's messianic politics recognizes that the Jewish people are both more and less than a *Volk*. The Jews are more than a *Volk* because Judaism does embody complete truth. At the same time, however, the Jews are less than a *Volk* because Judaism must wait for others to complete the world's redemption. As we saw in the last chapter, Judaism must wait for Christianity to do this work. Despite Christianity's religious and fanatical tendencies, which can be played out in both abstract theological and concrete political terms, Judaism must wait for Christianity, and all the world's nations, to redeem the world. It is here that we come to the first sense in which Rosenzweig argues that Judaism risks politics. Rosenzweig maintains that Judaism's messianic politics risks the wrath not only of antisemitism, but of modern nationalism also. The Jewish community is representative of all humankind and stands as a witness to the representational scheme of revelation.[34] This act of witnessing is an act fraught with risk. Rosenzweig suggests that Zionism is an idol because by defining Jewish existence only in political terms, it ironically forgoes the risk of politics.

## Risking Segregation: Aesthetics as Education

As discussed briefly in chapter 4, Rosenzweig argues that only by existing as a separate whole can the Jewish community provide the opportunity for the nations of the world to respond to God's revelation. Once again, the wholeness of Jewish existence is full of risk. Jews risk the wrath of the nations in order to give the nations the opportunity to make God's revelation their own. Rosenzweig argues that if Jews are to live as witness to the nations, Jewish life must restore, albeit in new form, the wholeness or the inner inseparableness of Jewish existence.[35]

The attempt to restore wholeness (*Ganzheit*) to Jewish life became the sole aim of Rosenzweig's program for Jewish education.[36] Shortly before he began work on *The Star of Redemption*, Rosenzweig wrote a short treatise on Jewish education, *It Is Time* (*Zeits ists!*).[37] He addressed his thoughts in an open letter to Hermann Cohen because "the majority of Jews in Germany who intend to live as Jews in Germany honor you [Cohen] as their intellectual leader."[38] Composed at the Balkan front, *It Is Time* outlines Rosenzweig's proposals for Jewish education in Germany. He begins by distinguishing between Christian and Jewish education, a distinction that points to Judaism's self-contained, inwardly connected essence. For Rosenzweig, the problem with previous approaches to Jewish education is that Jewish educators have failed to recognize the essential difference between Judaism and Christianity in regard to this fact:

> The resolutions of the Rabbinical Assembly which dealt with these things in the summer of 1916 make it appear, consciously or unconsciously, as if the main difficulty, aside from organizational ones, were the same with which Christian religious education [*Religionsunterricht*] is confronted: the difficulty of developing religious feeling by influencing the intellection. In reality, however, the problem of Jewish religious instruction is quite different. We are not concerned with creating an emotional center of this world to which the student is introduced by

other school subjects, but with his introduction into the "Jewish sphere" which is independent from, and even opposed to, his non-Jewish surroundings.[39]

Notice that Rosenzweig's claims for the differences between Jewish and Christian education hinges on his view of religion. He contends that Christian education is an attempt to develop religious feeling while Jewish education has nothing to do with this. Though Judaism is a religious denomination (*Konfession*), it is not a religion (*Religion*). We saw in the last chapter that Christianity necessarily risks becoming a religion. In contrast to Christianity, Rosenzweig argues that religion is not a risk for Judaism; its risk is found in relation to politics.

Rosenzweig maintains that the Jewish response to the Enlightenment and emancipation had destroyed the self-contained Jewish sphere. While Rosenzweig in no way sought to return to a pre-Enlightenment era, his plans for Jewish education are permeated with the desire to return Judaism's essential form—*Ganzheit*—to modern Jewish life. His practical plans for Jewish education were based on the notion of Judaism as self-contained world that must be repossessed:

"To possess" a world does not mean to possess it within another world which includes its possessor; thus the German may possess another civilization—ancient or modern—because or insofar as it also belongs to the spiritual universe which includes him; therefore he can acquire it without leaving his own world, maybe even without understanding its language; because in any event he will understand it only as translated into the "language" of his world. . . . With our problem, things are quite different. It is true that the world to be acquired also belongs, in a very important sense, to the fundamental forces of the surrounding world, but it is not to be acquired in that sense. Our own Jewish world ought not to be experienced as a mere preliminary stage to that other world. Such a procedure may be permissible for others, but not for us.[40]

A Jewish world is possible if and only if it is precisely that: a world that is Jewish. A Jewish world is separate from the rest of the world. As in the case of paganism, wholeness means separation and isolation.

Rosenzweig argues that while the pagan and the Christian create meaning through art, the Jew creates meaning through her language.[41] For Rosenzweig, an acquaintance and then intimacy with Hebrew is the only path to Jewish *Ganzheit*, as he wrote to his parents in October 1916 regarding the Rabbinical Assembly's debate on Jewish education: "The attitude toward Hebrew is the sore point, far more than the debate itself brought out. For Hebrew must be pursued not as the subject of study, but as the very medium through which the entire content of [Judaism] is presented."[42] Rosenzweig argues that Hebrew must be used as the language of Judaism, and not merely studied as a dead language. Rosenzweig suggests in *It Is Time* that if the classroom focused first on the Jewish sacred calendar and increasingly on Jewish texts, Hebrew would be learned as the language of the Jewish world and not as the dead grammar of the past. Only by acquiring a Jewish language through its use would it be possible to reacquire a Jewish world. The mere use of Hebrew would lead the way from text to life. The classroom would prepare the student for the learning that is Jewish life itself. In contrast to the modern world, the Jewish world knows no distinction between education and life.[43] Language is life and learning Hebrew allows Jews to live a Jewish life. For Rosenzweig, Jewish learning by way of the language of the past can develop into Jewish existence in the present.

For this reason, a return to Hebrew is not for Rosenzweig, as it is for the Zionists, the creation of a new language. In a 1925 review essay of the Zionist Jakob Klatzkin's translation of Spinoza's *Ethics* into Hebrew, Rosenzweig makes his position clear:

> Language cannot develop as it wants to but as it must. And for the Hebrew language, this "must" does not lie within itself, as in every normal national language but from something beyond its "spokenness," that is, from the heritage of the past, and the connection maintained with those whose Jewishness is essentially that of the heir.[44]

For Rosenzweig, a return to Hebrew is a return to the past. A return to the past, by way of a comprehensive approach to Jewish education could, Rosenzweig believed, recreate Jewish wholeness in the present.

The vision of Jewish education expressed in *It Is Time* was never achieved. As Rosenzweig recognized, if Jewish education was to proceed in the ways he hoped, a new training ground for Jewish teachers would first be necessary. The Jewish teacher, who would be a teacher-scholar, would have to be a new kind of person embodying similar tensions to those of *The Star of Redemption*'s new thinker. In his letter to Cohen, Rosenzweig proposed a new academy for the *Wissenschaft des Judentums* that would produce scholars who would equally be teachers for the Jewish community. Cohen was very enthusiastic about Rosenzweig's plan and was able to generate a great deal of support for a new academy from intellectuals and community leaders.[45] However, due to Cohen's death in April 1918 and to Germany's defeat in the Great War and the consequent economic crisis, the academy, though established, was different from what Rosenzweig had envisioned.[46] While committed to developing more fully engaged scholars, and consciously different from the *Wissenschaft des Judentums*, the academy ultimately was not interested in a comprehensive program for rejuvenating Jewish life in Germany.[47] When it became apparent that the new academy would continue to separate research from teaching, Rosenzweig, though still connected to it, turned to other projects. Recognizing that a comprehensive approach to Jewish education was not at that time possible, Rosenzweig founded, in 1920, the *Freies Jüdisches Lehrhaus*, which focused solely on adult education.

The plan for the *Lehrhaus* was an attempt to develop an alternative model of Jewish study from that of both the academy and the *Wissenschaft des Judentums*. It is in the context of the creation of the *Lehrhaus* that we find Rosenzweig's oft-quoted words: "Books are not now the prime need of the day. But what we need more than ever, or at least as much as ever, are people—Jewish people."[48] The *Lehrhaus* would begin modestly by simply introducing adults to Hebrew and to Jewish texts and history. The goal would be engagement with Judaism, involvement in Judaism, not mastery of Judaism. For this modest plan to affect and create a Jewish community, a new kind of teacher would be required. This teacher would have to be "much more and much less" than an ordinary teacher. The new teacher must be "a master and at the same time a pupil."[49] This new teacher would produce a new type of learning environment in which "the teachers will be discovered in the same discussion room and the same discussion period as the students."[50] The aim of discussion would not be to find a solution to a particular problem posed by Jewish texts, history, or existence, but rather to produce a conversation. For Rosenzweig, the essence and core of Jewish life is precisely an ongoing conversation about things Jewish, a conversation to which the Enlightenment had put a stop.

The modest prospect of an open engagement and dialogue with Jewish texts could, Rosenzweig argued, rejuvenate German Judaism. The reinstitution of the ongoing Jewish conversation could itself be the stepping stone toward the *Ganzheit*, the wholeness, of Jewish communal life. By beginning modestly, merely by making conversation possible, by merely being open to the possibility of Jewish life, the Jewish community could renew itself. Rosenzweig argued, however, that to renew itself, the Jewish community must recognize both the interconnected wholeness it had lost and the current dogmas that kept it from regaining this wholeness. Mere openness could, Rosenzweig suggested, open whole new possibilities for the Jewish community:

> I will dare to predict only this much: that each will see the whole [*das Ganze*]. For just as it is impossible to attain to the whole without modestly beginning with that which is nearest, so it is impossible for a person to attain to the whole, the whole that is determined for him, if he has found the strength to make that first simple and most modest beginning. It is necessary for him to free himself from those stupid claims that would impose Juda "ism" on him as a canon of a definite, circumscribed "Jewish duties" (vulgar orthodoxy), or "Jewish task"

(vulgar Zionism), or—God forbid—"Jewish ideas" (vulgar liberalism). If he has prepared himself quite simply to have everything that happens to him, inwardly and outwardly, happen to him in a Jewish way—his vocation, his nationality, his marriage, and even, if that has to be, his Juda"ism"—then he may be certain that with the simple assumption of that infinite "pledge" he will become in reality "wholly Jew" ["*ganz Jude*"].[51]

Rosenzweig argues that vulgar orthodoxy, vulgar Zionism, and, perhaps worst of all, vulgar liberalism keep Jews from being wholly Jewish. Each dogma imposes a limitation on Jewish existence, reducing Jewishness to some particular sphere of life, rather than allowing Jewish existence to exist in its wholeness. The establishment of the *Lehrhaus* rested upon this principle of wholeness, as Rosenzweig reminded everyone at the *Lehrhaus*'s opening: "You should regard every individual aspect, every individual lecture or seminar you attend, as a part of the whole [*das Ganze*], which is offered to you only for the sake of the whole."[52] To make oneself and all parts of oneself part of the wholeness of Jewish existence is the goal of all of Jewish life and education, for Rosenzweig.[53]

The word "goal" is important here. Rosenzweig maintains that Judaism, although complete and whole in and of itself, is not only a reality, but also always a goal. Like the witness, Judaism uses the past for the sake of the present. The present, however, is also always the future. The Jewish reflection upon the Jewish past forms at the same time the goal of the Jewish future. Historical time knows no future, but only the endless passing of time. To truly be future, then, Judaism must exist separately from the world of historical time. The future, for Rosenzweig, is a radical future; it is a time that is itself timeless. The future cannot exist in time, for time always passes away. Judaism for the Jew is thus both future and timeless: "For the Jew, Judaism is more than a power in the past, more than a curiosity in our own era; to us it is the goal of the future. And since it is future, therefore it is a world of its own, quite aside from the world which surrounds us."[54]

Rosenzweig's writings on "Judaism," as opposed to Jewish people or life, refer then to the idealized goal and meaning of Jewish existence. "Judaism," for Rosenzweig, is self-consciously idealized. This is nowhere as true as in Part 3, Book 1 of *The Star of Redemption*. Rosenzweig is aware that the discussion of Judaism in *The Star of Redemption* is wholly idealized and ahistorical. This, indeed, is his point. Rosenzweig argues that the goal of Judaism is to be beyond history; it is to be beyond the time of the nations. The time of the nations is the time of eternal war and strife; this is the meaning of history. Rosenzweig argues that Judaism ought to exist beyond history because Judaism is witness to the world of God's eternal revelation. Judaism represents that which is more than this world, that which is more than eternal human strife: the possibility of divine love.

Rather than reflecting a backward looking, idolizing perspective on the pre-emancipation era, Rosenzweig's discussion of Judaism in *The Star of Redemption* reflects what he believes is the foremost goal of Jewish education: the self-contained, interconnected wholeness that comes from Jewish language, learning, and life. For Rosenzweig, "Judaism" *qua* Judaism is always goal, always future. "Judaism" does not refer to the concrete reality of living Jews, but to the goal of Jewish life. Rosenzweig is quite aware of the historical reality of Jewish life and the ways in which Jewish reality changes throughout history. Indeed, his proposals for and work in Jewish education are premised on the historical reality of early twentieth century European Judaism. Rosenzweig claims that the Enlightenment and emancipation had destroyed the self-contained Jewish sphere not because Jews never, in the past, interacted with the external world. Again, Jews exist both in relation to and separately from the external world. His claim is rather that the Enlightenment, or more precisely the Jewish response to the Enlightenment, had destroyed the inner connections of the community:

> What is new is not so much the collapse of the outer barriers; even previously, while the ghetto had certainly sheltered the Jew, it had not shut him off. He moved beyond its bounds, and what the ghetto gave him was only peace, home, a home for his spirit. What is new, is not that the Jew's feet could now take him farther than before—in the Middle Ages the Jew was not an especially sedentary, but rather a comparatively mobile element of medieval society. The new feature is that the wanderer no longer returns at dusk. The gates of the ghetto no longer close behind him, allowing him to spend the night in solitary learning.[55]

Rosenzweig's hope was certainly not to have the gates of the ghetto return. This would be the vulgar solution of orthodoxy. At the same time, his hope was also not to pretend that the gates of the ghetto did not serve a positive end: they made the solitary learning of Judaism possible. The dishonesty that claims that gates never do any good is the vulgarity of liberalism. Rosenzweig sought a new future for Judaism, a future that was different from its past. This future, however, is not divorced from its past, as Rosenzweig argues the ideology of vulgar Zionism is. The new Jewish future is tied to the past; it uses the Jewish past to respond to the present and in so doing creates possibilities that never existed before for the future. Rosenzweig maintains that the open dialogue of education could aid in the anti-dogmatic (re)creation of the interconnected wholeness of a Jewish world.

Rosenzweig warns nonetheless that the interconnected wholeness of a Jewish world can become an idol. When Jewish existence is divorced from its outer reality it becomes idolatrous. When Jews approach the world with denial, disdain, and mortification, Judaism no longer plays its role as a messianic politics. Rosenzweig maintains that this is a Jewish danger consonant with Zionism's danger. Both Jewish segregation and Zionism turn Jewish revelation into an idol. Both deny the hermeneutical responsibility that Jews bear for the past legacy of Jewish revelation and its continuing mission to redeem an unredeemed world. Rosenzweig advocates a diaspora Judaism because he argues that the diaspora is best suited to avoiding the idolatrous tendency of complete segregation. By living a diaspora existence, Jews could risk politics for the sake of the redemption of the world.

Rosenzweig declared continually his commitment to the political risks of the separation and relation intrinsic to diaspora Jewish life. At the end of January 1923, he wrote to Rudolf Hallo:

> I am perhaps especially innocent with respect to the problem of *Deutschtum* and *Judentum*. I believe that my return to Judaism [*Verjudung*] has not made me a worse but a better German. I do not view the generation before us as better Germans. . . . Were someone to suspend me between tenterhooks, tearing me in two pieces, I would surely know with which of these two halves my heart . . . would go; I also know that I would not survive the operation.[56]

Rosenzweig saw himself as a Jew *and* a German. He believed that he made a contribution to Germany as a Jew. Indeed, in this letter he states, "*The Star* will surely one day and with justice be regarded with gratitude by the German spirit as a gift from its Jewish enclave." Including Cohen's *Religion* with *The Star of Redemption*, he adds, "Our work [however] will be honored by Germany only posthumously in some distant time." There is no ignoring the poignancy of Rosenzweig's prophetic comment. His and Cohen's work have come to be honored by Germany as a gift from its Jewish enclave only posthumously in some distant time. This distant time, of course, is the time after the German destruction of European Jewry. Though, as we have seen, Rosenzweig was aware of the potentially lethal dangers of Christian and German nationalist antisemitism, he certainly could not have foreseen the horrors to come. Indeed, in 1923 the German-Jewish community was experiencing a spiritual renaissance of sorts, due in no small part to the success of Rosenzweig's *Lehrhaus*. Tragically, Rosenzweig's description of the risk diaspora Jewry faced from politics has been verified by historical events. In the next chapter I turn to the question of whether Rosenzweig's view of the Jewish relation to politics can be said to be valid in any way after the Jewish political response to the Holocaust: the establishment of the State of Israel.

# *Eight*

## After Israel: Rosenzweig's Philosophy of Risk Reconsidered

IN THE LAST CHAPTER we explored what we might call Rosenzweig's "blood hermeneutic," his argument that blood, and not land, signifies hope for the future. Intimately connected to Rosenzweig's blood hermeneutic is the argument that Judaism's mission to the nations of the world is to risk and bear the often brutal and violent consequences of world politics. Rosenzweig argues that because they are the blood community and in this way representative for all humanity, the Jewish community suffers for the nations of the world. After the Holocaust and after the creation of the State of Israel how might we understand a contemporary application of Rosenzweig's hermeneutic? Does the existence of the State of Israel in light of the brutal murder of six million Jews show Rosenzweig's philosophy to be at best anachronistic or irretrievably flawed and even offensive at worst?

In order to consider a contemporary application of Rosenzweig's hermeneutic, it is essential that we recall first his emphasis on idolatry as a mistake in worship. This means that, unlike Cohen, for whom the eradication of idolatry begins with right thinking, Rosenzweig emphasizes that idolatry is something that is always risked, particularly by those closest to God's revelation. On a theoretical level, this already indicates the ways in which Rosenzweig's philosophy does not aim to develop a fixed set of dogmas, but rather attempts to provide resources for thinking about the complex relation between Judaism and modernity. We will see in this chapter that this theoretical framework was in fact already borne out in Rosenzweig's own thought about Zionism. Rosenzweig remained open to Zionism, despite his warnings about its potential dangers. This important point provides us a starting place for reconsidering his thought after the establishment of the State of Israel.

### Rosenzweig's Non-Zionism: The Historical Record

To consider the possibility of a contemporary application of Rosenzweig's blood hermeneutic, we turn first in this chapter to the practical question of the establishment of the State of Israel in light of Rosenzweig's non-Zionism. I begin to do so with a consideration of the recent remarks of the late Gillian Rose, whose criticism of Rosenzweig's view of politics, and Jewish politics in particular, has been among the most scathing. Rose seeks to challenge Rosenzweig's "project of expounding redemption and the Kingdom by elevating Judaism as 'life' beyond the political history of 'the world.'"[1] In keeping with her broad argument in *Judaism and Modernity*, Rose maintains that Rosenzweig misconstrues both "Judaism" and "modernity," along with their relation to each other.[2] In particular, Rose argues that "Rosenzweig's attempt to exorcise power from love, and love from power, to substitute love for 'freedom,' as the third which redeems 'the world,' spoils his theology, his anthropology, and his cosmology—his ideas of God and man and world."[3]

To put Rose's argument into more straightforward terms, she contends that Rosenzweig crudely splits Christianity and Judaism into worldliness and other-worldliness, in order to save Judaism from being dirtied by politics and history. From Rose's perspective, Rosenzweig's thought is a historical, philosophical, and ethical failure. She claims that Rosenzweig historically misconstrues Judaism, while philosophically and ethically he misconstrues the complex meanings and responsibilities of living in this world. Where Rose poses a theoretical challenge to Rosenzweig's view of Judaism and politics, the establishment of the State of Israel would seem to pose the practical, and in fact definitive, counterpart to Rose's critique.

Is Rosenzweig accused fairly, in Rose's words, of "elevating Judaism as 'life' beyond the political history of 'the world'"? The answer to this question is both yes and no. Rosenzweig does argue that Judaism challenges the political order. Indeed, the challenge that Judaism raises to the political order is the subject of Part 3, Book 1 of *The Star of Redemption*. As we saw in chapter 3, however, this argument is a philosophical argument and not a historical argument. Rosenzweig knows full well that Judaism has had political dimensions. His argument is that Jewish revelation offers the world the possibility of redemption. Redemption for Rosenzweig is not apolitical; it is, however, beyond politics. Before turning and returning to some of the philosophical underpinnings of Rosenzweig's arguments, however, let us turn first to what he actually said about Judaism's entry into the political world, that is, about Zionism. We saw in the last chapter that from Rosenzweig's perspective, Zionism is idolatry because it loses sight of the Jewish mission to the nations. Nonetheless, because of his emphasis on the openness of the future as well as his insistence on the distinction between Judaism and philosophy, two themes that we have seen are intimately connected in Rosenzweig's musings on idolatry, Rosenzweig remained open to Zionism. Where Rosenzweig's ethical monotheism differs from Cohen's is that Rosenzweig maintains that only by risking idolatry can Judaism fulfill its mission. In the final analysis, Rosenzweig's thought suggests that the Jewish people must risk the idolatry of Zionism.

To understand Rosenzweig's ambivalent embrace of Zionism, let us turn first back to his view of diaspora Judaism and to the vexed question of *Deutschtum* and *Judentum*, the German-Jewish relation. We cannot discuss the relation between *Deutschtum* and *Judentum* without turning to Cohen's 1915 essay "Deutschtum und Judentum" and to Rosenzweig's reply of the same title.[4] Cohen's essay was written as a wartime defense of Jewish loyalty to the German state. While many Jews had hoped that the war would unify them with their fellow Germans, the opposite seemed to have occurred. The war produced antisemitic complaints about perceived Jewish disloyalty and lack of participation in the war. This antisemitic backlash led in turn to growing support for Zionism among young German Jews. Disillusioned both by the war and increasing antisemitism, young German Jews identified increasingly with Zionism's fundamental premise, that Jews must create their own national identity, for nothing but antisemitism and suffering would come from diaspora existence.

Cohen's essay sought to show that Germanism and Judaism were not antithetical, a premise that both antisemites and Zionists shared. In "Deutschtum und Judentum" Cohen argues that Germanism and Judaism represent one confluent value. Deriving from Greek Platonism and biblical culture respectively, Germanism and Judaism are the complementary expressions of universal, rational, social ethics.[5] Germanism and Judaism find their most basic point of contact in the recognition that the human is never a "mere means":

> On this main point everyone should feel again the inner community [*Gemeinschaft*] between Germanism and Judaism. For the concept of humanity has its source in the Messianism of the Israelite prophets. And it stands outside of doubt, foreseen also by Herder, that the biblical spirit has had an effect also in German humanism as [its] deepest cause.[6]

Cohen derives the German concept of humanity from Kant and in fact often refers to Germany as "the nation of Kant." As Steven Schwarzschild has rightly pointed out,

> Germanism [for Cohen] does not designate the narrow and, as Cohen knew only too well from his own lifelong experiences, historically disastrous reality of Germany but the intermediate embodiment, as he wished to see it, of the

> progressive development of humanistic values from Plato through Maimonides to Kant, the French Revolution, and the socialist movement which had, by that time, achieved greater political successes in Germany than anywhere else.[7]

In philosophical terms, "Germanism" represents a regulative ideal, and not a normative reality. This point goes no less for Cohen's use of "Judaism." As Cohen makes abundantly clear, especially in his *Religion of Reason*, "Judaism" represents an ideal. From the sources of Judaism, we can derive the ethical ideals of biblical culture which have developed into the religion of reason. For Cohen, Judaism and the religion of reason are something we strive for. As Rosenzweig reiterates in his own terms, Judaism, like all regulative ideals, is always a goal. And the goal is always more than the reality.

Cohen's essay "Deutschtum und Judentum" incited tremendous controversy. Within Jewish circles, Martin Buber's response to it is perhaps best known. Writing in his journal *Der Jude*, Buber argued in 1916 that Cohen had failed to make a distinction between state and people. According to Buber, Cohen defined nationality as a purely natural fact, and thereby failed to understand the more far reaching reality of peoplehood, a reality that transcends natural fact and links the Jewish people to each other throughout history. Buber maintains that the Jewish people, "Judaism," should thus not be understood on par with the German state, "Germanism":

> The Jewish people—not a natural fact but a historical reality that can be compared to no other; not a concept but an awesome living and dying before your and my eyes; not the means for the transmission of the religion but the bearer of this religion and with it all Jewish ideology, all Jewish ethos, all Jewish sociality debased as it has been to the dust. Jews in this or that place, in this or that fatherland may "possess their political consciousness and feeling for a home state"; the Jewish people is the great homeless people.[8]

Because it pointed to the continuity of Jewish existence that depended on the historical reality of Jewish peoplehood, Buber's formulation was intended to be pro-Zionist. At the same time, and for the same reason, Buber suggests that Jewish peoplehood does not run the same risks of other forms of nationalism precisely because it is so much more than natural fact. Buber argues that Jewish peoplehood is an ethos that has spiritual and social implications far greater than any natural fact of statehood. The natural fact of Jewish statehood would always be subsumed under the reality of Jewish peoplehood.

Like Buber, Rosenzweig accuses Cohen of making a category error. Rosenzweig maintains that Germanism and Judaism are not two things that can be compared to each other; they are wholly different and should not be confused. But, whereas Buber accuses Cohen of not recognizing the breadth and depth of Judaism, Rosenzweig accuses Cohen of giving Germanism too much breadth and depth. Rosenzweig accuses Cohen not of denying the scope of Jewish peoplehood and Jewish religion, as Buber does, but of making Germanism into a religion:

> One may compare Germanism and Anglo-Saxonism, Germanism and Ottomanism [*Osmanentum*], not Germanism and Judaism. . . . [Judaism] is no nation like other nations and it has, despite the naiveté of vulgar Zionism, also never been. . . . Cohen . . . gives Germanism the dangerous honor of being assessed not as a nationality but as a religion [*Religion*]. The root of all the strangeness of Cohenian writing is laid out here.[9]

Notice that from Rosenzweig's perspective the danger of Cohen's approach is its religious dimension. In the context of Rosenzweig's remarks about religion, he seems to be indicating that Cohen is attributing a modern, Christian theological attribute to Germanism. Rosenzweig maintains that this is deeply dangerous. It is not Cohen's lack of recognition for the Jewish people that Rosenzweig finds disturbing, but rather Cohen's religious, quasi-theological embrace of Germanism that he argues is deeply troubling.

Though still not a Zionist, Rosenzweig's position in this essay in regard to Germanism and Judaism is closer in form to Buber's than to Cohen's. Like Buber, Rosenzweig argues that it is a category error to equate Germanism and Judaism. However, perhaps despite himself, in terms of content, Rosenzweig begins sounding more and more like Cohen. Ironically, Rosenzweig uses Cohen's own argument about the meaning of Judaism against him. Rosenzweig borrows from Cohen the criticism of nationalist aspiration on the part of the Jewish people and attributes it also to German nationalism. Of course, Cohen would contend that he is neither a Jewish nationalist nor a German nationalist but is rather presenting ideals, and not realities. In criticizing Cohen in the manner he does, Rosenzweig points to what he considers a major flaw within Cohen's thought. Though "Judaism" is also a goal for Rosenzweig, "Judaism" is never reducible to an idea. While "Judaism" is always future and goal, and while, in this very essay, he states that the Jewish people have never really "been," Judaism and Jews are also always in the here and now. For Rosenzweig, goals and reality can and do converge.

And it is here that we can understand an absolutely fundamental difference between Rosenzweig and Cohen: Rosenzweig thinks we can reach the goal in reality, while Cohen thinks we cannot. No matter how close we get, for Cohen, we will never achieve our goal, whether the goal is Germanism, Judaism, or social justice (all of which, by the way, turn out to be the same thing for Cohen). The Messianic era for Rosenzweig is the achievement of the goal. For Cohen, the goal will always remain goal. Cohen and Rosenzweig agree that nothing wholly new can happen in historical time. "Progress" of some kind can be made, but things essentially remain the same. Cohen, of course, has greater faith than Rosenzweig in the potential of worldly institutions to affect history. Cohen believes that progress can be made in history. Rosenzweig doubts this. Nevertheless, in the final analysis, both agree that historical time cannot itself produce the Messianic era. Cohen argues that the best we can do is put our energies into helping history move progressively along; Rosenzweig argues that Cohen's optimism is an illusion. For Rosenzweig, once naive optimism is gone, we are left only with history's bankruptcy of possibilities for the future. If something new is to happen, and if things are really to change, history must be interrupted. Judaism, claims Rosenzweig, offers this moment of interruption because it embodies the disruption of God's revelation into the human world.

Having rejected Cohen's rationalized scheme, we nonetheless hear Cohen's echo in the alternative that Rosenzweig proposes to a rationalized, generated God. Rosenzweig states that the Jewish *Volk* do not generate their God, but rather receive and witness God. In his 1914 essay "Atheistic Theology," which was written as criticism of Buber's notion of the Jewish *Volk*, Rosenzweig makes a suggestion consonant with his point here.[10] Atheistic theology, argues Rosenzweig, elevates the community's self-image and interests to the status of the divine. In so doing, atheistic theology in effect obliterates the distinction between the human and God. Arguing against Buber's conception of Jewish peoplehood, Rosenzweig draws on Cohen's insistence on the absolute difference between the human and the divine, a difference maintained by much of traditional Judaism.

Both Cohen and Rosenzweig base their rejection of Zionism on their insistence on the absolute separation between the human and God. Like atheistic theology, Zionism elevates the community's self-perception to the level of the divine. For Cohen and Rosenzweig, Zionism rejects the finitude of the human being, a finitude that always exists in relation to the infinite. By rejecting the finite human being's relation to the infinite God, Zionism at the same time rejects the relation between past and present. The Zionist asserts that the fate of the Jewish people is only in the here and now. Receiving God, for Rosenzweig, means also to witness God. And witnessing, as we have seen throughout this book, is a hermeneutical relation. To witness is to use the past for the sake of the present, and to thereby create a future. Rosenzweig's rejection of Cohen's overly cognitive view of generation (*Erzeugung*) leads him to an embrace of witnessing (*Zeugnis*) that comes from the procreation (*Zeugung*) of future generations.

But Rosenzweig also rebukes the liberal rejection of Zionism for Cohenian reasons. He writes in May 1927 to Benno Jacob, rabbi and representative of anti-Zionist liberal Jews in Germany:

> The anti-Zionist component of liberalism has become traditional, yet it is in need of revision. The reason being that this element of classical liberalism was not primarily religious but a tribute to the tendency toward political and social emancipation that went hand in hand with it. The survival of Jewish liberalism depends on its being able to disengage itself from these contexts. Just as it was a vital question for political liberalism to disengage itself from the economic ideas of its classical period, the Manchester movement and anti-socialism. Synagogical liberalism is now confronted by the same task that confronted Naumann and his fellow fighters: to break away from a classical alliance and a classical opposition, and to preserve its essential meaning for the future.[11]

For Rosenzweig, liberals are not wrong to reject Zionism, but they reject it for the wrong reasons. While the goals of political and social emancipation are worthy ones, Jewish liberals have focused on them at the expense of traditional Jewish values. Liberal Jews must return to the theological dimensions of the rejection of Zionism, and these are the dimensions of existing as witness to God's revelation in the world.

But although they both reject Zionism for this theological reason, Rosenzweig rejects what is ultimately Cohen's liberal critique of Zionism. Rosenzweig's argument suggests that Cohen is philosophically and politically inconsistent in his position. Cohen argues that we conceive rather than receive God. Moreover, while rejecting Zionism's intrinsic relation to Judaism, Cohen nonetheless argues for Germanism's intrinsic relation to Judaism. For Rosenzweig, Judaism is not only an idea but also an existence. So, too, witnessing is an actual, real, physical presence, and not a mental construct. For Rosenzweig, it is the lack of recognition of this basic fact that leads Cohen to make the category error of equating Germanism and Judaism. Cohen falls prey to liberalism which has for too long based itself on abstract ideas, and not on the existence and reality of real people.

As he came to modify his position in later years, Rosenzweig argues that he is not an anti-Zionist, but a "non-Zionist."[12] In a series of letters during May 1927 to Benno Jacob, from which we have already quoted above, Rosenzweig makes his position clear. He argues that he is a non-Zionist, and not an anti-Zionist, precisely because he recognizes the supremacy of existence over ideas.

> I do not believe that a movement should be judged by the standards of its extreme theoreticians. What I mean is that Zionism must not be judged by the theories of Klatzkin, nor the standpoint of the Central-Verein by the work of

> Naumann. We always find the characteristic feature of a movement at that juncture where the movement veers away from the theoretical conclusions and gravitates back to earth. The constant, which must be introduced into the formula before we can use it to calculate reality, is not made up of the little inconsistencies of current politics but of this one great inconsistency that is decisive for the effect, of this angle of refraction which is characteristic of the movement.[13]

Rosenzweig recognizes that, though theoretically flawed, Zionism in practice provides for the possibility of a Jewish reality. By gathering Jews together from all over the world, Zionism has recreated a Jewish world in Rosenzweig's sense, even if Zionist theories do not have this creation of a Jewish world as their specific aim. Rosenzweig offers Benno Jacob an example:

> As for Tel Aviv, the "town of speculators," which most Zionists view as a questionable Zionist achievement—I cannot help being impressed by the fact that all stores there close from *kiddush* to *havdalah*,[14] and that thus, at any rate, the mold into which the content of the Sabbath can flow is provided. Where could you, or one of your liberal colleagues, find so excellent an opportunity for crowded pews?[15]

Rosenzweig maintains that unlike Hermann Cohen, and liberal Jews in general, Zionism makes possible the physical reality of Jewish existence. This reality, as we saw in our discussion of Rosenzweig's views on Jewish education, is absolutely essential if Jewish life is to continue in the modern world. For Rosenzweig, reality is necessary if eternity is to be possible. Without the possibility of actual, existent Jewish life, the eternity of the Jewish people would have no value. Zionism makes this possibility possible; Hermann Cohen and liberalism do not. Zionism, therefore, perhaps despite itself, contributes to the creation of eternity in time. Rosenzweig thus ends his letter to Jacob with the following statement: "According to the words of a philosopher whom I regard as an authority even greater than Hermann Cohen, what is not to come save in eternity will not come in all eternity."[16]

We can now appreciate the interconnections between Rosenzweig's view of idolatry and his ambivalent embrace of Zionism. The philosopher whom Rosenzweig regards "as an authority even greater than Hermann Cohen" is the medieval Jewish philosopher Judah Halevi. Rosenzweig's point in the above quotation is that Cohen is the Jewish anomaly in disregarding the reality of Jewish existence in favor of Jewish ideas. For Rosenzweig, Cohen erred due to his absolute faith in "the false Messiah of the nineteenth century," the false Messiah of historical progress.[17] For Rosenzweig, liberalism of this form is and would be the death of Judaism.

Rosenzweig agrees with Halevi that without the blood of Jews, and the physical reality of Jewish life, Judaism is a meaningless idea that would soon become a non-existent reality.[18] It is here too that Rosenzweig's view of idolatry is in keeping with Halevi's. For both, idolatry is an error in worship. The human being's relation to God is defined through worship, and not through thoughts. Idolatry is always a risk precisely because worship of God is always required.[19] Rosenzweig agrees with Halevi that in order to worship God, the concrete existence of Jewish people is required. Zionism, Rosenzweig recognized, could sustain the Jewish people in a way that liberalism could not.

But Rosenzweig was still not a Zionist. As we have seen throughout this book, he regarded the non-"homey" aspect of Judaism, Jewish *Unheimlichkeit*, as essential to and definitive of Jewish existence. A Jewish home (*Heimat*) exists only in Jewish blood and never in land. Rosenzweig's positive assessment of the effects of Zionism were tempered by his claim that only in relation to diaspora Judaism could Zionism flourish:

> The Zionists would be lost once they lose touch with the Diaspora. Their contact with the Diaspora is the only thing that makes them hold fast to their goal, which means, however, that they must be homeless in time and remain wanderers, even there. Ahad Ha'am's conception of Zionism [as creating in Palestine a 'spiritual center' for world Jewry] is thus quite (unconsciously) correct; only by realizing its connection with Berlin, Lodz . . . will Palestine remain Jewish and also make life in the Diaspora really possible.[20]

Palestine would remain Jewish only in relation to the diaspora. The diaspora is a constant reminder to Zionists that even with a homeland, Jews remain homeless. The diaspora reminds Zionists of Jewish incompleteness, and the incompleteness of the redemption of the world.

But Zionism also makes life in the diaspora possible. The structures of Jewish life in Palestine furnish diaspora Jews with a model of Jewish life. By restoring the physical reality of Jewish life, Zionism allows the diaspora, which remains without physical reality, to strive for such a reality. Though not a Zionist, Rosenzweig actively supported the building up of Palestine as an economically and culturally vibrant Jewish community. He publicly endorsed *Keren Ha-Yesod* (Palestine Foundation Fund, founded in London in 1920 by the World Zionist Organization) and encouraged German Jews of all political persuasions to contribute to it.[21] In his educational work with German youth, Rosenzweig actively encouraged the support of Palestine, while remaining committed to diaspora existence.[22] For Rosenzweig, Zionism and Jewish life in the diaspora are dialectically complementary. Both aim to restore the wholeness to Jewish life and both were necessary for that wholeness. Vulgar liberalism, as much as vulgar Zionism, only further obliterates the possibility of Jewish wholeness. Vulgar liberalism implies that Germanism and Judaism can be mediated into a unified whole, but such a mediated whole could only destroy the separateness that is necessary for Jewish existence.

Rosenzweig rejects the paradox of "Deutschtum und Judentum" as misleading. Germanism and Judaism are not two different things to be mediated into something new. Rather, in their conjunction with one another, Germanism and Judaism remain wholly separate. The wholes of Germanism and Judaism are not comparable to each other; it is a category error to think that they are. Each represents a separate realm of life. Though Germanism and Judaism exist in tension with each other, Germanism does not limit Judaism. In "Bildung und kein Ende," Rosenzweig makes this point clear:

> The Jewishness of a Jew is done an injustice if it is put on the same level as his nationality. One's nationality—the German, for instance—is of necessity differentiated from other nationalities. The German nationality of a Jew excludes his being simultaneously of French or British nationality. A German is after all only a German, not a Frenchman or an Englishman too. . . . The relationship between one's German nationality and one's humanity is one that philosophers of history may meditate upon . . . but there is no "relationship" between one's Jewishness and one's humanity that needs to be discovered, puzzled out, experienced, or created. Here the situation is different: as a Jew one is a human being, as a human being a Jew. One is a *jüdisch Kind* with every breath. . . . Just as Jewishness does not know limitations inside the Jewish individual, so it does not limit that individual himself when he faces the outside world. On the contrary, it makes for his humanity. Strange as it may sound to the obtuse ears of a nationalist, being a Jew is no limiting barrier that cuts Jews off from someone who is limited by being something else.[23]

Rosenzweig contends that in its separateness, in its wholeness, Judaism embraces all. The dynamic of living the universal *through* the particular is, for Rosenzweig, the essence of bearing witness. The witness is always less than the universal but nonetheless represents more than the particular. Judaism contributes to German culture as witness to the universal.

For Rosenzweig, the particularity of concrete Jewish existence, which takes place in the passing on of blood from generation to generation, makes Jewish witnessing possible. Bearing witness takes place in bearing. It is on this issue of concrete existence that Rosenzweig differs from Cohen's liberal position. Cohen rejects Zionism because he argues that Judaism represents the universal and Judaism's universality cannot be limited to any particular existence, especially the existence of Jewish blood. Rosenzweig rejects Zionism not by way of a claim to Judaism's universality, but by way of a claim to Jewish particularity. It is the particularity of Jewish existence, and in particular of Jewish blood, that makes

Judaism incompatible with Zionism. For Rosenzweig, Judaism is not, and should not become, like the nations of the world. It is this same point, however, that allows Rosenzweig to become, toward the end of his life, open to Zionism's possibilities. Because Zionism offers a way toward the particularity of concrete Jewish existence, toward Jewish wholeness, Zionism could, for Rosenzweig, redeem itself.

## Risk and Judgment

Rose's argument about Rosenzweig is misleading not only in regard to the historical record of Rosenzweig's approach to Judaism's relation to politics but also in terms of the philosophical underpinnings of Rosenzweig's thought. Rosenzweig's ambivalence toward Zionism was not a late addition to his thought, but is consistent with *The Star of Redemption*'s philosophical approach. As we have seen throughout this book, *The Star of Redemption* consciously uses idealized models to make hermeneutical arguments about both Judaism and modernity.[24] Neither Judaism nor modernity is monolithic for Rosenzweig. As we have seen, Rosenzweig seeks in *The Star of Redemption* to think through both Judaism and philosophy by questioning their very identities. It certainly is possible to read Rosenzweig as Rose does. But to do so is to replace Rosenzweig's inherently hermeneutical argument, both within and beyond *The Star of Redemption*, with a purely reductive one.

Ironically, Rose's analysis of Rosenzweig violates her own recommendation for how to do philosophy. In *Mourning Becomes the Law*, her last book before her death, Rose criticizes precisely the deterministic approach that she herself takes toward *The Star of Redemption*:

> From Plato to Marx, I would argue, it is always possible to take the claims and conceptuality of philosophical works (I say "works" not "texts": the former implying the labour of the concept inseparable from its formal characteristics as opposed to the latter with its connotations of signifiers, the symbolic and semiotics) deterministically or aporetically—as fixed, closed conceptual structures, colonising being with the garrison of thought; or according to the difficulty which the conceptuality represents by leaving gaps and silences in the mode of representation.[25]

Rose reads *The Star of Redemption* deterministically as opposed to aporetically. As we have seen, especially in chapter 3, *The Star of Redemption*'s structure—that is the work itself ("the labour of the concept inseparable from its formal characteristics")—suggests a hermeneutical approach to the identities of Judaism, philosophy, and modernity. Rosenzweig's ability to think about Zionism in potentially positive terms is linked to *The Star of Redemption*'s philosophical arguments about idolatry and risk. Both the form and the content of *The Star of Redemption*'s argument emphasize the indeterminacy of the future and the risk and ambiguity intrinsic to human freedom.

In connection with *The Star of Redemption*'s argument about risk and the future, *The Star of Redemption*, despite Rose's claims, recognizes both violence and coercion. Rose contends that along with the dichotomy between Judaism and politics, Rosenzweig presents a dichotomy between love and violence:

> Without violence-in-love and coercion-in-commandment, Judaism and Christianity are deprived of their political history and hence of their sacred history; without coming to know his will to power, man is deprived of finding faith through his ambivalent love, and God is deprived of his freedom.[26]

Once again, Rose's argument is feasible only if we approach *The Star of Redemption* deterministically. As we have seen, especially in chapter 6, inherent in Rosenzweig's views of the Jewish-Christian relation, of interpersonal dialogue, as well as of the dynamics of revelation itself is the recognition of the relation between love and violence. Recall that for Rosenzweig love is inherently judgmental. Read aporetically, *The Star of Redemption* does not maintain a dichotomy between love and law or between revelation and coercion. Freedom, for Rosenzweig, is rooted in the ambiguity of loving and being loved by others. Both loving and being loved are inherently violent, argues Rosenzweig. In fact, the argument of *The Star of Redemption* suggests that love is commanding and revelation is coercive. The coercion intrinsic to love does not negate human freedom. Rather, it challenges us to choose our responses carefully. Moreover, we need not respond to God's revelation or to another person; this too is a choice. Indeed, we have seen repeatedly that paganism—not responding—is an authentically truthful and honest choice, for Rosenzweig.

Finally, and perhaps most tellingly, Rosenzweig's view of the necessity of risking idolatry points to *The Star of Redemption*'s conscious awareness of the uncertainty and ambiguity that permeates all human experience, especially of the divine. Indeed, the fanatic is someone who for Rosenzweig denies this uncertainty and ambiguity and in so doing creates the kinds of dichotomies Rose accuses *The Star of Redemption* of creating. Rose's reading of Rosenzweig is appealing because of its simplicity. *The Star of Redemption* is difficult because of its complexity. Even if it fails in making its arguments about Judaism and modernity, there can be no doubt that it succeeds in making us question both. This sort of questioning was precisely Rosenzweig's philosophical and hermeneutical goal. Like the great works Rose describes, *The Star of Redemption* leaves gaps "according to the difficulty that the conceptuality represents." The difficulty is over the definitions of Judaism, modernity, and philosophy themselves. *The Star of Redemption* does not try to resolve deterministically these difficulties but to question these determinations themselves. It is in this context that Rosenzweig's growing ambivalence about Zionism is in accord with the philosophical approach of *The Star of Redemption* itself, despite the differences between the two.

## A Jewish Return to History?

But what would Rosenzweig say about the establishment of the modern State of Israel? My interest is not in what the man Rosenzweig might say. This question cannot be answered and if it could, the answer would be beside the point. Here I would like again to endorse Rose's approach to philosophical works. If *The Star of Redemption* and Rosenzweig's other philosophical writings are great works, and I maintain they are, then where does the labor of Rosenzweig's concepts and their formal characteristics point us? The work of the contemporary Jewish thinker Michael Wyschogrod offers us an important opportunity to evaluate Rosenzweig's thought in a more contemporary context. Indeed, the parallel between Wyschogrod's and Rosenzweig's thought is striking. At the same time, there are some significant differences between the two, differences that should help us to think about Rosenzweig's ethical monotheism and its potential contemporary relevance.

Merely the title of Wyschogrod's book, *The Body of Faith*, alerts us to the deep affinity between his thought and Rosenzweig's.[27] It is interesting to note that Wyschogrod himself does not seem to notice this deep affinity. He mentions Rosenzweig in the context of twentieth-century Jewish thinkers who have put too much stress on ethics over and against carnal Israel. Wyschogrod is both wrong and right in his brief characterization of Rosenzweig. Let us turn first to why Rosenzweig is probably the Jewish thinker closest to Wyschogrod.

To begin with, reiterating Rosenzweig's view in *The Star of Redemption* of the blood community, Wyschogrod writes: "The being of Israel is embodied being. Jewish theology can therefore never become pure self-consciousness."[28] Moreover, Wyschogrod and Rosenzweig come to their positions from the same methodological point of view. For both, the Jewish philosophical tradition has for too long denied the living relationship between God and the people of Israel. Recall Rosenzweig's argument that "the 'anthropomorphisms' of the Bible are throughout assertions about meetings between God and man."[29] Arguing against the long line of Jewish rationalist criticism of anthropomorphism, Rosenzweig contends that "anthropomorphism" is necessary for the vital relationship between Israel and God. He contends that trust in God's ability to meet the human and the human ability to respond to God is a necessity of comparable importance "to the Law and the Prophets, for our continued existence as Jews."[30] Wyschogrod makes the same point:

> We cannot overlook a basic contradiction. The God of the Bible is a person. He is one of the characters who appears in the stories told in the Bible. He has a personality that undergoes development in the course of the story. . . . Against this simple fact, Jewish philosophy has marshaled all of its resources. The personality of God had to be demythologized. . . . When the philosophic critique of anthropomorphism comes into its own, the reality of God recedes.[31]

Rosenzweig and Wyschogrod agree that Israel experiences her relationship with God as a living relationship. This means that the reality of the relation, of God, and of Israel herself cannot be denied. In Wyschogrod's words, "Separated from the Jewish people, nothing is Judaism. If anything, it is the Jewish people that is Judaism."[32] Furthermore, Wyschogrod and Rosenzweig agree that God dwells in the people and not in the land. In Wyschogrod's words:

> While this people has a land because Hashem [God] ultimately gives it a land and dwells in it, its peoplehood is not coextensive with the land, as is the peoplehood of others, who cannot survive as a people once they are separated from their land.
>
> The Jewish people is the dwelling place of Hashem.[33]

Like Rosenzweig, Wyschogrod links antisemitism to Israel's carnal election:

> The pervasive hatred that has been directed at the Jewish people ever since it came into being is therefore first and foremost a hatred of Hashem, who is represented by the Jewish people and who can be gotten at only through the Jewish people.[34]

Wyschogrod's response to the Holocaust is also in keeping with the labor of Rosenzweig's concepts and their formal characteristics. Wyschogrod argues that Hitler rightly recognized the meaning of carnal Israel: that God dwells within the people of Israel:

> Sin does not drive Hashem out of the world completely. Only the destruction of the Jewish people does. Hitler understood that. He knew that it was insufficient to cancel the teachings of Jewish morality and to substitute for it the new moral order of the superman. It was not only Jewish values that needed to be eradicated but Jews had to be murdered. There are no Jewish values without

> Jews, and the most convincing intellectual refutation of Jewish values is worthless as long as the Jewish face is seen in the world.[35]

Commenting on a poem of Jehuda Halevi's, some fifty years and many atrocities earlier, Rosenzweig had made the same point:

> The unique characteristic of the people is this: that it looks at itself in about the same way as the outside world looks at it. A whole world asserts that the Jewish people is outcast and elect, both; and the Jewish people . . . only confirms it. Except that seen from the outside, the characterization assumes the form of external connectedness, while from within it represents an inner inseparableness, and the vessels of curse and blessing communicate so closely that the latter can overflow only when the former too is full to the brim.[36]

Both Wyschogrod and Rosenzweig attribute Jewish suffering and even, in Wyschogrod's case, the horror of the Holocaust to the election of Israel. Both argue that the antisemite recognizes correctly the uniqueness of the Jewish people and turns what could be a blessing for the world into a curse. Finally, Wyschogrod's attribution of a theological dimension to Nazi antisemitism is in keeping with Rosenzweig's analysis.[37] We have seen that the connections between Wyschogrod's and Rosenzweig's views of God, Israel, the relationship between them, the possibility of world redemption, and antisemitism all come down to an agreement about the carnal nature of Jewish election.

As we saw in the first section of this chapter, it is Rosenzweig's endorsement of the facticity of Israel's existence that allows him to be open to Zionism. Would he claim then, as Wyschogrod does, that the establishment of the State of Israel marks Judaism's reentry into history?[38] We saw in the last chapter that Rosenzweig argues that Judaism is a messianic politics. Would he agree with Wyschogrod's claim that the establishment of the State of Israel is a defining moment in Judaism's messianic history? Wyschogrod writes:

> Authentic Judaism must be messianic Judaism.
>
> Messianic Judaism is Judaism that takes seriously the belief that Jewish history, in spite of everything that has happened, is prelude to an extraordinary act of God by which history will come to its climax and the reconciliation between God and man, and man and man, realized. Messianism is therefore the Jewish principle of hope.[39]

Wyschogrod is well aware of the practical implications of his statement. Though defining himself as a left-wing Orthodox Jew, Wyschogrod writes:

> At this writing [1989], the critical issue is Judea and Samaria, the territories that came under Israeli control in the 1967 war and that, in Arab opinion, must

> become the territory of a Palestinian state. Since these territories are an integral part of the covenanted land of Israel perpetually bestowed by God on the Jewish people, to the degree that the messianic-biblical idea is operative in one's understanding of contemporary Jewish history, the relinquishing of these territories is inconceivable, being contrary to the messianic thrust of recent Jewish history.[40]

In the preface to the second edition of *The Body of Faith*, written in 1995, Wyschogrod states reluctantly that he is in favor of the "peace process," despite his reservations.[41] Presumably, this means he is in favor of returning land for peace. Nonetheless, the implications of Wyschogrod's position remain clear. His messianic Judaism is intimately linked with the messianic politics of Zionism.[42]

It is here that Wyschogrod is right to recognize that at bottom, he and Rosenzweig part ways. In Rose's terms, the labor of Rosenzweig's concepts and their formal characteristics cannot lead to an endorsement of Zionism as a messianic politics. The view that we can be sure of the divine significance of the establishment of the State of Israel, that God has returned to the Jewish people particular pieces of land, would smack of fanaticism for Rosenzweig. This view is fanatical because it suggests an absolute knowledge of God's will and an ability to manipulate that will. Rosenzweig would certainly reject this view. Indeed, the combination of political Zionism and "religion" for him would be disastrous. Such a lethal combination is precisely what Rosenzweig ascribes to the rise of modern nationalism, of whose dangers Rosenzweig was deeply aware.

It is here that Rosenzweig's relationship to Hermann Cohen is once again significant. "Judaism," though not reducible to concepts, nonetheless remains a concept for Rosenzweig in one very important sense. As we saw in the last chapter, "Judaism" for Rosenzweig is always ideal; it is always future. Rosenzweig self-consciously (and not naively as Rose would have it) idealizes "Judaism" in *The Star of Redemption* in order to reflect the fact that the Jewish people should always remember that the world is not yet redeemed. The Jewish people, though their revelation is complete, must spur on the rest of the world toward redemption. In this sense, "Judaism" is always future, and always ideal.

Rosenzweig's view that "Judaism" is also always ideal points to another important difference between him and Wyschogrod. Though Rosenzweig would agree with Wyschogrod that "the house of Israel is . . . not a voluntary association defined by acceptance or rejection of a set of propositions,"[43] Rosenzweig would disagree with the conclusion about Jewish unity that Wyschogrod draws from this point. Wyschogrod argues that Jewish identity is defined by God's covenant with the Jews; the Jews, then, are a natural family, identified by their common destiny.[44] For Rosenzweig, Jewish unity is ideal and realized. Wyschogrod recognizes the empirical problems that his position implies. He is in fact willing to take the issue of empirical verification head-on:

> If large-scale, organized violence between groups of Jews is possible, if war is possible among Jews, then the Jewish people is not one. I do not believe such violence is possible. Much to our horror, skirmishes, small-scale rock throwing, and individual crime among Jews are possible. But war is not. It is simply inconceivable.[45]

Unfortunately, reality may prove Wyschogrod wrong. War does seem possible among Jews, as the 1995 assassination of Israeli prime minister Yitzhak Rabin makes clear. Rosenzweig would not be surprised, though surely saddened, by recent events in Israel. Indeed, his warning against fanatical nationalism is a warning against the kind of internal conflict that has come to characterize Israeli life. From Rosenzweig's perspective, the Jewish people do not have a special immunity against nationalist politics (hence the particular irony of Rose's criticism). This is one of the reasons why Rosenzweig was apprehensive about Zionism.

The differences between Wyschogrod and Rosenzweig also point to the hermeneutical thrust of Rosenzweig's arguments. Wyschogrod defines Jewish identity as a given, for all Jews, at all times. Although Rosenzweig would agree with this on one level, he would also caution that the modern Jew does not experience his world in this way.[46] Rather than contending that only Orthodox Judaism is authentic Judaism, as Wyschogrod does, Rosenzweig, while still adhering to a traditionalist view of Jewish law, maintains an openness to inter-Jewish difference. This difference is more a matter of emphasis than content. Wyschogrod does advocate pluralism, but nonetheless maintains that only Orthodoxy is authentic Judaism. From a hermeneutical and pedagogical point of view, Rosenzweig's view may be more appropriate to the state of contemporary Jewry. It was in fact an openness to inter-Jewish difference that Rosenzweig found compelling about Zionism:

> Zionism, diagnostician of genius but most mediocre healer, has recognized the disease but prescribed the wrong treatment. What it recognized was the absence of a specific contemporary Jewish life having some common characteristics other than just the common possession of a dead scholarship called the "Science of Judaism" (which nobody is familiar with) and the common "defense against antisemitism." What Zionism also recognized—and here proved itself to be a real pathologist, not merely a diagnostician—is this: that the only

> healthy, the only whole thing about the Jewish person—is the Jewish person himself.[47]

Though Rosenzweig disagreed with Zionism's solution, he agreed, as we have seen, with Zionism's diagnosis of modern Judaism and of modern Jewish individuals:

> Expressly or unconsciously, Zionism has always emphasized that it is the integrity of the Jewish individual which has in reality held us together since the beginning, and offered the only solid ground upon which the several vessels of Jewish life could develop—land, state, and law in the old days; later, divine commandment, worship, and home. But as soon as the great question is posed as what should be done now, and how new vessels of Jewish communal life are to be planted in this devastated but indestructible soil in place of the shrunken ones . . . Zionism fails us. . . . Those who want to work for the movement, for today, without shifting the main burden to an uncertain tomorrow, must take the Jewish individual seriously, here and now, as he is in his wholeness.[48]

From the perspective of Rosenzweig's thought, Wyschogrod does not take the Jewish individual, in his wholeness, seriously enough. Not taking Jewish individuals seriously leads Wyschogrod to a position that is both hermeneutically and pragmatically problematic. Rosenzweig's program for adult Jewish education sought to meet individuals where they are. Rosenzweig recognized that Judaism, and indeed Orthodox Judaism, was not the only authentic mode of being in the modern world. Indeed, as we have seen throughout this book, Rosenzweig argues that recognition of irreducible particularity and finitude, what he calls neo-paganism, also constitutes an authentic, modern identity. Rosenzweig tolerated various non-halakhic, non-Orthodox forms of modern Judaism—what we might call Jewish paganism—for at least two reasons.[49] First, he argued that pagans always have the possibility of becoming witnesses. Political Zionism, though idolatry as an end in itself, could bring Jewish people together, which could bring Jews back to Judaism. Second, Rosenzweig argued that paganism was always preferable to fanaticism. Rosenzweig would certainly favor political Zionism over messianic Zionism. Wyschogrod's embrace of a messianic Zionism is aided by his advocacy of a Jewish unity that ultimately denies inter-Jewish difference. If there is only one authentic mode of Judaism—Orthodoxy—it becomes easier to believe that God's will has been expressed in a clear and direct way. Wyschogrod's messianic Zionism would be problematic for Rosenzweig both because it tends toward a fanatical politics and because it denies the reality of the modern, individual Jew.

Rosenzweig's philosophy remained a diaspora philosophy. Though he would embrace the practical reality and even necessity of the State of Israel, he would be highly critical of any theological valuation attached to the state. Rosenzweig would remind Israeli Jews that the meaning of the Jewish people is that it "never loses the untrammeled freedom of a wanderer who is more faithful a knight to his country when he roams abroad, craving adventure and yearning for the home [*Heimat*] he has left behind, than when he is at home [*zuhause*]."[50] Rosenzweig would remind Israeli Jews that "Judaism" and "Israel" remain goals that are not yet achieved. In order to remember this, diaspora Judaism is an essential counterpart to the modern Israeli State. Only in relation to the diaspora can the modern State of Israel remember the Jewish mission to the nations.

Of course, many Israeli Jews, secular and religious alike, would reject this view. Indeed, Rosenzweig's thought remains in the final analysis directed at the diaspora. His central question remains the question of the possibilities of Jewish meaning in the modern world. This question remains essentially a diaspora question because as Rosenzweig argues, too much of a focus on politics as an end in itself tends to distort the possibilities of Jewish (and for that matter any human) meaning in the modern world. This does not mean that Jews are not engaged in politics, both in the diaspora and in the State of Israel. It does mean, however, that lest Judaism become an idol, or even worse a kind of fanaticism, Jews must remember that Judaism's mission to the nations is beyond politics. Judaism represents all of humanity. Rosenzweig argues that by definition, political institutions do not have this representative ability.[51]

# *Conclusion*

## The Future of Monotheism

As we saw in the last chapter, Rosenzweig's thought remains in the final analysis directed at the diaspora. But is there a future for monotheism in an increasingly plural world and particularly for Rosenzweig's claims regarding the ethical content of monotheism? At the turn of the millennium, is it possible to claim that monotheism, whether Jewish or Christian, can make an ethical contribution to culture?

It would seem, in fact, that turn-of-the-millennium American culture, with its emphasis on the intrinsic values of pluralism and diversity, and indeed its quest for tolerance and distaste for judging others, might be inclined to think otherwise. In academic guise, Regina Schwartz has recently expressed some of these late twentieth century cultural values and questioned the link between ethics and monotheism. In *The Curse of Cain: The Violent Legacy of Monotheism*, Schwartz argues not only that no such link exists, but that properly understood, monotheism is responsible for the long legacy of violence in the West. She begins by suggesting that "some suspicion of the ancient biblical link between ethics and the myth of monotheism seems in order, along with some doubt about the wisdom of tying ethics to an understanding of identity that is agonistic by nature."[1]

Schwartz's criticism of monotheism on ethical grounds offers us a helpful starting point to begin to evaluate what Rosenzweig's ethical monotheism might look like in contemporary guise. As we saw particularly in chapter 6, Rosenzweig argues that monotheism gains its critical force not through affirmation but through judgment. In this sense, Rosenzweig would agree with Schwartz that monotheism is "agonistic by nature." Where Rosenzweig and Schwartz would disagree is whether this is a bad or good thing.

By way of conclusion, I consider briefly the possibilities for the future of monotheism in the context of late twentieth century American criticism that monotheism is anything but ethical. To do so, I compare Rosenzweig's thought to that of the contemporary American Christian theologian George Lindbeck. More than any other current thinker, the thrust and direction of Lindbeck's work in America at the end of the twentieth century parallels what Rosenzweig sought to accomplish in Germany at the beginning of the century. Reading Rosenzweig in light of Lindbeck allows us to examine anew the question of what the future of monotheism might look like from Rosenzweig's perspective.

## Monotheism and "Religion" Revisited

In order to begin to understand Lindbeck's conceptual relation to Rosenzweig, let us return to Schwartz's criticism of monotheism. According to Schwartz, there is an intimate connection between monotheism's belief in one God and its violent legacy toward "the other." "Monotheism is a myth that grounds particular identity in universal transcendence. And monotheism is a myth that forges identity antithetically—against the Other."[2] The connection between monotheism's belief in a transcendent other and the formation of monotheistic identity as against others is the root of monotheism's violence, argues Schwartz. She maintains that monotheism is predicated on an intrinsically violent conception of identity, a conception that reflects a narrative of "scarcity":

> The very idea that identity is constructed 'against' suggests scarcity, as though there were a finite amount of identity itself, and so a space must be carved out for it and jealously guarded, like finite territory. If there were no identity shortage, if Israelites could be Egyptians too, for instance, there would be no need for aggressive or defensive gestures to protect their space. That is, singularity joins hands with scarcity, and both are given powerful expression in monotheism's emphasis on allegiance to one and only one god.[3]

Ironically, Schwartz fails to realize that her very proposal that there would be "no identity shortage, if Israelites could be Egyptians too" is one that many contemporary advocates of monotheistic religion have advanced. Here Lindbeck is very helpful. In his now classic 1984 study *The Nature of Doctrine*, Lindbeck distinguishes between an "experiential-expressive model" of religion and experience and a "cultural-linguistic alternative." In short, the difference between these two models is one of cause and effect; the former understands "religious experience" as producing the possibility of religious language and/or community, while the latter understands the forms and languages of particular religious communities as producing any possibility of "religious experience." In Lindbeck's categories, the position that "Israelites could be Egyptians too" fits the experiential-expressivist model. This picture of monotheism is precisely what the dominant strand of twentieth-century Christian theology has sought.

Lindbeck notes that the "experiential expressive" model is "particularly well fitted to supply a rationale for the interreligious dialogue and cooperation that is so urgently needed in a divided yet shrinking world."[4] He suggests that Bernard Lonergan, a Catholic theologian, captures perhaps most fully the experiential-expressive approach. In particular, Lindbeck cites Lonergan's contention that religious experience is "God's gift of love." Lonergan writes:

> Inasmuch as it is conscious without being known, the gift of God's love is an experience of the holy, of Rudolf Otto's *mysterium fascinans et tremendum*. It is what Paul Tillich named a being grasped by ultimate concern. It is what corresponds to Ignatius Loyola's consolation that has no cause, as expounded by Karl Rahner.[5]

Lindbeck's analysis suggests that Lonergan, Otto, Tillich, and Rahner lay claim to, in Schwartz's terms, an ethic of plentitude rather than scarcity. Lindbeck describes the modern desire for an ethic of plentitude, a desire shared by Schwartz and the theologians cited by Lonergan:

> As we move into a culturally (even if not statistically) post-Christian period . . . increasing numbers of people regard all religions as possible sources of symbols to be used eclectically in articulating, clarifying, and organizing the experiences of the inner self. Religions are seen as multiple suppliers of different forms of a single commodity needed for transcendent self-expression and self-realization.[6]

From Lindbeck's perspective, the possibility of Israelites identifying as Egyptians too is predicated on the same assumption that underlies the experiential-expressive model of religion. Schwartz and the experiential-expressivist theorist of religion share the assumption that religious identity is both generic and multiple. Religious identity is multiple because it is generic and generic because it is multiple. Ironically, rather than offering a fresh insight into "monotheism," Schwartz's book reiterates a theme that has dominated twentieth-century Christian theology and hence by implication modern arguments about monotheism.[7]

Rosenzweig and Lindbeck reject both assumptions that religious identity is multiple and that it is generic. Before turning back to Lindbeck's and Rosenzweig's approaches to the issues of monotheism and identity, let us note that while the experiential-expressive model is advocated mainly by Christian theologians, some Jewish thinkers fit into this category also. Buber's thought could easily be included under the experiential-expressive rubric. As we saw particularly in chapter 5, Buber's "I and Thou" is a model of generic religious experience that neither dictates nor requires any particular communal identity. Like Lonergan, Otto, Tillich, and Rahner, Buber attempts to make possible a view of religious identity that is generous rather than limited. Recall Rosenzweig's comment to Buber: "What is to become of I and Thou if they will have to swallow up the entire world and Creator as well? *Religion? I am afraid so—and shudder at the word whenever I hear it.* For my and your sake, there has to be something else in this world besides—me and you!"[8]

Rosenzweig would agree with Lindbeck's statement that "adherents of different religions do not diversely thematize the same experience; rather they have different experiences."[9] As the argument of the structure of *The Star of Redemption* makes clear, personal revelation gains its meaning only through particular communal forms.[10] Schwartz makes a point with which both Rosenzweig and Lindbeck would agree. As against much of modern Christian theology, and some Jewish thought also, Rosenzweig, Lindbeck, and Schwartz agree that monotheism means a particular identity.

As we have seen throughout this book, Rosenzweig argues *against* an experiential-expressive model of religion (to use Lindbeck's terminology). Rosenzweig argues that Jewish monotheism has world redemptive possibilities not by way of its generic generality, but only by way of its particularity. It is not difficult to imagine how Rosenzweig's efforts at adult education, as well as his translation with Martin Buber of the Hebrew Bible into German, fit into Lindbeck's cultural-linguistic model. Rosenzweig's *Lehrhaus* sought not to provide the individual Jew with access to personal revelation but rather with the tools, or in Lindbeck's terms, skills, for returning to Jewish community, such as knowledge of Hebrew and Jewish texts. On a more theoretical level, the hermeneutics of the Buber-Rosenzweig Bible translation, which aimed for shocked attention in its readers, cohere well with Lindbeck's claim that "religions, like languages, can be understood only in their own terms, not by transposing them into an alien speech."[11] As we have seen throughout this book, Rosenzweig's view of the tasks of Jewish education and Bible translation is not at odds with the philosophical argument in *The Star of Redemption* about revelation. Rather, the hermeneutical argument of the structure of *The Star of Redemption* does not suggest that personal revelation makes community possible, as most interpreters of Rosenzweig have maintained. *The Star of Redemption* suggests that the historical realities of the Jewish and Christian communities make the experience of revelation possible for the modern person.

## Reconsidering Rosenzweig in Light of Lindbeck

We do not require Lindbeck's *Nature of Doctrine* to demonstrate the "cultural-linguistic" argument of *The Star of Redemption.* As we have seen, this can be done simply on the basis of the argument implicit in *The Star of Redemption*'s structure itself. However, Lindbeck's thought does help significantly to account for some of the reasons why Rosenzweig's thought has been so misunderstood. By way of concluding this study, let us analyze briefly the reception of Rosenzweig's thought via Lindbeck's categories. As Lindbeck argues in great detail, the "experiential-expressive model" of religion and experience enjoys its popularity both in the academic and public realms because of the perceived need to make "religion" universally accessible and defensible. Ironically, the "experiential-expressivist" approach to Rosenzweig inflicts Rosenzweig's thought with the very position that he, both in *The Star of Redemption* and beyond, sought to defeat. The recognition of this irony tells us as much about our cultural situation, and our continued need to understand "religion" in universal terms, as about Rosenzweig's own project.

Let us return to the historical context of Rosenzweig's argument. We have seen that Rosenzweig's thought is understood best as ethically monotheist in the tradition of Hermann Cohen. To use Lindbeck's terms, Cohen's ethical monotheism falls under the category of a "propositional understanding of religion." This means that for Cohen the propositional truths of religion are on par with the propositional truths of philosophical and scientific standards. In keeping with his view of idolatry, Cohen's approach to religion is a cognitive one. As Lindbeck remarks, "In modern times, propositional understandings of religion have long been on the defensive and experiential-expressive ones in the ascendancy."[12] This trend isn't surprising. As the last two centuries in particular have demonstrated, the cognitivist approach to religion has trouble meeting the demands of science and philosophy, as well as of "religion." Explaining the ascendancy of experiential-expressive models from the side of religion, Lindbeck notes that Immanuel Kant's "reduction of morality seemed to the sensibilities of most religious people to leave religion intolerably impoverished."[13]

We need but recall that Kant was Cohen's philosophical mentor. As discussed in chapter 1, Rosenzweig in his "Note on Anthropomorphism" responded precisely to what he argued was rationalism's impoverishment.[14] Of particular significance is his comment that "the assumption that [biblical anthropomorphisms] make is none other than the double one that the Bible commonly makes: namely that God is capable of what he wills . . . and that the creature is capable of what he should be."[15] Rosenzweig criticizes the rationalized view of "biblical anthropomorphism" which he contends destroys the meaning of God's revelation to human beings. Lindbeck argues that the rationalized, propositional approach to religion opened the door to experiential-expressive models that sought to restore some of the particular religious, and not merely rational or ethical, content of religion. Lindbeck locates Schleiermacher as the father of such an approach.[16] One need only call to mind Schleiermacher's most famous phrase, that religion is a "*feeling* of absolute dependence," to appreciate Lindbeck's point.[17]

We are now in a position to explain both Rosenzweig's relation to Cohen and the reasons for so much of the misunderstanding of Rosenzweig's thought. Rosenzweig responds precisely to what Lindbeck describes as the impoverishment of religion by the propositionalist approach. In the following quotation, Lindbeck contrasts the cognitivist approach to the cultural-linguist one. Lindbeck's contrast could easily be applied to the relation between Cohen's and Rosenzweig's thought, and in particular to their positions on idolatry:

> This stress on the code, rather than the (e.g. propositionally) encoded, enables a cultural-linguistic approach to accommodate the experiential-expressive concern for the unreflective dimensions of human existence far better than is possible in a cognitivist outlook. Religion cannot be pictured in the cognitivist (and voluntarist) manner as primarily a matter of deliberately choosing to believe or follow explicitly known propositions or directives. Rather, to become religious—no less than to become culturally or linguistically competent—is to interiorize a set of skills by practice and training. One learns how to feel, act, and think in conformity with a religious tradition that is, in its inner structure, far richer and more subtle than can be explicitly articulated. The primary knowledge is not *about* the religion, nor *that* the religion teaches such and such, but rather *how* to be religious in such and such ways.[18]

Where Cohen stresses the encoded, Rosenzweig stresses the code. This difference at once reflects their different approaches to philosophy and the problem of idolatry. For Cohen, there is a confluence between philosophy and Judaism: both express true knowledge about what there is in the world. For Rosenzweig, there is no such confluence. Philosophy is about what there is in the world, while Judaism's truth is contained in how Jews worship God, rather than in what they think. In keeping with his view of the confluence between philosophy and Judaism, Cohen contends that idolatry is wrong thinking. And in keeping with his view of the incommensurability between philosophy and Judaism, Rosenzweig's thought suggests that idolatry is wrong worship. Nonetheless, Rosenzweig maintains Cohen's problematic, which is the question of Judaism's contribution to the modern world. Rosenzweig follows Cohen in answering this question with an argument about idolatry and the proper concept of representation.

From Rosenzweig's perspective, he is replacing Cohen's faulty conceptual framework—what Lindbeck would call a propositionalist model—with a more adequate one, what Lindbeck would call a cultural-linguistic one.[19] This model does not deny the importance of the encoded (of reason or of religious experience) but argues instead that the code produces the encoded, and not the other way around. Content cannot be separated from form.[20] Without such a methodological corrective, Rosenzweig contends that Cohen's whole system is a distortion of Judaism, with not only theoretical but also practical consequences.[21]

Why has Rosenzweig so often been taken for an experiential-expressive thinker? Lindbeck's models are helpful here also. Historically, an experiential-expressive approach has been a logical consequence of the inadequacy of the propositional approach to religion. Rosenzweig was well aware of the attraction of romantic conceptions of religion, what Lindbeck would call the experiential-expressive model. Indeed, particularly in Part 2 of *The Star of Redemption*, Rosenzweig's discussion of "religious experience" is filled with romantic language and imagery. Rather than reflecting the fact that Rosenzweig was too much a creature of his times, his attention to romantic language and imagery only emphasizes the hermeneutical thrust of the work. *The Star of Redemption* contends that though the modern person may believe that she comes to religious community through personal religious experience, in truth it is the communal structures of the historical communities of Judaism and Christianity that make this personal experience possible in the first place. Rosenzweig would agree with Lindbeck's statement that "instead of deriving external features of a religion from inner experience, it is the inner experiences which are viewed as derivative."[22] The misunderstanding of Rosenzweig on this point is indicative of what Lindbeck calls the ascendancy of experiential-expressive models. Excessive attention to the romantic language and imagery in *The Star of Redemption* has eclipsed its philosophical argument about the priority of communal structures. Ironically, Rosenzweig's hermeneutic sensitivities have produced confusion for the contemporary reader (both his and our own) who still remains too much in the throes of the propositional-experiential dichotomy.[23]

## The Problem of Election: Ethics and Judgment Revisited

We can now return to Schwartz's criticism of monotheism. The question about particularism is nowhere so pronounced as on the issue of chosenness. From Schwartz's point of view, any notion of chosenness is predicated on a violent relation to "the other." She would insist that a necessary corollary to the chosen people's statement "we are chosen" is "and you are not." The problem of election seems, perhaps more than any other problem of monotheism, to raise the issue of "scarcity," of which Schwartz makes so much. Is the love of God so scarce that only a few can be especially beloved? As we have seen throughout this book, the notion of Jewish election is absolutely central to Rosenzweig's thought. A belief in Jewish election marks Rosenzweig's ethical monotheism; his argument, to put it concisely, is that the election of the Jewish people makes world redemption a possibility. Is Rosenzweig's argument about Jewish election, and hence his ethical monotheism, an arrogant, not to speak of outdated, position?

Before answering this question, it is significant to note that at the end of the twentieth century in America, Lindbeck, a Lutheran, seeks to reappropriate a conception of election for Christianity. Lindbeck's post-liberal theology is predicated not only on an embrace of a distinctive identity for Christians, but on the identity of an elect people, in fact of an Israel-like people.[24] Below, we will turn to the question of how a Christian appropriation of Israel's election complicates Rosenzweig's Jewish-Christian schema. Here, however, I would like to focus on the similarities between Rosenzweig's and Lindbeck's positions. Each contends that his tradition understands itself to be the tradition of an elect people. Are Rosenzweig and Lindbeck merely carrying on, to use Schwartz's term, monotheism's violent legacy?

The answer to this question is both yes and no. The "yes" part is simple. Rosenzweig's and Lindbeck's monotheisms *are* exclusive. Each maintains that his respective tradition gains its meaning through its particularity and exclusivity. But beyond this somewhat definitional understanding, it is unclear what it would mean to think of Rosenzweig's and Lindbeck's monotheisms as intrinsically violent in Schwartz's sense. Let us recall briefly Rosenzweig's view of judgment. We have seen that Rosenzweig argues that it is a distinctly modern view that suggests that our identities are not based on some prejudgments [*Vorurteil*]. This modern view distorts not only our self-conceptions but also our ability to affect and to be affected by others. Rosenzweig argues that judgment, and not affirmation, propels us toward redemption—for judgment, and not affirmation, can force us to change ourselves. Monotheism for both Rosenzweig and Lindbeck is judgmental; if it were not it would be both ineffective and dishonest. Most importantly in this context, if Jewish monotheism were not judgmental for Rosenzweig, there would be no possibility of interhuman relationships. Ethics itself is predicated upon judgment. Rosenzweig argues that to judge the other is to take the other seriously and to open up the possibility of love.[25]

Of course, we cannot stop here. We must ask Rosenzweig and Lindbeck the next rather obvious question: in a pluralistic society, and indeed in a pluralistic world, is it not perhaps better to be dishonest than to be arrogant and triumphant? On what ethical grounds could an adherence to a doctrine of election possibly rest? It is here that a striking similarity between Rosenzweig and Lindbeck becomes apparent. Neither Rosenzweig nor Lindbeck advocates an acontextual notion of election. Election is not a dogma that can be isolated from life lived in community. Both Rosenzweig and Lindbeck contend that to be elect is to be a witness to God's revelation. Divorced from witnessing, which comes only from *living* a Jewish or a Christian life, the notion of election loses its meaning. Lindbeck echoes Rosenzweig's arguments about the connections between witnessing, language, and translation when he writes:

> To be unique witness to salvation is quite different from being the unique means or vehicle. Witnessing to salvation is a matter of pointing all things to the true God who, in view of what we have called untranslatability, can be rightly identified only in the unique language of the elect peoples.
>
> The interreligious importance of this shift from soteriology to untranslatability or, in this context, from means to witness to salvation, is that it is a move from triumphalism to modesty which nevertheless remains faithful to the Bible. If it is true, as we can plausibly postulate, even if not prove, that all religions of world importance affirm a comprehensiveness which implies untranslatability, then the biblical affirmation of uniqueness is not longer uniquely offensive. When uniqueness is thought of in terms of means of salvation, as Christians (but not Jews) have usually done, it becomes difficult to avoid unbiblically arrogant claims for the church and, at the same time, retain the exclusivist biblical understanding of election. In so far as the appeal of pluralism and to a lesser degree inclusivism is owing to their opposition to arrogance, they are biblically justifiable, but this appeal is purchased, it seems, at the cost of incoherence: the basic grammar of election, which is central to biblical faith, is shattered.[26]

Lindbeck argues that if biblical faith is to have any coherence it must do so within the "basic grammar of election." The cultural-linguist position implies not only that the "grammar of election" is untranslatable but that perhaps all grammars are. From Lindbeck's perspective, this position avoids arrogance for three reasons. First, if it is possible that "all religions of world importance affirm a comprehensiveness which implies untranslatability," then the claim to uniqueness is not offensive. We will elaborate below on this claim in the context of Rosenzweig's ethical monotheism. Second, and here Lindbeck is very close to Rosenzweig, witnessing is performative. Outsiders can join the community precisely by imitating communal practices. Conversion, for both Rosenzweig and Lindbeck, is the learning of the grammar of the community; it is to make the community's past, present, and future one's own.[27] And third, both Jewish and Christian election are predicated on a future judgment. This emphasis on the future avoids triumphalism. The redemption of the world is not yet complete. Lindbeck follows the spirit of Rosenzweig's criticism of Christianity in insisting that Christians must ever remind themselves that their revelation is not complete and neither is the redemption of the world.

Rosenzweig and Lindbeck's views of election and the untranslatability of religious traditions converge on the issue of the ethical effect Jewish and Christian monotheism can have on the world. Both insist that the witnessing community make a contribution to world culture and the possibility of world redemption precisely by not seeking to do so in such terms. The integrity and hence ethical and redemptive possibilities of the witnessing community are predicated upon the adherence to the language game of the community itself. Just as Rosenzweig maintains that Judaism remain self-contained for the sake of the redemption of the world, Lindbeck argues that

> provided a religion stresses service rather than domination, it is likely to contribute more to the future of humanity if it preserves its own distinctiveness and integrity than if it yields to the homogenizing tendencies associated with liberal experiential-expressivism.
>
> This conclusion is paradoxical: Religious communities are likely to be practically relevant in the long run to the degree that they do not first ask what is either practical or relevant, but instead concentrate on their own intratextual outlooks and forms of life.[28]

But even if we grant that Rosenzweig and Lindbeck each move toward a position on election that is modest rather than arrogant, we are still left with a fundamental objection from someone like Schwartz. Recall her equation of monotheism's violent legacy toward others and monotheism's adherence to a transcendent deity: "Monotheism is a myth that grounds particular identity in universal transcendence. And monotheism is a myth that forges identity antithetically—against the Other." From Rosenzweig's perspective, Jewish monotheism is violent in this sense. As we saw in chapter 6's discussion of judgment, Rosenzweig does not shy away from the ambiguity, what he in fact calls the dreadful (*grauenhaft*) dynamic of human and divine love.[29] In fact, he argues that revelation, love itself, is a kind of violent act because it forces a judgment upon the self. Love is born of judgment, not affirmation. In this sense, monotheism does forge "identity antithetically."

Indeed, Rosenzweig goes so far as to argue in *The Star of Redemption* that monotheism is the originator of the concept of "holy war."[30] Recall, however, that he argues at the same time that the Jew is the only true pacifist because he cannot take war seriously.[31] Rosenzweig's contention here is consistent with his argument about the relation between judgment and love. Monotheism begins in the judgment of holy war but leads to the love of true pacifism. Significantly, Lindbeck's "post-liberal" Christianity may be described as the very movement from judgment to love that Rosenzweig describes—from, in Rosenzweig's view, Christianity's severe judgment in its conflation of holy war and ordinary war, to the true love of pacifism.[32] In keeping with Rosenzweig's arguments about Christian idolatry, Lindbeck argues that Christianity can only make this move by recognizing its link to Judaism and by becoming more "Israel-like."

This dynamic from judgment to love describes the election of the Jewish people as well. Here Michael Wyschogrod is very close to Rosenzweig when he remarks that election "is not hard to understand: it is a scandal."[33] From the perspective of reason, God's revelation is scandalous but that is also why it is miraculous. Reason and revelation do not add up to one whole for Rosenzweig as they do for Cohen. As Rosenzweig puts it, "A miracle does not constitute history, a people is not a juridical fact, martyrdom is not an arithmetical problem, and love is not social."[34] Rosenzweig contends that revelation makes human freedom truly possible. The possibilities that revelation brings to humanity can neither be calculated nor controlled. This is at once revelation's promise *and* revelation's danger.

We could say that Schwartz could just call a truce with Rosenzweig and Lindbeck, saying that they could agree on the description of monotheism as identity oriented and worshiping a transcendent God, but that they would disagree on whether monotheism contributes violence or the possibility of universal redemption to the world. Rosenzweig and Lindbeck would find this proposition reductive. They would argue that because Jewish and Christian monotheisms are bound to a future that is not yet, it is too soon to make a judgment about monotheism's violence or ethics. But their objection would go deeper than this. From Rosenzweig and Lindbeck's point of view, Schwartz's argument about plentitude versus scarcity is hermeneutically problematic. She concludes her book:

> And so here I have offered my small contribution to that far more illustrious history of rewritings, one in which Luther read all of the Bible through his belief that faith is the promise of redemption, in which Milton read the Bible as asserting individual moral victories in the face of constant struggles against the chaos of sin. . . . My revision would produce an alternative Bible that subverts the dominant strand of violence and scarcity with an ideal of plentitude and its corollary ethical imperative of generosity. It would be a Bible embracing multiplicity instead of monotheism.[35]

On what basis does Schwartz make her interpretation? From where is she standing? Lindbeck and Rosenzweig would maintain that Schwartz's position is a feasible one but it is not biblical. They would acknowledge that their responses come from within the Christian and Jewish traditions. But they would contend further that Schwartz's position comes from her position in some tradition. This tradition, however complex and historically situated, needs to be articulated. If it is not articulated, it remains at best weak and at worst incoherent. Rosenzweig's argument, as we have seen throughout this book, is that the crisis of modernity is a crisis of meaning. The modern notion that we can stand from nowhere and offer interpretations distorts the ways in which human meaning is created and transformed. Indeed, we have seen that Rosenzweig argues that the claim for unsituated points of view is the marker of modern idolatry.

Schwartz may be surprised to have her position equated with a "modern" one. Most likely, she would consider her interpretation "postmodern," meaning that rather than subscribing to some universal notion of reason she represents a particular point of view. She lists her interpretation as one of many and does not claim that it is the only one. But as we saw in chapter 2, Rosenzweig argues that a point-of-view position such as Schwartz's (which has an important affinity with much of those who claim a "postmodern" position today) is dialectically related to the claims of the historical enlightenment. Both the philosopher of the historical enlightenment and the point-of-view thinker disregard the hermeneutical underpinnings of their own identities. Neither position can acknowledge its debts to its past and thus to its present and future. This would be Rosenzweig's general criticism of Schwartz's position. His particularly Jewish position would parallel Lindbeck's Christian one. From the perspective of the Jewish and Christian traditions, Schwartz's "alternative Bible that subverts the dominant strand of violence and scarcity with an ideal of plentitude and its corollary ethical imperative of generosity" is not the Bible. If the Bible is to have a future, argue both Rosenzweig and Lindbeck, its adherents must return to it its own voice.[36]

## Concluding Thoughts: Jewish Thought and Apologetic Thinking

A comparison of Lindbeck and Rosenzweig is complicated, of course, not only because of the differences between late twentieth century America and early twentieth century Germany, but also because of Lindbeck's and Rosenzweig's respective commitments to Lutheranism and Judaism. But rather than detracting from a better understanding of Rosenzweig's thought, the complexity of the comparison between him and Lindbeck should aid us in thinking about the implications of at least two issues of great urgency to Rosenzweig himself and to current debates in religious studies today. These are the issues of, first, the possibility and nature of Jewish philosophy, and, second, the possibility and nature of interreligious dialogue.

The careful reader may have noticed that I glossed over a point above. I claimed a bit too quickly that Rosenzweig would concur with Lindbeck's statement—that "if it is true, as we can plausibly postulate, even if not prove, that all religions of world importance affirm a comprehensiveness which implies untranslatability, then the biblical affirmation of uniqueness in not [*sic*] longer uniquely offensive." I have after all given ample suggestion throughout this book that Rosenzweig's ethical monotheism might not affirm a "comprehensiveness which implies untranslatability" to "all religions of world importance." We need but recall in particular chapter 3's discussion of the philosophical import of carnal Israel in *The Star of Redemption* and chapter 6's discussion of Christianity, in which I argued that for Rosenzweig Christianity only gains its redemptive potential through its relation to Judaism. There hardly seems room for the kind of pluralism about which Lindbeck writes.

This issue is complicated for a number of reasons. There are at least two questions about pluralism that must be asked of Rosenzweig's thought. The first is the general question: can his ethical monotheism tolerate plurality? The second is what happens to the Jewish-Christian relation for Rosenzweig when Christians begin to understand themselves as "Israel-like" communities? The first question is actually a question about method for Rosenzweig. The proper way to ask this question is to ask instead: what kind of argument is Rosenzweig making? Is his ethical monotheism a kind of dogmatic theology or is it something else? The second, more specific question about Christianity is a question about the content of Rosenzweig's thought. Does Rosenzweig's understanding of Judaism require Christianity to be universal in a way that Lindbeck and other Christians today would reject? Let us turn to the question about method first and second to the question about content.

In 1923, two years after the publication of *The Star of Redemption*, Rosenzweig published an important essay called "Apologetic Thinking" in Buber's journal *Der Jude*.[37] A brief analysis of this essay will allow us to consider the ethically monotheistic argument of *The Star of Redemption* both in its context and in our own. In this essay, Rosenzweig distinguishes apologetics from dogmatics and argues that, in contrast to Christian theology, Jewish thought is always the former and never the latter. Rosenzweig argues that while dogmatic thinking is the systematic attempt to elucidate the inherited dogmas of a tradition, apologetic thinking is always occasional:

> No one became a Jewish thinker within the private domain of Judaism. Thinking was not thinking about Judaism (which was simply taken for granted, and was more of an existence than an "ism"); it was thinking within Judaism, learning—ultimately ornamental, rather than fundamental, thinking. Anyone who was to think about Judaism, somehow had to be drawn to the border of Judaism, if not psychologically then intellectually. His thinking was thus

> determined by the power that had brought him to the border and the horizon of his gaze was defined by the degree to which he had been carried to, near, or across it.
>
> Apologetics is the legitimate strength of this thinking, but also an inherent danger.[38]

Rosenzweig contends that Jewish thought is ornamental rather than fundamental because it is always produced as a response to some external context. Thinking from an internal Jewish perspective is thinking within Judaism and not about Judaism. Thinking about Judaism happens in response to some external circumstance. This does not mean that Jewish thought is by definition illegitimate from an internally Jewish perspective. We have seen that Rosenzweig argues that Judaism must always remain in relation with its external world. Apologetic thinking is in this sense a strength for Judaism from an internal perspective. Properly understood Jewish thought displays the interaction between Judaism and some particular occasion. However, Rosenzweig argues, apologetic thinking also has an inherent danger. This danger is that it is possible to equate thinking about Judaism with thinking within Judaism. As Rosenzweig's philosophy of translation, his approach to the German-Jewish symbiosis, and *The Star of Redemption*'s argument about the philosophical import of carnal Israel all show, the equation of thinking about and thinking within Judaism is a troubling category error with grave practical consequences. Rosenzweig maintains that this was precisely the error committed by German-Jewish rationalists of the nineteenth and twentieth centuries. He contends further that the crisis of modernity for Judaism has been the loss of a particularly Jewish language or, in other words, the replacement of thinking within Judaism for thinking about Judaism.

Viewing Rosenzweig's ethical monotheism in the context of his understanding of Jewish thought allows us to see that *The Star of Redemption* does not try to present eternal dogma about Judaism or anything else. This emphasizes one of the main contentions of this book: *The Star of Redemption* is a hermeneutically oriented work that self-consciously asks questions about the meanings of Judaism and philosophy in the modern world. Rosenzweig sees himself as self-consciously working within a tradition of Jewish thought that is occasioned by historical circumstances.[39]

*The Star of Redemption*'s arguments and conclusions are valid for us in as much as we take its circumstances to be our own. Certainly arguments about the nature of hermeneutics and tradition and their relation to ethics, aesthetics, and politics are still very much with us today. Rosenzweig's thought anticipates much of the current debate of the late twentieth century and may remain a resource for continuing to think about these matters. However, Rosenzweig's arguments and conclusions are only as valid as his questions. *The Star of Redemption*'s occasional thinking is as valid as is its occasion. Indeed, Rosenzweig's philosophical legacy is found in his questions rather than in his answers. The contemporary reader must decide whether Rosenzweig has described adequately the crisis of meaning of the modern world and whether his responses to this crisis are in any way adequate. This is the question that should be asked of Rosenzweig today and not the question that has too often been asked of him regarding a description of the veracity of religious experience over and against reason.

Rosenzweig's thought does not offer any straightforward, practical solutions to the problem of religious authority in the modern world. Here too Lindbeck's project parallels Rosenzweig's. Lindbeck writes that "a Christian postliberal consensus on the primarily cultural-linguistic character of religions would not by itself overcome substantive disagreements between conservatives and progressives, feminists and antifeminists, Catholics and Protestants."[40] Rosenzweig's thought does not by itself offer solutions to internal Jewish issues, such as the status of particular Jewish laws and their relation to contemporary issues such as the status of women, homosexuality, reproductive technology, or anything else. What Rosenzweig's thought does offer is the possibility of thinking about how religious authority may be *possible* in the modern world. Again the hermeneutical thrust of Rosenzweig's argument becomes apparent. Rosenzweig takes modernity seriously. He takes seriously the impact that modern worldviews and particularly the historicist and scientific worldviews have had on modern people. This crisis of meaning is the occasion to which his thought responds. As he writes, the thinking of a Jewish thinker is "determined by the power that had brought him to the border and the horizon of his gaze was defined by the degree to which he had been carried to, near, or across it."

Rosenzweig's argument for a return to an internal Jewish language is not an ahistorical or uncritical approach to Judaism but is rather intimately connected to his hermeneutical musings on the hermeneutical condition of the modern person. The strength of Rosenzweig's thought is that he is consciously aware of the complex interaction between Judaism and modern thought. Rosenzweig writes after the crisis of historicism, which means that he is deeply cognizant of the difficulty, if not impossibility, of separating a pure "Judaism" from its many external influences. His call for an internal Jewish language, for a thinking within, rather than about, Judaism, is hermeneutically sophisticated. Again, Lindbeck is helpful. The cultural-linguist approach to religious traditions is not an argument for a separation between religious tradition and the world.[41] The cultural-linguist approach argues for the give and take of translation as the hermeneutical engine that moves a tradition in and through history.

Very much in keeping with Rosenzweig's theory of translation, Lindbeck's cultural-linguistic model is a call not for isolation but for a reassessment of where the burden of translation should lie.[42] In Lindbeck's words:

> A scriptural world is . . . able to absorb the universe. It supplies the interpretive framework within which believers seek to live their lives and understand reality. This happens quite apart from formal theories. Augustine did not describe his work in the categories we are employing, but the whole of his theological production can be understood as a progressive, even if not always successful, struggle to insert everything from Platonism and the Pelagian problem to the fall of Rome into the world of the Bible. Aquinas tried to do something similar with Aristotelianism, and Schleiermacher with German romantic idealism. The way they described extrascriptural realities and experience, so it can be argued, was shaped by biblical categories much more than was warranted by their formal methodologies.[43]

Recall Rosenzweig's comment:

> What is new [in the modern era], is not that the Jew's feet could now take him farther than before—in the Middle Ages the Jew was not an especially sedentary, but rather a comparatively mobile element of medieval society. The new feature is that the wanderer no longer returns at dusk. The gates of the ghetto no longer close behind him, allowing him to spend the night in solitary learning.[44]

Like Rosenzweig, Lindbeck argues that scriptural traditions gain their meaning through their interaction with, and not denial of, the outside world. Both reiterate that what is needed for the modern person is a way to close the gates of religious tradition, if only for the evening.

Let us return then to the question of Jewish election and pluralism in Rosenzweig's ethical monotheism. Rosenzweig's argument is that these are internal matters for the elect people of God. Though he certainly does not demonstrate sensitivity toward multiple religious traditions in *The Star of Redemption*, Rosenzweig's arguments about Jewish election and ethical monotheism do not preclude a social and cultural openness to a society of plural and diverse religious traditions. What his arguments do preclude is a distortion of the internal workings of Jewish monotheism. From within the language of Judaism, the Jews are an elect people who witness God's revelation for the sake of the redemption of the world. Until this truth is verified in the redemption of the world, this only has meaning from within the witnessing community. Moreover, if there is no community to witness God's word, there is no meaning to Jewish election. The strength of Rosenzweig's argument is that he does not seek to distort the fact that there is an internal Jewish perspective that is untranslatable though not entirely closed off to others. We have seen that his argument is against a wholly apologetic approach to Judaism and philosophy, an approach that cannot but distort both. This is the methodological issue at stake in Rosenzweig's understanding of Jewish election.

We must now turn briefly to his view of the Jewish-Christian relation, which in the contemporary context cannot but raise the issue of the content of Rosenzweig's notion of Jewish election. We have seen that Rosenzweig contends in *The Star of Redemption* that Christianity furthers Jewish revelation by acting as the rays of the fire of Judaism. Let us call to mind Gillian Rose's harsh criticism:

> In two ways *The Star of Redemption* reaffirms the abyssal opposition of grace and law which is the legacy of the self-definition of Christianity against Judaism: by inverting their bearers so that Judaism qualifies for eternal grace while Christianity struggles with the state and law.[45]

In chapter 8, I tried to demonstrate that Rose draws such conclusions by reading Rosenzweig's views of Judaism reductively rather than aporetically. But what should we make of Rosenzweig's contention about Christianity's relation to the state and law? Does Rosenzweig require Christianity to be worldly in order that Judaism can be other-worldly? Does Rosenzweig require Christianity to be universal so that Judaism may remain particular?

Here my answer is similar to the answer I offered in chapter 8. Though in *The Star of Redemption* Rosenzweig does ascribe to Christianity a political worldliness and to Judaism an anti-political unworldliness, understanding the work as an apologetic text in Rosenzweig's sense allows us to read it aporetically rather than reductively. Just as Rosenzweig showed openness to the political and cultural realities of Zionism, so too his thought could show openness to the political and cultural realities of a Christian return to Israel-like communities. Indeed, Rosenzweig maintains that Judaism *and* Christianity are the future of monotheism. It is very much in the spirit of Rosenzweig's arguments about Christian idolatry that many post-Holocaust, Christian thinkers have advocated a Christian return to its Jewish origins.

However, the significance of this claim is not, as most proponents of Jewish-Christian dialogue in Rosenzweig's name have maintained, that Judaism and Christianity are mutually affirming. Rather, the significance of the dialogical relation between Judaism and Christianity is that these two traditions exist in an eternally judgmental relation to one another. The fact that they both strive to be Israel-like forms the basis of this judgment. What true dialogue between Judaism and Christianity provides is recognition of this tension, and not a dismissal of it.[46] There is an insurmountable tension between Judaism and Christianity not because they are so different but because they share so much. In keeping with Rosenzweig's view of the Jewish-Christian relation, dialogue between Judaism and Christianity means not mutual affirmation but the recognition that God "has set enmity between the two for all time and has withal most intimately bound each to each."[47]

Judaism and Christianity have overlapping language games, and nowhere does this tension arise more profoundly than on the issue of election. Lindbeck recognizes this very problem when he argues: "Clarity grows and honesty increases when each religion considers its relation to others in terms of its emic categories, its native tongue, instead of contorting and distorting its heritage to fit the constraints of a purportedly universalizable etic idiom of salvation."[48] It is a distortion of both the Jewish and Christian traditions to ignore the fundamental tension that arises between them, in their own theological terms, over the issue of election. The fact that they both strive to be Israel-like forms the basis of their judgment of each other.

Lindbeck's arguments about Christian election are in the spirit of Rosenzweig's appreciation of the tension between Judaism and Christianity—a tension that for each is productive for his own religious tradition. In attempting to correct the supersessionist reading of Christian election, Lindbeck writes: "The church of believers in Christ has never been scripturally or normatively the fulfillment of Israel. . . . The light of the Messianic dawn which, Christians believe, shines more brightly in the church than in Israel before, or unbelieving Israel after Christ, also makes the Christian potential for unfaithfulness greater."[49] The key point in this statement is that Lindbeck combines a criticism of Christian supersessionism with the honest statement that "the light of the Messianic dawn . . . , Christians believe, shines more brightly in the church than in Israel before." The cultural-linguistic model does not and cannot deny the literal grammars of its respective tradition. Reading Rosenzweig in light of Lindbeck reiterates, among other things, that the cultural-linguistic model will be disappointing for those who are looking for mutual affirmation between Judaism and Christianity. Neither Rosenzweig, who argues for the world-historical significance of Christianity, nor Lindbeck, who argues that Christians must model themselves and become an Israel-like community, believes that the relation between Judaism and Christianity eradicates his tradition's judgment of the other or founds a universal, Judeo-Christian discourse.[50]

We can now return one last time to the question of Rosenzweig's construction of the Jewish and Christian communities. Significantly, Lindbeck, despite (or perhaps because of) his shared recognition of the irreconcilable tension between Judaism and Christianity, provides an important antidote to the reductive reading of Rosenzweig's constructions of both Judaism and Christianity that Rose offers. Lindbeck writes:

> Faithfulness *in extremis* leads to martyrdom. . . . Faithfulness, however, is not foolhardiness. It must be exercised with prudence: wise as serpents and harmless as doves . . . the test in terms of which prudence is to be exercised. It may sound repellently ethnocentric, but the survival and welfare of the chosen people is a criterion for distinguishing between the prudent and imprudent. That special concern for one's own group should be part of one's social and political responsibilities has become foreign to many Christians, but it remains familiar to Jews. Especially since the Holocaust, they have had to relearn that insuring communal survival may sometimes take precedence over other duties.[51]

"The labor of the concept inseparable from its formal characteristics" of Rosenzweig's work (to use Rose's formulation) leads to Lindbeck's view that the question of Israel's peacefulness and relation to politics cannot be answered with blanket statements. Rosenzweig and Lindbeck agree that the future of monotheism is a risk, politically, theologically, and in every other human way. In keeping with his most fundamental commitments, Rosenzweig's thought leads to the conclusion that the future of monotheism is not something that can be determined in advance. By definition, monotheism itself is a risk. As we have seen throughout this book, a non-idolatrous life for Rosenzweig is a life of risk. It is a life that risks the "ever-new will of God's revelation." Perhaps most profoundly, a non-idolatrous life, in its willingness to takes risks, is a life that must always risk idolatry.

# *Notes*

All citations to Rosenzweig are to the recent edition of his collected works, entitled *Franz Rosenzweig: Der Mensch und sein Werk: Gesammelte Schriften*, published in four volumes (Boston and The Hague: Martinus Nijhoff, 1974–1984). These texts are cited by volume and page numbers as follows:

| | |
|---|---|
| GS 1:1 | *Brief und Tagebücher*, vol. 1 |
| GS 1:2 | *Brief und Tagebücher*, vol. 2 |
| *The Star of Redemption* | *Der Stern der Erlösung*, trans. William W. Hallo |
| GS 3 | *Zweistromland. Kleinere Schriften zu Glauben und Denken* |
| GS 4:1 | *Sprachdenken im Übersetzen 1. Band Hymnen und Gedichte des Jehuda Halevi* |
| GS 4:2 | *Sprachdenken im Übersetzen 2. Band Arbeitspapiere zur Verdeutschung der Schrift* |

References to Rosenzweig's work cite the page number of the original German text followed by the page number of a published English translation. Where no published English translation is available, translations are those of the present author. Hebrew transliterations from quoted material follow that author's transliterations. Otherwise, transliterations are my own.

**Introduction**

1. See Franz Rosenzweig, "Das neue Denken," in GS 3, pp. 139–161.

2. The argument that "Rosenzweig should be read as a philosopher—specifically, a postmodern philosopher" is one of two major themes of Robert Gibbs's *Correlations in Rosenzweig and Levinas* (Princeton: Princeton University Press, 1992), p. 10. Yudit Kornberg Greenberg, *Better than Wine: Love, Poetry, and Prayer in the Thought of Franz Rosenzweig* (Atlanta: Scholars Press, 1996), also claims that Rosenzweig can and should be read as a postmodern philosopher (see pp. 129–138).

3. In this sense, this study is indebted to Stéphane Mosès' *Système et révélation: La philosophie de Franz Rosenzweig* (Paris: Les Editions du Souil, 1982; translated into English as *System and Revelation: Philosophy of Franz Rosenzweig* by Catherine Tihanyi [Detroit: Wayne State University Press, 1992]), in terms of Mosès' overall theme, as elucidated in its title, of the complex ways in which Rosenzweig's thought is animated by an irresolvable tension between "system" and "revelation."

4. See Julius Guttmann's treatment of Rosenzweig in *Philosophies of Judaism*, translated from the German and Hebrew by David W. Silverman, with an introduction by R. J. Zwi Werblowsky (New York: Holt, Rinehart and Winston, 1964).

5. See, for example, Else-Rahel Freund, *Franz Rosenzweig's Philosophy of Existence*, trans. Stephen L. Weinstein and Robert Israel from the German revised

edition, ed. Paul Mendes-Flohr (Boston and the Hague: Martinus Nijhoff Publishers, 1979).

6. Robert Gibbs writes: "Jewish particularity needs to be juxtaposed to other particularities, and a logic that can open to generality without dissolving particularity will be the hallmark of PJP [postmodern Jewish philosophy] logic. Rosenzweig devoted much of his thought to the logic of 'and' (parataxis), allowing independent entities to stand in relation with each other without combining to form a third. Even as he explored universality, he maintained the prior independence of the existing person" (in Steven Kepnes, Peter Ochs, and Robert Gibbs, *Reasoning After Revelation* [Boulder: Westview Press, 1998], p. 23). Yudit Kornberg Greenberg also attributes a shared approach to Judaism and particularity in "postmodern Jewish philosophy." She writes: "Postmodernism doesn't exclude in advance; it has no conceptual a priori. It demands neither certain attributes nor their opposites" (in *Reasoning After Revelation*, p. 11).

7. Steven Kepnes comes close to Rosenzweig's view of the importance of Jewish texts for reorienting the Jewish person in the modern world. Nonetheless, Kepnes's analysis remains one-sided; he does not consider the continuing interaction between the newly oriented Jewish person and his/her external world. Moreover, the term "postmodern Jewish thinking" remains problematic, for it implies a linearity and indeed a stasis between Judaism, philosophy, and modernity. I turn to these issues in greater detail in the conclusion of this book. Kepnes writes: "Postmodern Jewish thinking is most lively for me at the conjunction of Jewish subjectivity and Jewish textuality. At this juncture, the modern, autonomous self passes into the postmodern twilight and becomes subject to the play of speech, text, and interpretation; the self-enclosed, rational, liberal, universal self loses its confidence and sets off to find itself in and through dialogue with the textual and human other. The self no longer recognizes itself in itself but through manifold, refracted linguistic forms. . . . In decentering the self, this hermeneutical process recenters Jewish texts, or Torah, as the fulcrum around which Jewish existence revolves" (*Reasoning After Revelation*, p. 24).

8. "Idolatry as a modern possibility" is Fackenheim's phrase. It is discussed further below.

9. Moshe Halbertal and Avishai Margalit, *Idolatry* (Cambridge, Mass.: Harvard University Press, 1992), do mention Emil Fackenheim in a footnote on page 293, as well as Yeshayahu Leibowitz in the text of page 229. I turn to these comments below.

10. See Francis Bacon, *The Essays* (Harmondsworth: Penguin Books, 1985). See Halbertal and Margalit's brief discussion of Bacon in *Idolatry*, p. 242.

11. *Writings of the Young Marx on Philosophy and Society*, trans. L. D. Easton and K. H. Cuddat (New York: Doubleday, 1967), p. 245.

12. Ibid., pp. 289–290. Halbertal and Margalit quote this passage in their discussion of Marx, arguing that for Marx the error of idolatry is an issue of proper worship (*Idolatry*, pp. 241–242). One of the key theses of this book is that this is also always a hermeneutical issue.

13. My intention is not to conflate MacIntyre and Gadamer but to paint some broad strokes about common aspects of their respective projects.

14. Hans-Georg Gadamer, *Truth and Method*, 2nd ed., trans. Joel Weinsheimer and Donald G. Marshall (New York: Crossroads, 1989), p. 301, emphasis in the original.

15. Alasdair MacIntyre, *After Virtue*, 2nd ed. (Notre Dame: University of Notre Dame Press, 1984), p. 221.

16. Among the text scholars whom Ochs includes under the rubric "post-critical" are Steven Fraade, Michael Fishbane, and Moshe Greenberg. He includes Hans Frei and George Lindbeck as "post-critical" Christian theologians. See Ochs's introduction in Peter Ochs, ed., *The Return to Scripture in Judaism and Christianity* (New York: Paulist Press), pp. 3–51.

17. See chapter 5 for an extended discussion of this point.

18. The term "language game" brings to mind, of course, the philosophy of the later Wittgenstein. When I use the term, I do so in the sense implied by Hans Frei, George Lindbeck, and Peter Ochs in their recent readings and uses of Wittgenstein, as opposed to those of D. Z. Philips. An account of the differences between these views, as well as their relation to Wittgenstein's thought, is beyond the scope of this book. I endorse Frei's, Lindbeck's, and Ochs's views of a language game in the sense that for each of them, the language game of Christianity or Judaism is always in interaction with its external society. In other words, the argument that Judaism is a language game is not an argument for relativism. As I will argue in the context of Rosenzweig's thought, this view of Judaism as a language game is consistent with Rosenzweig's views of the relation between "religion" and science, Judaism and Germanism, and, indeed, Judaism and modernity. See Dewi Zephaniah Philips, *Religion Without Explanation* (Oxford: Basil Blackwell, 1975), and Peter Ochs, *Peirce Pragmatism and the Logic of Scripture* (New York: Cambridge University Press, 1998). I refer to Frei and Lindbeck below.

19. Clifford Geertz, "From the Native's Point of View: On the Nature of Anthropological Understanding," in *Interpretive Social Science*, ed. P. Rabinow and W. M. Sullivan (Berkeley: University of California Press, 1979), pp. 240ff., as quoted in Ochs, *The Return to Scripture*, pp. 21–22.

20. Halbertal and Margalit, *Idolatry*, p. 244.

21. Ludwig Wittgenstein, *The Big Typescript*, Manuscript 213 and 413, as quoted in Halbertal and Margalit, *Idolatry*, p. 244.

22. Halbertal and Margalit suggest that Wittgenstein's thought has affinities with Maimonides on negative attributes (*Idolatry*, p. 245). What may be more relevant to this discussion is that Wittgenstein's comments may have affinities with Hermann Cohen's view of idolatry. I turn to Cohen below.

23. Paul Tillich, *Systematic Theology* I (Chicago: University of Chicago Press, 1951), p. 13.

24. Franz Rosenzweig, *Hegel und der Staat* (Munich and Berlin: R. Oldenbourg, 1920), 2:243.

25. Halbertal and Margalit, *Idolatry*, p. 246.

26. In his provocative essay, "Idolatry as a Modern Possibility," Emil Fackenheim argues that idolatry is something that takes on particular forms (*Encounters Between Judaism and Modern Philosophy* [New York: Basic Books, 1973], pp.

171–198). Fackenheim rightly points out that the prohibition against idolatry adequately understood is not today's secularized cliché of generic iconoclasm. So too, theologically, every sin and every folly is not idolatry. The argument of this book suggests, however, that Rosenzweig's thought differs from Fackenheim's in the end on the issue of the relation between Judaism and philosophy. In a footnote, Halbertal and Margalit describe Fackenheim's view of idolatry in the following way: "For a modern theological articulation of idolatry as granting absolute value to the state, see E. Fackenheim" (*Idolatry*, p. 293). Though I think Halbertal and Margalit are reductive in describing Fackenheim's view in this way, precisely because Fackenheim does argue emphatically that his view is an attempt to counter generic iconoclasm, there is some truth to their reduction. In the end, Fackenheim's approach to idolatry does begin to sound formulaic. Though he criticizes Tillich in particular, Fackenheim's view of idolatry sounds quite similar to Tillich's. Like Tillich, Fackenheim suggests that "idolatry is the literal identification of finiteness and infinitude" (*Encounters Between Judaism and Modern Philosophy*, p. 189). It is interesting that Halbertal and Margalit do not categorize Yeshayahu Leibowitz in the same way as Fackenheim: "There are some thinkers (such as the contemporary Israeli philosopher Yeshayahu Leibowitz) who claim that . . . [w]hat characterizes God is not an ontological proposition, an exclusive collection of attributes, but the attitude of unconditional obedience to him" (p. 229). This would seem to qualify Leibowitz for Halbertal and Margalit's category of "extension." David Biale has written about the tension between Leibowitz's view of idolatry as an attitude and his general definition of Judaism as practice. See his "Homage to Yeshayahu Leibowitz: Israeli Public Intellectual" in *Religious Studies Review* 22, no. 4 (October 1996): 309–312.

27. See Peter Berkowitz, *Nietzsche: The Ethics of an Immoralist* (Cambridge, Mass.: Harvard University Press, 1995), for an analysis of the ways in which the strength of Nietzsche's arguments rests on the attempt to invert traditional values.

28. See in particular Friedrich Nietzsche, *Twilight of Idols*, in *The Portable Nietzsche*, ed. and trans. Walter Kaufmann (New York: Viking, 1954).

29. David Hume, *Dialogues Concerning Natural Religion and the Natural History of Religion*, ed. J.C.A. Gaskin (New York: Oxford University Press, 1983), pp. 48–56.

30. GS 2, p. 768.

31. Halbertal and Margalit, *Idolatry*, p. 241.

32. Ibid., p. 5.

33. Ibid., p. 241.

34. Wendell Dietrich, *Cohen and Troeltsch: Ethical Monotheistic Religion and Theory of Culture* (Atlanta: Scholars Press, 1986), p. 1.

35. Halbertal and Margalit, *Idolatry*, p. 7.

**Chapter One**

1. The *Wissenschaft des Judentums* developed as a historiographical school that was dedicated to the modern and critical study of Judaism in all its aspects. It developed initially in Germany, in the 1820s, as part of the Berlin *Haskalah*

(enlightenment) movement. Its historiographical methods centered on understanding Judaism in all of its manifestations—theology, religious worship, Jewish law, Hebrew literature, ethics, education, and so forth. The *Wissenschaft des Judentums* came to understand Jewish history as the evolution of one period into the next. In this sense, it was tied to notions of linear, historical progress and for this reason, Rosenzweig was critical of it. Gershom Scholem shared this criticism, and it forms the basis of his work on the Kabbalah. However, as a number of recent scholars have reiterated, the *Wissenschaft des Judentums* was historically more complex than its critics have presented it. See Susannah Heschel, *Abraham Geiger and the Jewish Jesus* (Chicago: University of Chicago Press, 1998). See also "Modern Jewish Studies," in *The Jew in the Modern World*, ed. Paul Mendes-Flohr and Jehuda Reinharz, 2nd ed. (New York: Oxford University Press, 1995), pp. 207–210. For a helpful discussion of Scholem's critique of *Wissenschaft des Judentums*, see David Biale, *Gershom Scholem, Kabbalah, and Counter-History* (Cambridge, Mass.: Harvard University Press, 1982).

2. Cohen was a professor at Marburg from 1873 to 1912.

3. As cited in Nahum Glatzer, *Franz Rosenzweig: His Life and Thought* (New York: Schocken, 1953), p. 29.

4. Ibid.

5. According to Glatzer, "During a furlough at the end of January and into February 1918, F. R. [Franz Rosenzweig] was twice in Berlin, where he visited Hermann Cohen. . . . In Cohen's bathroom F.R. happened by chance upon a discarded carbon manuscript copy (on very thin paper) of Cohen's *Religion der Vernunft aus den Quellen des Judentums*, which he appropriated." Rosenzweig wrote to Cohen on March 9, 1918: "All I can do is thank you. These pages have helped me through dark days" (*Franz Rosenzweig*, p. 65). See Hermann Cohen, *Religion der Vernunft aus den Quellen des Judentums* (Leipzig: G. Fock, 1919); translated as *Religion of Reason out of the Sources of Judaism*, by Simon Kaplan (Atlanta: Scholars Press, 1995) (hereafter cited by the page number in the German original first, followed by the English translation). See especially chapters 1 and 2 ("God's Uniqueness" and "Image Worship"), which form the foundation of Cohen's entire argument in *Religion of Reason*. Arguably, the problematic of idolatry and representation is central to Cohen's entire system.

6. See Cohen, *Religion of Reason*, chapter 12, "The Idea of the Messiah and Mankind."

7. In the first chapter of *Religion of Reason*, Cohen follows Maimonides and argues not only that God cannot be represented in physical form but that most generally God can only be known negatively, by what God is not. Cohen concisely sums up his views on images:

> Michael Sachs, in a sensitive anticipation of the iconoclastic turmoil, produced the hymn "And All Shall Come" for the services of the New Year and the Day of Atonement.
>
> In this hymn there is one word that makes a corresponding word in the prophets and the psalms more intelligible. And this deeper understanding brings to light the aesthetic consciousness that nourished the fight against the images of the gods. This hymn says: "They will be *ashamed* of their images."

> The images must be ashamed of themselves because they are merely illusions. But, above all, the image worshipers and, indeed, the image makers must be ashamed of the illusory images they produce in order to worship them.
>
> When image worship begins to produce shame, then idol worship declines. [Cohen, *Religion of Reason*, p. 64/55; emphasis in the original.]

(Michael Sachs [1808–1864] was a German rabbi and scholar. He succeeded Leopold Zunz in Prague in 1836 and then went to Berlin in 1840 where he was also a *dayyan* [judge]. Sachs worked on a German Bible translation with Zunz. His major work is *Religiöse Poesie der Juden in Spanien*, published in 1845.)

8. See Andrea Poma, *The Critical Philosophy of Hermann Cohen*, trans. John Denton (Albany: State University Press of New York, 1997), for the most comprehensive overview in English of Cohen's critical idealism. For a critical analysis of Cohen's logic, see especially Helmut Holzhey, *Cohen und Natorp*, vol. 1, *Ursprung und Einheit* (Basel: Schwabe, 1986).

9. See Poma, *Critical Philosophy of Cohen*, especially pp. 87, 238.

10. See Harry van der Linden, *Kantian Ethics and Socialism* (Indianapolis: Hackett, 1988), especially chapter 4, "Hermann Cohen: From Social Ethics to Socialist Ethics."

11. As Halbertal and Margalit report in *Idolatry*, this question is asked and answered in many different ways throughout rabbinic and Jewish literature, which they explore in their book.

12. We will see that for Rosenzweig and Cohen, and for their medieval predecessors, Judah Halevi and Moses Maimonides, all four configurations are possible; there is a right God, there are wrong gods, there is right worship, and there is wrong worship.

13. I refer here to Maimonides' argument for the confluence between Judaism and philosophy on the issue of idolatry, as he develops it in *The Guide of the Perplexed*, trans. S. Pines (Chicago: University of Chicago Press, 1963). Here I take Maimonides' argument at face value and do not deal with the question of the *Guide*'s relation to Maimonides' nonphilosophical works. This is an enormous subject that this study does not attempt even to broach. My purpose is to provide a basic backdrop to Cohen's and Rosenzweig's arguments. Cohen himself took Maimonides' comments about the confluence of Judaism and philosophy at face value. See Cohen's "Charackteristik der Ethik Maimunis" (1908) in Hermann Cohen, *Jüdische Schriften* (Berlin: C. A. Schwetschke & Sohn, 1924), 3:221–289. For Leo Strauss's famous articulation of the alternate view—that Maimonides' argument in the *Guide* should precisely not be taken at face value—see his "Literary Character of the *Guide of the Perplexed*" in *Persecution and the Art of Writing* (Chicago: University of Chicago Press, 1980), pp. 38–94. See Ehud Benor, *Worship of the Heart: A Study in Maimonides' Philosophy of Religion* (Albany: State University of New York Press, 1995), for a recent argument that religion and philosophy complement each other for Maimonides. See also David Novak's argument in *Natural Law in Judaism* (New York: Cambridge University Press, 1998), pp. 115–121, that Cohen misreads Maimonides not on the confluence between Judaism and philosophy, but on the confluence between Judaism and ethics.

14. See the first few lines of *The Guide of the Perplexed*: "Image [*selem*] and likeness [*demuth*]. People have thought that in the Hebrew language image denotes the shape and configuration of a thing. This supposition led them to the pure doctrine of corporeality of God, on account of His saying: Let us make man in our image, after our likeness" (21). Maimonides goes on to attempt to show that this view is a misunderstanding of both Hebrew and the biblical text and that *selem* refers to function. Note that the problem begins for Maimonides with what people *think* God *is*.

15. See *Guide*, chapter 35, pp. 79–81.

16. For anthropomorphic biblical conceptions of God, see most especially Exodus 24:10, 1 Kings 22:9, Isaiah 6:1, Ezekiel 1:26, and Daniel 7:9. Rabbinic sources too speak of God's image. For a midrashic description of the fact of God appearing in images, see for example *Pesiqta Rabbati* 31, 155b: "'What can I liken to you?' [I have appeared] to you in several forms. At the sea I appeared to you as a warrior engaged in war. . . . At Sinai I appeared as an elder teaching Torah. . . . At the Tabernacle I appeared as a bridegroom entering his nuptial chamber." Also, much of kabbalistic literature in particular is rife with anthropomorphic descriptions of God. See Elliot Wolfson, *Through a Speculum That Shines* (Princeton: Princeton University Press, 1994), for a thorough discussion of the role of images in Kabbalah.

For an overview of the use of images in Jewish practice, see the following by Menahem Haran: "The Ark and the Cherubim: Their Symbolic Significance in Biblical Ritual," *Israel Exploration Journal* (1959), part 1, 9:1, pp. 30–38, part 2, 9:2, pp. 89–94; "The Divine Presence and the Cultic Institutions," *Biblica* 50 (1969): 251–267; and *Temples and Temple-Service in Ancient Israel* (Oxford: Clarendon Press, 1978). Also see Baruch Levine, *In the Presence of the Lord* (Leiden: Brill, 1974).

17. *Guide*, I:26, p. 56.

18. Ibid., I:1, p. 21.

19. Within Maimonides scholarship, there is a debate over which is the proper interpretation of Maimonides' doctrine of negative attributes: is it a critique of the human ability to know God's essence, or is it a critique of language? This issue is beyond the scope of this book. My only goal in discussing Maimonides here is to set up the context for Rosenzweig's discussion of anthropomorphism. For the view that Maimonides seeks to critique first and foremost the possibility of human knowledge of God, see Shlomo Pines, "The Limitations of Human Knowledge according to al-Farfabi ibn Bajji and Maimonides," in *Studies in Medieval Jewish History and Literature*, ed. I. Twersky (Cambridge, Mass.: Harvard University Press, 1979), pp. 89–110. For more on Maimonides and language see H. A. Wolfson, *Studies in the History of Philosophy and Religion*, ed. I. Twersky and G. Williams, vol. 2 (Cambridge, Mass.: Harvard University Press, 1977), chapter 5.

20. *Guide*, I:59, p. 140.

21. See chapter 2 of Cohen's *Religion of Reason*, "Image Worship."

22. See ibid., and note 7 above.

23. Azade Seyhan, *Representation and Its Discontents: The Critical Legacy of German Romanticism* (Berkeley: University of California Press, 1992), p. 4. See

also Martha B. Helfer, *The Retreat of Representation: The Concept of Darstellung in German Critical Discourse* (Albany: State University of New York Press, 1996); Christiaan Hart Nibbrig, ed., *Was heisst "Darstellung"?* (Frankfurt am Main: Suhrkamp, 1994); Philippe Lacoue-Labarthe and Jean-Luc Nancy, *The Literary Absolute*, trans. Philip Barnard and Cheryl Lester (Albany: State University of New York Press, 1988).

24. GS 3, pp. 735–746. See Michael Oppenheim, *Speaking/Writing of God: Jewish Philosophical Reflections on the Life with Others* (Albany: State University of New York Press, 1997), chapter 2, for a discussion of Rosenzweig's view of anthropomorphism.

25. GS 3, p. 737.

26. Ibid.

27. Ibid., p. 739.

28. See Stéphane Mosès' essay, "Franz Rosenzweig in Perspective: Reflections on His Last Diaries," in *The Philosophy of Franz Rosenzweig*, ed. Paul Mendes-Flohr (Hanover, N.H.: Brandeis University Press, 1988), pp. 185–201.

29. GS 1:2, pp. 770–771.

30. As Mosès explains, "Against . . . [Freud's] understanding of the role of religious symbols Rosenzweig posits a natural relation to the real world, which, in its living immediacy, has the character of an authentic revelation. The aim of biblical monotheism is to eliminate the 'projective' symbolism, in order to re-endow the natural experiences with a spontaneously divine character" ("Franz Rosenzweig in Perspective," p. 190).

31. GS 3, p. 741.

32. Ibid.

33. See GS 4:2, pp. 114, 166, for the German translations of Luther and Buber and Rosenzweig cited above.

34. Franz Rosenzweig, *Jehuda Halevi: Zweiundneunzig Hymnen und Gedichte, Deutsch, mit einem Nachwort und mit Anmerkungen* (Der Sechzig Hymnen und Gedichte Zweite Ausgabe) (Berlin: Verlag Lambert Schneider, 1927). Reprinted as GS 4:1.

35. GS 3, p. 152. As translated in Barbara Galli, *Franz Rosenzweig and Jehuda Halevi: Translating, Translations, and Translators* (Montreal and Kingston: McGill-Queen's University Press, 1995), p. 290. See Galli's book for an excellent account of Rosenzweig's translation of Halevi and of the relation of the translation to Rosenzweig's thought.

36. See Dorit Orgad's argument that prior to translating Halevi's poems, Rosenzweig was influenced by Halevi's philosophy while writing *The Star of Redemption*, in "Rosenzweig and Halevi: Similar Ideas in Their Training" (Hebrew), *Da'at* 21 (Summer 1998), pp. 115–128. While I agree with Orgad's thesis, I disagree with her characterization of Halevi and Rosenzweig's thought as leading to irrational conclusions (though grounded in rational proof). I address this issue most directly in chapter 3. For an argument that Rosenzweig's relation to Zionism was also shaped by his encounter with Halevi, see Ehud Luz, "Zionism and Messianism in the Thought of Franz Rosenzweig" (Hebrew), *Jerusalem Studies in Jewish Thought* 2, 3 (Nisan 1983): 472–489. I discuss Rosenzweig's position of Zionism in chapter 8.

37. Judah Halevi, *The Kuzari: In Defense of the Despised Faith*, trans. and annotated by N. Daniel Korobkin (Northvale, N.J.: Jason Aronson, 1998).

38. On Halevi's specific criticism of the attempt to find a rational for the commandments, see A. Jacobus, "The Kuzari's Attitude toward Philosophy"(in Hebrew), *Alumah* (1936): 61–62. See also Leo Strauss, "The Law of Reason in the *Kuzari*," in *Persecution and the Art of Writing*, pp. 95–141. The argument I make in this book about Rosenzweig's relation to philosophy could parallel Strauss's argument about Halevi. In Rosenzweig's terms, Judaism provides an ethical orientation in life, an orientation that philosophy cannot provide.

39. Halevi, *Kuzari*, 4:13, pp. 221–222.

40. Ibid., 1:97, pp. 40–41.

41. Cohen's arguments about the confluence between Judaism and philosophy are both explicit and implicit. See for example his statement, a few pages into the *Religion of Reason*, that "Religion is not philosophy. However, the religion of reason, by virtue of its share in reason, has at least some kinship with philosophy. It is therefore not surprising that this share in reason, akin to that of philosophy, begins to stir within religion, starting, it would seem, with its concept of God" (*Religion of Reason*, p. 42/36).

42. Halbertal and Margalit, *Idolatry*, pp. 186–190.

43. GS 3, p. 740.

44. Ibid., p. 740.

45. GS 1:2, p. 587.

46. Halbertal and Margalit also only deal with the problem of representation from a cognitive point of view. See their chapter "Idolatry and Representation" in *Idolatry*, pp. 37–66.

47. The interconnection between Cohen's conceptions of proper thinking and monotheism, and idolatry as their opposite, is reflected even in Cohen's definition of monotheism: "Monotheism is not the thought of one man, but the development of this thought which impregnates the entire thinking of the people" (*Religion of Reason*, pp. 42–43/36).

48. Although *The Star of Redemption* does not advocate a normative ethics, it is replete with ethical implications. As Robert Gibbs has shown, Rosenzweig's dialogical conception of ethics is intimately linked and indebted to Cohen's understanding of ethics, as expressed both in Cohen's *Religion* and in his earlier *Ethik*. See Gibbs, *Correlations in Rosenzweig and Levinas*, pp. 178–181. But Rosenzweig's link to Cohen goes beyond a dialogical ethics. For Rosenzweig, representation is always ethical and political in nature. Rosenzweig's understanding of what it means to represent others, what it means to be a representative, what he also calls a witness, is fundamentally an ethically monotheistic concept.

49. Halbertal and Margalit, *Idolatry*, p. 8.

50. The blood community, and the critical import of the blood community, is discussed in greater detail in chapters 3 and 7.

51. Almut Sh. Bruckstein would dispute the reading of Cohen that I offer here. She has argued recently that Cohen's philosophy forms the basis of a "Post-Talmudic Hermeneutics" which is "neither apologetic nor assimilationist in nature: It insists upon the specificity of Jewish and Talmudic culture and upon the responsibility of Jews to engage in that culture" ("Joining the Narrators: A Philosophy

of Talmudic Hermeneutics," in Kepnes, Ochs, and Gibbs, *Reasoning After Revelation*, p. 118). In my view, Cohen himself does not make such a claim for Jewish particularity and remains instead committed to a confluence between Judaism and philosophy that can only undermine such particularity. This is nowhere as true as in his discussion of idolatry. Nonetheless, I agree with Bruckstein that Cohen's thought forms the basis of such a post-assimilationist commitment to Jewish particularity. This is one of the great ironies and tensions of Cohen's thought. I discuss this further in the next chapter.

**Chapter Two**

1. See Moses Mendelssohn, *Jerusalem*, trans. Allan Arkush (Hanover, N.H.: Brandeis University Press, 1983); Abraham Geiger, "A General Introduction to the Science of Judaism," in *Abraham Geiger and Liberal Judaism*, ed. Max Wiener (Philadelphia: Jewish Publication Society of America, 1962), pp. 149–157; Heinrich Graetz, "The Structure of Jewish History," in *The Structure of Jewish History*, ed. and trans. Ismar Schorsch (New York: Jewish Theological Seminary of America, 1975), pp. 63–124; Leo Baeck, *The Essence of Judaism*, trans. V. Grubenwieser and L. Pearl (New York: Schocken, 1948).

2. See in particular Hermann Cohen, *Der Begriff der Religion* (Giessen: Verlag von Alfred Topelmann, 1915), pp. 120–122.

3. Steven S. Schwarzschild, "The Title of Hermann Cohen's 'Religion of Reason Out of the Sources of Judaism,'" introductory essay to Cohen, *Religion of Reason*, p. 11, n. 16. See especially *The Star of Redemption*, pp. 443–448/399–402.

4. My claim is not that Rosenzweig self-consciously follows Mendelssohn, but rather that Mendelssohn and Rosenzweig mark the beginning and the end of German-Jewish thought and that this tradition of thought is more internally coherent than is ordinarily supposed. As Amos Funkenstein has remarked, "Seldom can the historian indicate the beginning and the end of a movement with such a precision as in the case of German-Jewish philosophy. It started with Mendelssohn's *Jerusalem* (1783) and ended with Rosenzweig's *Stern der Erlösung* (1921)" ("Franz Rosenzweig and the End of German-Jewish Philosophy," in *Perceptions of Jewish History* [Berkeley: University of California Press, 1993], p. 257). Rosenzweig himself was favorably disposed to Mendelssohn and was in fact planning to give a course at the *Lehrhaus* on him. See Paul Mendes-Flohr, "Mendelssohn and Rosenzweig," in *Der Philosoph Franz Rosenzweig. Internationaler Kongress, Kassel 1986*, ed. Wolfdietrich Schmied-Kowarzik (Freiburg and Munich: Verlag Karl Alber, 1988), 1: 213–223.

5. See Alexander Altmann, *Moses Mendelssohn: A Biographical Study* (Philadelphia: Jewish Publication Society, 1973), especially chapter 3, pp. 194–263, for an account of this.

6. Ibid., pp. 201–209.

7. John Casper Lavater, *Aussichten in die Ewigkeit, in Briefen an Hrn. Joh. Georg Zimmermann*, First Part, Zürich, 1768; Second Part, Zurich, 1769; Third Part, Zurich, 1772; 2nd ed. of all three parts, Zurich, 1773.

8. Mendelssohn, *Jerusalem*, p. 100.

9. Ibid., p. 89.

10. Ibid., pp. 89–90.

11. Ibid., p. 114.

12. Ibid., p. 113, emphasis in the original.

13. Ibid., pp. 102–103.

14. Ibid., p. 111.

15. As Halbertal and Margalit point out in *Idolatry*, the two senses of *avodah zarah* as alien object of worship and an alien kind of worship are often intertwined in the Jewish tradition. I discuss this in chapter 1.

16. *Writings of the Young Marx on Philosophy and Society*, pp. 245–246.

17. Marx, *Capital*, vol. 1, trans. Ben Fowkes (London: Penguin, 1976), pp. 163–164. I thank David M. Craig for some helpful discussions of this issue in Marx.

18. Ibid., p. 167.

19. "Contribution to the Critique of Hegel's Philosophy of Right" (1843), in Karl Marx and Friederich Engels, *Collected Works* (London: Lawrence and Wisheart, 1975), 3.175.

20. See Van Harvey, *Feuerbach and the Interpretation of Religion* (Cambridge: Cambridge University Press, 1995), especially p. 32, for a discussion of the translation of *Vergegenständlichung* as "projection."

21. Even by the time Lessing had written *The Education of the Human Race*, Mendelssohn's view of progress would seem outdated. See G. E. Lessing, *Werke*, vol. 8 (München: Carl Hanser Verlag, 1979).

22. Mendelssohn, *Jerusalem*, p. 97.

23. Alexander Altmann, "Moses Mendelssohn as Archetypal German Jew," in *The Jewish Response to German Culture*, ed. Jehuda Reinharz and Walter Schatzberg (Hanover, N.H.: University Press of New England, 1985), pp. 17–31. See in particular Altmann's comment (p. 27): "In Mendelssohn's view, the survival of Israel as a separate nation was a matter of religious concern. It was bound up with an ideal to be achieved. It had an ultimate purpose beyond the natural instinct for self-preservation, national identity, or sentimental considerations. It was an idea that compelled Jews to remain Jews. . . . It is reechoed in Hermann Cohen's discussion of 'The Law' in his *Religion of Reason from the Sources of Judaism* (1919). After praising Mendelssohn's 'great messianic tendency,' Cohen pleads for the recognition of the need for maintaining a measure of separateness, even 'isolation,' in cultural respects, seeing that, ultimately, the future of pure monotheism was at stake."

24. Mendelssohn, *Jerusalem*, p. 118, emphasis in the original.

25. Ibid., p. 119.

26. Ibid.

27. The creation of signs and meaning is by definition communal because without public understanding of signs and language, language would mean nothing. Implicit in Mendelssohn's view of language and signs is a denial of the possibility of a private language. This point of view is consistent with what we will see in Rosenzweig (and Cohen, for that matter).

28. See chapter 1.

29. David Sorkin, *Moses Mendelssohn and the Religious Enlightenment*

(Berkeley: University of California Press, 1996); Allan Arkush, *Moses Mendelssohn and the Enlightenment* (Albany: State University of New York Press, 1994). Sorkin's argument is based on an assessment of Mendelssohn's Hebrew writings together with the German ones. Arkush's argument is based on Leo Strauss's framework for approaching certain philosophical/political tracts as esoteric, that is, as reading differently to the masses and the elite. Strauss himself does not include Mendelssohn as an esoteric writer. Arkush argues that Mendelssohn is a more complex thinker than has been acknowledged. See Leo Strauss, "Persecution and the Art of Writing," in *Persecution and the Art of Writing*, pp. 22–37.

30. Mendelssohn, *Jerusalem*, p. 99.

31. Mendelssohn's philosophical argument for the complementarity of religion and reason in the second part of *Jerusalem* is the same argument for the complementarity of church and state in the first part.

32. See Moshe Schwarcz, *Mi'mitos Le'hitgalut* (From myth to revelation) (Tel Aviv: Ha-kibbutz ha-me'uhad, 1978), pp. 238–242, for a discussion of the theological problem of miracles in Rosenzweig's thought. See also Yhoydah Amir, "Miracle as Epistemological Category" (Hebrew), *Da'at*, Summer 1993, for a further discussion of the epistemological role of miracle in Rosenzweig's thought.

33. *The Star of Redemption*, p. 109/98.

34. For more on Rosenzweig's understanding of ideological developments around 1800, see Stéphane Mosès' discussion in "'1800': Goethe, Hegel, and the Accomplishment of the System," in *System and Revelation: Philosophy of Franz Rosenzweig*, pp. 37–38.

35. *The Star of Redemption*, p. 110/99.

36. Of course, even scientists were forced, along with theologians, to recognize the pitfalls of an emphasis on the present. After all, the present always becomes the past. The problem that Rosenzweig is pointing out here has implications, as will be discussed, for all forms of knowledge. His point, as we will see, is that the present needs the past in order to create meaning in the present. This point is his emphasis in "The New Thinking."

37. *The Star of Redemption*, p. 112/101.

38. For Rosenzweig, Schleiermacher's theological attempts epitomize this effort at neutralizing the past by way of the present, and for this reason became the standard by which all theology after him had to define itself (*The Star of Redemption*, pp. 111–112/100–101). See Friederich Schleiermacher, *Hermeneutik und Kritik* in *Werke* (Berlin: Reiner, 1842), vol. 3, translated as *Hermeneutics* (Missoula, Mont.: Scholars Press, 1987). Gadamer sums up the thrust of Schleiermacher's hermeneutics in accordance with Rosenzweig's point: "It is ultimately a divinatory process, a placing of oneself within the whole framework of the author, an apprehension of the 'inner origin' of the composition of a work, a recreation of a creative act" (*Truth and Method*, p. 187). All possible tension with past interpretation is neutralized by Schleiermacher's view of "inner origin."

39. *The Star of Redemption*, p. 105/95.

40. This issue is especially central in Rosenzweig's discussion of prophecy. See especially ibid., p. 105/95.

41. Ibid., p. 116/104.

42. For Rosenzweig, just as we must ask Schleiermacher, "Is this still belief?" we must ask Nietzsche, "Is this still science?" (ibid., p. 117/105).

43. Ibid., p. 107/97. Rosenzweig goes on: "The testimony of oath and the testimony of blood thus amalgamate and after several centuries both ultimately become a single proof in Augustine's famous appeal from all individual reasons to the present historical overall-manifestation, the *ecclesiae auctoritas*, without which he would not credit the testimony of Scripture" (ibid., p. 107/97). Rosenzweig's comments about Augustine in this context are significant, especially in light of Amos Funkenstein's contention that Rosenzweig may have translated Augustine's view of Christianity expressed in *The City of God* to Judaism. See Amos Funkenstein, *Perceptions of Jewish History*, pp. 291–301.

44. *The Star of Redemption*, p. 107/97.

45. GS 3, p. 561.

46. Gadamer, *Philosophical Hermeneutics*, trans. David E. Linge (Berkeley: University of California Press, 1976), p. 9. For a more extended discussion, see Gadamer, *Truth and Method*, especially pp. 276–277.

47. GS 3, p. 159.

48. Gadamer, *Truth and Method*, p. 302

49. See Gadamer's comment that "every finite present has its limitations. We define the concept of 'situation' by saying that it represents a standpoint that limits the possibility of vision. Hence essential to the concept of situation is the concept of '*horizon*.' The horizon is the range of vision that includes everything that can be seen from a particular vantage point. Applying this to the thinking mind, we speak of narrowness of horizon, of the possible expansion of horizon, of the opening up of new horizons, and so forth" (*Truth and Method*, p. 302). Rosenzweig does not speak of a visual horizon but of a calling and hearing that orients the modern person. The issues of sight and sound, and their significance for ethical monotheism, are discussed further in chapter 4.

50. See in particular Nietzsche's *Twilight of Idols*.

51. See chapter 1.

52. *The Star of Redemption*, pp. 302/271–272.

53. GS 3, 153.

54. See Paul Mendes-Flohr, "Franz Rosenzweig's Concept of Philosophical Faith," *Leo Baeck Institute Yearbook* 34 (1989): 357–369, for a helpful overview of the relation between philosophy and theology in Rosenzweig's new thinking.

55. *The Star of Redemption*, p. 118/106. This point is significant for the question of Rosenzweig's so-called existentialism. He adds one page later, "But truth will not be denied, not for the sake of the ideal, *least of all for the sake of experience*" (emphasis added, *The Star of Redemption*, p. 119/107).

56. Ibid., pp. 134/120–121.

57. For Rosenzweig, in its critique of the dogmatism of German idealism, philosophy had rightfully come to understand that we must aim at grasping existence (*Dasein*) rather than being (*Sein*). Recognizing the distinctive, ever-changing, process of being-there is at the same time the recognition of the human inability to understand existence from the point of view of Being (*Sein*) without reference to the distinctive. For Rosenzweig, the attempt to describe the being-there (*dasein*) of

existence (*Dasein*), in contrast to the attempt to capture the being (*sein*) of Being (*Sein*), is fundamentally true because it can grapple with the distinctive, ephemeral nature of life: "The world is neither shadow nor dream nor picture; its being is being there, real being there" (*ihr Sein ist Dasein, wirkliches Dasein*) (p. 147/133, translation altered).

58. There is, of course, much more to say about Rosenzweig's relation to Heidegger. Rosenzweig himself claimed in a short essay published shortly after his death an affinity with Heidegger's thought, claiming moreover that Heidegger was the proper inheritor of Cohen's thought (see "Vertauschte Fronten," in GS 3, pp. 235–238). See Karl Löwith, "M. Heidegger and F. Rosenzweig on Temporality and Eternity," *Philosophy and Phenomenological Research* 3, no. 1 (September 1942), reprinted with modified title as "M. Heidegger and F. Rosenzweig: A Postscript to *Being and Time*," in Karl Löwith, *Nature, History, and Existentialism*, ed. Arnold Levison (Evanston: Northwestern University Press, 1966), pp. 51–78. See also Alan Udoff, "Rosenzweig's Heidegger Reception and the Re-Origination of Jewish Thinking," in *Der Philosoph Franz Rosenzweig (1886–1929)*, pp. 923–950, as well as, in the same volume, Steven S. Schwarzschild, "Franz Rosenzweig and Martin Heidegger: The German and Jewish Turn to Ethnicism," pp. 887–889.

59. *The Star of Redemption*, p. 122/110.

60. Ibid., p. 302/271.

61. Ibid., p. 296/266.

62. Halevi, *Kuzari*, 1:97, p. 41.

63. The "whether she knows it or not" is the subject of the next chapter.

64. As quoted in Nahum Glatzer, *Franz Rosenzweig, His Life and Thought*, p. 136. Rosenzweig continues: "This, if anything, is what will remain of me. I don't take it personally, but consider it part of my destiny."

65. Emil Fackenheim, *To Mend the World* (New York: Schocken, 1982), p. 69.

66. *The Star of Redemption*, p. 361/325.

67. Cohen's point here is a critique of Marx and Marx's Hegelianism. It goes back to Kant's discussions of historical progress in which he (Kant) argues that the notion of "real" progress is a dangerous idea and revolution especially dangerous. This argument corresponds to Kantian metaphysics, in which the dangers of dogmatism loom large: it would be dogmatic, in its worse sense, to ever think we *know* that history is progressing. See most specifically Kant's "Idea of a Universal History," "What is Enlightenment?" and "Perpetual Peace." These are all included in *Kant's Political Writings*, ed. Hans Reiss, trans. H. B. Nisbet (Cambridge: Cambridge University Press, 1975).

68. For the theological implications of this aspect of Cohen's thought, see David Novak, *The Election of Israel: The Idea of the Chosen People* (New York: Cambridge University Press, 1995).

69. In his introduction to the collection of Cohen's Jewish writings, Rosenzweig writes: "Was Cohen als Philosophiegeschichte erstrebt, ist nicht mehr und nicht weniger als eine Geschichte der einen menschlichen Vernunft, also nichts andres als was bei Hegel Kern und Stern des Systems ist. Und gewiß, Cohen ist Kantianer, aber sein Kantianismus ist trotz aller auch bei ihm vorhandenen Be-

tonung der kritischen Vorsicht, die er nie aufgegeben hat, doch etwas ganz andres als die sauersüße Verlegenheitsbescheidung vor den hohen Trauben des Systems" ("Einleitung in die Akademieausgabe der Jüdischen Schriften Hermann Cohens," GS 3, p. 181). In Cohen's effort to move away from any notion of the "given" in experience, and thereby away from any notion of the "thing-in-itself" which reason can never know except through its knowing of its not knowing, Cohen's critique of Kant ends up resembling Hegel's critique of Kant in significant ways. Charles Taylor's summary of Hegel's critique of the Kantian concept could easily apply also to Cohen's approach to Kant: "What for Kant is a structure of the mind is for Hegel an ontological foundation. The concept is the basis of things, the Idea is that which posits reality. It is not simply an unfulfilled tendency; it *is* in a more fundamental sense than anything else" (*Hegel* [Cambridge, Mass.: Harvard University Press, 1975], p. 529). The ultimate difference between Cohen's and Hegel's understanding of dialectic is that Cohen claims the dialectic is infinite, while for Hegel, dialectical mediation has a final endpoint. For more on this, see Jakob Gordin, *Der Ichbegriff bei Hegel, bei Cohen und in der Südwestdeutschen Schule hinsichtlich der Kategorienlehre untersucht.* Erster Teil: *Der Begriff des Denkens bei Hegel und Cohen* (Berlin, 1927). From Rosenzweig's perspective, this is not a big difference.

70. Again, see Rosenzweig's "Einleitung in die Akademieausgabe der Jüdischen Schriften Hermann Cohens," GS 3, pp. 177–224. Of special interest is Rosenzweig's comment about Cohen's aesthetics: "Die Ästhetik selber—auch das ist bezeichnend für die Schärfe der biographischen Wendung—ist ganz erfüllt von der Abweisung eigener systematischer Ansprüche der Religion" (p. 204). In my view, much of Cohen's *Religion of Reason* is anticipated by his *Aesthetics*. This is a point that Rosenzweig, despite his comments about Cohen's existential turn, seemed to grasp.

71. See also Natan Rotenstreich, "Religion of Reason," in *Jews and German Philosophy* (New York: Schocken, 1984), pp. 60–71, for a brief analysis of Rosenzweig's allegations about Cohen's thought. For a detailed philosophical analysis of the development yet consistency of Cohen's position from his system to his religion, see Sinai Ucko, *Der Gottesbegriff in der Philosophie Hermann Cohens*, Ph.D. diss., Albertus-Universität zu Königsberg, 1927. See also Alexander Altmann, "Hermann Cohens Begriff der Korrelation," in *In Zwei Welten—Bishnay Olamot: On S. Moser's 75th Birthday* (Tel Aviv: Bitaon Verlag, 1962), pp. 377–399. Regarding Rosenzweig's remarks about Cohen's person, see Steven Schwarzschild, "F. Rosenzweig's Anecdotes about Hermann Cohen," in *Gegenwart im Rückblick*, ed. H. A. Strauss and K. Grossman (Heidelberg, 1970), pp. 209–218. For a contemporary argument that sides more with Rosenzweig, see Hugo Bergman, *Toldot Ha-filosofya Ha-hadashah* (The history of modern philosophy) (Jerusalem: Mosad Bialik, 1979), pp. 172–192.

72. Hermann Cohen, *Ethik des reinen Willens*, *Werke* (Hildesheim; New York: Olms, 1981), vol. 7, p. 212.

73. Ibid. This is not a sufficient account of Cohen's position of the self. The self, for Cohen, is a task that is never completed. See most specifically *Ethik*, introduction (pp. 1–82) and chapter 8, "das Ideal" (pp. 389–427).

74. Though a fascinating topic, a comprehensive account of the hermeneutical

aspects of Cohen's thought is beyond the scope of this study. Recently, Peter Schmid made a fascinating argument that Cohen's whole ethic, which includes first and foremost his philosophy of law, could be read as a hermeneutic in line with Gadamer and Heidegger. See Peter A. Schmid, *Ethik als Hermeneutik: Systematische Untersuchungen zu Hermann Cohens Rechts und Tugendlehre* (Würzburg: Königshausen and Neumann, 1995).

75. See the introduction to Cohen's *Religion of Reason*, especially this comment: "For consciousness is, properly speaking, only another expression for history. As all culture is developed by history, so also is it developed by consciousness; the only difference is that consciousness actualizes the narrower history of man. . . . Reason is the rock out of which the concept originates for the sake of systematic examination, if the course the concept takes in the river basin of history is to come to view" (*Religion of Reason*, pp. 5–6/4–5).

76. Ibid., p. 367/316, translation altered.

77. Ibid., p. 368/317.

78. He goes on that the merit of the fathers is "always related, however, only to the positive moral achievement, and in no way to the negative one, to the sin for which a vicarious substitute may be sought" (ibid., p. 370/318). The context of Cohen's discussion is his interpretation of Ezekiel.

79. Ibid., p. 369/317.

80. Again, see Mendes-Flohr and Reinharz, "Modern Jewish Studies," in their edited volume, *The Jew in the Modern World*, for a good overview of some of the contradictions inherent in the *Wissenschaft des Judentums*.

81. Cohen, *Religion of Reason*, p. 372/320.

82. Ibid., p. 372/320.

83. Ibid., p. 63/54.

84. Ibid., p. 61/52.

85. On my reading, Cohen's emphasis on performance here is in tension with his general emphasis on cognition. Almut Sh. Bruckstein and Avi Bernstein-Nahar have each convinced me through extensive conversations that it may be possible to reread Cohen (though I remain skeptical that it can be done on Cohen's own terms) so as to emphasize the performative dimensions of his work and to overcome the tensions that I see. Such a rereading is beyond the scope of this study, though I greatly anticipate learning much from such a study.

86. Cohen, *Religion of Reason*, p. 313/268.

87. *The Star of Redemption*, pp. 340–341/306–307.

88. Cohen, *Religion of Reason*, p. 274/235.

89. Ibid., pp. 274–275/234–235.

90. *The Star of Redemption*, p. 361/325.

91. Recall again Cohen's definition of monotheism: "Monotheism is not the thought of one man, but the development of this thought which impregnates the entire thinking of the people," cited in chapter 1.

**Chapter Three**

1. See Mosès, *System and Revelation: Philosophy of Franz Rosenzweig*, especially the conclusion.

2. See most recently Almut Sh. Bruckstein, "On Jewish Hermeneutics: Mai-

monides and Bachya as Vectors in Cohen's Philosophy of Origin," in *Hermann Cohen's Philosophy of Religion* (Hildesheim, Zürich, and New York: Georg Olms Verlag, 1997), pp. 35–50. See also Yoseph Ben-Shlomo, "Cohen's Philosophy of Religion and Conception of Judaism" (in Hebrew), in Hermann Cohen, *Religion of Reason out of the Sources of Judaism*, ed. Shmuel Hugo Bergman and Natan Rotenstreich (Jerusalem: Mosad Bialik, 1971), pp. 481–482, as well as Sinai Ocko's "Hermann Cohen and his Religious Teaching" (in Hebrew) in the same volume, pp. 7–30. For a recent view that criticizes Cohen for suggesting this confluence, from the perspectives of both philosophy and Judaism, see Gillian Rose, "Hermann Cohen—Kant among the Prophets," in *Judaism and Modernity* (Cambridge: Blackwell, 1993), pp. 111–125. Avi Bernstein-Nahar's 1998 dissertation, *Accounting for Modern Jewish Identity: Hermann Cohen and the Ethics of Self-Responsibility* (Department of Religious Studies, Stanford University), addresses the confluence between philosophy and Judaism in Cohen and its implications for contemporary conceptions of Jewish identity. I return to Bruckstein and Rose below.

3. See in particular Rosenzweig's essay "Scripture and Luther," in *Scripture and Translation*, ed. Everett Fox, trans. Lawrence Rosenwald (Bloomington: Indiana University Press, 1994), pp. 47–69. This hermeneutical issue is discussed further in chapter 5.

4. See Else-Rahel Freund, *Franz Rosenzweig's Philosophy of Existence*, p. 5.

5. Much has been written on Rosenzweig's philosophical relation to Hegel. See in particular Stéphane Mosès, "Hegel beim Wort genommen. Geschichtskritik bei Franz Rosenzweig," in *Zeitgewinn. Messianisches Denken nach Franz Rosenzweig*, ed. Gotthard Fuchs and Hans Hermann Henrix (Frankfurt am Main: Verlag Josef Knecht, 1987), pp. 67–89, as well as, in the same volume, Heinz-Jürgen Göritz, "Der Tod als Krisis geschichtlicher Synthese. Der Begriff der Erfahrung bei Hegel and Rosenzweig," pp. 91–126. See also Shlomo Avineri, "Rosenzweig's Hegel Interpretation: Its Relationship to the Development of His Jewish Thinking," and Otto Pöggeler, "Rosenzweig and Hegel," both in *Der Philosoph Franz Rosenzweig*, 2: 831–853.

6. GS 3: 141.

7. *The Star of Redemption*, p. 180/161.

8. Ibid., pp. 203–204/182–183.

9. See "Das neue Denken," GS 3, especially p. 141.

10. GS 3: 142–143.

11. See Moshe Schwarcz, *Mi'mitos Le'hitgalut* (From myth to revelation), especially pp. 244–253, for an extended analysis of Rosenzweig's relation to Schelling. See also Robert Gibbs's analysis of Rosenzweig's logic in *Correlations in Rosenzweig and Levinas*, pp. 40–53. The view of the structure of *The Star of Redemption* that I am presenting here does not conflict with analyses of the particulars of what is going on in Rosenzweig's logic. I am trying instead to point to the relative weight that logic is given in *The Star of Redemption*. Reading *The Star of Redemption* progressively skews, among other things, the importance that Rosenzweig places on logic. I return to this point in my discussion of Cohen.

12. The gendering is intentional. For the way in which this gendering plays out philosophically in *The Star of Redemption*, see Leora Batnitzky, "Judaism, Ethics, and the Feminine: Perspectives from Levinas and Rosenzweig," unpublished

manuscript, presented at the Twenty-eighth Annual Conference of the Association for Jewish Studies, Boston, December 1996.

13. *The Star of Redemption*, pp. 439/394–395.

14. Hans-Georg Gadamer, "The Universality of the Hermeneutical Problem," in *Philosophical Hermeneutics*, p. 9.

15. See the postscript that Rosenzweig adds to "The Unity of the Bible," originally published in *Der Morgan*, October 1928, translated in *Scripture and Translation*, pp. 25–26.

16. Gadamer, *Philosophical Hermeneutics*, p. 9.

17. An important difference between Rosenzweig and Gadamer is that Rosenzweig argues, especially in the case of the Bible, that for relation to be possible, distance must be emphasized rather than downplayed. This is the topic of chapter 5.

18. *Philosophical Hermeneutics*, pp. 22–23.

19. Both Gadamer and Rosenzweig agree that returning to tradition is not a wholesale embrace of tradition. Gadamer sums up this point well: "My thesis is . . . that the thing which hermeneutics teaches us is to see through the dogmaticism of asserting an opposition and separation between the ongoing, natural 'tradition' and the reflective appropriation of it" (*Philosophical Hermeneutics*, p. 28).

20. Robert Gibbs adheres to the progressivist argument when he writes that "the third part of the *Star* shows us the need to ground both logic and linguistic theory in social experience" (*Reasoning After Revelation*, p. 24). This statement is partially right, but it misses the fact that *The Star of Redemption*'s argument is multidirectional. The modern person believes in this kind of progress, but upon her return to community realizes that "the need to ground both logic and linguistic theory in social experience" is a grounding that has already taken place. In fact, logic and linguistic theory are only possible because they are already grounded as such. It is because he reads *The Star of Redemption* progressively that Gibbs places so much emphasis on the logic.

21. An important exception to those who argue that *The Star of Redemption* advocates two separate but equal communities is David Novak who, both in *Jewish-Christian Dialogue: A Jewish Justification* (New York: Oxford University Press, 1989), especially p. 110, and in *The Election of Israel: The Idea of the Chosen People*, especially p. 101, acknowledges that Rosenzweig privileges Judaism over Christianity. Novak nonetheless suggests that a kind of Jewish-Christian mutuality can be developed in accordance with Rosenzweig's view of Jewish election. I offer an alternate view in chapter 6.

22. *The Star of Redemption*, p. 368/331.

23. Ibid., pp. 331–332/298–299, translation altered. Again, Rosenzweig's views of gender are complex and beyond the scope of the present study. When I am not quoting him, I use gender neutral terms.

24. See in particular Cohen, *Der Begriff der Religion*, pp. 120–122, and Rosenzweig, *The Star of Redemption*, pp. 443–448/399–402.

25. I thus agree partially but not entirely with Almut Bruckstein's assertion that "Rosenzweig inaugurated a philosophical revolution that, in fact, transcends

the 'literal meaning'—the *peshat*—of Cohen's logic, while keeping its method alive. Rosenzweig simply radicalizes Cohen's own claim concerning the creative power of 'alterity'—in other words, of 'otherness,' or 'that which differs.' For Cohen, 'alterity' is identical with the 'limit of thought'; it is a 'nought of knowledge' that assumes creativity in that it triggers a process in which 'pure thinking' produces meaning that is ever new. Rosenzweig, however, reads 'alterity' or 'the nought of knowledge' as the end of thought—that is, the end of 'my' thoughts" (*Reasoning After Revelation*, p. 116). On my reading, Rosenzweig's methodological break with Cohen is more radical. As I argue below, it goes beyond the attempt to articulate the "limit of thought" and is an attempt to completely reorient philosophical thinking away from philosophy.

26. "Das neue Denken," GS 3: 140.

27. Bruckstein, "On Jewish Hermeneutics: Maimonides and Bachya as Vectors in Cohen's Philosophy of Origin," p. 37. Bruckstein praises this confluence in Cohen while Rose is highly critical of it. Rose writes that "*as a reader* of Kant, Cohen destroys critical Kantianism, while as *a reader* of the sources of Judaism, he appears to overlook commandment and law" ("Hermann Cohen—Kant among the Prophets," in *Judaism and Modernity*, p. 124). Bruckstein and Rose agree, though neither elaborates in detail, that Rosenzweig shares Cohen's project. This chapter suggests that Rosenzweig does not share with Cohen the attempt to harmonize Judaism with philosophy.

28. See Gadamer, "The Phenomenological Movement," in *Philosophical Hermeneutics*, pp. 130–181, for a good overview of the development of phenomenology in the context of Husserl and Heidegger.

29. Letter dated November 8, 1916, in Rosenzweig and Rosenstock-Huessy, *Judaism Despite Christianity*, ed. Eugen Rosenstock-Huessy (Tuscaloosa: University of Alabama Press, 1969), p. 138.

30. Hermann Cohen, *Deutschtum und Judentum* (Giessen, 1915); reprinted in *Jüdische Schriften*, ed. B. Strauss, 3 vols. (Berlin, 1924).

31. "Das Volk erzeugt nicht seinen Gott, sondern es empfängt und bezeugt ihn," in GS 3: 169.

32. *The Star of Redemption*, p. 331/298.

33. George Mosse, *German Jews Beyond Judaism* (Bloomington: Indiana University Press, 1985), p. 47.

34. Schwarzschild, "Franz Rosenzweig and Martin Heidegger: The German and the Jewish Turn to Ethnicism," in *Der Philosoph Franz Rosenzweig*.

35. GS 1:2, p. 736.

36. GS 1:2, pp. 735–736. Rosenzweig writes that the contrast to "life" is "die Schau," a term that is used in a variety of ways throughout *The Star of Redemption*, as evidenced well by the fact that it is translated there as "view," "vista," "observation," "glimpse," "vision." Its immediate reference, in opposition to "life" on *The Star of Redemption*'s last page, is to viewpoints, *Weltanschauugen*. Rosenzweig contends that the new thinking is a movement away from both Hegelian philosophy and point-of-view philosophy but that it is philosophical nonetheless. See Barbara Galli, "Rosenzweig's *Lehrhaus* Lectures on the Science of God, Man, and World" in *Paradigms in Jewish Philosophy*, ed. R. Jospe

(Madison, Wisc.: Associated University Press, 1997), pp. 198–218, for an elaboration of Rosenzweig's view of this matter.

37. GS 3: 140.

38. Ibid., 142.

39. Ibid., 140.

40. Ibid., 151.

41. It is here that Rosenzweig's remarks about the textuality of *The Star of Redemption* are most significant. See especially GS 3: 140. For a discussion of the textuality of *The Star of Redemption*, see Greenberg, *Better Than Wine*. In the context of the argument of this chapter, I suggest that the philosophical implications of the textuality of *The Star of Redemption* should cause us to rethink the importance of logic for Rosenzweig. Although, as a number of interpreters have noted, especially Bruckstein (1997) and Gibbs (1992), Rosenzweig relies heavily on Cohen's logic of anticipation in Part 1 of *The Star of Redemption*, I have argued in this chapter that Rosenzweig gives his logic not only little existential weight, but also very little philosophical weight. Rosenzweig differs fundamentally from Cohen on the issue of the importance of logic. This is what Rosenzweig means when he writes, as quoted above, that *The Star of Redemption* does *not* "want to bring a mere 'Copernican turn' of thinking" about. Rosenzweig's system of philosophy is not merely a reversal of Cohen's logic, but rather an undoing of the epistemological priority of logic itself.

42. See especially Franz Rosenzweig, "Scripture and Word," in *Scripture and Translation*, pp. 40–46.

43. Letter dated August 30, 1920, in *Franz Rosenzweig: His Life and Thought*, p. 97, as quoted in Galli, "Franz Rosenzweig's *Lehrhaus* Lectures," p. 214.

44. This point about carnal Israel has an important epistemological affinity with Lurianic Kabbalah's notion of the revealed and hidden God. Carnal Israel is that which is revealed; nonetheless, that which is revealed is always limited by that which is hidden. As Moshe Idel has so clearly pointed out, Rosenzweig distinguishes between two types of mysticism: the negative theory of Ekhart, Boehme, and Schelling and the positive theory of Lurianic Kabbalah. For Lurianic Kabbalah, God exists before *any* relation with the existence of the world or even God's self. Rosenzweig discusses this issue most extensively in a letter to Rudolf Ehrenberg of November 18, 1917, called the "Urzelle," or "Germ Cell" of *The Star of Redemption*. See GS 3: 125–138. See Moshe Idel, "Franz Rosenzweig and the Kabbalah," in *Philosophy of Franz Rosenzweig*, ed. Paul Mendes-Flohr, pp. 138–168, for a very helpful discussion of Rosenzweig's criticism of "mysticism" and embrace of certain kabbalistic concepts. See also Greenberg, *Better Than Wine*, and Elliot R. Wolfson, "Facing the Effaced: Mystical Eschatology and the Idealist Orientation in the Thought of Franz Rosenzweig," *Journal for the History of Modern Theology* 4, no. 1 (1997): 39–81, for more extensive discussions of Rosenzweig's relation to kabbalistic thought.

45. It is useful to recall here the epigraph Rosenzweig uses for the introductory first page to the first part of *The Star of Redemption*: "*In philosophos*," which means "against philosophers." Shmuel Hugo Bergman suggests that Rosenzweig uses these words because he is "conscious of his opposition to the entire philo-

sophical tradition" (*Dialogical Philosophy from Kierkegaard to Buber*, trans. Arnold A. Gerstein [Albany: State University of New York Press, 1991], p. 176). On my reading, Rosenzweig's relationship to philosophy is much more ambiguous, and reflects a criticism of a certain type of philosophical tradition (that of the "philosophers") rather than an opposition to philosophizing per se. Nonetheless, Rosenzweig's "new thinking" is only possible in relation to the "old thinking" of the philosophers. Again, the hermeneutical perspective is important here: *The Star of Redemption* suggests that modern readers can neither avoid nor fully overcome philosophy. Once again, this return is not an uncritical return. The strength of Rosenzweig's hermeneutical approach is that he is always fully conscious of the tension in the modern person's relation to tradition.

**Chapter Four**

1. Buber also aimed to take aesthetics seriously. Rosenzweig's criticism of Buber's aesthetic approach—on Jewish grounds—is made clear in the next chapter. For more on Buber, see Buber's introduction to *Jüdischer Künstler*, ed. Martin Buber (Berlin: Jüdischer Verlag, 1903), pp. 1–6. Buber's writing in this short piece reflects some agreement with Wagner's depiction of the Jews as uncreative. Buber attributes this lack of creativity to the influence of the Jewish legal tradition and praises Ḥasidism in contrast. Buber suggests that contemporary Jewry could and should begin to create visual art. See Avram Kampf, *Jewish Experience in the Art of the Twentieth Century* (South Hadley, Mass.: Bergin and Garvey, 1984), pp. 15, 203, for a discussion of the early Buber's attitudes toward Judaism and art. See also Gavriel D. Rosenfeld, "Defining 'Jewish Art' in Ost und West, 1901–1908: A Study in the Nationalisation of Jewish Culture," in *Leo Baeck Institute Yearbook* 39 (1994): 83–110. For the later Buber's discussion of art, see his *Moses: The Revelation and the Covenant*, introduction by Michael Fishbane (Atlantic Highlands, N.J.: Humanities Press International, 1989), pp. 115–118, 125–127.

2. Again, see Schwarcz, *Mi'mitos Le'hitgalut* (From myth to revelation), for a comprehensive account of Rosenzweig's relation to Schelling. For a very helpful account of the relation between Schelling's and Rosenzweig's theories of art, see Schwarcz, *Safah, Mitos, Omanut* (Language, myth, art) (Jerusalem and Tel Aviv: Schocken Books, 1966).

3. *The Star of Redemption*, p. 465/418, translation altered slightly.

4. Again, see Elliot Wolfson, *Through a Speculum That Shines*, for a broad overview of vision in Kabbalah.

5. *The Star of Redemption*, p. 470/422.

6. For a brief and helpful discussion of these issues, see Jacob Katz, "German Culture and the Jews," in *Jewish Response to German Culture*, pp. 85–99.

7. Hermann Cohen, *Religion of Reason*, p. 402/346.

8. Heinrich Graetz, "The Structure of Jewish History," in *The Structure of Jewish History*, p. 68. The issue of modern Jewish polemics about visual art has recently drawn much attention. For the historical record regarding the modern Jewish relation to visual art, see Richard Cohen, *Jewish Icons: Art and Society in Modern Europe* (Berkeley: University of California Press, 1998). See also Kalman

Bland's recent "Anti-Semitism and Aniconism: The Germanophone Requiem for Jewish Visual Art," in *Jewish Identity in Modern Art History*, ed. Catherine M. Soussloff (Berkeley: University of California Press, 1999), pp. 41–66.

9. Graetz, *Structure of Jewish History*, p. 68.

10. Cohen, *Religion of Reason*, p. 67/58.

11. Ibid., p. 62/53.

12. See chapter 1.

13. See chapters 3 and 8.

14. *The Star of Redemption*, p. 471/424.

15. Ibid., p. 212/190.

16. Dietrich, *Cohen and Troeltsch*, p. 1. See chapter 1.

17. In this sense, Rosenzweig's thought also has an interesting relation to the (in my view) too often neglected thought of Leo Baeck. Note for instance Baeck's characterization of a dichotomy between ethics and art in his criticism of "Romantic Religion," which he argues characterizes much of Christianity. Baeck writes: "The desire to yield to illusion, justifiable in art, here characterizes the entire relation to the world. . . . Romanticism therefore lacks any strong ethical impulse, any will to conquer life ethically. . . . All law, all that legislates, all morality with its commandments is repugnant to it; it would rather stay outside the sphere of good and evil; the highest ideal may be anything at all, except the distinct demands of ethical action" (Leo Baeck, "Romantic Religion," in *Judaism and Christianity*, trans. Walter Kaufmann [New York: Atheneum, 1981], pp. 191–192). Baeck's views were of course deeply indebted to Cohen's.

18. *The Star of Redemption*, pp. 83–84/77.

19. See ibid., p. 84/77. In his *Origin of German Tragic Drama* (trans. John Osborne [London: Verso, 1977]), Walter Benjamin draws on, and acknowledges, Rosenzweig's interpretation of the silence of Attic drama.

20. *The Star of Redemption*, p. 89/82.

21. Ibid., p. 88/81.

22. Ibid., p. 65/60.

23. Ibid., p. 420/377.

24. Ibid., p. 393/354.

25. See chapter 7, as well as my "Dialogue as Judgment, Not Mutual Affirmation: A New Look at Franz Rosenzweig's Dialogical Philosophy," *Journal of Religion* 79, no. 4 (October 1999): 523–544, for more on this point.

26. "A Note on Anthropomorphism," GS 3, p. 741.

27. See chapter 1.

28. *The Star of Redemption*, p. 459/413, translation altered.

29. Rosenzweig and Rosenstock-Huessey, *Judaism Despite Christianity*, p. 114.

30. *The Star of Redemption*, pp. 331/298–299. See chapters 3 and 8 for more extended arguments about how the "blood community" functions in *The The Star of Redemption*.

31. This does not mean that Rosenzweig believes that individual Jews abstain from art, but only that the ideal of Judaism does.

32. *The Star of Redemption*, pp. 333, 371, 270/300, 334, 243.

33. GS 3, p. 559.

34. Richard Wagner, "Das Judentum in der Musik," *Gesammelte Schriften*, vol. 13, p. 11, ed. Julius Kapp (Leipzig: Hesse & Becker, 1911). The essay is translated as "Judaism in Music," in *Judaism in Music and Other Essays*, trans. W. Ashton Ellis (Lincoln: University of Nebraska Press, 1995).

35. *The Star of Redemption*, p. 371/334.

36. Richard Wagner, "Das Judentum in der Musik," pp. 12–13/"Judaism in Music," p. 85, translation altered.

37. *The Star of Redemption*, pp. 334–335/301.

38. Rosenzweig, GS 4:1, p. 159, cited here as translated by Glatzer, *Franz Rosenzweig*, pp. 335–336, translation altered.

39. As quoted in Sigmund Freud, "The 'Uncanny,'" in *Collected Papers*, trans. Joan Riviere (New York: Basic Books, 1959), 4: 375. See Friedrich Wilhelm Joseph Schelling, *Philosophie der Mythologie* (Darmstadt: Wissenschaftliche Buchgestellschaft, 1996), 2: 649.

40. Freud, "The 'Uncanny,'" p. 394.

41. Daniel Boyarin, *Unheroic Conduct* (Berkeley: University of California Press, 1997), pp. 234–235. Of related interest, see Jay Geller, "A Paleontological View of Freud's Study of Religion: Unearthing the Leitfossil Circumcision," *Modern Judaism* 13 (1193): 49–70, and "'Glance at the Nose': Freud's Inscription of Jewish Difference," *American Imago* 49, no. 4 (1992): 427–444. In the spring of 1995, I benefited from extended conversations with Susan Bernofsky, Talia Bloch, and James Goldwasser on the relation between Freud's and Rosenzweig's view of the uncanny. In the fall of 1995, Susan Shapiro shared with me a six-page research proposal on Freud and the uncanny, while I shared with her my work on Rosenzweig and the uncanny. She has included a discussion of Rosenzweig and the uncanny in "The Uncanny Jew: A Brief History of an Image," *Judaism* 46, no. 1 (1997): 63–78.

42. Boyarin, *Unheroic Conduct*, p. 235. Boyarin connects Freud's ambivalence about his Jewishness with his fear of castration and his disgust at his circumcised penis: "The 'appearance' that Freud thoroughly dislikes, on this reading, is the appearance of his own circumcised penis" (p. 235).

43. Ibid.

44. Gordon C. F. Bearn, "Wittgenstein on the Uncanny," *Soundings* 17, no. 1 (Spring 1993): 33.

45. Martin Heidegger, *Sein und Zeit* (Tübingen: Max Niemeyer Verlag, 1953), p. 128, trans. John Macquarrie and Edward Robinson as *Being and Time* (San Francisco: Harper and Row, 1962), pp. 165–166.

46. GS 3, p. 560.

47. Rosenzweig suggests cryptically that antisemites believe that Jews are all the same and thus are shocked by their experience of intra-Jewish difference. See James Goldwasser, "Franz Rosenzweig's *Zweistromland*: German *and* Jew," in *Answering to the Name: German-Jewish Identity and Individual Identity in Franz Kafka, Gustav Landaver, and Franz Rosenzweig*, Ph.D. diss., Princeton University, 1999, for more on this point.

48. Buber, *Werke* (München: Lamber Schneider, 1964), 1: 101, trans. Walter

Kaufmann as *I and Thou* (New York: Charles Scribner's Sons, 1970), pp. 84–85 (emphasis added).

49. GS 3, p. 560.

50. In the context of Wittgenstein's thought, Bearn captures the general characteristic of the uncanny that Rosenzweig ascribes not to experience in general, but to the experience of the Jewish people in particular. Bearn writes: "A canny place is where it is easy, as Wittgenstein might have put it, to know your way about. It is homey. Thus an un-canny place is one that unsettles our attempt to find our way about. It is not homey. To this extent, the un-canny repeats the semantic space of its German relation: Das Un-heimliche" ("Wittgenstein and the Uncanny," pp. 33–34).

51. Gadamer, *Philosophical Hermeneutics*, pp. 100–101.

52. "Das neue Denken," in GS 3, pp. 155–156.

53. *The Star of Redemption*, p. 42/38.

54. Stéphane Mosès, *System and Revelation*, pp. 73–74.

55. Friedrich Wilhelm Joseph Schelling, *System of Transcendental Idealism*, trans. Peter Heath, with an introduction by Michael Vater (Charlottesville: University of Virginia Press, 1981), p. 231.

56. *The Star of Redemption*, p. 163/146.

57. Rosenzweig's use of Schelling's thought first to establish a truth and then to show the limitation of that truth is actually quite consistent with the structure of *The Star of Redemption*. Part 2's aesthetic theory rests upon the truth of paganism developed in Part 1. But the theory of revelation of Part 2, which is one and the same with Rosenzweig's theory of language, seeks to show the limitation of aesthetics qua aesthetics. See chapter 3.

58. *The Star of Redemption*, pp. 162–164/145–147.

59. Ibid., p. 163/147.

60. Friedrich Wilhelm Joseph Schelling, *Philosophy of Art*, trans. Douglas W. Stott (Minneapolis: University of Minnesota Press, 1989), p. 32.

61. Ibid., pp. 32, 102.

62. *The Star of Redemption*, p. 278/249.

63. Ibid., p. 276/248.

64. "Ja, es ist wirklich un-heimlich; es hat kein Heim, kein Zuhause; es weiß kein Dach einer Gattung, wo es unterkriechen könnte" (ibid., p. 270; the translation is mine).

65. Ibid., p. 270/243.

66. *The Star of Redemption*, p. 271/243.

67. Ibid., p. 272/244.

68. Boyarin, *Unheroic Conduct*, p. 224.

69. "Anleitung zum Jüdischen Denken," GS 3, p. 615. Schoken Verlags used a text sample (*Textproben*) from this series of lectures in their Almanac for the year 5699, 1938–39, under the title "Fragmente aus dem Nachlaß" (Fragments from the Estate).

70. Richard Wagner, *Dichtungen und Schriften*, ed. Dieter Borchmeyer (Frankfurt am Main: Insel, 1983), 7: 153–155.

71. Ibid., 5: 277.

72. Ibid., 6: 39.

73. Though obviously relevant, the specifics of Wagner's antisemitism are beyond the scope of this book. Judaism is the difference that Wagner wants beaten. The best and most comprehensive recent book on this topic is Marc A. Weiner, *Richard Wagner and the Anti-Semitic Imagination* (Lincoln: University of Nebraska Press, 1995). See also Paul Lawrence Rose, *Wagner: Race and Revolution* (New Haven: Yale University Press, 1992), and Jacob Katz, *The Darker Side of Genius: Richard Wagner's Anti-Semitism* (Hanover, N.H.: University Press of New England, 1986).

74. As Rosenzweig wrote to his parents in October 1916 regarding the Rabbinical Assembly's debate on Jewish education: "The attitude toward Hebrew is the sore point, far more than the debate itself brought out. For Hebrew must be pursued not as the subject of study, but as the very medium through which the entire content of [Judaism] is presented" (GS 1:1, p. 257).

75. GS 3, p. 463, trans. William Wolf in *On Jewish Learning*, ed. N. N. Glatzer (New York: Schocken, 1965), pp. 29–30.

76. *The Star of Redemption*, p. 333/300.

77. Schelling, *Philosophy of Art*, p. 35.

78. *The Star of Redemption*, pp. 341–342/308.

79. Ibid., p. 339/305.

## Chapter Five

1. Franz Rosenzweig, *Der Tischdank* (Jüdische Bücherei: Berlin, 1920), volume 22.

2. As quoted in Glatzer, *Franz Rosenzweig*, p. 102.

3. Rosenzweig began work on the Judah Halevi translations in 1921, worked on the translations primarily in 1922, wrote an epilogue in 1923, and published them all the same year (now published in GS 4:1). His work on Judah Halevi was inspired by his irritation with the translation by Emil B. Cohen, published in 1921. Rosenzweig wrote that Cohen's translation "annoyed me so much that verse came from it" (as quoted in Glatzer, *Franz Rosenzweig*, p. 122). A year and a half after translating the Grace after Meals, Rosenzweig translated the Friday night service in connection with his adult education efforts at the *Lehrhaus*. See Franz Rosenzweig, "Häusliche Feier; Lern Kaddisch," in *Gabe, Herrn Rabbiner Dr. Nobel zum 50. Geburtstag dargebracht* (Frankfurt am Main, 1921). See also Rosenzweig's unpublished translation of the Kol Nidre prayer, which he included in a letter to Martin Buber (GS 1, bd 2, pp. 832–833). In this chapter, we will only be concerned with Rosenzweig's translation of the Bible.

4. For an account of Rosenzweig's illness, see Glatzer, *Franz Rosenzweig*, pp. 108–143.

5. Gershom Scholem to Buber, April 27, 1926 (emphasis added); *Martin Buber Briefwechsel II 1918–1938*, Erste Auflage (Heidelberg: Verlag Lambert Schneider, 1973), p. 252, ed. Nahum N. Glatzer and Paul Mendes-Flohr, trans. Richard and Clara Winston and Harry Zohn as *The Letters of Martin Buber: A Life of Dialogue* (Syracuse: Syracuse University Press, 1996), p. 338. I have altered the translation slightly.

6. See W. Gunther Plaut's excellent monograph, *German-Jewish Bible Trans-*

*lations: Linguistic Theology as a Political Phenomenon* (New York: Leo Baeck Institute, 1992).

7. Buber and Rosenzweig, *Die Schrift und ihre Verdeutschung* (Berlin: Schocken Verlag, 1936), translated by Lawrence Rosenwald with Everett Fox as *Scripture and Translation* (Bloomington: Indiana University Press, 1994).

8. This essay also appears in English in Buber's *On the Bible*, trans. Olga Marx (New York: Schocken, 1968), pp. 1–13. The translations vary.

9. As *Die Schrift und ihre Verdeutschung* is now out of print, I cite Buber's and Rosenzweig's collected works in German first, followed by Rosenwald's English translation (see n. 7). The German original of Buber's essays on the Bible can be found in the second volume of his collected works, *Schriften zur Bibel*, while the German original of Rosenzweig's essays can be found in GS 3. Martin Buber, *Werke* (München: Lamber Schneider, 1964), 2:849/4–5.

10. Ibid., p. 16/8.

11. Ibid., p. 18/10.

12. Gadamer, *Truth and Method*, pp. 264–265.

13. Ibid., p. 384.

14. Ibid., pp. 384–385.

15. GS 3, p. 749/*Scripture and Translation*, p. 47.

16. Ibid.

17. Ibid., pp. 758/56–57.

18. Buber, "On Word Choice in Translating the Bible," *Werke* 2:1111/*Scripture and Translation*, p. 73.

19. Ibid., p. 1112/74.

20. GS 3, p. 751/*Scripture and Translation*, p. 49.

21. Ibid., p. 753/51.

22. Ibid., p. 758/56.

23. For an argument about Rosenzweig's and Heidegger's affinity on the issue of translation, see Peter Eli Gordon, "Translation and Ontology: Rosenzweig, Heidegger, and the Anxiety of Affiliation," in *New German Critique* 77 (Spring-Summer 1999). I agree with Gordon about Rosenzweig's affinity with Heidegger, though I believe important differences remain, such as Rosenzweig's ethical monotheistic commitments—which, on my reading, completely alters Rosenzweig's and Heidegger's perspectives. Perhaps more significantly in the context of the Bible translation, Gordon does not treat Buber's role or thought and analyzes the translation project as if Rosenzweig worked alone. On my reading, Buber's philosophical views, both in terms of the translation and beyond, bear a closer affinity to Heidegger's than Rosenzweig's do, for reasons detailed in this chapter as well as in chapter 4's brief discussion of the uncanny.

24. Heidegger, *Being and Time*, p. 220/262, translation altered.

25. For a very helpful account of this issue in Heidegger, see Jan Aler, "Heidegger's Conception of Language," in *On Heidegger and Language*, ed. Joseph Kockelmans (Evanston: Northwestern University Press, 1972), pp. 33–66.

26. Martin Heidegger, *Poetry, Language, and Thought*, trans. A. Hofstadter (San Francisco: Harper and Row, 1971), p. 190.

27. Martin Buber, "The Word That Is Spoken," trans. M. Friedman and

Ronald Gregor Smith, in *The Knowledge of Man* (Atlantic Highlands, N.J.: Humanities Press International, 1988), p. 117.

28. *The Star of Redemption*, p. 221/198.

29. *Werke* 2:857/*Scripture and Translation*, p. 11, emphasis in the original.

30. Buber, *I and Thou*, trans. Walter Kaufmann (New York: Charles Scribner's Sons, 1970); *Ich und Du* (Berlin: Schocken Verlag, 1922); *Werke* 1:79–170.

31. In an otherwise helpful article, Martin Jay perpetuates this myth by writing, "In many way similar to Buber's I-Thou philosophy, 'The New Thinking' stressed the whole man over the intellect and saw dialogue as the central religious experience" ("Politics of Translation: Siegfried Kracauer and Walter Benjamin on the Buber-Rosenzweig Bible," *Leo Baeck Institute Yearbook* 21 [1976]: 7–8).

32. See Rivka Horwitz, *Buber's Way to I and Thou* (Heidelberg: Lambert Schneider, 1978), chaps. 5 and 6 and especially p. 222. See also Steven Kepnes, *The Text as Thou: Martin Buber's Dialogical Hermeneutics and Narrative Theology* (Bloomington: Indiana University Press, 1992). I follow Kepnes's analysis of the development of Buber's hermeneutics and draw from his book for this analysis.

33. Horwitz, *Buber's Way to I and Thou*, chap. 5, especially p. 194.

34. As quoted from ibid., p. 196.

35. Buber, *Werke* 2:83/*I and Thou*, p. 59.

36. GS 1:2, pp. 736–737.

37. On Buber's use of creation, revelation, and redemption, see Paul Mendes-Flohr, "Martin Buber's Conception of God," *Teologia Filosofica E Filosofia Della Religione*, ed. A. Babolin (Perugia: Editrice Benucci, 1986).

38. For Buber and Rosenzweig's discussion of their differences about the emergence of the notions of creation and redemption from revelation, see their letters of September 1922 in Buber, *Briefwechsel*, pp. 124–131, translated in *Letters of Martin Buber: A Life of Dialogue*, pp. 278–290.

39. In Glatzer, *On Jewish Learning*, pp. 72–92.

40. Buber, *Werke* 1:152–154/*I and Thou*, pp. 158–160. For more on Buber's view of law, see Maurice S. Friedman, "Revelation and Law in the Thought of Martin Buber," *Judaism* 3:1 (1954): 3–19; Ernst Simon, "Martin Buber and the Faith of Israel" (Hebrew), *Iyyun* 9 (1958): 13–25; Hillel Goldberg, "The Early Buber and Jewish Law," *Tradition* 21:1 (Spring 1983): 66–74. Simon's analysis is of particular interest as it bears a conceptual affinity to Rosenzweig's criticism of Buber in their 1922 correspondence.

41. Buber, *Briefwechsel*, 2: 126/*Letters of Martin Buber*, p. 279.

42. See Poma's *Critical Philosophy of Hermann Cohen* for an overview of the relation of Cohen's *Religion of Reason* to his system.

43. Cohen regarded Kant's distinction between logic and ethics, between being and what ought to be, as the lasting hallmark of Kant's philosophy. This led Cohen to reassess completely Kant's conception of law and to make the science of law the focus of his ethics. See Cohen, *Ethik*, 7:267ff.

44. Buber, *Briefwechsel*, 2: 128/*Letters of Martin Buber*, p. 280, emphasis added.

45. See Richard A. Cohen's discussion of this difference between Buber and

Rosenzweig in his essay, "Rosenzweig contra Buber: Personal Pronouns," in *Elevations: The Height of the Good in Rosenzweig and Levinas* (Chicago: University of Chicago Press, 1994), pp. 67–89.

46. I thus agree with both Eliezer Schweid's thesis that Rosenzweig's approach to biblical interpretation should be understood in relation to his conception of revelation and Shemaryahu Talmon's thesis that Buber and Rosenzweig's approach was a rejection of both a Protestant approach and a Modern Orthodox approach. I argue throughout this book, and especially in chapter 3, that Rosenzweig's approach is fundamentally a hermeneutical one. The modern person experiences the Bible as new revelation but this revelation is only possible, the modern person realizes later, because of the historical community of Jews who have read the text. This hermeneutical sensibility becomes possible by way of Buber and Rosenzweig's hermeneutical approach, which is meant to put into question modern approaches to the Bible (specifically those of Protestantism and Modern Orthodoxy). See Eliezer Schweid, "Franz Rosenzweig k'mefaresh filosofy shel ha mikra" (Franz Rosenzweig as philosophical exegete of scripture), in *Miluot: Mechkarei ha'universita ha'ptucha b'toledot am yisrael v'tarbuto* (Tel Aviv: Ha'universita Ha'ptucha, 1984). See also Shemaryahu Talmon, "Zur Bibleinterpretationsmethode von Franz Rosenzweig und Martin Buber," in *Der Philosoph Franz Rosenzweig*, pp. 273–285.

47. As translated in Glatzer, *On Jewish Learning*, p. 116. See Paul Mendes-Flohr, "Law and Sacrament: Ritual Observance in Twentieth-Century Jewish Thought," in *Divided Passions: Jewish Intellectuals and the Experience of Modernity* (Detroit: Wayne State University Press, 1991), pp. 341–369, for a more extended discussion of Buber and Rosenzweig on Jewish law.

48. *The Star of Redemption*, p. 374/337.

49. Ibid., p. 224/201.

50. Ibid., p. 334/301.

51. Ibid., p. 222/199.

52. Ibid., pp. 227–228/203–204.

53. See Paul Mendes-Flohr, *From Mysticism to Dialogue: Martin Buber's Transformation of German Social Thought* (Detroit: Wayne State University Press, 1989), for an extended discussion of the development of Buber's view of *Erlebnis* and his dialogical philosophy.

54. See their correspondence for Buber's response: "I would almost plead with you to take me at my word when I say that I was not for a moment 'intoxicated.' "

55. See especially pp. 231–232/207–208 of *The Star of Redemption* for Rosenzweig's description of how the "mystic" gets stuck in the lyrical relation. In sum, Rosenzweig writes: "This thoroughly immoral relationship to the world is thus utterly essential for the pure mystic if he wants, for the rest, to assert and preserve his pure mysticism" (p. 232/208).

56. See chapter 8.

57. Rosenzweig's view of the reading of the Bible as drama, and not narrative, is similar to Alasdair MacIntyre's view of dramatic narrative. MacIntyre describes dramatic narrative in the following terms: "We enter upon a stage which we did not design and we find ourselves part of an action that was not of our making. Each of us being a main character in his own drama plays subordinate

parts in the dramas of others, and each drama constrains the others" (*After Virtue*, p. 213). MacIntyre emphasizes the unpredictability of drama. His emphasis is on the formation of identity in a context that we ourselves do not create. One of the important differences between Rosenzweig and MacIntyre is that Rosenzweig emphasizes the discontinuity of tradition not as the exception but the norm.

58. Kepnes concurs with this description; see *Text as Thou*, especially pp. 98–121. Kepnes emphasizes that while Buber's hermeneutics is very much in keeping with narrative structures, Buber emphasizes the middle and not the beginning and end, in accordance with the modern anti-novel.

59. The difference between Buber and Rosenzweig is one of degree and not kind. They agree both that the past makes demands on the present but more importantly that identities are transformed through the relation to the text. On this issue, Rosenzweig is much closer to Buber than he is (to cite an extreme case) to Richard Wagner, for whom art has the task of confirming and restoring the ontological identity of its audience.

60. *The Star of Redemption*, p. 221/198.

61. Steven Kepnes has documented the development of Buber's hermeneutics, and I rely on the very helpful analysis of his *Text as Thou* for the following discussion.

62. One important way to understand the difference between Rosenzweig and Buber is to understand their respective allegiances to the Marburg neo-Kantian school (Cohen) and the Southwest Baden neo-Kantian school (Dilthey). While Rosenzweig and Buber each criticize their predecessors (Cohen and Dilthey), each also remains closely tied in important ways to his initial allegiance. See also chapter 3.

63. Martin Buber, "My Way to Hasidism," in *Hasidism and Modern Man*, trans. M. Friedman (Atlantic Highlands, N.J.: Humanities Press International, 1988), p. 54.

64. See Dilthey, "The Hermeneutics of the Human Sciences," in *The Hermeneutics Reader*, ed. and trans. Mueller-Vollmer (New York: Continuum, 1985).

65. Martin Buber, *The Tales of Rabbi Nachman*, trans. M. Friedman (New York: Horizon, 1956), p. i.

66. Martin Buber, *Briefwechsel aus sieben Jahrzehnten*, Vol. 1, p. 244 (emphasis added).

67. Ibid., p. 88/81 (cited the other way around in chapter 4).

68. Buber, *Werke* 1:81–82/*I and Thou*, pp. 57–58.

69. Martin Buber, *Hasidism and Modern Man*, p. 16.

70. I take this to be one of the central points of Kepnes's *Text as Thou*; see especially pp. 22 and 31.

71. Buber, *Werke* 1:81/*I and Thou*, p. 57.

72. Martin Buber, "Dialogue," in *Between Man and Man*, trans. R. G. Smith, ed. Maurice Friedman (New York: Macmillan, 1965), p. 25, translation altered slightly.

73. Kepnes, *Text as Thou*, p. 32.

74. Kepnes writes: "What we find in Buber's writings on the Bible is an extension of the principles of interpretation of works of art developed in *I and Thou* to

the sacred text, the Hebrew Bible. Like the work of art the Bible can be regarded as a Thou and the process of interpretation phrased as a 'dialogue with the text' " (ibid., p. 58).

75. There is an excellent discussion of this point in chapter 5 of Horwitz, *Buber's Way to "I and Thou"*; see pp. 193–206.

76. "The ways of God are different from the ways of man, but the word of God and the word of man are the same. What man hears in his heart as his own speech is the very word which comes out of God's mouth" (*The Star of Redemption*, pp. 167–168/151).

77. GS 3, p. 834/*Scripture and Translation*, p. 5.

78. Ibid., p. 151, cited in chapter 3.

79. For more on the erosion of belief in liberalism in early twentieth century German Jewry, see Uriel Tal, *Christians and Jews in Germany: Religion, Politics and Ideology in the Second Reich, 1870–1914*, trans. Noah Jonathan Jacobs (Ithaca: Cornell University Press, 1975).

80. See David Sorkin, *Moses Mendelssohn and the Religious Enlightenment*, pp. 53–79.

81. GS 3, pp. 749–750/*Scripture and Translation*, p. 48.

82. Ibid. Ironically, the translator of these essays translates this line poorly. Instead of "the world was not created without form," "the world was not made an empty desert" is rendered for "*In der Welt, die nicht zur Wüste geschaffen wurde.*" While "empty desert" is technically a correct translation of "*Wüste*," it misses the fact that Rosenzweig, in alluding to the verse in Isaiah, is referring to the Hebrew *tohu*, the same word that is used in Genesis 1:2, which describes the earth as being without form.

83. In their first translation of Genesis, Buber and Rosenzweig translated Genesis 1:2 as "Und die Erde war Wirrnis und Wüste; Finsternis allüber Abgrund; Braus Gottes brütend allüber den Wassern," thus using Wüste for *tohu*. The notes to the first edition, which are in the Buber archives in Jerusalem, show Buber citing Isaiah 45:18. Buber writes, "It must read 'Wüste und Wirrnis' for in Isaiah 45:18, *tohu* clearly means Wüste" (cited and translated in Everett Fox, *Technical Aspects of the Translation of Genesis of Martin Buber and Franz Rosenzweig*, Ph.D. diss., Brandeis University, 1975, p. 85). However, in 1930, the *Logenausgabe*, a second edition of the Buber-Rosenzweig Pentateuch, was published by the B'nai B'rith Lodge of Berlin. Rosenzweig had died in 1929, but this edition contained the revisions that he had made before his death. The translation of "Wirrnis und Wüste" is changed to "Irrsal und Wirrsal." The reason for the change was that Rosenzweig felt that the rhyme of *tohu vevohu* was as important as the content. Therefore, the sound of Wüste was wrong and they changed "Wirrnis und Wüste" to "Irrsal und Wirrsal" because "Irrsal und Wirrsal" rhyme. Rosenzweig's notes to the revisions of the translation are now published in the fourth volume of his collected works. For the discussion of Genesis 1:2, see GS 4:1, pp. 3–6.

84. See Edward L. Greenstein's discussion of diversity and translation in his essay "Theories of Modern Bible Translation," in *Essays on Biblical Method and Translation* (Atlanta: Scholars Press, 1989), especially p. 114.

85. *The Star of Redemption*, p. 328/295.

86. *Der Pentateuch ubersetzt und erklaert*, 5 vols., 1867–78; English translation of the commentary, 1956–62.

87. *The Nineteen Letters of Ben Uziel*, trans. Bernard Drachman (New York: Funk and Wagnalls, 1899).

88. This letter was originally published in *Der Morgen*, October 1928.

89. GS 3, p. 831/*Scripture and Translation*, p. 22.

90. Ibid., p. 831/22.

91. Rosenzweig adds a postscript to "The Unity of the Bible" in order to emphasize that he is not making a distinction between *Wissenschaft* and "religion." If such a distinction is ever made, it is a Protestant, and not a Jewish, distinction. From a Jewish point of view, Rosenzweig writes, God is both transcendent and transcendental to *Wissenschaft*. Scientific statements, the sort *Wissenschaft* claims to make, are only possible in relation to God. In the language of *The Star of Redemption*, descriptive statements are only possible because of imperatives. The imperative marks the relation between the human and God and is the basic human orientation. See chapter 2.

92. GS 3, p. 833/*Scripture and Translation*, p. 24.

93. Ibid., p. 762/60.

94. Ibid., p. 827/140.

95. Ibid., p. 763/61.

96. Ibid., p. 765/63.

97. Peter Ochs, *The Return to Scripture in Judaism and Christianity*, p. 3. More technically, Ochs claims: "The postcritical claim is that modern scholarship tends to define rational inquiry on the model of everyday inquiry: as if reason operates only when a community's deep-seated rules of knowledge are in place and when the task of inquiry is strictly referential. . . . Modern scholarship therefore tends to reduce the pursuit of knowledge to the terms of a binary opposition between referential, rational inquiry (when the deep rules are in place) and non-referential irrational inquiry (when they are not). . . . The postcritical complain is that this binary opposition excludes the possibility that scriptural texts may have pragmatic reference: that is, that they may represent claims about the inadequacy of certain inherited rules of meaning and about ways of transforming those rules or adjusting them to new conditions of life" (p. 39).

98. David Weiss Halivni, for example, comes to the problem of text criticism from within the tradition. See his "Plain Sense and Applied Meaning in Rabbinic Exegesis," ibid.

99. GS 3, p. 819/*Scripture and Translation*, p. 131.

100. Buber, *Werke* 2:1131–1149; *On the Bible*, pp. 22–43.

101. *The New English Bible* (New York: Oxford University Press, 1971).

102. For a discussion of the similarities between Buber and Rosenzweig and midrash, see Edward L. Greenstein's "Theories of Bible Translation," in *Essays on Biblical Method and Translation*, especially pp. 109–110.

103. English translations, except for the translation of Exodus 3:14–15, are from Everett Fox, *In the Beginning* (New York: Schocken, 1983).

104. GS 3, p. 779/*Scripture and Translation*, p. 42.

105. Again, see Fox, *In the Beginning*. Also see his *Five Books of Moses* (New York: Schocken, 1995).

106. Fox cites a fragment of the Buber Archives (box #4a 3) entitled *"Einige Sätze über den byblischen Rhythmus": Prosa-Poesie* (cited in Fox, *Technical Aspects*, 32).

107. This example is from ibid., p. 40.

108. GS 3, p. 803–804/102.

109. Ibid., p. 806/104, translation altered.

110. Ibid., p. 805/*Scripture and Translation*, p. 104.

111. Ibid., p. 806/104.

112. Buber and Rosenzweig first included the word "aber" ("but") in their translation of Exodus 3:14—"Gott aber sprach zu Mosche"—but later dropped it, in keeping with both the Hebrew text and Luther's translation. See GS 4:2, pp. 93–96. I follow Rosenwald's translation here (*Scripture and Translation*, p. 102). In *In the Beginning*, Fox does not translate the tetragrammaton with a capitalized pronoun. And he uses a transliteration, along with a translation, in his translation of "Eheyeh Asher Eheyeh." Finally, Fox translates "Eheyeh Asher Eheyeh" with the future—"I-WILL-BE-THERE"—while Buber and Rosenzweig use the present, "I AM THERE." Fox's translation of Exodus 3:14–15 is as follows:

> God said to Moshe:
> Eheyeh Asher Eheyeh/I will be-there howsoever I will be-there.
> And he said:
> Thus shall you say to the Children of Israel:
> Eheyeh/I-WILL-BE-THERE sends me to you.
> And God said further to Moshe:
> Thus shall you say to the Children of Israel:
> YHWH,
> the God of your fathers,
> the God of Avraham, the God of Yitzhak, and the God of Yaakov,
> sends me to you.
> That is my name for the ages,
> that is my title (from) generation to generation.

In an earlier translation, Fox translated in accordance with Buber and Rosenzweig's principles. See *Response* 14 (1972): 3–160.

113. All quotations from "The Bible in German" are from Siegfried Kracauer, *The Mass Ornament*, trans. with an introduction by Thomas Levin (Cambridge, Mass.: Harvard University Press, 1995).

114. GS 3, p. 797/*Scripture and Translation*, p. 157.

115. See Edward L. Greenstein's recent article, "On the Ethics of Translation: A Response" *SEMIEA* 76: 127–134.

116. Kracauer, *The Mass Ornament*, translation altered slightly.

117. Buber, *I and Thou*, p. 120/113.

118. *The Star of Redemption*, pp. 231–232/207–208.

119. I am referring here to the status of Buber's philosophy in 1926. While Buber had always criticized institutions, at the time of Kracauer's review he had not yet developed any sort of positive notion of community.

120. It is rather odd that Kracauer seems to have missed the fact that Rosenzweig was not a Zionist. Aside from the strong emphasis on diaspora Judaism in

*The Star of Redemption*, Rosenzweig, as early as 1915, had publicly criticized nationalist aspirations on the part of the Jewish people. I return to this point in brief below and in great detail in chapters 7 and 8.

121. *The Star of Redemption*, pp. 323–325/290–292.

122. Walter Benjamin, *Illuminations*, trans. Harry Zohn, ed. Hannah Arendt (New York: Schocken, 1986), thesis 6, p. 261.

123. Ibid., p. 258.

124. Ibid., p. 184.

125. I take this point from Lawrence Rosenwald's discussion in "On the Reception of Buber and Rosenzweig's Bible," *Prooftexts* 14, no. 1 (1994): 48–49.

126. Franz Rosenzweig, "The Unity of the Bible," in GS 3, p. 834/*Scripture and Translation*, p. 25. See also Rosenwald, "On the Reception of Buber and Rosenzweig's Bible," pp. 48–49.

127. GS 3, pp. 817–818/*Scripture and Translation*, p. 130. For Rosenwald, these comments in the context of Rosenzweig's comments in "The Unity of the Bible" reflect an "Emersonian freedom from consistency" ("On the Reception of Buber and Rosenzweig's Bible," p. 48). In my view, this claim is consistent with Rosenzweig's approach to both "religion" and art.

128. GS 1, bd 2, p. 1171/*Letters of Martin Buber*, p. 353.

129. Greenstein, "On the Ethics of Translation," pp. 128–129.

130. Rosenzweig, letter of August 18, 1929, cited ibid., pp. 322–343, translated in *Letters of Martin Buber*, p. 368.

131. For more on this see William Cutter, "Ghostly Hebrew, Ghastly Speech: Scholem to Rosenzweig, 1926," *Prooftexts* 10 (1990): 413–433.

**Chapter Six**

1. Franz Rosenzweig, *Hegel und der Staat* (Munich and Berlin: R. Oldenbourg, 1920). A chapter of the book was Rosenzweig's 1912 doctoral dissertation. The book was written primarily in 1914 and published in 1920.

2. See Glatzer, *Franz Rosenzweig*, pp. 20–25.

3. Ibid., pp. 23–24.

4. To Rudolf Ehrenberg, October 31, 1913, ibid., pp. 24–25.

5. Ibid., p. 28.

6. Ibid., p. xviii. Glatzer goes on to write that Rosenzweig "never mentioned this event to his friends and never presented it in his writings. He guarded it as the secret ground of his new life" (xviii). By October 23, 1913, Rosenzweig had reported his change of heart toward Judaism in a letter to his mother.

7. Ibid., p. 28. See Aharon Shear-Yashuv's discussion of the fascinating relationship between Rosenzweig and his cousin, Hans Ehrenberg, who, after converting to Christianity, gave up his professorship at the University of Heidelberg to become a Lutheran minister in Bochum ("The Theological Discussion between Franz Rosenzweig and Hans Ehrenberg" [Hebrew], *Da'at* 21 [Summer 1998], pp. 103–114). As should be clear in this chapter, however, I do not agree with Yashuv's characterization of Rosenzweig's view that the synagogue and the church are complementary.

8. Rosenzweig notes some of Cohen's comments for his lectures: "'God be

what He be, but He must be One. . . . On this point we cannot come to an understanding with Christianity. . . . The whole of Nature, the model of art, is opened up in the Second Commandment—and sealed. This is something for which the world has never forgiven us' " (Glatzer, *Franz Rosenzweig*, p. 30). We will return to this last point.

9. Their letters are collected and translated in *Judaism Despite Christianity*, edited by Rosenstock-Huessy.

10. *The Star of Redemption*, pp. 469–470/422.

11. Tillich, like Rosenzweig, was influenced heavily by both Cohen and Schelling.

12. Paul Tillich, *Dynamics of Faith* (New York and Evanston: Harper and Row, 1957), p. 42.

13. See especially *The Star of Redemption*, p. 222/199 and pp. 327/294–295.

14. Tillich, *Dynamics of Faith*, pp. 41–43.

15. Ibid., p. 393/354, as quoted in chapter 4.

16. See chapter 4.

17. *The Star of Redemption*, p. 420/377.

18. Ibid., pp. 418–419/376.

19. Ibid., p. 419/376.

20. Ibid., p. 419/377.

21. Tillich, *Dynamics of Faith*, p. 52.

22. Ibid., p. 45.

23. Ibid., pp. 97–98.

24. *The Star of Redemption*, pp. 398–399/359.

25. See chapter 1.

26. See chapter 2.

27. *The Star of Redemption*, pp. 462/415–416.

28. Buber, *Werke* 1:88/*I and Thou*, p. 67.

29. For a survey of appropriations of Rosenzweig's thought in Christian arguments for theologies of the Jewish-Christian relation, see "Recent Theologies of Jewish-Christian Relations" by both Peter Haas and Rosemary Radford Ruether, in *Religious Studies Review* 16, no. 4 (October 1990): 316–323. I refer below to a number of particular appropriations of Rosenzweig's thought. For a recent Jewish appropriation of Rosenzweig for the sake of Jewish-Christian dialogue, see Michael S. Kogan, "Toward a Jewish Theology of Christianity," *Journal of Ecumenical Studies*, 32, no. 1 (Winter 1995): 89–106. David Novak, *Jewish-Christian Dialogue: A Jewish Justification*, is an important exception to this view of Rosenzweig. He rightly argues that Rosenzweig does not offer the basis for Jewish-Christian dialogue. In particular, Novak notes, "Can any Christian be expected to accept the primacy of Judaism for his or her own relationship with God? If a Christian were to accept this primacy, then why should that Christian not actually become a Jew?" (p. 110). Novak nonetheless argues for a Jewish justification of Jewish-Christian dialogue that moves beyond Rosenzweig's particularism. In my view, this position remains problematic. See Leora Batnitzky, "Dialogue as Judgement, Not Mutual Affirmation: A New Look at Franz Rosenzweig's Dialogical Philosophy," *Journal of Religion* 79:4 (October 1999): 523–544, for a fuller articulation of my position on the contemporary implications of Rosenzweig's thought for Jewish-Christian dialogue.

30. Paul M. van Buren, *A Theology of the Jewish-Christian Reality,* Part 1, *Discerning the Way*; Part 2, *A Christian Theology of the People of Israel*; Part 3, *Christ in Context* (San Francisco: Harper and Row, 1987–88).

31. Rosenzweig and Rosenstock-Huessy, *Judaism Despite Christianity,* p. 113.

32. "To the Jew," Rosenzweig continues in this same letter, "that God is our Father is the first and most self-evident fact—and what need is there for a third person between me and my father in Heaven?"

33. GS 1:1, p. 142.

34. Rosenzweig and Rosenstock-Huessy, *Judaism Despite Christianity,* p. 114, as quoted in chapter 4.

35. See Rosenzweig's letter to Rudolf Ehrenberg, November 4, 1913: "To us, our 'stubbornness' is fidelity and our 'infidelity towards God' is remedied—just because it is infidelity and not an original primeval estrangement ('Adam's' fall into sin!)—only by repentance and return, not by a transformation of conversion" (GS 1:1, p. 142).

36. Rosenzweig and Rosenstock-Huessy, *Judaism Despite Christianity,* p. 112.

37. *The Star of Redemption,* p. 462/415.

38. Given Rosenzweig's striking characterizations of the unrelenting judgmental relationship between Judaism and Christianity, it is surprising to read the following statement in a collection of contemporary essays devoted to Jewish-Christian dialogue: "Most importantly for Franz Rosenzweig, the . . . essential self-affirmation of one's religious particularity entailed an equally important second obligation: the acceptance and recognition of the value and validity of the religious particularity of one's neighbor." See Gerhard E. Spiegler, "Dialogue as Affirmation: Franz Rosenzweig's Contribution to Christian-Jewish Conversations," in *Religious Issues and Inter-religious Dialogues: An Analysis and Sourcebook of Developments Since 1945,* ed. by Charles Wei-hsun Fu and Gerhard E. Spiegler (New York: Greenwood Press, 1989), p. 432.

39. Rosenzweig and Rosenstock-Huessy, *Judaism Despite Christianity,* p. 136.

40. *The Star of Redemption,* p. 459/413.

41. Ibid., p. 459/413.

42. Ibid., p. 339/305.

43. Judaism's self-judgment drives Judaism inwards, just as Christianity's self-judgment drives Christianity outwards. We will discuss this more fully below in the last section of this chapter.

44. Ibid., p. 264/237.

45. Ibid., p. 200/180.

46. Ibid., pp. 200/179–180.

47. Ibid., pp. 200–201/180.

48. Ibid., pp. 201/180–181.

49. Ibid., p. 204/183, translation altered.

50. Ibid.

51. Ibid., p. 460/414.

52. Ibid., p. 447/402.

53. It is significant to note in this context that Rosenzweig's understanding of

antisemitism as something that is intrinsic to Christian civilization differs not only from Cohen's more rationalist approach, but from Theodor Herzl's also. See Theodor Herzl, *Der Judenstaat* (Leipzig and Vienna: Breitenstein, 1896), translated as *The Jewish State* by Sylvie D'Avidgdor (New York: Dover, 1988), for Herzl's argument that once Jews stop competing economically with non-Jews, antisemitism will disappear.

54. G.W.F. Hegel, *Philosophy of History*, trans. C. J. Friederich (New York: Dover, 1956), p. 424.

55. *The Star of Redemption*, p. 390/352.

56. Ibid., p. 446/401.

57. Rosenzweig and Rosenstock-Huessy, *Judaism Despite Christianity*, p. 131.

58. *The Star of Redemption*, p. 367/330, translation altered.

59. G.W.F. Hegel, *Elements of the Philosophy of Right*, trans. H. B. Nisbet, ed. Allen W. Wood (Cambridge: Cambridge University Press, 1991), pp. 361–363.

60. *The Star of Redemption*, p. 365/329.

61. George Mosse, *The Jews and the German War Experience, 1914–1918* (New York: Leo Baeck Institute, 1977), p. 22.

62. In some important ways, Cohen shares Rosenzweig's view of Judaism as the center of the star, and Christianity its rays. For an interesting discussion of Cohen's mixed view of Christianity, see John C. Lyden, "Hermann Cohen's Relationship to Christian Thought," *Journal of Jewish Thought and Philosophy* 2 (1994): 279–301.

63. *The Star of Redemption*, p. 461/415, translation altered slightly.

## Chapter Seven

1. *The Star of Redemption*, p. 452/407.

2. GS 3, p. 557. See Dana Hollander, "Franz Rosenzweig on Nation, Translation, and Judaism," *Philosophy Today* 38, no. 4 (1994): 380–389, for a provocative argument about the interrelation between these issues in Rosenzweig's thought.

3. GS 3, p. 557, emphasis added.

4. *The Star of Redemption*, p. 270/243.

5. See Theodor Herzl, *Der Judenstaat*.

6. "Uncanny" literally means "beyond ken." "Uncanny," of course, comes from "canny," which means possessing knowledge or skill. "Can" is from the Anglo-Saxon "can" or "cann," the present indicative of "cunnan," meaning to know or to be able, which is related to the Dutch "kunnan" and to the German "können." See Anthony Vidler, *The Architectural Uncanny* (Cambridge, Mass.: MIT Press, 1992), pp. 3–14.

7. *The Star of Redemption*, p. 272/244, as quoted in chapter 4.

8. This does not imply that Rosenzweig sees Zionism and racism as one and the same thing. Rather, as elaborated below, Zionism does have some very positive possibilities, while racism obviously does not.

9. Martin Buber, "Judaism and the Jews" in *On Judaism*, trans. Eva Jospe, ed.

Nahum N. Glatzer (New York: Schocken, 1967), p. 16, originally published under the title *Drei Reden über das Judentum* (Frankfurt am Main, 1911). I thank Steven Kepnes for drawing my attention to this reference.

10. Ibid., p. 15.

11. *The Star of Redemption*, pp. 331/298–299, as quoted in chapter 3.

12. Buber, "Judaism and the Jews," p. 16.

13. See chapter 5's discussion of the differences between Buber and Rosenzweig.

14. *The Star of Redemption*, pp. 332–333/299–300.

15. Rosenzweig's point is exemplified by the Zionist argument of Theodor Herzl, *Altneuland* (Leipzig: Seemann, 1902). In a 1925 review essay of the new Hebrew translation of Spinoza's *Ethics* by the Zionist Jakob Klatzkin (who was a student of Hermann Cohen), Rosenzweig makes this same point: "Klatzkin is the leading representative of what he himself calls a 'formal nationalism,' i.e. a nationalism that denies the Jewish heritage any claim whatsoever on the new generation about to assume it" (GS 3, p. 724/Glatzer, *Franz Rosenzweig*, p. 264, translation modified). We will return to this issue in our discussion of Hebrew language and Jewish education below.

16. Buber argues for a new future while Rosenzweig argues for a future out of the sources of Judaism.

17. *The Star of Redemption*, p. 333/300, translation altered. Hallo translates *Heimat* as "land" and *zuhause* as "in that land."

18. *The Star of Redemption*, p. 333/300.

19. The essence of the Jewish people is contrasted to the existence of the nations. In other words, the conception of Judaism in *The Star of Redemption* is idealized, while the view of the nations of the world is realistic. Rosenzweig is aware of this tension (GS 3, pp. 154–155). In the next chapter we will turn to Rosenzweig's own critique and account, in his later writings, of *The Star of Redemption*'s description of Judaism's essence. For now, however, we can recount Stéphane Mosès' succinct summary of this tension in *The Star of Redemption*: "What Rosenzweig means to say is that the Nations are determined by their political destiny whereas the Jewish people is essentially ruled by its religious vocation" (*System and Revelation*, p. 217).

20. Rosenzweig, *Hegel und der Staat*, 2:243.

21. GS 3, p. 156.

22. Ibid.

23. Ibid., pp. 155–156.

24. *The Star of Redemption*, pp. 64/59–60; pp. 59/55–56.

25. Ibid., p. 60/55. Hallo's translation leaves out a comma in the original between "Volk" and "Staat," which I have replaced.

26. Ibid., pp. 60/55–56.

27. "For the peoples of antiquity, war was after all only one among other natural expressions of life: it held no fundamental contradictions. To the nations war means staking life in order to live. A nation that fares forth to war accepts the possibility of dying. This is not significant so long as nations regard themselves as mortal" (ibid., p. 366/329).

28. Ibid., p. 366/330.

29. Ibid., p. 367/331, translation altered.

30. Ibid., p. 368/331.

31. Ibid., pp. 368/331–332.

32. "For the state is the ever changing guise under which time moves step by step toward eternity. So far as God's people is concerned, eternity has already come—even in the midst of time! For the nations of the world there is only the current era. But the state symbolizes the attempt to give nations eternity within the confines of time, an attempt which must of necessity be repeated again and again. The very fact that the state does try it, and must try it, makes it the imitator and rival of the people which is in itself eternal, a people which would cease to have a claim to its own eternity if the state were able to attain what it is striving for" (ibid., p. 369/332).

33. GS 3, p. 156.

34. See chapter 2.

35. See chapter 4.

36. For a discussion of Rosenzweig's conception of *Ganzheit* in Jewish education in the context of reforms in adult education in Germany, see Michael Brenner, *The Renaissance of Jewish Culture in Weimar Germany* (New Haven: Yale University Press, 1996), p. 281.

37. GS 3, pp. 461–482. Translated as "It Is Time" in *On Jewish Learning*, pp. 27–54. The letter was first published as a pamphlet in 1917.

38. GS 3, p. 461/Glatzer, *On Jewish Learning*, p. 27.

39. Ibid., p. 462/28.

40. Ibid., pp. 462–463/29–30.

41. "Language and meaning are co-related, and we underestimate the intimate relation between Christianity and the German language, if we think that Jewish contents can be clothed in German language without admitting connotations foreign to them" (ibid., p. 466/34).

42. GS 1:1, p. 257.

43. "For it is a secret, though a quite open one, to these times of ours—obsessed and suffocated as they are by education—that books exist only to transmit that which has been achieved by those who are still developing. While that which exists today, at this moment—life itself—needs no books. If I myself exist, why ask for something to 'educate' me? But children come and ask; and the child in myself awakes—and it asks and wants to be educated and to develop—into what? Into something living, into something that exists. But just here is where an end is put to the making of books" ("Bildung und kein Ende," GS 3, p. 494/"Towards a Renaissance of Jewish Learning," in Glatzer, *On Jewish Learning*, p. 58).

44. Ibid., pp. 728/269–270. Rosenzweig argues that the consequences of making Hebrew wholly modern are disastrous: "If the new Hebrew, the Hebrew spoken in Palestine, should set out to evade this law of Jewish destiny, it might indeed achieve its purpose theoretically, but it would have to bear the consequences. Nor would these consequences be merely what some of our young and old radicals actually desire: that the new Hebrew should no longer be the language of the old Jewish people. More than that, there would probably be no time to realize the

hope of a new 'indigenous,' 'truly national' culture which would automatically solve the problem never yet solved in the entire history of our race of fusing normality and individuality: for when we are normal, we are exactly like anyone else, and when we are individual, we are a 'proverb and a byword' (Deut. 28:37) among nations" (ibid., p. 726–727/268). See William Cutter, "Ghostly Hebrew, Ghastly Speech: Scholem to Rosenzweig, 1926."

45. See Cohen's essay on the plan for the new academy "Zur Begründung einer Akademie für die Wissenschaft des Judentums," *Jüdische Schriften*, bd 2, pp. 210–217.

46. See Rivka Horwitz, "Franz Rosenzweig—On Jewish Education," *Journal of Jewish Thought and Philosophy* 2 (1993): 201–218, for a discussion of some of the politics that led to the changes in the structure of the academy.

47. For an articulation of the academy's approach, see Julius Guttmann, "Die Akademie für die Wissenschaft des Judentums," in *Der Jude* 7 (1923). See also Glazter's discussion of the academy in *On Jewish Learning*, pp. 12–16. The academy closed in 1934.

48. "Bildung und kein Ende," in GS 3, 491–492/55, translation altered.

49. Ibid., p. 502/69.

50. Ibid.

51. Ibid., p. 499/66, translation altered.

52. "Neues Lernen"/"Upon the Opening of the Jüdisches Lehrhaus," ibid., p. 509/101.

53. This is the context of Rosenzweig's oft-quoted dictum, "Nothing more is assumed than the simple resolve to say 'Nothing Jewish is alien to me'" (ibid., p. 499/65).

54. Ibid., p. 463/30.

55. Ibid., p. 506/96.

56. GS 1:2, pp. 887–888.

## Chapter Eight

1. Rose, *Judaism and Modernity*, pp. 129–130.

2. See especially the introduction to *Judaism and Modernity*, pp. 1–10.

3. Ibid., p. 131.

4. Hermann Cohen, "Deutschtum und Judentum, mit grundlegenden Betrachtungen über Staat und Internationalismus," *Jüdische Schriften*, 2: 237–302. Franz Rosenzweig, "'Deutschtum und Judentum'," GS 3, pp. 169–175). At first Rosenzweig requested that his essay not be published. However, in a letter to his cousin Gertrud Oppenheim from October 1917 (GS 1:1, pp. 456–459) he already takes back this wish. The first part of the essay was first published in *Kleinere Schriften* in 1937 under the title "Jüdische Volkstum." A full version was first published in the collected works cited above.

5. Cohen begins his argument by showing the complementarity of biblical and Greek notions of transcendence: "That is the sense of the uniqueness of God: that his being [*sein Sein*] is unique being; that outside of his being there is no other being; that all other being, as Plato would say, is only appearance" (*Jüdische*

*Schriften*, 2:243). The coincidence of biblical and Greek notions of transcendence leads into Cohen's argument about subsequent Jewish and German conceptions of humanity.

6. Ibid. 2:264.

7. Steven Schwarzschild, "'Germanism and Judaism'—Hermann Cohen's Normative Paradigm of the German-Jewish Symbiosis," in *Jews and Germans from 1860 to 1933: The Problematic Symbiosis*, ed. David Bronson (Heidelberg: Universitätsverlag, 1979), p. 144.

8. Martin Buber, *Der Jude und Sein Judentum*, "Völker, Staaten und Zion, I. Begriffe und Wirklichkeit [Letter to Hermann Cohen (July 1916)], II. Der Staat und die Menschheit. Bemerkungen zu Hermann Cohens 'Antwort' [September 1916]," as quoted in Maurice Friedman, *Martin Buber's Life and Work, The Early Years, 1878–1923* (New York: E. P. Dutton, 1981), pp. 216–217.

9. GS 3, p. 173.

10. Ibid., pp. 687–698.

11. GS 1:2, p. 1138/Glatzer, *Franz Rosenzweig*, p. 159. Friedrich Naumann (1860–1919) was the co-founder and leader of the German Democratic Party, German National Assembly, Weimar.

12. For a discussion of the evolution of Rosenzweig's attitude toward Zionism see Stéphane Mosès, "Politik und Religion. Zur Aktualität Franz Rosenzweigs," in *Der Philosoph Franz Rosenzweig*, 2: 855–875.

13. GS 1:2, p. 1138/Glatzer, *Franz Rosenzweig*, pp. 157–158.

14. From the prayer that is recited at the beginnning of the Sabbath to the prayer that is recited at the end, that is, from Friday evening to Saturday night.

15. GS 1:2, p. 1148–1149/Glatzer, *Franz Rosenzweig*, p. 357.

16. Ibid., p. 1149/358. The philosopher whom Rosenzweig regards "as an authority even greater than Hermann Cohen" is Judah Halevi. Again, see Ehud Luz's argument that Rosenzweig's position in regard to Zionism changed significantly as a result of working on the poems of Halevi: "Zionism and Messianism in the Thought of Franz Rosenzweig" (Hebrew).

17. Rosenzweig writes:

> Hermann Cohen once said to me—he was over seventy at the time: "I am still hoping to see the dawn of the messianic era." What Cohen, who believed in the false Messiah of the nineteenth century, meant by that was the conversion of Christians to the "pure monotheism" of his Judaism, a conversion which he thought the liberal Protestant theology of his day was initiating. I was startled by the vigor of his belief that it would happen "speedily in our days," and did not dare tell him that I did not think these indications were true signs. All I said was that I did not believe I should live to see it. At that he asked: "But when do *you* think it will be?" I did not have the heart to mention any date at all, and so I answered: "Perhaps in hundreds of years." But he understood me to say: "Perhaps in a hundred years," and cried: "Oh, please say in fifty!"

GS 4:1, p. 155/Glatzer, *Franz Rosenzweig*, p. 351. Steven Schwarzschild argues that this oft-cited story by Rosenzweig is fictional. Schwarzschild suggests that many of Rosenzweig's anecdotes about Cohen tell us more about Rosenzweig's concerns than about anything having to do with Cohen. See Schwarzschild,

"Franz Rosenzweig's Anecdotes about Hermann Cohen" in *Gegenwart im Rückblick: Festgabe für die Jüdische Gemeinde zu Berlin 25 Jahre nach dem Neubeginn.*

18. Rosenzweig's view of the bodily nature of Jewish existence for the sake of world redemption is in keeping with Halevi's description in the *Kuzari* of the Jewish people in physical and indeed biological terms. Note that Halevi's use of biological terms to describe the people of Israel is intimately linked with the fate of all humanity. Note also Halevi's interpretation of the suffering servant, which is also very similar to Rosenzweig's early twentieth century view. For both Rosenzweig and Halevi, Judaism can only perform its world-historical mission if it itself has a physical reality. Halevi writes:

> We [the people of Israel] are therefore not at the level of a corpse, but rather at the level of a sick man who has wasted away. . . . This is what Scripture means in saying, "Can these bones live?" [Ezekiel 37:3]. It is detailed further in the section of "Behold, my servant shall prosper" [Isaiah 52:13–53:12] specifically from the verses "He has no form nor beauty. . . . It was as if we hid our faces from him, he was despised, and we did not esteem him." This [turning away] is because of the sick person's visible deterioration and poor appearance, much like a fastidious person will turn away from dirty things—"Despised and rejected by people, a man of pains and well acquainted with illness." . . . Israel amongst the nations is like a heart amongst its organs—[the heart is a very sensitive organ, in that] it becomes considerably ill from the influence of the other organs and also considerably healthy from their influence. . . . The Divinity in relation to us is like the soul in relation to the heart [—just as the soul first connects to the heart and then spreads to the rest of the body, so does God's influence in the world connect first to Israel and then spread to the rest of the world]. . . . Just as the heart's inherent equilibrium and pure makeup allows the soul to attach to it, so, too, does the Divinity attach Itself to Israel because of their inherent nature. But [despite the heart's inherent purity], it still becomes tainted at times because of the other organs, such as from the desires of the liver or stomach, or from the poor makeup of the testicles. Similarly, Israel becomes tainted from their assimilation with the other nations, as it says, "And they assimilated with the nations, and they learned from their ways" [Psalms 106:35]. (Halevi, *Kuzari*, 2:35, pp. 90–92).

19. Here Rosenzweig is again quite close to Halevi. Recall that for Halevi the Israelites created and worshiped the golden calf in the context of their expectation that they (the Israelites) are always in the process of relating to God. See chapter 1.

20. GS 1:2, p. 400/Glatzer, *Franz Rosenzweig*, p. 54. Elsewhere, Rosenzweig explains what he means by his statement that Aḥad Ha'am's conception of Palestine as a "spiritual center" is *unconsciously* correct:

> For the center which the new Palestine might at best become in a pre-messianic period would never, in this day and age, be a center in the sense of Aḥad Ha'am, who wished to curb premature messianisms only to fall prey to it out of delight in "culture"—it would become a center in the mathematical sense. For, a circle

> is indeed drawn around its center, but in terms of construction the center does not in the least determine the area the circle will occupy, while the smallest arc of its periphery indicates the location of the center quite unambiguously. Thus a spiritual center such as we have in mind in regard to Palestine can be seen at a great distance and so become representative for all Jewry. But if it is to be a real center, it must depend on the periphery. To express it plainly and dryly to the point of blasphemy: the spirit of this spiritual center cannot grow in the direction of pure, uninhibited nationalism avid for its own development, no matter how much it would like to; just because of its focal character it must constantly keep in sight the periphery which can never be governed by pure nationalism but will always be constrained to regard the national as a function of the religious, and for very simple reasons based on the sociology of minorities. As one probes more deeply into these reasons, they rapidly lead out of the realm of blasphemy, into that of metaphysics: Why have we always been a minority? And why can we not stop being one? (GS 3, p. 728/Glatzer, *Franz Rosenzweig*, p. 269)

21. See Rosenzweig's letter to Julius Blau, the president of *Keren Ha-Yesod* in Frankfurt, GS 1:2, pp. 1123–1124. See also a letter to his mother of May 1924, GS 1:2, p. 964.

22. For a discussion of Rosenzweig's ideological influence on the German youth movement, see Paul Mendes-Flohr, "Rosenzweig and the Kameraden; a Non-Zionist Alliance," *Journal of Contemporary History* 26, nos. 3–4 (1991): 385–402.

23. GS 3, p. 492/Glatzer, *On Jewish Learning*, pp. 56–57. See Rosenzweig, "Hic et ubique" (Here and everywhere), in which he discusses what he perceives as the crisis of the publishing industry in these terms (GS 3, pp. 413–421).

24. See chapters 3 and 4.

25. Gillian Rose, *Mourning Becomes the Law* (Cambridge: Cambridge University Press, 1996), pp. 7–8.

26. Rose, *Judaism and Modernity*, p. 135.

27. Michael Wyschogrod, *The Body of Faith: God and the People Israel*, 2nd ed. (Northvale, N.J.: Jason Aronson, 1996).

28. Ibid., p. 26.

29. GS 3, p. 737, as cited in chapter 1.

30. Ibid., p. 740, as cited in chapter 1.

31. Wyschogrod, *Body of Faith*, pp. 85–86.

32. Ibid., p. 174.

33. Ibid., p. 103.

34. Ibid., p. 103.

35. Ibid., p. 223.

36. GS 4:1, p. 159/Glatzer, *Franz Rosenzweig*, pp. 335–336, translation altered, as quoted in chapter 4.

37. See Wyschogrod's preface to the second edition of *Body of Faith*, p. xxix.

38. Ibid., p. 235.

39. Ibid., pp. 245–255.

40. Ibid., p. 237.

41. Ibid., p. xxix.

42. Wyschogrod states, "The Zionist idea at first appeared in a perfectly secular and practical guise. Yet, perhaps from the very first, it was not difficult to detect messianic energies at work. However secularly disguised, a Jewish movement that spoke of the return of a dispersed Jewish people to its natural homeland, which would be turned into a moral paradigm for all humanity, could not for long be interpreted without reference to the messianic idea"(ibid., p. 237).

43. Ibid., p. 175.

44. Ibid., p. 242.

45. Ibid., p. 243.

46. See chapter 3 for a discussion of the relation between Rosenzweig's phenomenological and philosophical accounts of Jewish identity.

47. Glatzer, *On Jewish Learning*, p. 64, translation altered.

48. Ibid., pp. 64–65.

49. Neither reason reflects a kind of relativism Orthodox thinkers sometimes accuse non-Orthodox thinkers of advocating. This is discussed in the conclusion.

50. *The Star of Redemption*, p. 333/300, translation altered.

51. Once again, of course, Rosenzweig follows Cohen. Even if one interprets Cohen's *Religion of Reason* as an existential turn (which I believe is not the case), Cohen's approach to the question of "religion" is to argue that it has a representative ability that political and legal institutions do not have.

## Conclusion

1. Regina Schwartz, *The Curse of Cain* (Chicago: University of Chicago Press, 1997), p. 38. For a good overview of both the methodological and substantive shortcomings of Schwartz's book, see Peter Berkowitz's review in the June 23, 1997, issue of *The New Republic*. Despite these problems, her analysis is useful because it raises some of the basic issues that "monotheism" faces today.

2. Ibid., p. 16.

3. Ibid., p. 20.

4. George Lindbeck, *The Nature of Doctrine* (Philadelphia: Westminster Press, 1984), p. 23.

5. Bernard Lonergan, as quoted ibid., p. 31.

6. Ibid., p. 22.

7. "Monotheism would make an ontological claim that only one god exists. Monolatry or henotheism would better describe the kind of exclusive allegiance to one deity (from a field of many) that we find in, say, Deuteronomy 28:14, 'Do not turn aside from any of the commands I give you today to the right or to the left, following other gods and serving,' but it sounds cumbersome, and since everyone uses monotheism to mean monolatry (thereby, with a sleight of vocabulary, turning allegiance to one god into the obliteration of other gods), I will stick to customary usage" (Schwartz, *Curse of Cain*, p. 17).

8. Emphasis added, as quoted in chapter 5.

9. Lindbeck, *Nature of Doctrine*, p. 40.

10. See chapter 3.

11. Lindbeck, *Nature of Doctrine*, p. 129.

12. Ibid., p. 19.

13. Ibid., p. 21.

14. See chapter 1.

15. GS 3, p. 741.

16. See Hans Frei, *Types of Christian Theology* (New Haven: Yale University Press, 1992), for a more extended and nuanced discussion of Schleiermacher.

17. Again, see Frei's more nuanced discussion, ibid.

18. Lindbeck, *Nature of Doctrine*, p. 35.

19. Though it is not the criterion for this reading, I believe that this reading of Rosenzweig is in accord with Rosenzweig's own self-understanding of what he was doing.

20. See in particular Rosenzweig's essay, "Scripture and Luther," in *Scripture and Translation*, pp. 47–69.

21. Lindbeck's models help us to see not only where Rosenzweig breaks with Cohen but also where Rosenzweig remains linked to his mentor, and for that matter to the tradition of German-Jewish rationalism.

22. Lindbeck, *Nature of Doctrine*, p. 34.

23. This also has the effect of producing two Rosenzweigs, the one of *The Star of Redemption* and the one of the *Lehrhaus*. No one, I think, would deny the plausibility of my account for the Rosenzweig of the *Lehrhaus*. While I acknowledge that Rosenzweig's thought may well have evolved, I maintain nonetheless that there is enough philosophical evidence in *The Star of Redemption* to support my reading. In making this suggestion, I also subscribe to Gillian Rose's view of a philosophical work as "the labour of the concept inseparable from its formal characteristics" (see chapter 7).

24. George Lindbeck, "The Gospel's Uniqueness: Election and Untranslatability," *Modern Theology* 13, no. 4 (October 1997): 423–450.

25. See chapter 6.

26. Lindbeck, "The Gospel's Uniqueness," p. 444.

27. See the discussion of Rosenzweig's view of conversion in chapter 3.

28. Lindbeck, *Nature of Doctrine*, p. 128.

29. See chapter 6.

30. *The Star of Redemption*, pp. 367–368/330–331.

31. See chapter 7.

32. See chapter 6.

33. Review of David Novak, *The Election of Israel* in *Modern Theology* 12, no. 4 (October 1996): 491.

34. Glatzer, *On Jewish Learning*, p. 80.

35. Schwartz, *Curse of Cain*, p. 176.

36. This is the case for Rosenzweig and Lindbeck, even if some modern people find the biblical voice repulsive. As Edward L. Greenstein writes in a recent article on Bible translation, "An alternative to hiding the text, or to disavowing it, however, is to confront it honestly, to evaluate it, and to deal with it" ("Race, Class, and the Politics of Biblical Translation," p. 130).

37. *Der Jude*, Jahrgang 7 (1923): 457–464, translated in *The Jew: Essays from*

*Buber's Journal Der Jude*, selected, edited, and introduced by Arthur A. Cohen, translated from the German by Joachim Neugroschel (Tuscaloosa: University of Alabama Press, 1980), pp. 262–272.

38. Rosenzweig, "Apologetic Thinking," p. 267.

39. The occasional nature of Jewish thought does not mean, however, that there are no coherent traditions of Jewish thought. As I have attempted to demonstrate, Rosenzweig continues Cohen's ethical monotheism not in content but in form. This relationship of both continuity and discontinuity is consistent with what Rosenzweig describes as apologetic thinking:

> Why has the word apologetics acquired such a bad reputation? The same seems to be true of the apologetic profession par excellence, that of the lawyer. A general bias against him sees his legitimate task, as it were, as lying. Perhaps a certain professional routine appears to justify this prejudice. Nevertheless, defense can be one of the noblest of human occupations—to wit, when it goes to the very bottom of issues and souls, and ignoring the petty device of lies, exculpates itself with truth, the whole truth. In this broad sense, literary apologetics also can defend. In so doing it would not embellish anything, much less evade a vulnerable point. Instead, it would make the basis of defense the points of greatest jeopardy. In a word: it would defend the whole, not this or that particular. It would not be a defense in the usual sense, but an open presentation—not of some random thing but of one's own province. ("Apologetic Thinking," pp. 271–272)

40. Lindbeck, *Nature of Doctrine*, p. 113. In keeping with Lindbeck's own self-description, I suggest that Rosenzweig's thought is better considered "postliberal" than "postmodern" as a number of recent interpreters have maintained.

41. Nor is it an argument that modern Jews can do without philosophy. Recall Rosenzweig's comment to Meinecke: "[Philosophy's] questions are meaningless to me. On the other hand, the questions asked by human beings have become increasingly important to me. This is precisely what I meant by 'cognition and knowledge as service'; a readiness to confront such questions, to answer them as best I can out of my limited knowledge and my even slighter ability" (letter dated August 30, 1920, in Glatzer, *Franz Rosenzweig: His Life and Thought*, p. 97, as quoted in chapter 3).

42. Lindbeck writes: "One can speak of all life and reality in French, or from an American or a Jewish perspective; and one can also describe French in French, American culture in American terms, and Judaism in Jewish ones. This makes it possible for theology to be intratextual, not simply by explicating religion from within but in the stronger sense of describing everything as inside, as interpreted by the religion, and doing this by means of religiously shaped second-order concepts" (*Nature of Doctrine*, pp. 114–115).

43. Ibid., p. 117.

44. GS 3, p. 506/Glatzer, *On Jewish Learning*, p. 96, as cited in chapter 7.

45. Rose, *Judaism and Modernity*, p. 137.

46. As I have suggested elsewhere, Rosenzweig's thought on the Jewish-Christian relation is closest to Jon D. Levenson's, especially in *The Death and Resurrec-*

*tion of the Beloved Son* (New Haven: Yale University Press, 1993). See Leora Batnitzky, "Dialogue as Judgment, Not Mutual Affirmation: A New Look at Franz Rosenzweig's Dialogical Philosophy."

47. *The Star of Redemption*, p. 462/415, as quoted in chapter 6.

48. Lindbeck, "The Gospel's Uniqueness," p. 427.

49. Ibid., p. 437.

50. It seems to me that the cultural-linguistic model is most in keeping with Rabbi Joseph B. Soloveitchik's 1964 position on interfaith dialogue: "We cooperate with the members of other faith communities in all fields of constructive human endeavor, but, simultaneously with our integration into the general social framework, we engage in a movement of recoil and retrace our steps. In a word, we belong to the human society and, at the same time, we feel as strangers and outsiders" ("Confrontation," *Tradition* 6:2 [Spring-Summer 1964]: 29).

51. Lindbeck, "The Gospel's Uniqueness," p. 447.

# *Index*